Subsidies in the Context of the WTO's Free Trade System

Gurwinder Singh

Subsidies in the Context of the WTO's Free Trade System

A Legal and Economic Analysis

Springer

Gurwinder Singh
Faculty of Law
University of Turku
Turku, Finland

ISBN 978-3-319-62421-1 ISBN 978-3-319-62422-8 (eBook)
DOI 10.1007/978-3-319-62422-8

Library of Congress Control Number: 2017947452

Printed on acid-free paper

This Springer imprint is published by Springer Nature
The registered company is Springer International Publishing AG
The registered company address is: Gewerbestrasse 11, 6330 Cham, Switzerland

Acknowledgements and Thanks Giving

What remains unforgettable....

Every research goes through stages and seeks needful support before it is finally a complete story. With respect, I express my gratitude to Prof. Jukka Mähönen for supervising me and ensuring constant funding throughout this project. Mr. Mähönen's friendly attitude and constant inspiration even during difficult times were a great support and will remain part of my vivid memories. I am immensely thankful to Prof. Petros Mavroidis, Edwin B. Parker Professor of Law, Columbia Law School, New York, for being kind enough to give his valuable time to finalize this project. I am also thankful to Dr. Luca Rubini, Reader at Birmingham Law School. Pekka Riekkinen, who has been my friend ever since I started the research on the topic of subsidies in Turku, kept me motivating for the successful completion. Tuomas has always inspired me in the successful completion of the work and has been friendly with me. An another colleague Katja Lindroos used to have discussions with me during lunch hours and has also wished for my comfortable and long-term stay in Turku. All of them deserve special thanks.

My personal opinion on the WTO and a few words on research: Freedom to trade and free entrepreneurship are age-old market claims, but what becomes interesting and adventurous is that every nation, big or small, developed, developing or less developed, is provided equal opportunity to trade through a free trade system, and the market system is regulated by one institution, that is, the WTO. By no stretch of imagination can I say how the great communist leaders would have reacted on the issue of farm subsidies during the Doha deadlock, but one thing is certain, that is, the leaders of the world despite so much economic disparity and social, cultural and political difference have repeatedly put their faith in this trade regulating institution, the WTO.

The book on *Subsidies in the Context of the WTO's Free Trade System, A Legal and Economic Analysis* has seen its own courses of ups and down before reaching conclusion. However, the constant motivation from supervisors and many of the administrative staff, several of them having retired, acted as a strong pillar of support.

In research, discussions act as essential tools, so they are required, if not frequently, at least when a person's thoughts are at crossroads and they are looking for the right direction. When I was in such situations, I contacted Prof. (retd) Paavo Okko—my thanks to him, for giving me time and patiently listening to my views, despite his busy schedule. Another person with whom I have had substantial discussions with is Mr. Diwakar Dixit, who works in the WTO office in Geneva. He not only gave his personal time but also engaged some of his work colleagues in these discussions.

The journey to any kind of success is not possible without the blessings of parents and the best wishes of friends and other near and dear ones. I recall the days at Delhi University, When three of my friends, Laxmi Shanker, Sudhakar Pandey and Dheeraj Lather, put trust in me and always inspired me. My parents and younger brother Charanpreet Singh were in my thoughts even though they were far from me, in India. At the time of this writing, turning the clock back reminds me of my school days friend Hirday Gill. School days memories have their own charm, especially when one is away from home. I owe a debt of gratitude to all well-wishers and feel short of words to express my gratitude. Shri S.K. Banerjee deserves a high level of respect after my parents, so I would like to also mention his name here.

When a person is given moral encouragement and is also helped during a crisis, he knows what such support really means. I am thankful to Prof. Jussi Tapani, Dean, Faculty of Law, for the moral encouragement during the need of the hour and the support given by him for finalizing this work.

What is most charming during research work is the frequent interaction with colleagues and making discussions outside the field of research or even outside the legal discipline. Colourful and cheerful colleagues from diverse cultures, some of them I met during the summer school seminars, are no less than a garden with a collection of a wide variety of flowers and so deserve to be named here: *Ahmad Ghouri*, *Alian Ancery*, *Anne-Wietske-Enequist*, *Anna Krizsan*, *Ali Imran, Daniel Acquah*, *Delhi Darbar (Hameed) George Maude*, *Hisaya Hatanaka*, *Ida Sulin*, *Janne Salminen*, *Johanna Friman*, *Jari Murto*, *Jarna Petman*, *Martin Bjorklund*, *Maija Halminen*, *Mira Turpenine*, *Matti Urpalinen*, *Manjinder Samra*, *Mirtunjay jee (neighbour)*, *Oleksandr*, *Rebecca*, *Stephen Davis*, *Stephen Egharevba*, *Satu Lidman*, *S.M Lauttamäki*, *Silke Trommer*, *Tuomas Metsäranta*, *Ville Sinkkonen*, and others from e-coherence group.

Without critical evaluation, a work does not become refined or polished, so I respond with thanks to Prof. Mary E. Footer and Pernille Wegener Jessen for the critical evaluation of my work.

Without funding, the wheel of fortune does not move forward as we all know. The generous funding support from various foundations and from the Faculty of Law, Turku University, has played a key role in accomplishing this research work and also enabling my comfortable stay in Finland. These funding sources deserve my sincere thanks for counting on me. I owe a debt of gratitude to the following foundations and sources of funding: Jenny ja Antti Wihurin rahasto; Werner Hacklin Säätiö; Suomen Kulttuurirahasto; Faculty of Law, University of Turku; Suomen Kulttuurirahasto (regional funds); and Niilo Helander Foundations.

To be fair, I would like to express my gratitude to many more who are directly or indirectly linked to me, and thanks to all who have given considerable support to me while writing this work. However, the list would really go long, so I apologize if I have missed someone's name.

Before embarking upon the theme of this work, I would like to express these lines that came into my mind as I was abstractly thinking while travelling from Turku to Helsinki by train.

> The values of fair trade are concepts based on morality. Fair trade is also a question of far-reaching milestones for assumptions based on economics. As a safeguard for fairness and equity, which are the universally-accepted legal values among the nations, it is natural that legal rationality will give an interpretation whenever an occasion arises to meet these objectives.[1]

Gurwinder Singh

[1]Quotations in this work are based on the author's own thoughts.

Contents

List of Abbreviations

AB	Appellate Body of the WTO
ACP	African, Caribbean and Pacific Group of States
ACT	Advanced Composite Technology
AD Agreement	Anti-Dumping Agreement
AD Duties	Anti-Dumping Duties
AMS	Aggregate Measure of Support
AoA	Agreement on Agriculture
APEC	Asia Pacific Economic Cooperation
ASCM	Agreement on Subsidies and Countervailing Measures
ASEAN	Association of Southeast Asian Nations
ASI	Advertisement Research Institute
ASP	Aviation Safety
AST	Advanced Subsonic Technology
AU	African Union
B&O tax rate	Business and Occupation tax rate
BAN	Basel Action Network
BCA	Boeing Commercial Airplanes
BSES	British Steel Engineering Steels
BSplc	British Steel plc
CAFTA	Central American Free Trade Agreement
CAP	Common Agriculture Policy
CDSOA	Continued Dumping and Subsidies Offset Act
CEC	Commission for Environmental Cooperation
CES	Constant Elasticity of Substitution
CFR	Code of Federal Regulations
CFTA	Canada Free Trade Area
CITES	Convention on International Trade in Endangered Species
CKDkit	Complete Knock Down Kit
Cl	Clause
CMLR	Common Market Law Report

CMO	Common Organisation
CNOOC	China's National Offshore Corporation
CNPC	China's National Petroleum Corporation
Co	Company
COM	Committee
COMECON	Council for Mutual Economic Assistance
CPC	Central Pay Commission
CREST	Core Research for Evolutionary Science and Technology
CRS	Congressional Research Service
CTE	Community Test for Environment
CUTS	Consumer Unity & Trust Society
CVA	Canadian Value Added
CVD	Currency Value Devaluation
CWP	Circular Welded Carbon Quality Steel Pipe
DIPP	Defence Industry Productivity Programme
DISC	Domestic International Sales Corporations
DOC	Department of Commerce
DOD	Department of Defence
DOL	Department of Labor
DRAMS	Dynamic Random Access Memory Semiconductors
DSB	Dispute Settlement Body of the WTO
DSTI	Directorate for Science, Technology and Industry
DSU	Dispute Settlement Undertaking of the WTO
EAAE	The European Association of Agricultural Economists
EADS	European Aeronautic Defence and Space Company
EAEC	European Atomic Energy Community
EC	European Community
ECJ	European Court of Justice
ECR	European Court Reports
ECS	Engineering and Chemical Supplies
ECSC	European Coal and Steel Community
EDF	European Development Fund
EEC	European Economic Community
EIB	European Investment Bank
EPA	Environment Protection Agency
EPZ	Export Promoting Zone
ERG	Expert Review Group
ETC	Energy Tax Credit
ETI	Extraterritorial Income Exclusion Act (US)
ETLA	Elinkeinoelämän Tutkimuslaitos (The Research Institute of the Finnish Economy)
EU	European Union
FAO	Food and Agriculture Organisation
FIT	Feed In Tariff Program

FNCE	French Conseil d' Etat
FSC	Foreign Sales Corporation
FSRI	Farm Security Rural Investment Act
GATS	General Agreement on Trade on Services
GATT	General Agreement on Tariffs and Trade
GDP	Gross Domestic Products
GOES	Grain Oriented flat rolled Electrical Steel
GSM	General Sales Manager
GSP	Generalized System of Preference
GTZ	German Technical Corporation (Deutsche Gesellschaft für Technische)
HIID	Harvard Institute for International Development
HPCC	High Performance Computing and Communications
HS System	Harmonized Commodity Description and Coding System
HSR	High Speed Research/Computing Technology
IBRD	International Bank for Reconstruction and Development
ICT	Information and Communication Technology sector
IFAD	International Fund for Agriculture Development
IFPRI	International Food Policy Research Institute
IMF	International Monetary Fund
Inc	Incorporation
INSEAD	Institut Européen d'Administration des Affaires or *European Institute of Business Administration*
Int Law Rev	International Law Review
IOI	Industrial Oxygen Incorporated
IP	Intellectual Property
IRB	Industrial Revenue Bond
ISBN	International Standard Book Number
ISP Collection	Independent Study Project Collection
ITO	International Trade Organisation
JSTOR	Journal Storage
KFW	Kreditanstalt für Wiederaufbau (Deutsche Airbus)
LA/MSF	Launch Aid, Member State Financing
LCA	Large Civil Aircraft
LDC	Less-Developed Countries
LDP	Local Development Programme
LTD	Limited
LWR	Light Walled-Rectangular pipe and tubes
LWS	Laminated Woven Sacks
MC	Marginal Cost
MEA	Multilateral Environment Agreement
MEMO	Memorandum
MET	Multilateral Environment Treaties
MFN	Most Favoured Nation

MOFCOM	Ministry of Commerce China
MOISA	Markets Organisations Institutions and Stakeholders Strategies
MR	Marginal Revenue
MRTP	Monopolies and Restrictive Trade Practices Act
MVTO	Motor Vehicle Tariff Order
NAEX	Net Agricultural-Exporters
NAFTA	North America Free Trade Agreement
NAIM	Net Agricultural-Importers
NASA	National Aeronautic and Space Administration
NBER	National Bureau of Economic Research
NFEX	Net Food-Exporters
NGO	Non-Governmental Organisation
NME	Non-Market Economy
NPRO	Non-Preferential Rules of Origin
NRCS	Natural Resource Conservation Service
NTN-I	National Treasury Note-Series-I (Brazil)
OECD	Organisation for Economic Co-operation and Development
OH	Ohio
OJ	Official Journal (Eur Lex)
OLCC	Online Computer Library Centre
OTR	Off-the Road Tires
PCB	Poly-Chlorinated Biphenyls
PME	Palm–Methyl Ester
POP	Persistent Organic pollutants
PROEX	Programa de Financiamento às Exportações (Brazil)
PTC	Production Tax Credit
PV energy	Photovoltaic energy
QAT	Quiet Aircraft Technology
R&D	Research and Development
R&TB	Research and Technology Base
R&TD	Research and Technology Development
REEP	Research and Educational Expedition Programs
RIRDC	Rural Industries Research and Development Corporation
RSPO	Roundtable on Sustainable Palm Oil
RSPO	Roundtable Sustainable Palm Oil
S.A. de C.V.	Sociedad Anonima de Capital Variable (Spanish to English: a variable capital corporation)
SAA	Statement of Administrative Action
SAIL	Steel Authority of India Ltd
SAM	State Aid Modernisation initiative
SC	Steel Committee (on steel making)
SCGP	Supplies Credit Guarantee Programme
SCM Agreement	Subsidies and Countervailing Measures Agreement
SDI	Ship Decommissioned Industry

SDT	Special and Differential Treatment
SECOFI	Secretaría de Comercio y Fomento Industrial (Secretariat of Commerce and Industrial Development)
SIDS	Small Island Developing States
SKDkit	Semi Knock Down Kit
SME	Small and Medium Enterprise
SOCB	State Owned Commercial Banks
SPS	Sanitary and Phytosanitary Measures
SRO	Special Remission Order
SSG	Special Agriculture Safeguard
SSJ	Shandong Shouguang Jianyuanchun Co., Ltd (People's Republic of China)
STE	State Trading Enterprises
TEC	Treaty Establishing European Community
TED	Turtle Excluding Device
TEU	Treaty on European Union
TFEU	Treaty on the Functioning of European Union
TNC	Trade Negotiating Committee
TPC	Technology Partnership Canada
TRIPS	Trade Related Aspect of Intellectual Property Rights
UES	United Engineering Steels Limited
UK	United Kingdom
UN	United Nations
UNCTAD	United Nation Conference on Trade and Development
UNDP	United Nations Development Programme
US	United States
US.C.C.P.A	United States Court of Customs and Patents Appeal
USC	United States International Trade Commission
USCA§	United States Code Annotated
USDA	United States Department of Agriculture
USDOC	United States Department of Commerce
USIRC	United States Internal Revenue Code
USLCA	United States Large Civil Aircraft
USSR	Union of Soviet Socialist Republic
VCLT	Vienna Convention on the Law of Treaties
VSP	Vehicle System
WFP	World Food Programme
WGTCP	Working Group on Trade and Competition Policy
WISCO	Wuhan Iron and Steel (group) Corporation
WTO	World Trade Organisation

Chapter 1
Regulating Free Trade from the WTO Perspective

Abstract The international legal framework plays a significant role in regulating business, not only within nations but also across national boundaries. No country in the world is sufficient in itself and so everyone has to depend upon each other. It is widely presumed that international trade helps a nation to satisfy the demands of their consumers and supply the surplus to other nations in efficient and economical ways. As the laws relating to trade and commerce can influence the economic, political and social aspects of an individual and society, the Developing and Developed nations considered that the regulation of trade, required some well-developed organization. All the visionary ideas, goals and experiences from earlier discussions took place at the erstwhile GATT, from 1986–1994. During the Uruguay Round, based on the preliminary work and based on formative discussions, it led to the formation of the WTO. This organisation, the WTO began to function, on 1st January 1995. The discussion in this chapter briefly deals with cross border trade issues, the background information preceding the WTO trading system and then formally in the context of the WTO. Within these discussions, a brief reference to the WTO institutional set up, policy mechanisms, promotion of free trade among the Member State and the links established through provisions that forms part of one trading system is covered.

Free trade promotes private entrepreneurship, hence allows each country to specialize in producing the product in regard to which it has a comparative advantage. The free trade market system promoted by the WTO covers both industrial and agricultural sectors of any economy. Along with the promotion of free trade as a key trading principle, creation and generation of wealth by the nations, through procedural checks and balances is a matter of shared concern between the Member States. These concerns are derivatives of fair trade principles. The discussion in this chapter also attempts to figure out historical link for the present day challenges in the matters of trade across borders and between Developed, Developing and the Less Developed countries. The past connection with the issues lead to the formation of the WTO objectives. The study of subsidies is one such key issue. The area of discussion in the chapter briefly touches the specific issue of subsidies which is one of the key subject area of the international trading system based on the principle of free trade.

G. Singh, *Subsidies in the Context of the WTO's Free Trade System*,
DOI 10.1007/978-3-319-62422-8_1

How far have the forces unleashed by promoting free trade, helped in bringing distributive fairness...

1.1 General Discussion on Trading Activity from the Historical and Modern Perspective

Trade between business units is regulated by executives as a part of their collective responsibility, whereas between nations, it is a matter of large-scale economic activity. This explains why there are institutions established by the treaty agreements to regulate trade according to the agreed rules. Presently, it is the WTO that acts as the international-trade regulatory institution.[1] For the promotion of free trade, the WTO is based on the premise for the creation of a market environment through an approach of cooperation among the nations.

The WTO more or less operates on a self-election basis. Respecting the sovereign status of the Member States, institutions like the IMF classify nations as Developed, Developing and Less-Developed. Characterising their status from the WTO perspective, the nations, which are ahead in the use of technology are referred to as the Developed countries and the nations depending mainly upon a rural economy are called Less-Developed countries, while those in between are referred to as Developing nations. This can be better explained by economic reasoning. The underlying, economic rationality that suggests the link between productivity, efficiency, and wealth has been explained by several economists. Robert Solow's point of view, for instance is that "... [i]mprovement in productivity can make a nation richer on a per capita basis, it is not how much capital a country has that makes it rich, rather it is how productive that capital is, and according to him the key to productivity is technology."[2] While making this point, he further asserts that the United States and other Western countries are not rich because of their natural resources or because of capital gained from somewhere, but rather that they are rich because of the continual improvement in the technological sector. This can also be explained by taking into account the historical facts. The industrial achievements that we see today are due to the perpetual efforts of humans in acquiring knowledge and making practical use of it. The first step started with the concepts of mechanics, next came the age of electronics and today it is the age of computers. All this is the result of group efforts. Nowadays, we have attained the position where human skills, manufactured products, resources, raw materials, have all become a part of trading activity among the nations.[3]

---

[1]Beinhocker (2007), p. 269.

[2]Robert Selow quoted in Eric Beinhocker's book (Beinhocker 2007, p. 41).

[3]R. Selow referred to in, "Technology and International Differences in Growth Rates." Fagerberg (1994), pp. 1147–1175.

As a matter of fact, technology leads to a greater productivity from resources and capital investment, enhances profits, and promotes methods for more savings and greater capital formation. Without technological advancement, capital can only have a restricted growth in proportion to the population. The progressive use of scientific knowledge in the production sector primarily requires a conducive environment and the unhindered economic support that can be provided by the institutions. This is one of the key reasons that in the pursuit of innovation and technological progress, the TRIPS[4] agreement is included in the WTO. In addition to this it is also worth mentioning, that from the perspective of equity based principles, along with technological advancement, the fundamentals of the WTO are also based on features supporting long-term progressive and welfare policies for the Member States through free trade.

1.2 Previous Trade Regulating Institutions Before the WTO, the ITO and GATT

The foundations of the WTO, which began to function on 1st January 1995, were laid down in 1986–1994. The negotiations termed as the *Uruguay Round* started in the preceding trade institution known as GATT. GATT was established in 1947 and lasted until 1994. GATT as an institution was created specifically, for trade-related issues, and for the economic co-operation among the Member States.

The origin of GATT can be traced to the US Government's proposals for the expansion of World Trade and Employment. The proposal was published in December 6, 1994 and subsequent to the publication of the proposal at the first meeting of the Economic and Social Council (ECOSOC) of the United Nations (UN) in 1946, the United States introduced a resolution calling for an international conference on trade and employment.[5] The resolution was unanimously adopted and the ECOSOC appointed a preparatory committee. During the same time interval, the US government also developed a Suggested Charter for an International Trade Organization (hereafter, Suggested Charter) and circulated it to the preparatory committee. The first meeting of the preparatory committee, except for adding a chapter on *economic development*, essentially adopted most of the US draft. The Developing countries including India criticised the Suggested Charter, as lacking a development agenda for the Developing countries and considered that it was rather designed mainly to support the policies of the industrial countries.[6]

[4]TRIPS:- "Agreement on Trade-Related Aspects of Intellectual Property Rights." The TRIPS agreement is Annex 1C of the Marrakesh Agreement Establishing the World Trade Organization, signed in Marrakesh, Morocco on 15 April, 1994.

[5]Srinivasan (2009), p. 9.

[6]Srinivasan (2009), pp. 9–10.

The negotiations that led to the formation of GATT and the discussions on a draft charter for the ITO were conducted simultaneously at the second meeting in Geneva. The meeting that was held for the preparatory committee of the Havana conference.[7] The aim was to create the ITO at the UN Conference on Trade and Employment in Havana, Cuba in 1947.[8] However, in the draft charter for the ITO, the authorisation for negotiating a tariff reduction delegated by the US congress to the president was restrictive. The power delegated did not authorised the US president to negotiate an agreement to establish an international organisation with the United States as a member. Thus ITO could not came into function.

As a result of all these ups and downs, it was decided that GATT was only to be a multilateral agreement and not an organisation although, it was designed to operate under the umbrella of the ITO once it came into being.[9]

As the ITO practically could not came into existence, the combined package of trade rules and tariff concessions in the ITO Charter, that Member Nations had negotiated exclusively, led to the working of a General Agreement on Tariffs and Trade (GATT). GATT's basic legal principles remained the same as they were in the previous ITO.

The formation of GATT was like an attempt to establish a forum, so as to take preliminary steps in the direction of finding economic and political solutions to the problems of the nations by negotiations. The basic objectives of GATT was to promote trade among the nations and provide technical assistance for the development of the nations and an upliftment of the standards of citizens.[10]

From its very inception, GATT brought together a diverse group of countries. Its wider scope of objectives and procedural effectiveness supported the common goal of *multinational trade liberalisation* and encouraged the new countries to join this trade-regulating institution. In the decades that followed, the momentum of trade liberalisation led to an exponential trade growth within the Members States, surpassing the consumer demand. This made it clear that despite its heterogeneity, the Member State's ability to trade with each other and to share the benefits of trade was established. GATT succeeded in reducing tariffs to lower levels. Nevertheless, a series of economic recessions in the 1970s and early 1980s, forced the governments to devise other forms of protection for sectors facing increased foreign competition.

Since, the Bretton Woods International Monetary System,[11] there have been substantial changes in trading patterns and the basic conditions of the economy of

---

[7]Srinivasan (2009), p. 10.

[8]United Nations Conference on Trade and Employment. Final Act and the related Documents. New York. April, 1948 https://www.wto.org/english/docs_e/legal_e/havana_e.pdf.

[9]Srinivasan (2009), pp. 10–11.

[10]Mavroidis (2005), p. 3.

[11]Bretton Woods Conference, officially called the United Nations Monetary and Financial Conference was held on July 1–22, 1944. The Bretton Woods system was the world's most recent experiment with a fixed exchange rate regime. Although it was originally designed as an adjustable peg, it evolved in its heyday into a de facto fixed exchange rate regime. The architects of the

nations. The emerging economies of the world, often categorised as Developing and Less-Developed have experienced these sudden changes and also the unexpected effects of market buoyancy. Undoubtedly, these changes have generated high hopes for some nations, but on the other hand, there are many nations that consider themselves trapped in this vicissitude due to many factors.

However, it is widely presumed that international trade helps a nation to satisfy the demands of their consumers and supply the surplus to other nations in efficient and economical ways. As the laws relating to trade and commerce can influence the economic, political and social aspects of an individual and society, the Developing and the Developed nations[12] considered that the regulation of trade required some well-developed organisation. This organisation was to consist of experts that could work beyond political considerations, and its goal would not be, simply short-term perspectives rather it could make objective analyses whenever required. As a part of regulatory measures these experts were to be capable of interpreting and enforcing treaties and agreements and can penalise in the case of aberrations. All the visionary ideas, goals and experiences from earlier discussions took place at the erstwhile GATT as a discussion form, from 1986 to 1994. During the Uruguay Round this led to the formation of the WTO. This organisation, the WTO began to function, on 1st January 1995.[13]

1.3 What Is the WTO?

The WTO is a multilateral trading system that developed from GATT. Despite several odds in the beginning, it has striven for its objectives and has kept its members in a progressive framework towards liberal trading principles. The system, developed over the years both in terms of membership and issue coverage, culminating in the establishment of the WTO in 1995.[14]

From an international law perspective, the WTO/GATT are treaty-based organisations, in the light of the fact that all the WTO agreements and treaty provisions are binding on the Member States.[15] When signing the Uruguay Round Agreement, all the parties agreed that the WTO treaty agreement was to be accepted in a

---

Bretton Woods system wanted a set of monetary arrangements that would combine the advantage of the classical gold standards (i.e. exchange rate stability) with the advantage of floating rates (i.e., independence to pursue national full employment policies). They sought to avoid the defects of floating rates (destabilising speculation and competitive beggar thy-neighbor devaluations).Bordo and Eichengreen (1993), pp. 3–5. http://www.nber.org/chapters/c6867.

[12]Developing and Developed nations based on the WTO classification.

[13]Bossche (2008), p. 77.

[14]World Trade Report (2007), p. xxx. www.wto.org.

[15]WTO Agreement Art II. (2).

comprehensive manner, which is also designated as a single undertaking.[16] After attaining membership, a Member State has an inherent obligation to ensure the conformity of its domestic legal system and the related statutory provisions and regulations with the WTO agreements.[17] Nevertheless, exceptions are allowed depending upon the economic and political situation of the nations.

The ability of the GATT/WTO system, to accommodate the different needs of Member States, has been an important factor in its success. All the decisions concerning the rules for framing new provisions are taken collectively by the Members as a whole, either by ministers, who gather at least once every 2 years or by their ambassadors or delegates who meet regularly in Geneva. There are two modes of decision-making in the WTO, the consensus method and the voting method. Decisions are deemed to be decided by consensus, if none of the Member State present at that meeting objects to the proposal. Where a decision cannot be taken by consensus, the decision in the ministerial conference is taken by a majority of the votes cast, unless otherwise specified in the WTO agreement.[18] Although, there is a possibility to choose voting in the WTO system, in a situation where a consensus cannot be reached, however, the preference to resolve issues through consensus remains the priority. On the contrary, GATT 1947 covered mainly the voting method and there was no explicit reference of the word consensus in this previous institution.[19]

The WTO is specifically a trade-regulatory organisation, however, it is different from the other organisations. Structured in such a way that it virtually covers both legal and economic issues of international trade, which is also evident from the procedural aspect followed by the DSB. Briefly, the WTO can also be regarded as a set of rules and agreements negotiated by a group of the world's trading nations.

With the formation of the WTO, the discussions on the unsettled issues among the Member States remains ongoing. The primary function of the WTO as a multilateral organisation is to regulate trade amongst the Member States, and this also means a forum for the discussion of many crucial matters such as subsidies.

In comparison to other global institutions, the WTO has distinct objectives; the main objectives of the WTO are to promote free trade, and create fair opportunities for development among its Member States.

---

[16]Article XI, 1.The contracting parties to the GATT 1947 as of the date of entry into force of this Agreement and the European Communities, which accept this Agreement and the Multilateral Trade Agreements and for which Schedules of Concessions and Commitments are annexed to GATT 1994 and for which Schedules of Specific Commitments are annexed to GATS shall become original Members of the WTO.

2. The least-developed countries recognised as such by the United Nations will only be required to undertake commitments and concessions to the extent consistent with their individual development, financial and trade needs or their administrative and institutional capabilities.

[17]WTO Agreement Art XVI.4.

[18]Matsushita et al. (2003), p. 12.

[19]Ehlermann & Ehring (2005), pp. 51–75.

1.3.1 From the Perspective of the WTO Objectives

The WTO was formed after the Uruguay round, 1986–1994, and based on earlier negotiations held during GATT conferences resulting in the following core objectives being adopted.

First, to liberalise trade among Member States.

Second, to ensure that Developing nations and the Less Developed countries obtain a level of share in the growth of international trade.

Third, that due importance should be given to sustainable development, sustainable development is important for the protection and preservation of the environment along with the overall economic growth of countries.[20]

Fourth, after signing the TRIPS agreement, a minimum standard for various forms of intellectual property (I.P) regulations has to be maintained by the Member States.[21]

However, it must be highlighted that the overarching role of this multilateral institution cannot be confined to these objectives only. WTO policies take into account the specific needs of Developing and Less-Developed countries, and also considers other matters of primary concerns such as, raising standards of living, creation of jobs, creating economic prosperity, equitable distribution of resources, placing a check on environmental degradation and the protection of public health. The fulfilment of the WTO objectives is a step-by-step process, which also requires an understanding of the market forces in the Member States.

1.4 International Law Norms and the WTO

The WTO, being a treaty-based organisation, specifically formed to regulate trade among Member States, is in principle part of international law, as any other international organisation. As an international institution, the WTO derives legality from the general principles of international law and treaty agreements which is clear from the working procedure of the dispute settlement body. Even though the establishment of this organisation has created a new system of international trade,

[20] In fact, within the WTO framework, there is no specific agreement dealing with the environment. The objectives of Sustainable Development and Environmental Protection are stated in the preamble to the Marrakesh Agreement establishing the WTO. The Doha Round of the WTO negotiations has linked certain aspects of trade with the environment and also assigned some task to a regular environment committee.

[21] Agreement on Trade Related Aspects of Intellectual Property Rights (TRIPS), is an international agreement administered by the World Trade Organization that sets down minimum standards for many form of intellectual property regulation. It was negotiated at the end of the Uruguay Round of the General Agreement on Tariffs and Trade (GATT) in 1994.

so as to promote free trade among its Member States, nevertheless, the general treaty rules of international law[22] are still the legally-binding rules.[23]

The WTO is part of the international legal system, therefore the peremptory norms of international law have the same non-derogatory status in the WTO system. These norms cannot be violated by any Member State either through international treaties or local or special customs, nor can an interpretation be made in clinical isolation from public international law.[24] An alternative explanation might be that the relevance of peremptory norms, i.e., *jus cogens*, carries the same significance as it has with other international organisations.[25] Certain norms are considered as the basis of international law, so there is customary prohibition against any violation of *jus cogens*.[26] However, it is difficult to conceive the real status of *jus cogens* and demarcate its boundaries. The DSB of the WTO, with the primary objectives of settling trade disputes between the Member States, accepts the status of *jus cogens*. As the human rights aspects are part of the general principles of international law (*jus cogens*), so on several occasions, they become linked to international trade issues.

Occasionally, human-right dogmas are quite widely interpreted, thus creating normative crisis because of the conflict of interest, for examples the issue of child labour, women's rights and several other similar issues. So far as the legal eligibility of entertaining a plea for the settlement of a trade dispute is concerned, litigation on the grounds of human rights violation cannot be entertained in the WTO dispute settlement body,[27] nevertheless, it is expected that the interpretation of the WTO provisions should be made in good-faith and consistent with human rights treaties. As a matter of fact, the WTO members do not appear to have granted any responsibility to the dispute settlement body for adjudicating matters concerning human

---

[22]Article 3.2 of the DSU: The Dispute settlement system of the WTO is a central element in providing security and predictability to the multilateral trading system. The members recognise that it serves to preserve rights and obligations of members under the covered agreements, and to clarify the existing provisions of those agreements in accordance with customary rules of interpretation of public international law. Recommendations and rulings of the DSB cannot add to or diminish the rights and obligations provided in the covered agreements.

[23]Article 26, Vienna Convention on the Law of Treaties. *Pacta sunt servanda.*

[24]In the case of *United States–Standards for Reformulated and Conventional Gasoline, WT/DS2/AB/R*, (see page no 17, of the AB report) AB in the matter before it, concerning the interpretation of Article XX by the Panel, in relation to the baseline establishment rule applied by the US for the conservation of natural resources, stated, the general rule of interpretation has attained the status of a rule of customary or general international law. As such, it forms part of the customary rules of interpretation of public international law which the Appellate Body has been directed, by Article 3 (2) of the DSU, to apply in seeking to clarify the provisions of the General Agreement and the other covered agreements of the Marrakesh Agreement Establishing the World Trade Organization. This direction reflects a measure of recognition that the General Agreement is not to be read in clinical isolation from public international law. The Appellate Body observes that the Panel Report failed to take adequate account of the words actually used by Article XX in several paragraphs.

[25]See preamble of the WTO.

[26]Gabrielle (2002), pp. 753–814.

[27]Abbott et al. (2006), p. 188.

rights. Issues such as human rights are seen more as value based.[28] In the case of a normative conflict, *jus-cogens* often enjoys primacy, either through binding obligation by adopting interpretation of provisions of the agreements in harmony with- *jus cogens*, or, by invalidating a conflicting WTO provision."[29] The prevalence of this feature can be seen in various WTO conferences where issues, such as labour standards, the banning of child labour and so on, are discussed.

Another debatable issues, involving normative interpretation, that needs to be discussed here can be classified as (1) the choice between trade and social values and (2) the interaction of MEA with the WTO aims of free trade. Environmental issues are relevant to the protection of nature. The protection of nature requires that there should be value based trade policies. With regard to trade between Developed and Developing countries, it is important to highlight these issues as well, because often the environmental conditions are tampered with due to trade benefits. International law governs both the WTO Agreement and its interaction with Multilateral Environment Agreements, (MEAs). In cases where an Appellate Body or panel has to establish priorities between the MEA and the WTO provisions, the panel and Appellate Bodies for applying fairness as a regulatory measures, attempt to strike a harmony between free trade and fair trade values. The concept of free trade does not prevail over other values. **Article XX of GATT, lists certain exceptions to free trade.**[30] The question of a balance between legal principles promoting free trade

[28]Value-based here means, that; the concept and realization of human rights are relative for the different societies.

[29]Gabrielle (2002), pp. 753–814.

[30]Subject to the requirement that such measures are not applied in a manner which would constitute a means of arbitrary or unjustifiable discrimination between countries where the same conditions prevail or a disguised restriction on international trade, nothing in this agreement shall be construed to prevent the adoption or enforcement by any contracting party of measures:

a) necessary to protect public morals;
b) necessary to protect human, animal or plant life or health;
c) relating to the importations or exportations of gold and silver;
d) necessary to secure compliance with laws or regulations which are not inconsistent with the provisions of this Agreement, including those relating to customs enforcement, the enforcement of monopolies operated under paragraph 4 of Article II and Article XVII, the protection of patents, trademarks and copyrights, and the prevention of deceptive practices;
e) relating to the products of prison labour;
f) imposed for the protection of national treasures of artistic, historic or archaeological value;
g) relating to the conservation of exhaustible natural resources if such measures are made effective in conjunction with restrictions on domestic production and consumption;
h) undertaken in pursuance of obligations under any intergovernmental commodity agreement which conforms to the criteria submitted to the contracting parties and not disapproved by them or which is itself so submitted and not so disapproved;
i) involving restrictions on exports of domestic materials necessary to ensure essential quantities of such materials to a domestic processing industry during periods when the domestic price of such materials is held below the world price as part of a governmental stabilization plan; Provided that such restrictions shall not operate to increase the exports of or the protection afforded to such domestic industry, and shall not depart from the provisions of this Agreement relating to non–discrimination;

and issues of sustainability arose in the case of **United States-Standards for Reformulated and Conventional Gasoline,**[31] and in the **United States-Import Prohibition of Certain Shrimp and Shrimp Products.**[32] It is likely that the Article XX exception clause is circumvented for protectionism and the issue in the first case was somewhat like this. The Appellate Body in this case followed an approach *of lifting the veil* and stated "disguised restriction on free trade is like disguised discrimination." Further, the Appellate Body added that if a Member State allowed the imports on a conditional basis, that the environment criteria should be fulfilled; however, this can be justified only if the same environment standards are applied to similar domestic products, thus fulfilling the national treatment criteria and giving equal treatment to the imported products.

This matter concerned the protection of an endangered species. Finally, the Panel in (United States-Import Prohibition of Certain Shrimp and Shrimp Products) urged "Malaysia and the United States to cooperate fully, in order to conclude, an agreement which would permit the protection and conservation of sea turtles to the satisfaction of all interests involved and taking into account the principle that states have common goals but differentiated responsibilities to conserve and protect the environment."[33]

---

j) essential to the acquisition or distribution of products in general or local short supply; Provided that any such measures shall be consistent with the principle that all contracting parties are entitled to an equitable share of the international supply of such products, and that any such measures, which are inconsistent with the other provisions of the agreement shall be discontinued as soon as the conditions giving rise them have ceased to exist. The contracting parties shall review the need for this sub-paragraph not later than 30 June 1960.

[31]In the case between, US and Brazil, WT/DS2/9, para 6.39, the Appellate body partly upheld the panel´s decision and directed modification to the rest. The Panel, referring to the Herring and Salmon case, stated that as the preamble of Article XX indicates, the purpose of including Article XX (g) in the General Agreement was not to widen the scope for measures serving trade policy purposes but merely to ensure that the commitments under the General Agreement, do not hinder the pursuit of policies aimed at the conservation of exhaustive natural resources. Para.6.40, the panel then proceeded to examine whether the baseline establishment methods can be linked to "primarily aimed at" achieving the conservation objectives of Gasoline rule.

[32]Case between Malaysia and U.S: See WT/DS58/RW.

[33]Appellate Body stated in its report, para 156, turning then to chapter XX, "we consider that it embodies the recognition on the part of WTO members, of the need to maintain a balance of rights and obligations between the right of a member to invoke one or another of the exceptions of Article XX, specified in paragraphs (a) to (j) on the one hand, and the substantive rights of the other members under the GATT 1994, on the other hand. Exercise by one Member of its rights to invoke an exception, such as Article XX (g) if abused or misused, will to that extent, erode or render naught the substantive treaty rights in, for example, Article XI:1, of other Members. Thus, a balance must be struck between the right of a Member to invoke an exception, under Article XX and the duty of that same Member to respect the treaty rights of the other members. To permit one member to abuse or misuse its right to invoke an exception would be effectively to allow that member to degrade its own treaty obligations as well as to devalue the treaty rights of other members."

The decisions in these cases made the position clear that the WTO as an institution promoting trade between the nations also acts as a regulatory organisation within the parameters of the general principles of international law. The significance of this organisation can be objectively measured as it takes into account other issues beyond free trade. These issues seem to be value based and can be termed as an approach towards fair trade values, hence, more or less pursuing the principles of "free and fair trade complementing each other."

1.4.1 The WTO and the Domestic Legal System

International institutions expect compliance of the treaty provisions and this requires a legal support base. With regard to creating legal certainty, states are bound by the provisions of Article 26, 27, 28 and 31 of the Vienna Convention on the Law of Treaties. Article 26 covers the principle of *Pacta sunt servanda*. Practically for the application of these treaties, the WTO provisions have to face differing legal systems,[34] within the Member States before a treaty is finally adopted or harmonised, which, indeed, is a complicated process. On the basis of a general comparison with the existing legal systems of the Member States, it is presumed that the domestic policies of Member States may not be conducive for accomplishing the WTO objectives of free trade during the initial phases. Member States may be required to make changes in their internal legal system, so that treaty provisions are in harmony with their domestic legal system. The different methods for implementation depend upon the constitutional structure adopted for treaty implementation and has been described in detail by international law theories on Monoism[35] and Dualism.[36]

1.4.2 Flexibility at the Normative Level, an Economic Necessity

The issue of normative flexibility, in international law, has again arisen as a matter of debate after the formation of GATT/WTO. The primary objective of this organisation is to deal with the problems of the international trade of its Member States, which makes it a system of choices and arrangements. When tested as regards new situations, the existing defined area of international legal norms cannot

[34]Sauve & Grasstek (2006), pp. 837–864.

[35]Monoism maintains that national legal rules and international law rules or treaty obligations that a state has accepted can be directly applied.

[36]In the case of dualism, international agreements are brought into a domestic legal system for implementation after harmonizing them with national law. This means that an act of parliament has been passed on the matter.

provide the appropriate level of support to the social, political, and economic basis, in order to meet the WTO objectives, as they are based on old propositions. The nature of the existing normative system seems to be facing deficiencies in reaching the appropriate conclusions, and this often leads to a debate about the relevancy of the existing norms. With the specific objectives of the WTO i.e., to promote free trade market principles, at an equal level, among all the nations despite their diversity, this will undoubtedly demand the potential for an evolution of new rules at the normative level. The need to create flexibility at the normative level and can be marginalised after has to be faced, while interpreting and applying both domestic law and international law for the fulfilment of the WTO objectives.

1.5 The Political Economy Dimension

The WTO is also viewed as an outcome of globalisation, and in this regard, an outlook from a political and economic perspective also takes account of the realities, such as, sovereignty, drawing a balance between globalisation and domestic policies, the relationship between Developed, Developing and Less-Developed countries, and between the IMF and the WTO. The extent of the influence on the state's political system, subsequent to acquiring membership of the WTO also necessitates consideration from the political perspective. The issue of political economy has become a topic of debate among constitutional lawyers, as to test whether the constitutional concepts of sovereignty remains at the same level after the ratification of the WTO, as before. During the WTO conference negotiations, it is often noticed that the position of the advanced economies is dominant. At times, the dominant economic position of the advanced nations within the WTO impinges on the present sovereign status of smaller nations. This has become a source of political and economic debate. In the strict constitutional sense, the term sovereignty has been interpreted as non-interference in the matters of nation-state, but, it often occurs that the WTO tries to create an order of the nations based on economic groups such as the G8, G8+5, G 14 and G 20 and by this means influences the policies of smaller economies. In the wake of economic globalisation, there are several instances where the market measures adopted by one nation influences the policies of other nations.

The contribution of the newly formed market mechanism to economic growth has proved significant. Subsequent to the Member States signing the WTO Agreement, it is hard to imagine that any process of substantial development could be accomplished without these market liberalization policies. The role of the constitutional mechanism however cannot be sidelined. After attaining membership, Member States are expected to reduce tariffs, complimented by non-discriminatory practices to like products from other Member States. This new feature of the market system is characterized by treaty based norms. In addition to this norm, there has been an institutionalization of development norms. These Development norms support flexibilities being extended to the Developing and Less-Developed countries. The development objectives also have constitutional support base within the Member States. The multilateral norms supporting market liberalization policies are different in character from the development norms supported by constitutional objectives, reason being that the constitutional objectives are based on the rights of the individuals.

It is often the case that the market liberalization agenda is heavily supported by the Developed countries. The interface between the normative aspects, multilateral and the domestic agenda based, often create complexities, as the domestic issues are compelled to a bargain, such as in the matters of food security, subsidies for development, product standards, and several others.

The concept of sovereignty also gets challenged internally within a Member State, as a free market requires a decentralised decision-making process so as to counter protectionist policies, risk of monopolies, actions by some political or economic (governmental or non-governmental) entities, as these can challenge the accomplishment of the objectives of the WTO.[37]

Despite the promotion of free trade, nations need to exist within the political reality that trade agreements reduces market barriers, but political barriers still remain. These political barriers cannot be ignored, as in the absence of state structures, the GATT/WTO based market concepts cannot work. Globalisation in political terms requires the right kinds of policies to maintain the balance between the objectives of the WTO and the national interest of the Member State. Using international agreements as a commitment device for increasing the market size in order to ascertain bargaining power, are less likely to motivate smaller nations to be part of multilateral-trading system, as there are high risks of losses for the Developing and Less-Developed countries.

The primary objective of economic globalisation is the removal of protectionist measures and also creating possibilities for economic development. This idea is basically-an outcome of neo-liberalism.[38]

In order to establish any assumed level of International market environment, the removal of trade barriers is required, no matter how gradually. Moreover, the economic globalisation is based on the assumption that market forces and commercial activities are efficient methods for producing and supplying goods and services. By adopting liberal trade policies, this will create an environment of competition at the production level, and eventually resolve production in an efficient manner on a natural basis. Concisely, it can be said that free trade can possibly help to secure the exchange of different goods, at the real value market price.

[37]Hudec and Southwick (2002), p. 29. www.cambridge.org/9780521813198.

[38]Neo-liberalism comprises two notions "neo" and "liberal" meaning free from government intervention. Adam Smith advocated the abolition of government in economic matters so that trade could flourish and first introduced liberalism in mid-1770. Sue L.T. Mc-Gregor, Janice Doull and Larry Fisk, "Neoliberalism, Microbes, and Peace: A human ecological perspective," p. 1. http://www.kon.org/archives/forum/14-1/McGregor.html, forum paper.

1.5.1 Free Trade Promoting Efficient Production

Traditional economics emphasises that markets are the best methods for allocating resources in a way that optimizes the welfare of society under equilibrium condition.[39] The assumption of attaining equilibrium, for all types of goods produced is practically illusive and neither the equilibrium position of market, anyway can be considered as remedies for all kinds of social, economic, environmental and other problems. Production of goods and putting it before the market forces is basically an issue that lays centre of the free market concepts, however, to measure the extent of market regulation requires streamlining of market policies.

Key role of the WTO is, regulation of international trade and setting a basis for attaining its objectives. Trading between nations, on the basis of the WTO principles has attained practical relevance because every economy has limited resources. There are limits to what a nation can produce efficiently, so for the rest of the products, trade-offs is the option followed. The general rule of the market system that remains prevalent is that in order to, produce more of one product, the economy must sacrifice some production of another product.

From the WTO perspective, free trade, promotes private entrepreneurship; hence each country needs to specialize in producing a product with regard to its comparative advantage. A country has a comparative advantage in producing a product if the opportunity cost[40] of producing those goods in terms of other goods is lower in that country than it is in other countries.[41]

The principles of economics, to a great extent, cover how we benefit ourselves, when these goods and services are traded. If we apply the economic principle of *comparative cost advantage,*[42] which states, that a market system can be established at the global level, by applying the concept that countries prosper first by taking advantage of their assets, in order to concentrate on what they can produce best, and then by trading these products with the products of other countries.

It was Ricardo who first advocated that free trade was a viable solution in the current times for growth and prosperity. He propounded the theory of comparative-cost advantage. The comparative-cost advantage theory is one of the key theories on the basis of which the WTO Member nations have developed their export oriented products.

---

[39]Beinhocker (2007), p. 294.

[40]Opportunity Cost:—Any decision that involves a choice between two or more options has an opportunity cost. Opportunity cost is useful when evaluating the cost and benefit of choices. By expressing the cost of one option in terms of forgone benefits of another, the marginal cost and marginal benefits of the options can be compared. www.netmba.com/econ/micro/cost/opportunity.

[41]Gregory (2007), p. 28.

[42]This theory was an improvement of Absolute advantage theory. In the WTO trading system absolute advantage is not relevant. For detail references see, www.wto.org. Also see, Krugman and Obstfed (2009), pp. 32–35.

According to the comparative-cost advantage theory, gains from trade are possible even though a country does not have an absolute advantage in the production of any commodity. This proposition is based on the fact that so long as there is a difference in the price ratios of products between the nations, which can be due to the several factors, there is a great trading possibility. The first reason is that money is used as a medium of exchange, which strengthens the possibility of making a comparison between the costs of similar products across borders.[43] Secondly, every country tries to export that commodity which has a relatively low cost of production.

The reason why the comparative-cost advantage theory is a better option can be further illustrated. If there are two countries, one producing product "A" and another producing product "B." then according to the absolute-advantage theory, gains from trade depend on the fact that one specialises in product A, and the other specialises in product B. Theoretically, this seems fine, but practically the situation precipitates in a way, that after several years of manufacturing product A, a saturation point of market demand is reached beyond which production of this product means no profit. Consumer requirements and shifting demands also force the manufacture of some other products besides product A, by combining different factors of production. This new factor-combination for production can consist of some previous elements combined with new elements, and even some imported from another place if available at a cheaper price. In terms of modern day economics, this is defined as an efficient mode of production. The market behaviour of consumers is varied and this demands that a variety of new products need to be developed.[44]

While discussing international trade, it is important to bear in mind that the relative costs of production in a market are also based on exchange rates, labour costs, availability of resources, and the advancement of technology.[45] In other words, theories based on the comparison of cost or market comparisons try to explain that the value of an export commodity is also to be understood in relation to other system's demand and supply and these influence the price of that commodity and the price based on the cost of production. The costs of production can be adjusted while trading with other nations. The application of this theory also gives some clue of which commodities are to be exported and why. As a guiding measure, it also helps to calculate the limits of exports and imports that, a market can sustain. Despite the application of the comparative-cost advantage theory, the question of how a general free trade theory can fit all countries with so much economic variance remains a problem to be resolved by economists and trade law specialist.[46]

[43]Kindleberger & Lindert (1986), pp. 23–24.

[44]Mankiw (2007), p. 48.

[45]Mason (1926), pp. 63–93.

[46]Södersten and Reed (1994), p. 18.

1.5.2 The Relationship Between the IMF and the WTO; Identifying the Need for International Financial Coordination

The policy co-ordination through institutions has its background, even before the formation of the WTO. Through the International legal system, there is also a possibility for the interrelationship between the institutions. During the post-World War I and at the time of, great depression scenario, the US concluded several bilateral trade agreements, but ironically, it had little success in formulating a multilateral trading system. Nevertheless, the Roosevelt administration as a part of post Second World War planning, formulated a multilateral trade regulating body, i.e., GATT, in 1947. In order to improve the chances of free trade among the Member States, GATT sought to establish an MFN clause, as part of the basic measures to encourage trade relations among the Member States. As a supportive measure, and in order to strengthen the possibility of flexibility in cross border free trade, GATT also solicited additional rules to restrain the use of trade intervention measures, by limiting the application of quota measures and other forms of administered protection.[47] A stable monetary system was essential both for free trade, and in order to remove competitive currency devaluation. Along with these developments, an international monetary system, the Bretton Woods system[48] was formed, which was more flexible than the gold standard.

One of the main objectives for establishing the Bretton Woods system[49] was to establish a sort of monetary arrangement, based on both the gold standard and the free floating exchange rate. This new arrangement was basically the gold exchange standard of 1920s, but with the fundamental change that the dollar displaced the British pound as one of the key currencies. After this change, the dollar was valued at 1/35 of a gold ounce, and was to be the only key currency. An additional feature added to this system, distinguishing it from the previous system in 1920 was that dollar was no longer redeemable in gold by private citizens. The dollar was redeemable in gold only by foreign governments and their Central Banks.[50] By

---

[47] Irwin and O'Rourke (2011), p. 20. www.nber.org/papers/w17598.

[48] Established in 1944 and named after the New Hampshire town where the agreements were drawn up, the Bretton Woods system created, an international basis for exchanging one currency for another. It also led to the creation of International Monetary Fund and the International Bank for Reconstruction and Development, now known as the World Bank. Stephey (2008).

[49] The new international monetary order was conceived and then driven through by the United States at an international monetary conference at Bretton Woods, New Hampshire, in mid-1944, and ratified by the Congress in July, 1945.

[50] Rothbard (2008), pp. 93–95.

introducing such an arrangement, the architects of the system designed a monetary system which excluded the shortcomings of both the gold standard[51] and floating exchange[52] rate system.[53] Eventually, they set up an adjustable peg system. As an outcome of this system, the dollar became the key reserve currency, supported by the American Gold reserve.[54] This new system was also a form of monetary experiment. Ironically, it did not function as expected. The dollar remained artificially undervalued and the other currencies remained overvalued and in 1945, this lead to a dollar deficit.

Despite the shortcomings, the dollar remained the key reserve currency, backed by the American Gold reserve, and the US payment deficit of 1950 was temporarily solved by a dollar glut. However, this led to another policy shortfall as, foreign holdings of the dollar surpassed by far the US gold reserve. This, created another risk that the US would not be able to meet its obligations to exchange gold for dollar reserve if the central banks of other nations started demanding gold for all their dollar reserve.[55] To overcome this dilemma, the US adopted a shortcut method of addressing this payment imbalance through a tighter monetary policy and higher interest rates. As the dollar was the pillar of the International monetary system, concern grew about the changes in the exchange rate, as a consequence of this policy shift. US policy makers recognised two policy options, (1) an adjustment in the exchange rate or (2) the imposition of import surcharges.US officials were reluctant to devalue the dollar in terms of gold, as this would particularly put the US prestige at stake.[56] The economy managed somehow for a few years. However, in 1969, when President Nixon came to power, the US economy was placed under great stress. The American gold reserve was at risk due to the high accumulation of dollars abroad and Nixon eventually decided to adopt changes in the international monetary system. In 1971, this led to the US decision to close the gold window and an imposition of surcharges on imports. In the same year, there was also a proposal by the Williams Commission, recommending that the US should adopt a uniform import tax on a temporary basis and also provide an export subsidy to stabilise its exchange rate.[57] This unilateral decision to impose surcharges led to resentment

---

[51]The defects of a fixed exchange rate gold standard is the subordination of national monetary policies to the dictates of an external balance and the subjugation of the economy to international transmission.

[52]Defects of the floating rate are, destabilising speculation and competitive beggar thy-neighbour devaluations.

[53]Bordo and Eichengreen (1993), p. 5. http://www.nber.org/chapters/c6867.

[54]Douglas (2012), pp. 2–3. www.nber.org/papers/w17749.

[55]Douglas (2012), p. 4. www.nber.org/papers/w17749.

[56]Douglas (2012), p. 3. www.nber.org/papers/w17749.

[57]Douglas (2012), p. 8. www.nber.org/papers/w17749. The Smithsonian Agreement, hailed by President Nixon as the "greatest monetary agreement in the history of the world," was even more shaky and unsound than the gold exchange standard of the 1920s or than Bretton Woods. For once again, the countries of the world pledged to maintain fixed exchange rates, but this time with no gold or world money to give any currency backing. Furthermore, many European currencies were

among the other GATT members, and even from within the USA. Questions were raised as to whether the US president had such authority. Based on institutional set up within the GATT system, there existed the possibility to impose quantitative restrictions. According to Article XII of GATT, any contracting party, in order to safeguard its external financial position and for its balance of payments problems, may restrict the quantity or value of merchandise to be imported. Additionally, in order to know the factual status, GATT under Article XV[58] enables to consult with IMF on matters involving the exchange rate. GATT in this case requested the IMF to investigate the US position, and submit a report. The IMF, in this case, supported the US measures, but despite this support GATT reached differing conclusions.[59]

Once membership is attained, the need for policy coordination is required for being part of the mainstream system and also that every individual gets benefitted out of the objectives. The matter of financial stress and shocks can be traced on a prior basis, once the interaction between the WTO treaty provisions starts with the existing market system of a Member States. The WTO trading system comprises of sovereign nations, who have domestic trade policies, that are expected to be consistent with international trade policies, but who are also free to choose their own economic policies. Economic policies among the nations are not similar, as the situation in every society is different, nevertheless, a certain level of understanding among the nations has finally led the WTO to work as a trading system.

As an after effect of WTO membership, the economic policy of the nations inevitably becomes affected by the treaty provisions. The reason for this being the required coordination with the international macroeconomic policies, is a more recent development and seem uncertain. International trade, apart from dealing with import and export, is also influenced by the balance of payments and the growth of money supplies at home and abroad.

In the context of the present-day international trade order, we can say that the WTO is a multi-currency based trading system, in which the business leaders/ traders, of each country are free to decide how to project and adjust, the price of products, the profits/loss-data, and also the amounts of debts. In the present day

---

fixed at undervalued parities in relation to the dollar; the only US concession was a puny devaluation of the official dollar rate to $38 an ounce. However, while much too little and too late, this devaluation was significant in violating an endless round of official American pronouncements, which had pledged to maintain the $35 rate forever more. Now at last the $35 price was implicitly acknowledged as not being engraved on tablets of stone.

[58]Article XV clause 1. The contracting party shall seek co-operation with the International Monetary Fund to the end that the Contracting Parties and the Fund may pursue a co-ordinated policy with regard to exchange questions within the jurisdiction of the Fund and the questions of quantitative restrictions and other trade measures within the jurisdiction of the contracting parties.

[59]The working party took note of the findings of the IMF and recognised that the United States has found itself in a serious balance-of-payment situation which required urgent action. While noting the contrary views of the United States, the other members of the Working party considered that the surcharge, as a trade restrictive measure was in-appropriate given the nature of the United States balance-of-payments situation and the undue burden of adjustment placed upon the import account with consequent serious effects on the trade of other contracting parties.

international trade, currencies establish their level of value depending on their demand. For the purpose of import and export of goods, the demand for a currency depends upon the range of goods, the services and assets that the currency has potential to buy[60] and this is termed as the exchange rate.[61] The coordination of various types of currencies in terms of exchange rate values is a complex process and is an institutional responsibility. The link which is established between trade and the interest rate of money eventually affects the overarching issue of free trade; a key agenda of the WTO. In fact, the treaty provisions and agreements that formed the WTO do not explicitly cover these issues, however, the IMF is the recognised responsible body for money value standardization.

Furthermore, it is also noteworthy that the IMF, which has as its primary purpose, the development of policies regarding money monitoring and stable payment systems, and by virtue of this is expected to be acceptable to all its Member countries nevertheless, has a restrictive role in matters of the WTO. The IMF cannot modify, add to or diminish the rights and obligations of the Member States. However, a specific agreement between the IMF and the WTO enables the staff of the IMF and the WTO secretariat to consult in the concerned matters,[62] thus it can be said that there is some kind of confined role for the IMF in the matters of the WTO.

1.6 The WTO System Based on Country Classification; The Developing, Developed and Less-Developed Countries

The traditional method of trading among nations is based on trade agreements with each country asserting their respective market power. The WTO as an institution, following treaty obligation is committed to providing equal opportunities to trade

---

[60]Rochan and Rossi (2006), pp. 1–15.

[61]The exchange rate of a currency is divided into two categories, fixed and flexible. In a purely fixed exchange rate regime, economic activity adjusts to the exchange rate. In a purely floating regime, the exchange rate is a reflection of economic activity.

[62]*Argentina-Measures Affecting Imports of Footwear Textiles Apparel and Items*, WT/DS56/AB/R, para 84–85. The only provision of the WTO Agreement that requires consultations with the IMF is Article XV: 2 of the GATT 1994.This provision requires the WTO to consult with the IMF when dealing with "problems concerning monetary reserves, balances of payments or foreign exchange arrangements..."As in the WTO Agreement, there are no provisions in the agreement between the IMF and the WTO that require a panel to consult with the IMF in a case such as this. Under Para 8 of this later agreement, in a case involving "exchange measures within the fund's jurisdiction," the IMF shall inform in writing the relevant WTO body (including dispute settlement panels)... whether such measures are consistent with the articles of agreement of the fund. Evidently, the IMF has not been authorised to provide its views to a WTO dispute settlement panel on matters not relating to exchange measures within its jurisdiction, unless it is requested to do so by the panel under Article 13 of the DSU.

through free trade principles. To ensure, that these opportunities are equal for all the Member States, the procedure adopted to attain this objective, is based on common legal principles determined by an assumed set of values, agreeable to all. As an international trade institution, the WTO tries to regulate trade practices despite these diversities and imbalances, by creating exceptions to the MFN clause for the Developing and Less-Developed countries. These exceptions should be applied in a non-discriminatory manner.

Despite the fact that the WTO provisions try to create support for the Developing and Less-Developed countries, the economic position of these nations also demands consideration based on import and export trends. Several Developing countries and Less-Developed countries operate under the risk of having extensive financial outflows due to the import of technology and technological products. To defend these situations, countries are left with two options: (1) Either borrowing from international financial institution or having an inflow of capital from the Developed countries. (2) Under certain circumstances, a country may have to depreciate its currency value. The latter option is adopted mainly where a country is left with very little liquid foreign-exchange reserves, and hence has no means to repay the lenders who have previously extended short-term foreign currency loans.[63] This transpires to be an awkward situation for the countries with the debt, since the amount of debt keeps on increasing. It is clear that the economic structure of Developing countries is in the need of concessionary measures.

The situation comparatively is such that the industrial sector in many of the Developing and Less-Developed countries are relatively weaker with regard to the capital formation. Therefore, the opportunities for earning profits at the initial stages of any industry can be disregarded. The financial burden also get compounded by the fact, that, the economies of some Developing and Less-Developed Countries also get constrained by the additional oil import bills. Consequently, the money that could be otherwise invested in development, is frittered away each time on paying for the increasing oil prices. Ironically, these countries have often borrowed money on interest to pay these bills.

1.6.1 The Less-Developed Countries

In 1971, the weaker economies of the world were designated by the United Nations as the Less-Developing countries.[64] The Economic and Social Council of the United Nations used the following three criteria to determine the new list, as proposed by the committee for development policy: (1) Low income, (2) weak human resources, and (3) economic vulnerability.

[63] A country's exchanged rate regime under which the government or central bank ties the official exchange rate to another country's currency.

[64] Macrory et al. (2005a), p. 343.

The Less-Developed nations suffer from serious social, economic, political and structural weaknesses, which are responsible for their slow pace of development. The WTO, which promotes the idea of free trade, is also trying to promote competition in industrial production, and also in human skills and knowledge. Besides the lack of a technological base, the uncertain socio-economic situation, and the structural bottlenecks, force these Less-Developed countries into a weaker competitive position as regards their level of technological competition. This also makes it a matter of necessity to give concessions to the Less-Developed nation, as a measure of support and so as to bring them to a certain level of industrialisation. The supportive concessions are even extended up to the procedural stage which can be observed, as a matter of reference in the case of the **United States–Subsidies on Upland Cotton.** "Benin and Chad, the two Less-Developed country members, involved in these proceedings as the third parties, were given differential treatment in accordance with Article 24.1[65] of the DSU."[66] With regard to the support for development and welfare through legal provisions, reasonable policy space has been given to the Less-Developed countries and taking into account the WTO objectives, these considerations are relevant.

1.6.2 The Developing Countries

In the WTO, there is no such specific definition of Developing countries; rather a Member State declares itself whether it should be categorised as a Developing country. As a matter of fact, Developing Countries form a heterogeneous group because of the diverse features creating different kinds of economic situations in these countries. The Developing countries category includes a large group of nations, and a simple classification is unable to reflect all the different interests and objectives, so they are further sub-classified as,[67] (a) classification on the basis of GDP

---

[65]Article 24.1, "At all stages of the determination of the causes of a dispute and of dispute settlement procedures involving a Less-Developed country member, particular consideration shall be given to the special situation of Less-Developed country members. In this regard, the member shall exercise due restraint in raising matters under these procedures involving a Less-Developed country member. If nullification or impairment is found to result from a measure taken by a Less-Developed country member, complaining parties shall exercise due restraint in asking for compensation or seeking authorization to suspend the application of concessions or other obligations pursuant to these procedures."

[66]*United States–Subsidies on Upland Cotton* WT/DS/267/R, para 512. The Panel in this case explicitly mentioned that at all the stages of the determination of the cause of dispute. . .particular consideration should be given to the special situation of Less Developed country.

[67]Kasteng et al. (2004), pp. 15–21. www2.jordbruksvert.se/webdav/files/SJV/trycksaker/pdf.

per capita,[68] (b) classification on the basis of net trade position,[69] (c) classification on the basis of common characteristics,[70] (d) classification on the basis of human development,[71] (e) classification on the basis of geographic location.[72] Member States that are categorised as Developing, can claim various kinds of exceptions to the MFN clause. These exceptional clause are mainly, in the form of a Generalised System of Preference (GSP), Special and Differential Treatment (SDT), both of which act in support of Developing and Less-Developed countries.

1.7 Free Trade and Fair Trade; A Brief Discussion

The transformation of the trading system, from GATT to the WTO, occurred not only for political [or legal] reasons but for economic reasons as well. Free trade, which is the primary objective of the WTO, is an advanced market concept based on the fact that nations usually do not consume all their current output; some of it is traded to other nations or can even be stored.

However, simply trading with short term objectives may be insufficient to accord a viable solution for the welfare of individuals in general through free trade. The WTO is thus based on much wider and long term objectives, these objectives focus on the principle that trade should be without discrimination, and beneficial to the Developing and Less-developed countries. In order to achieve these goals, the methods to be adopted are also specified: 'trade should be free and decrease in barriers through negotiations.'

Along with the promotion of free trade as a key trading principle, creation and generation of wealth by the nations, and having procedural checks and balances[73] are matters of shared concern between the Member States. Although, the WTO does not have any strict codified provisions to draw a distinction between fair-trade and unfair trade, the SCM Agreement, Agreement to check the dumping practices

---

[68]The World Bank uses the following categories: low-income countries, lower middle income countries, upper middle income countries or high income countries.

[69]According to the FAO trade statistics, the Developing countries can be classified in the following categories: Net Agricultural-Exporters (NAEX), Net Agricultural-Importers (NAIM), and Net Food Importers (NFIM) Net Food Exporters (NFEX).

[70]The United Nations system defines several categories of Developing countries according to common characteristics: Less-Developed countries, land-locked Developing countries, small island Developing countries, Transition markets and Low-income food deficit countries.

[71]The UNDP uses the human development index to classify the countries into the following groups: low human development, medium human development or high human development.

[72]The United Nations also group the countries according to their geographic location in different regions: Latin America and the Caribbean, Sub-Saharan Africa, East Asia and the Pacific, Europe and Central Asia, the Middle East and North America and South America.

[73]The term "checks and balances" signify, the regulatory restrictions on the nations that have prevailing potentials in the market economies because of technological advancement.

entitled as Agreement on Implementation of Article VI of the General Agreement on Tariffs and Trade 1994, and several other WTO Agreements are regulatory measures based on fair trade concepts. Both the trade practices of Dumping and Subsidies are regarded as unfair:-

1. in the light of the basic objectives of the WTO
2. in the context of transparent trade practice and
3. because these practices lead to the allocation of scarce resources in an inefficient manner.

No doubt it would be an Utopian ambition to say that free trade will make everyone better off. The question arises as to how this is possible without promoting the fair trade concepts. Free trade indeed creates more opportunities, as Member States try to follow an International trade market system based on comparative cost advantage, thus increasing productivity; however uncertainty and scepticism are also part of this debate. The issue of gains from free trade also leads to further questions, such as; who benefits from trade? How can income be distributed to reduce income inequality and poverty? It is indeed an important point to evaluate, that market liberalisation policies goes contrary to the WTO objectives, if the benefits of trade are not distributed across different regions uniformly within a Member State. The case is often such, that within a Member State the level of interaction of the domestic markets with international trade varies. Market systems within a Member State are driven by several factors that somehow does not fit into the general theory of free trade. Trade liberalisation based on common theories, faces the challenges of the high proportion of a population, the cultural differences and issues related to factor mobility.[74] However, despite several limitations, free trade has also shown substantive effects. As a natural consequence of its operations, the monopoly power of domestic firms has been diminished.[75] Even if a firm is the only producer of a product in a country, there may be several foreign suppliers once non-protectionist trade policies are followed. Free trade keeps the prices of imports low and increases the choice of goods for consumers. Trade liberalisation complemented by fair trade values, shall automatically check the effects of trade expansion, such as a market dominating strategy that free trade will otherwise produce.[76] Fairtrade also gives some insight into "*sustainable development, cautioning primarily with regard to the effect on the environment and the use of natural resources, promoting business transparency and the efficient use of resources.*"

It is noteworthy that even if fair trade objectives are not currently the core aspects of the WTO trading system, the promotion of free trade at an equitable level among the Member States requires the WTO to encompass fair trade values up to a certain level. A certain consistent level of approach between free trade and fair

[74]Krishna et al. (2010), pp. 5, 11, 12. http://www.nber.org/papers/w16322.

[75]Krugman and Obstfed (2009), p. 208.

[76]Drezner (2006), p. 1. ISBN 0876093497 www.cfr.org/content/publications/attachments/CPCTrade.

trade objectives is necessary to form a bridge between the objectives, so that free trade keeps advancing in order to accomplish the objectives. Basically, through the fair trade approach, the objectives that the WTO wishes to achieve are the economic advancement of Developing and Less-Developed countries. These aims can be realised when the Member States start working on policies, by enacting the primary and secondary rules,[77] with these objectives in mind.

1.8 Subsidies as a State Support Between Free Trade and Fair Trade

The discussion on state support and subsidies has conceptual basis in the context of free trade and fair trade, where free trade is the primary frame of reference and fair trade acts as a regulatory measures. While studying the specific issue of subsidies, a comparison between the objectives of fair trade and free trade also includes, the testing of standards, values, and policies of the Member States. There is doctrinal difference between free trade and fair trade, which is obvious in the objectives. By applying fair trade concepts[78] through a rules based instrument in the form of the ASCM, the WTO tries to regulate the state support, given in the form of subsidies. Agricultural or Industrial trade subsidies supported by the nation-governments leads to *protectionist* measures, and are also discriminatory trade practices, leading to trade distortion, therefore they violate the objectives of the WTO free trade system. The norms of fair trade depend on individual ethics and morality, established legal norms, and economic and social principles. However, the fair trade values for justifying the level of subsidies, are based on the following features.

1.8.1 The Underlying Features of Fair Trade

1. The significant features of fair trade are, promoting market transparency, creating efficiency based on fair competition, and the efficient use of resources. Although the use of subsidies expands trade, the unregulated use of subsidies is at odds with these principles.

[77]Footer (2006), p. 183.

[78]Fair trade concepts such as, equitable distribution of resources, reducing poverty by creating more trading opportunities, creating fair chance for the development of Developing and Less Developed countries, can be defined in the light of the objectives mentioned in the preamble of the WTO such as 'raising standards of living, ensuring full employment, expanding production of trade in goods and services and to enhance the means for doing so in a manner consistent with their respective needs and concerns at different level of economic development. Recognising that there is need for positive efforts to ensure that developing countries and especially the least developed countries, secure a share of growth with the needs of their economic development.'

2. It is expected that fair trade will promote equitable market conditions. Equitable market conditions from the WTO perspective also means, creating trade opportunities for the Developing and Less-Developing countries. This aspect is emphasised by the inclusion of specific provisions within the ASCM, supporting subsidies for Developing and Less-Developed countries.
3. As a result of shifting the production centers to the Developing and Less-Developed countries, and because of the trade liberalisation policies, problems concerning the environment are also increasing and this requires due consideration. Fair trade values also specify that due care should be taken for the minimum impact on environment because of the trading activity. The policy mechanism supporting state aid and subsidies for trade should be consistent with the sustainable development objective.

1.8.2 MFN Clause for Promoting Free Trade

For trade to be based on efficiency and the maximum utilisation of resources, free trade demands, that a trading environment should be non-discriminatory and for this objective, two main principles have been adopted by the WTO. (1) The (MFN) Most Favoured Nation clause and (2) the National treatment principle. The MFN principle prohibits like goods from being discriminated against by the goods of other countries or any country being given special consideration, other than through exceptions or special agreements. To make the fundamentals of trade liberalisation concrete, the "National treatment clause"[79] further prohibits imported products from being treated less favourably than domestic products of the same kind.

The MFN clause adopted by the WTO, which is the main pillar supporting free trade, also contains some provisions supporting exceptions for the Developing and Less-Developed countries. The most favoured nation's clause explicitly mentions that the importing country should not accord any discrimination against the like product of any other Member State, or in other words, equal favour should be provided to the like products of other Member States. In order to impress upon the development and welfare measures, and that such chances are not missed in the free trading system; the preamble of the WTO agreement in the light of these needs,

[79]Article III of the GATT 1994. 1) The members recognize that internal taxes and other internal charges, and laws regulations and requirements affecting the internal sale, offering or sale, purchase, transportation, distribution or use of products, and internal quantitative regulations, requiring the mixture, processing or the use of products in specified amounts or proportions, should not be applied to imported or domestic products so as to afford protection to domestic production.

2) The products of the territory of any member imported into the territory of any other member shall not be subject, directly or indirectly, to internal taxes or other internal charges of any kind in excess of those applied, directly or indirectly, to like domestic products. Moreover, no member shall otherwise apply internal taxes or other internal charges to imported or domestic products in a manner contrary to the principles set forth in para 1.

refers to the provision of a special relaxation.[80] In this regard, cross border trade rules and regulations should be framed consistent with the MFN clause. For the effective application of the MFN clause, tariffs and other charges should not be discriminatory, nor should any internal regulations be discriminatory.[81] The exceptions to the MFN clause, act as counterbalancing provisions between nations with a different economic status trading with each other. The exceptions are those of "Generalised system of preference," "Special and differential treatment," and other provisions which respond to the development needs, that are expected to be for a transition period only. For the gradual, step by step economic progress of the Developing and Less-Developed countries, it is essential for the global institutions to accept these exceptions as the necessary flexibilities.

1. SDT, "Special and Differential Treatment." The acceptance by many Developing Countries of the IMF's structural programming in their adoption of trade liberalisation-oriented development measures also sought further Special and Differential Treatment.[82] Special and Differential Treatment (here after referred to, SDT.) provisions allow countries to provide more favourable treatment to the Developing Countries than to the remainder of the membership. These are provisions within the various WTO Agreements, providing special dispensations/exemptions to the Developing countries in order to provide special

[80]The parties to this agreement, Recognizing that their relations in the field of trade and economic endeavor should be conducted with a view to raising standards of living, ensuring full employment and a large and steadily growing volume of real income and effective demand, and expanding the production of trade in goods and services, while allowing for the optimal use of the world's resources in accordance with the objective of sustainable development, seeking both to protect and preserve the environment and to enhance the means for doing so in a manner consistent with their respective needs and concerns at different levels of economic development.

Recognizing further that there is need for positive efforts designed to ensure that Developing countries and especially the Less-Developing countries among them, secure a share in the growth in international trade commensurate with the need of their economic development.

[81]GATT Article I. (1) Provides for WTO members to accord Most-Favoured-Nation treatment to "like products" of other WTO members regarding tariffs, regulations on exports and imports, internal taxes and charges, and internal regulations. In other words, "like products" from all WTO members must be given the same treatment as the most advantageous treatment to the product of any state.

Should an importing country accord differential treatment to "like products" of the exporting country, i.e., by setting different tariff rates, it would be clearly a violation of GATT Article I.(1). However, Article I.(1) violations can also occur even when there is no ostensible discrimination against the product of a Most-Favoured Nation, such as when an importing country accords differential treatment among products that are considered to be "like products," which ultimately results in the de-facto discrimination against products of specific contracting parties. For instance, a country may apply a different tariff rate to a particular variety of raw coffee bean, but if that variety and other varieties of coffee beans were considered to be like products using criteria such as consumer tastes and end-use, the differential tariffs may have an effect on imports from different countries.

[82]As early as in 1947–48 at the Havana Conference, some Developing countries challenged the assumption that trade liberalisation on an MFN basis would automatically lead to their growth and development. Source www.wto.org/english/tratop_e/devel_e/sem01_e/gibbs_e.doc.

considerations, such as (a) a longer time period for implementing agreements and commitments (b) measures to increase trading opportunities for the Developing countries, (c) special provisions requiring the WTO Members to safeguard the trade interests of the Developing countries, (d) support to help the Developing countries building the capacity to carry out the WTO work, while also handling disputes and implementing technical standards.[83] From the perspective of the WTO objectives of welfare and development, SDT provisions are the main provisions creating the possibilities for economic and technological advancement of the Developing countries. This favourable treatment is based on the relative level of development and different kinds of requirements for the development within the Developing and Less-Developed countries.

2. GSP, "Generalised System of Preference." Basically, the concept of GSP was introduced by UNCTAD in 1964, and in 1970, the GATT contracting parties adopted it. It is a system that grants to products exported, from the Developing countries, lower tariff rates than those normally required from other countries. Developed countries, by virtue of this provision based mechanism, follow the concessionary approach, such as lower tariffs or even duty free treatment to the specific imported products from the Developing countries with whom the trade preference agreement is signed.[84] This special measure is granted to the Developing countries in order to have a better chances to boost their exports and hence buy or invest the money in technological advancement. The sort of extensive waivers granted through these supporting provisions were not renewed during the Tokyo Round discussions of November 18, 1979 and as a result were minimised as an enabling clause. With this status, the provision was enabled but no longer obligates the Developed countries to accord preferential tariff treatments.[85] Therefore, in their present capacity, the GSP are more like concessional measures based on the ambit of SDT policies.

In addition to these relaxations for the Developing and Less-Developed economies, the core issue of making the international trading system efficient, remains the priority. Efficient functioning means here the adopting of measures to increase global production and consumption by adopting cost effective methods. This objective can be realised if the market system of the Member States modifies itself to adopt the pattern of an increase in global production and consumption in a global economy, by greater *flexibility in cross border* flows of trade in goods, services, assets and intellectual property. Following the liberal market policies based on the WTO system, the trading opportunities for the Member States has indeed grown, but they are obliged to follow a specific set of rules for trade. These rules act as checks and balances restricting discriminatory, market distortionary, and other inefficient trade practices.

---

[83]For reference see, www.wto.org/english/tratop_e/dev_special_different.

[84]Macrory et al. (2005b), p. 1540.

[85]Macrory et al. (2005b), p. 1542, also see, www.wto.org/english/tratop_e/dev_special_different.

1.9 Subsidies for Development and Welfare; A Brief Discussion

The study about state support and subsidies is an attempt to analyse, the various causes of trade distortion, trade-discriminatory practices, and other issues linked with subsidies that often arises as a consequence of unregulated free trade. Additionally, the study about contemporary trade practices, attempts to determine how these issues fall within the ambit of subsidies described under the SCM Agreement. This comparison is pursued with the objective of testing how far the free trade system as promoted by the WTO, succeeds in terms of limiting the use of subsidies and creating a kind of equation between the objectives of free trade and fair trade values. Since the subject area of International trade or trade between the nations is vast, therefore a broader perspective on international trade is applied as a measure to cover the state support and to study the regulatory role of fair trade values. The regulatory measures based on fair trade concepts and values are the positive criteria used to determine the role of the WTO, and specifically the SCM Agreement, to regulate state support in the form of subsidies.

State support can be in many forms, and to analyse the extent of this support through fair trade values, such as efficiency based on fair level of competition, it requires a level of comparison between various WTO objectives and the international trade in practice. Fair trade values from the WTO perspectives are relative. From the perspective of international trade, it demands, the comparative analysis of the state support from the perspective of the Developed, Developing, and Less-Developed countries, and the limits of justification for their use. State aid and subsidies affects market competition, nevertheless, there is a need to exempt several types of state aid when considering the wide economic inequality and disparity among the Member States because of several factors.

While making comparison we also need to take into account the indispensable reliance on rural economy by the Less–Developed and the Developing nations, which is the key reason for state support being given in the form of subsidies for the purpose of agriculture. Developed economies are already ahead in the industrial and technological sectors and the use of subsidies by them to prevail in the export market, creates a rift between the Developed and Developing economies. During the WTO ministerial conferences, it can be observed that because of the general free trade policy approach, Member States, also in the matters concerning agriculture trade, try to bargain between farm products with the industrial products and this leads to polarization of debate. The question remains between the Member States, '*is it possible to meet the WTO development and welfare objectives, if the farm subsidies promoted by the Developed economies are not regulated.*'

In the free trade system promoted by the WTO, subsidies are also used for the strategic purposes, such as dumping. Subsidies, either used directly or through policy measures can be an attempt to encourage trade in export and formally dumping the products to capture any foreign market. This is contrary to the market transparency, efficiency principles, efficient allocation of resources, and, in particular, it challenges the basic objectives of the WTO. Such policy measures both by the Developed and Developing countries that promote exports by overstepping/tampering with the WTO rules through policy mechanism can be termed as unjustifiable subsidies.

State support for welfare and development can also be a dilemma for the WTO, as several forms of trade concessions are allowed to the Developing nations, but how to draw the limits to the extent of these concessions, at the back of fair trade values is not clear in the present SCM Agreement. Bearing in mind the WTO objectives, the issue arises whether the justifiable use of subsidies for the promotion of export by the Developing countries can legally be used for exporting goods at a price cheaper than the domestic price of that product.

Among the Developed nations and the Developing nations, the newly developed trade practices such as the intermediate parts being purchased from the places where the production cost is relatively lower; however, this location is usually not disclosed to the customers. This becomes a matter of analysing the role of subsidies. In terms of present day international trade, such business practices are in the form of outsourcing, offshore assembly, and product sharing agreements. The significance of fair trade values, as trade regulatory measures entails that transparency in cross border trade is an essential requirement, meaning that consumers should know the nationality of the product. With the lack of transparency, such cross border business practices by the multinationals are used to reduce the cost of production and this is a form of financial benefit to them. At the abstract level, it can be said, that these are the forms of benefit not covered by the SCM Agreement, but nevertheless, such trade advantages have commonalities with the subsidy practices. From the perspective of fair trade values, it becomes an issue for analysis whether, in the case of obtaining imported intermediate products, either on the basis of discrimination of place or obtaining intermediate inputs on the basis of mutually agreed concessions by the Member States, does that confer benefit to any export industry.

The impact of trade subsidies on the environment also need to be analysed from the perspective of the WTO objectives. The main objective of the WTO is to promote free trade and along with free trade to promote sustainable development in principle. This is easy to discuss at the horizontal level, however, construction of both the objectives, the sustainable development and free trade are different and possible coherence seems difficult to reach. Free trade literally means no protectionist policies or no restrictions on trade; on the other hand the goal of sustainable development means qualitative measures, based on certain agreed standards to be adopted before the promotion of trade. Based on this, it can be construed, that trade practices for the attainment of benefits can aberate environmental standards. The far reaching negative effects of unregulated trade, on the environment are revealed. The economic impact can be determined once the instances of the effects are analysed and compared with economic terms, such as "financial contribution´ and 'benefit.'"

While justifying subsidies for Welfare and Development, the main consideration is that the majority of the WTO Members comprise of Developing and Less-

Developed countries and this being the position, the economic growth and advantages for social improvement are considered to be the preferable issues. With the aspiration, to attain this objective, the challenge is to overcome the conventional attitude 'that business only meant profits and that taking into account welfare along with business is paradoxical.'

This issue can be clarified as follows.

1. How can a nation benefit from the economic growth of other nations?
2. What kind of trade pattern should be the basis of growth (from the perspective of Developing and Less-Developed countries)?

These questions demand flexibility from both the Developing and the Developed countries side. Within the WTO, several concessions that are given to Developing and Less-Developed countries are an illustration of the affirmative action taken in the light of welfare policies.

Ironically, there is a growing attitude among the policy-makers of the Developed countries, that the import of products from the Developing nations is a challenge for their domestic markets products. People in the technologically-advanced nations, where workers earn high wages, often fear that trading with lower-wage countries will reduce their standard of living. This is leading to protectionist policies for the sake of short-term gains on both the sides. Within the WTO, this difference of opinion between Developed and a Developing country is termed the "North-South divide."

1.9.1 State Support Whether Justifiable or Non-justifiable

Trade issues related to subsidies are part of the profound discussion on fair trade measures that are based upon the implied ethos, acting as regulatory measures for realising the objectives of the WTO.[86] The discussion on trade subsidies at the horizontal level, covers both industrial and agricultural issues in international trade and at vertical dimension, further analysing the justifiable and non-justifiable use of these subsidies. Trade subsidies can be compared to the two sides of the same coin. For practical reasons, there seems to be some justification for giving subsidies, for

[86]Preamble of the WTO, "The parties to this Agreement, recognizing that their relations in the field of trade and economic endeavor should be conducted with a view to raising standards of living, ensuring full employment and a large steadily growing volume of real income and effective demand, and expanding the production of trade in goods and services .... Recognizing further that there is a need for positive efforts designed to ensure that developing countries, and especially the least developed countries among them, secure a share in the growth of international trade commensurate with the needs of their economic development. Being desirous of contributing to these objectives by entering into reciprocal and mutually advantageous arrangements directed to the substantial reduction of tariffs and other barriers to trade and to the elimination of discriminatory treatment in international trade relations."

example, during the initial phase of industrialisation and also when society is transforming from an agricultural economy to a free market economy. This support can be categorised as justifiable state-aid,[87] justifiable and non-justifiable subsidies from the WTO perspective. It is noteworthy, that the term state-aid[88] is a term used within the EU system, but is not used under the WTO SCM Agreement.[89] Within the WTO framework, subsidies to the extent that they are a necessity are valid, however, if this state support is given at subsequent intervals, similar to any form of deliberate normative exercise,[90] specifically, for the promotion of export, then, then these are subsidies barred by the WTO.

The WTO trading system is classified based on economic and technological criteria, the term justifiable and non-justifiable are used as hypothetical parameters to determine the extent of state support considering the country classification. These parameters are distinct from the prohibited, actionable, and non-actionable subsidies,[91] as classified under the SCM Agreement. Within the SCM Agreement, the provisions describing actionable subsidies are open ended and thus gives the DSB the possibility to make interpretations whenever a dispute arises concerning the extent of the use of subsidies. Therefore, these parameters are applied mainly in the case of actionable subsidies, or to create a distinction as to when state support can be considered actionable.

From the Developed nation's perspective, the demarcation of justifiable and non-justifiable subsidies to the Developing and Less-Developed countries can be seen as a level of concession, or a policy level institutional support measures. The state support given to attain the WTO objectives of welfare and development is promoted as a positive and an equitable aim of the WTO.[92] Justifiable subsidies and non-justifiable subsidies, or the instances the justifiable subsidies will take the form of non-justifiable, depends very much on the cause and effect relationship in a market system. From the WTO perspective, trade subsidies are also regarded as protectionist measures adopted to safeguard domestic industry and hence, are a hindrance to free trade.

---

[87]The term state-aid is used in the EU.

[88]Luca (2009), p. 149. "Unlike in the WTO law, there is only one provision featuring a definition of State aid in the EC. Article 87(1) EC regulates 'any aid granted by the State or through State resources in any form whatsoever."

[89]There are several agreements annexed to the Marrakesh Agreement signed in 1994. Agreement on Subsidies and Countervailing Measures is covered under Annex 1A, covering Multilateral Agreements on Trade in Goods. SCM Agreement: Subsidies and Countervailing Measures Agreement. This agreement is based on outlines determining the justifiable and non-justifiable use of subsidies. The provisions in this agreement classify subsidies as, prohibited, actionable and non-actionable, and restricts the use of subsidies in order to avoid trade distortion.

[90]Footer (2006), p. 3.

[91]For non-actionable subsidies see Article 8 of the SCM Agreement. Article 8 is obsolete since 1999.

[92]Luca (2009), p. 22.

1.10 Subsidies from the WTO Perspective

The basic question of fair trade is derived from certain assumed values that touch the core economic idea of free trade. Free trade under the WTO covers all kinds of goods, and is not confined to trade in traditional goods such as raw materials and agricultural products; rather nowadays it is also to promote trade in technological products, which needs to be competitive at the global level. Attaining this level of competitiveness requires a specialisation in production and this plays a key role in the creation of wealth. Creating wealth for welfare and, subsequently, its proper distribution, needs fair regulation. In this context, the making of a distinction between fair trade and unfair trade is a complex issue for both lawyers and economists.

From the perspective of the WTO trading system, it is mainly the export subsidies or the special favours to domestic products or the inducing of local contents[93] in the final production that is considered unjustifiable under the WTO law. Since, an export subsidy can be in a covert form, to determine the practice of subsidies and its effects, the focus is placed on the "financial contribution" and "benefit"[94] obtained by any industry.

As the Member States are classified as Developed, Developing and Less-Developed countries, subsidies in the WTO context need to be seen from two different dimensions. First, they need to be seen from the economic position of the Less-Developed countries and second, from the stand point of the Developed countries. The Less-Developed countries face several kinds of challenges that are recognised by the WTO. The economic structure in these countries is in a transformation stage; from agricultural to industrial, which in itself suggests that the industries are at an infant stage and in need of various kinds of support. For example, economic policies can support subsidies for production in general, or can focus on the use of subsidies for the export of some specific manufactured type of goods by which, it is believed, a comparative advantage can be developed.

Although the Developed nations do have a comparative advantage in many sectors of production, they seek concessions in the form of subsidies for research and development, classified as non-actionable subsidies (now support in the form of non-actionable subsidies has been reduced). The significance of these kinds of concessions is questionable from the point of fairness in trade. Funding for research and development overlaps with other kinds of investment, for example, deduction from corporate profit tax and this may take the form of practising covertly, what can be called unfair-trade. In similar cases, the Agreement on Subsidies and Countervailing Measures has provisions for remedies in the case any party that is affected. Nevertheless, there are several kinds of policy measures that become linked with export promotion measures and which take the form of export subsidies.

[93]For details see, Article 3 of the SCM Agreement.

[94]Article 1.1(b) of Subsidies and Countervailing Measures Act.

These latter issues need to be analysed in the light of present-day international-trade practices based on some accepted values by the Member States of the WTO.

1.10.1 The Regulation of Subsidies from the WTO Perspective

The Subsidies and Countervailing Measure Agreement is an instrument for the classification of subsidies, policy coordination, and for the regulation of cross border trade. In this study, while analysing several issues, observing practical implications of the policies in support of subsidies, and assessing the extent of trade regulations through SCM Agreement, has raised new queries.

There are several reasonable grounds for the concessions, but the most significant is that development requires market stability, which justifies the concessions in favour of Developing and Less-Developed countries, however, on occasions; these concessions are used to circumvent the accepted rules on trade.

"Financial contribution" and the "benefit" are the key factors taken together to determine the subsidy practices. These two factors are also used to test the indirect forms of state support, which may not be categorised as trade subsidies as per the SCM Agreement. These trade practices can however be tested, if they are contrary to the assumed fair trade values and concepts.

1.11 Conclusions

This chapter briefly covers how far the SCM Agreement is able to achieve its primary objectives, such as, the restrictive use of subsidy practices, promoting efficiency in the free trade system, creating possibilities for development by the expansion of trade opportunities for the Developing and Less-Developed countries. From the discussions, the inference drawn is that the SCM Agreement, in the present context, is not comprehensive enough to cover several forms of subsidies and further suggestions are also proposed in the following chapters. The chapter also tries to develop a proposition based on the critical evaluation of the SCM Agreement, as some of the trade related issues seems beyond the reach of the provisions of the Agreement, in its present form. Keeping in view the objectives of the WTO, subsidies for the development and welfare of the Developing and Less-Developed nations are advocated. Along with the conclusions, there are other suggestions mainly supporting a widening of the scope of the SCM Agreement. On this basis, we start the discussion on various forms of subsidies in the next chapter.

References

Abbott FM, Breinning-Kaufmann C, Cottier T (2006) International Trade and Human Rights: foundations and conceptual issues. University of Michigan Press, Ann Arbor

Beinhocker E (2007) The origin of wealth: evolution complexity and radical remaking of economics. Harvard Business Press, Boston

Bordo MD, Eichengreen B (eds) (1993) A retrospective on the Bretton Woods System: lessons for International Monetary Reform. University of Chicago Press, Chicago

Bossche P (2008) The law and policy of the World Trade Organization. Cambridge University Press, Cambridge

Ehlermann C-D, Ehring L (2005) Decision-making in the World Trade Organization. J Int Econ Law 8(1):51–75

Fagerberg J (1994) Technology and international differences in growth rates. J Econ Lit 32 (3):1147–1175

Footer ME (2006) An institutional and normative analysis of the World Trade Organization. Martinus Nijhoff, Leiden

Gabrielle M (2002) WTO dispute settlement and human rights. Eur J Int Law 13(4):753–814

Gregory MN (2007) Principles of economics. South Western Thomson publication, Mason

Hudec RE, Southwick JD (eds) (2002) Essays in honour of Daniel M. Kennedy – the political economy of International Trade Law. Cambridge University Publication, Cambridge

Kindleberger CP, Lindert PH (1986) International economics. Irwin Publishers, Illions

Krugman P, Obstfed M (2009) International economics: theory and policy. Pearson Addison Wesley, Boston

Luca R (2009) The definition of subsidy and state aid: WTO and EC law in comparative perspective. Oxford University Press, New York

Macrory P, Appleton AE, Plummer MG (eds) (2005a) The World Trade Organization: legal economic and political analysis, vol II. Springer, New York

Macrory P, Appleton AE, Plummer MG (eds) (2005b) The World Trade Organization: legal economic and political analysis, vol I. Springer, New York

Mason ES (1926) The doctrine of comparitive costs. Q J Econ 41(1):63–93

Matsushita M, Schoenbaum TJ, Mavroidis P (2003) The World Trade Organization: law practice and policy. Oxford University Press, Oxford

Mavroidis PC (2005) Oxford commentaries on the GATT/WTO Agreements. The general agreements on tariffs and trade: a commentary. Oxford University Press, New York

Rochan LP, Rossi S (2006) Monetary and exchange rate systems: a global view of financial crisis. Edward Elgar Press, Cheltenham

Rothbard MN (2008) What has government done to our money? Ludwig von Mises Institute Press, Albama, pp 93–95

Sauve P, Grasstek CV (2006) The consistency of WTO rules: can the single undertaking squared with variable geometry? J Int Econ Law 9(4):837–864

Södersten B, Reed G (1994) International economics. The Macmillan Press Ltd, London

Srinivasan TN (2009) Developing countries and the multilateral trading system: from the GATT to the Uruguay round and the future. Westview Press, Colarado

Stephey M (2008) A brief history of Bretton Woods System. TIME, 28 October 2008. http://content.time.com/time/business/article/0,8599,1852254,00.html

Cases

Argentina-Measures Affecting Imports of Footwear Textiles Apparel and Items WT/DS56/AB/R
United States-Import Prohibition of Certain Shrimp and Shrimp Products WT/DS58/R
United States-Standard for Reformulated and Conventional Gasoline WT/DS2/AB/R
United States-Subsidies on Upland Cotton WT/DS267/R

Reports and Electronic Sources

Douglas IA (2012) The Nixon shock after forty years: the import surcharge revisited. National Bureau of Economic Research, Cambridge. www.nber.org/papers/w17749

Drezner DW (2006) U.S. trade strategy, free versus fair. Council on Foreign Relations, New York. www.cfr.org/content/publications/attachments/CPCTrade

Irwin DA, O'Rourke KH (2011) Coping with shocks and shifts: the multilateral trading system in historical-perspective. National Bureau of Economic Research, Cambridge. www.nber.org/papers/w17598

Kasteng JA, Karlsson A, Lindberg C (2004) Differentiation between developing countries in the WTO

Krishna P, Devashish M, Sundram A (2010) Trade, poverty and the lagging regions of-South Asia. Cambridge. NBER Working Paper Series. http://www.nber.org/papers/w16322

Swedish Board of Agriculture International Affairs Division. http://www2.jordbruksverket.se/webdav/files/SJV/trycksaker/Pdf_rapporter/ra04_14Epdf

World Trade Report (2007) www.wto.org

Chapter 2
Subsidies in International Trade from the WTO Perspective

Abstract The trade practices of giving subsidies are normally defined as financial support in cash or in kind, if made in favour of an undertaking by the state. This support can either be direct or indirect in form, for the goods or services that any such industry produces. Trade-subsidy supported by the national government often leads to the distortion of efficient and competitive market system or can either be a protectionist measures, and hence, violates the underlying principles of fair-trade. Fair trade principle although not emphasised as the main trading principles of governing free trade, however is effectuated as a regulatory measure through the SCM Agreement provisions.

This chapter starts with a discussion on state-aid, as state-aid is one of the primary aspects of subsidies, and although not explained in the SCM Agreement in a distinct manner, it is, however, used in EU law.

Further, the study covers a brief reference to some economic principles as premises for a better understanding of international trade in practice. The analysis broadly covers the use of subsidies in international trade, investigating the reason for the differences of opinion between the Developed and Developing nations, the extent of justification in the form of justifiable subsidies for its use, as well as how the non-justifiable use of subsidies affects market efficiency. Although, the primary function of the WTO as a multilateral organisation is to regulate trade amongst the Member Nations, it is also a forum for the discussion of such crucial matters. Placing at the forefront the mentioned objectives of the WTO, this study will analyse various forms of state support as the causes of trade distortion and how they fall within the ambit of subsidies.

2.1 New Trends in International Trade

The approach towards international trade adopted by the WTO is based, primarily on the economic theory of free trade.[1] These free trade promoting ideas followed by the WTO are underpinned by further legal concepts and by provisions based on research and reflections developed through the economic, historical, and political evaluation of the phases that the world trading system and its practices have passed

[1]The theory of free trade was first propounded by Adam Smith and later applied by David Ricardo.

G. Singh, *Subsidies in the Context of the WTO's Free Trade System*,
DOI 10.1007/978-3-319-62422-8_2

through. When the Member States, started inducing liberal trade policies in the light of the WTO rules, they faced two noteworthy challenges. First, while re-structuring the markets for promoting free trade policies, the Member States were obliged neither to apply discriminatory tariffs nor to increase the existing levels of tariffs. Ironically, this is easy in theory but difficult in practice, because of certain inherent conflicting situations and due to the lack of an unequivocal approach by the Member States. Following this, the second challenge, states faced was lowering the existing tariffs, as it became likely that a number of industries, both domestic and foreign, would be required to adjust to competition based on fluctuating demand and supply in the market. As a result, this type of market environment led to unregulated competition among the Member States. For those economies based on industrial production and featuring high import and exports of industrial goods, the growing market uncertainty, as a result of shifting trends in international trade, was the primary reasons for the use of subsidies.

2.1.1 Practices Versus Obligations

In the present-day trade practices, there is an invariable use of subsidies by, Developed, Developing, and Less-Developed nations, even for trivial reasons. This creates the risk of a *de facto* use of subsidies claiming *de jure* status after long-term use. Over time, this unjustified use of subsidies can acquire legal support by becoming precedents. Ironically, such a use of subsidy can retain its legal support despite a vagueness of purpose.

The 'WTO Subsidies Agreement' is based on the concept that indiscriminate use of subsidies by any Member States is contrary to the basic objectives of the WTO. This Agreement is an instrument with prescribed regulatory measures, classifying subsidies broadly, and conditionally restricting their use. However, the demand has grown for broader legal claims and support, in the case of the new types of subsidies with unclear objectives that are not covered within the descriptions in the Agreement. There is a possibility that such a use rather enhances complexities of regulating international trade. To understand the far-reaching effects of subsidies in international trade, we start with a discussion about state-aid. The term State-aid as such is not applied in the SCM Agreement; it is derived from EU law and is used for the purpose of explanation.

2.2 Subsidy and State-Aid, General Discussion. The WTO and EU as an Instance

A subsidy can generally be expressed as the opposite of a tax. Referring this practice from the broader perspective of *industrial trade production* and *free movement of goods*, the term "subsidy" in general can be construed as conforming to a meaning with a wider coverage, such as *"aid," "bounty" and "grant"* on a collinear basis.[2] However, such a wide interpretation is not used to determine fairness in international trade.

Aid in general can be defined as a necessary form of assistance and state-aid as government assistance. The term state-aid is mainly used in EU law. The extent of justification for such assistance depends very much on the amount, volume, quality, and several other factors that can be categorised within cause and effect relationship.

Depending upon the circumstances, state-aid is legally valid to a certain extent, but, when the validity of the state-aid ceases in precise terms, it is a difficult matter, to ascertain and requires further discussion on a case by case basis. In the matters of international trade, the intricate link established between subsidies and state-aid, necessitates that the two terms be discussed comparatively, usually when such a policy measure is adopted or framed, and several clauses are added justifying state support. Such state support occasionally takes the form of subsidies and thus challenges the main objectives of the WTO.

Bounty is a term used for some kind of award or benefit given after an act—is performed.[3] In the context of WTO trading system, it can be described as a reward by a government to any industry in the form of concession after achieving export targets.

On the basis of general observation as presented above, one can say that it is difficult to define the term subsidy in a precise manner, however, interpretation of the term can be somewhat relative to the context and approach and can also be analysed in relation to perceptions of economic and market concepts. As a matter of fact, GATT, the trade regulating institution preceding the WTO lacked the proper definition of subsidies. Subsidies under GATT were described at the general level, under Article XVI[4] and were subdivided into five clauses. Later on during the

[2]Webster's New World Dictionary defines "grant" as "something granted" and "bounty" as "something given freely as a generous gift."

[3]Thomas (2001), p. 341.

[4]Article XVI cl (1) If any contracting party grants or maintains any subsidy, including any form of income or price support, which operates directly or indirectly to increase exports of any product from, or to reduce imports of any product into, its territory, it shall notify the CONTRACTING PARTIES in writing of the extent and nature of subsidization. . .the possibility of limiting the subsidization. (2) The contracting party recognize that the granting by a contracting party of a subsidy on the export of any product may have harmful effects for other contracting parties, both importing and exporting. . .. (3) Accordingly, contracting parties should seek to avoid the use of subsidies on the export of primary product. (4) Further, as from 1 January 1958 or the earliest

Tokyo Round,[5] a specific Subsidies Code was established with further addition in provisions and procedures to deal with the subsidy practices of the Member State. The 1979 Tokyo Round code did not succeed, as it faced several challenges. After going through mixed experiences, another round of discussions was held in 1985, during the Uruguay Round in which the issue of subsidies was given a specific reference.[6] It was during December 20, 1991, that the final draft, exhibiting the outcome of the negotiations, known as the Dunkel Draft was tabled in Geneva.[7] The difference of opinion among the Member states on several issues was apparent in this draft. With regard to the subject of subsidies, which was indeed widely discussed, two major viewpoints emerged. One of them, put forward by the US, laid emphasis on the existing inadequacy of the established legal measures to check subsidies. The other group consisting of several members considered the lack of a proper legal base to apply countervailing measures. The negotiating parties could not reach a unanimous approach, so the difference of opinion on various topics was the only final outcome of the Dunkel Draft.[8] In order to attain consistency, the Trade Negotiations Committee advanced a suggestion to re-launch the Uruguay Round multilateral trade negotiations. On July 28, 1993, Director-General Sutherland, as the chairperson of the TNC, took the initiative to attain 'substantial and concrete' progress.[9] Finally, on December 15 1993, Director-General Sutherland announced the successful conclusion of the Uruguay Round negotiations.[10] It was on April 15 1994, in Marrakesh, that the Final Act based on the Uruguay Round Multilateral Trade Negotiations was signed.[11]

The WTO ASCM (Agreement on Subsidies and Countervailing Measures) nowhere mentions the term state-aid or bounty; however, it classifies subsidies

---

practicable date thereafter, contracting parties shall cease to grant either directly or indirectly any form of subsidy on the export of any product other than primary product which subsidy results in the sale of such product for export at a price lower than the comparable price charged for the like product to buyers in the domestic market.... (5) The CONTRACTING PARTIES shall review the operation of the provisions of this Article from time to time with a view to examine its effectiveness...contracting parties.

[5]Tokyo Round in 1979.

[6]Stewart (1993), p. 70.

[7]Stewart (1999), p. 221.

[8]Stewart (1993), p. 70.

[9]Stewart (1999), p. 226.

[10]Stewart (1999), p. 233. In remarks before the TNC, Chairman Sutherland noted that: "The Round went further than any previous negotiation to extend and strengthen the rule of law in international trade, both by bringing GATT principles to apply in areas where they have been lacking, and by strengthening the existing rules, especially by ensuring their application through a more effective dispute settlement system...."

[11]For reference see, www.wto.org see Uruguay Round Agreement, Marrakesh Declaration of 15th April 1994. The Declaration cl(2) Ministers affirm that the establishment of the World trade Organization ushers in a new era of global economic cooperation, reflecting the widespread desire to operate in a fairer and more open multilateral trading system for the benefit and welfare of the people.

into three categories. (1) Prohibited subsidies,[12] (2) Actionable subsidies,[13] (3) Non-actionable subsidies.[14] Comparing these three terms (Aid, Bounty and Subsidy), it can be seen that they have in common, "financial contributions" and "benefits" as a basic feature, thus, naturally demanding the wider interpretation of the provisions describing subsidies.

Furthermore, it is significant to note that the possibility of applying any legal standard as regards an insightful distinction, or whether it is a matter of semantic overlap, between aid, bounty and subsidy, any such reference, to distinguish, seems missing in the SCM Agreement. Once a matter is brought before the DSB and the case in question requires interpretation of substantive law during the court procedures, for this understanding of the scope and objectives of the policies is necessary to reach the right conclusions.

An advantage of this purposive distinction can be observed while applying the SCM provisions. Further to mention, the wider scope of interpretation also helps in understanding the cause of disagreement between the parties, from several dimensions.

2.2.1 *State-Aid and Subsidy, the EU Approach (General Comparison)*

The formation of the European Union is a sort of supra-national, political, and legal order, as the member countries, after the formation of union have restricted the interpretation of sovereignty. It is not only the member countries, but also the nationals of the member countries, that are expected to follow the EU guidelines. Further, it is to be taken into account that EU free trade, works on the system of duality. Basically, it is based on a common internal market system, however member countries of the EU retain the ability to negotiate trade with non-member countries on an individual basis.[15] Within the EU law, the normative aspect of state-aid lies in the integration of the states into one common market.[16]

Traditionally, the state aid monitored by the Commission has been classified into four broad categories: (1) aid to horizontal objectives, (2) regional aid, (3) sectoral aid, and (4) aid to individual firms for rescue and restructuring.[17] In the present

[12]Prohibited subsidies are defined under Article 3 of the SCM agreement.

[13]Actionable subsidies are discussed under Article 5 & 6 of the SCM agreement.

[14]Non-actionable subsidies are defined under Article 8. The provisions regulating non-actionable subsidies expired at the end of the year 1999. Matsushita et al. (2003), p. 282.

[15]Barnard (2010), p. 8. According to Article 28(1) TEFU, the EU comprises a CU where customs duties are prohibited between Member States and a common customs tariff is adopted in respect of the third countries. However, EU law also permits the use of non-tariff barriers i.e. quantitative restrictions.

[16]Luca (2009), p. 16.

[17]Riess (2006), p. 83.

context, the EU system has structured its state aid policy mainly in the form of a horizontal and vertical level. Horizontal aid includes aid to horizontal objectives or for general policy purposes such as R&D, environment and energy savings, SMEs (small and medium enterprise), employment, and training.[18] State aid is classified as vertical in the case of sectoral aid and aid for rescue and reconstruction. As the sectoral aid is given to firms of certain classified sectors, therefore, because of its specific effectiveness, it is termed vertical aid.[19]

Despite the fact that EU is a Member State of the WTO, there are still possibilities of tension between the EU state aid rules and the WTO subsidy provisions.[20] This is partly due to a certain level of differences in the normative level and differences in the aims and objectives of the WTO. Within the EU system, justification for state-aid is mainly an attempt to create a balance between the common market and welfare measures on the one hand and maintaining the competitive level and market efficiency on the other.[21] The justifiability criteria for state aid are based on the factors outlined in Article 107cl (2)[22] of the TEFU. Whether any kind of state support meets the justifiability criteria or not,[23] the Market Investor principle[24] is one of the key yardsticks applied by the European Court of Justice

[18]Riess (2006), p. 83.

[19]Riess (2006), p. 85.

[20]Differences discussed in the Chapter on Agriculture Subsidies.

[21]Funta (2009), pp. 311–322.

[22]TEFU, Article 107cl(2) The following shall be compatible with the internal market:

(a) aid having a social character, granted to individual consumers, provided that such aid is granted without discrimination related to the origin of the products concerned;
(b) aid to make good the damage caused by natural disasters or exceptional occurrences;
(c) aid granted to the economy of certain areas of the Federal Republic of Germany affected by the division of Germany, in so far as such aid is required in order to compensate for the economic disadvantages caused by that division.

(3) The following may be considered to be compatible with the internal market:

(a) aid to promote the economic development of areas where the standard of living is abnormally low or where there is serious underemployment, and of the regions referred to in Article 349, in view of their structural, economic and social situation;
(b) aid to promote the execution of an important project of common European interest or to remedy a serious disturbance in the economy of a Member State;
(c) aid to facilitate the development of certain economic activities or of certain economic areas, where such aid does not adversely affect trading conditions to an extent contrary to the common interest;
(d) aid to promote culture and heritage conservation where such aid does not affect trading conditions and competition in the Union to an extent that is contrary to the common interest;
(e) such other categories of aid as may be specified by decision of the Council on a proposal from the Commission.

[23]Biondi et al. (2004), p. 8.

[24]According to this principle, the Member State must prove that, it considered the measure as an investment on market terms and not as financial support by a public authority. See *European Commission v EDF* C-124/10 [2012] ECR I-0000.EDF case.

In the case of **Italy v Commission**,[25] "The European Court of Justice, in reply to the primary Italian claims,[26] stated (see paragraph 14, 15 of this case) that aid granted by states or through state resources that could affect competition, was incompatible with the Common Market. From this judgement, it seems that the court reached the conclusion that any such aid having the possibility of breaching the common market system of the EU, based on competition policy and efficiency principle cannot be justified. The effect on the competition policy and market efficiency is an implied limitation drawn by the interpretations of the provisions and may vary from case to case.

Comparing the EU system with the WTO trading system, there is no agreement among the Member States concerning the competition policy or any such provisions that creates a legal obligation among the Member States to determine the effects of subsidies on the level of competitiveness in the market. Moreover, the EU is a sort of centralised system and the control mechanism is based on levels, regional, national, and at the EU level, whereas, the WTO is not structured in the form of tier system, but is rather simply based on Member States categorisation and the schedule of commitment.

Within the WTO framework, the subsidies are regulated more or less through the fair trade market concept imbibed as the underlying principles in the form of clauses and provisions. As the Member States within the WTO system are categorised as Developed, Developing, and Less-Developed, so the provisions within the SCM Agreement are more like tools that permit judges of the DSB for creating a certain level of balance between the free trade objectives of the WTO and the fair trade principles supporting the trade mechanism with the development objectives. These provisions within the agreement acts as checks and balances, in the WTO free trade system.

Trade subsidy is a questionable issue within the WTO trading system; however, it can be posited that state support in the form of aid[27] can be provided by the Member States for various justifiable reasons.[28] In theory, this may sound simple but whenever the matter is raised for adjudication, drawing a line of distinction between justifiable aid and a disguised form of aid that may finally turn out to be non-justifiable subsidies in the context of the WTO, is difficult to analyse. There can be occasions when the motive behind the aid may remain obscure (as discussed in the Airbus case, later in this chapter). Within the WTO trading system, there is no reference to the term state aid. In the lack of strict rules of interpretation, legal

---

[25]See Case *C-6/97 Italy v Commission* [1999] ECR I-02981, paragraph 61 (Common Market Law Reports).

[26]Para 10 Judgment of the Court (sixth chamber) 1999.The Italian Republic claims that the tax-credit scheme does not constitute state-aid, in compatible with the Common Market, since there is no allocation direct or indirect of state resources which distort or threaten to distort competition by affecting intra-community trade.

[27]The term aid is used as a necessary form of state support. Also see *C-379/98, Preussen Elektra AG v Schhleswag AG* [2001] EUECJ. Para 63, 73 and 74 of the judgment.

[28]Biondi et al. (2004), pp. 14–15.

rationality in the cases may help to draw a certain level of distinctions between the terms.[29] The relative differences between the two terms, state-aid and subsidies were discussed in the case of **European Coal and Steel Community (ECSC) Treaty case.**[30]

> A subsidy is normally defined as a payment in cash and kind made in support of an undertaking other than the payment by the purchaser or consumer for the goods or services produced. An aid is a very similar concept that, however, places emphasis on its purpose and seems especially devised for a particular objective, which cannot normally be achieved without outside help. In terms of justifiable support, the concept of aid is nevertheless wider than that of a subsidy because it embraces not only positive benefits, such as subsidy, but also interventions which, in various forms, mitigate the charges (financial) that are normally included in the budget of an undertaking. Without such considerations, therefore, aid being subsidies in the strict meaning of the word, are similar in character and have the same effect.

It is thus evident, that in the broader context, to attain state's basic objectives, the use of aid is not confined to positive benefits but also to other measures having similar characteristics.

The EC/EU court, in this case, made a distinction between these two terms, mainly based on the objectives of the policies. State-aid and subsidies have common basic features, i.e., payment in kind or any other form of support. Practically, the use of state-aid is restricted to a certain specific purpose, whereas the use of support without any necessity—based specifications may be called a subsidy.

State aid policies of the EU also have a political aspect, as in the realm of EU law, there are regulations to check state aid through competition policy objectives; however, there are no strict regulations in many of the Member States of the WTO. As a result, EU firms while trading with the other Member States of the WTO faces competition in the market, as they will be in disadvantaged position. Therefore, occasionally, state aid rules are planned accordingly to face the market competition outside the EU on the one hand, and on the other to develop the industrial policies of the member countries in harmony with each other.[31]

The checks and balances on state aid, within the EU trading system are by and large regulated at the EU level and the Commission is the key regulator.[32]

In the case of **Fédération Nationale du Commerce Extérieur des Produits Alimentaires and Syndicat National des Négociants et Trsnsformateurs de**

[29]Luca (2009), p. 11.

[30]*Case C-390/98, Banks v British Coal and Secretary of State* [2001] ECR I-6117 (summaries of State-Aid judgments at the national level see, 20th September 2001, para 30).

[31]Blauberger and Rike (2010), p. 6.

[32]In accordance to Article 108(3) TEFU and Article 2.1 of the Regulation No 659/1999, member states must notify any measure that falls under the state aid definition to the European Commission and they must not implement measures without prior approval by the Commission. The Commission has the exclusive right to examine whether a notified measure is compatible with the common market, subject to Article 107(2) and (3) TEFU.

Saumon v French Republic,[33] the French Conseil d' Etat[34] referred to the Court, for a preliminary ruling, a question on the interpretation of the last sentence of Article 93(3)[35] of the EEC Treaty.

With regard to the issue of determining the jurisdiction of a national court and the Commission, in this case it was stated by the EC that by virtue of Article 93 of the EEC treaty,[36] supervision of the system of providing state aid is a subject within the purview of the Commission and for national courts.[37] Further, the point of distinction was elaborated in para. 14 of the case document. Advocate General F.G. Jacobs refers to the fact that the exclusive role conferred on the commission by virtue of Article 92, Article 93, of the EEC treaty, 107, 108 of the TEFU, is to discover whether the aid is compatible with the common market.[38] From the court's decision, it can be established that jurisdictional division of the courts on the matters of state aid is one at the commission's level and the second lies with the national courts of the members. However, the jurisdiction of the national court is subsidiary, as these courts have no jurisdiction to decide on the compatibility of any such measure with the common market. National courts of the member countries can make a general application for the procedure to interpret the concept of aid while introducing any such aid related[39] policy matter.[40]

Another significant feature in the EU system of state aid is the use of the *de minimis* clause. The *de minimis* clause exempts trivial quantities of state support from the restrictive level of EU rules and there is no need for it to be notified for its approval.[41]

---

[33] *C-354/90, FNCE,* [1991] ECR 1-5505.

[34] The Highest court in France.

[35] Article 93(3) The Commission shall be informed, in sufficient time to enable it to submit its comments, of any plans to grant or alter aid. If it considers that any such plan is not compatible with the common market having regard to Article 87, it shall without delay initiate the procedure provided in para 2.

[36] (Ex-Article 88 TEC-108 TEFU) para 8, para 11 (The involvement of national courts is the result of the direct effect which the last sentence of Article 93(3) of the treaty has been held to have).

[37] See Para 8, Case C-354/90.

[38] See Para 14, Case C-354/90, the views of the Advocate General.

[39] As mentioned previously, Article 92. Presently, Article 107 of the Treaty on the Functioning of the European Union and Regulation 994/98. The Commission may declare some state as being compatible with common market and exempt it from the obligation to notify.

[40] Advocate General Jacobs has tried to clarify the issue of the jurisdiction of national courts. See Para 9. Opinion of Mr, Advocate General Jacobs Case C-354/90.

[41] See Commission's State Aid Modernisation initiative (SAM, see IP/12/458) In 2006, the Commission adopted the current *de minimis* Regulation for the period 2007–2013 (See IP/06/1765 and MEMO/12/936). The current regulation exempts aid amounting to €200,000 per undertaking over a 3 year period. Companies undergoing financial difficulties are no longer excluded from the scope of the regulation and will be allowed to receive *de minimis* aid. Additionally, subsidised loans of up to €1 million may also benefit from the *de minimis* Regulation if certain conditions are met.

In contrast to the *de minimis* clause in the EU system, where the amount of support under the *de minimis* clause is quantified in the provisions and the limits are defined primarily, the *de minimis* clause within the SCM Agreement is mainly affect based, relying much on the purpose and the consequences of such policy measures. Article 11.9[42] of the SCM Agreement comes into effect once the investigation starts and at the preliminary level it is determined that the amount of subsidy is of insignificant effect and the quantity of the imported product can have a negligible effect on the established pattern of the market where such product is imported.[43] Finally, the difference in the level of determination opens new forms of questions for the WTO trading system and specifically for the WTO SCM Agreement.

Within the EU system, justifiable aid, is classified on specific grounds mentioned in Article 107 and Article 108 of the TEFU. However, within the WTO system, the non-actionable subsidies identified under Article 8 of the SCM Agreement are presently obsolete. On the other hand, there are different forms of subsidies within the Agreement on Agriculture still exempted from the strict regulations, discussed in the next chapter. Seemingly, Article 11cl(9) of the SCM Agreement recognises the need for exemption from the restrictive provisions of the certain amount of state support.

Considering the WTO objectives and comparing it with EU objectives on aid, the concessions and aid of these undertakings are legally justified within the limits of the stipulated provisions, but beyond that threshold they are subsidies not valid under the ASCM.

While attempting to establish the nexus between state-aid and subsidies, one can observe that both are a charge on public funds, hence share a common source, but with different objectives. Due to the common basis and several other similarities, it is difficult to make a differentiation between the two and the exact instances when state-aid takes the form of a subsidy. The accepted practice is such that aid is given to support a policy measure or for any welfare purposes, which is in the larger interest of society.[44] In these cases, social benefits can overshadow the prohibitive levels of a subsidy, based on the use of funds from the public account.

Within the EU system, the justification of state aid on sociological grounds lies in the objectives mentioned in Article 107 of the TEFU, such as, (1) aid to promote

---

[42]An application under para 1 shall be rejected and an investigation shall be terminated promptly as soon as the authorities concerned are satisfied that there is not sufficient subsidisation or of injury to justify proceeding with the case.

[43]Article 11.9 There shall be immediate termination in cases where the amount of subsidy is *de minimis*, or where the volume of subsidized imports, actual or potential or the injury, is negligible. For the purpose of this paragraph, the amount of the subsidy shall be considered to be *de minimis* if the subsidy is less than 1% ad valorem.

[44]The use of state-aid for welfare measures is also supported for social welfare grounds. Relevant here from this perspective is Roscoe Pound's idea of *social engineering* and Rudolf Von Jhering's idea in his book *Der Zweck im Recht* translated into English as ("Law as a Means to an End") also Amartya Sen, J. Rawls and J. Bentham as quoted in this context, see first chapter.

economic development of the areas that are under-developed (2) aid to make good the damage caused by natural disasters and etc.[45]

The flexibilities within the SCM Agreement created for the Developing and Less Developed countries to promote welfare measures, such as in order to construct infrastructure or setting up of the basic level of industrial economic system, are some of the aspects that can be compared with the justifiable limits of state aid. Although, there exist the probability of variance, but at the conceptual level there also exists some level of similarities with the EU state aid. A broader classification of such types of exemptions was, in the subsidies classified as non-actionable, within the WTO SCM Agreement, which are however now obsolete.

Some authors are of the view that EU institutions have consistently differentiated the notion of state-aid in EU law, from the notion of subsidies in the WTO Agreements[46]; however, it seems rather that the difference between the two terms remains fragile.

The legal approach used to describe the subsidies, is a partial explanation concerning the role of state-aid and subsidies. Further insights about subsidies and state aid and additionally its level of affect in the market system also requires discussions from an economic perspective.

2.3 Economic Aspects for Checking Subsidies

Economic concerns about checking subsidies are related to the approach that subsidies can distort a market system that is established on the levels of efficiency. The term efficiency can be used in the context of fair trade as well as free trade. For the explanation of subsidies in this chapter and the following chapters, it is used in the context of fair trade objectives as enshrined in the preamble of the WTO. The unregulated use of subsidies undermines the norms of fair competition that support production and supply of goods to the consumers, both at the domestic level and abroad, within the price range resultantly fixed by market forces of demand and supply. In the long run, the trade practice of subsidies also prevents markets from attaining optimal-resource allocation. Supplementing these economic concerns with the attainment of the WTO welfare objectives, and the efficient working of the market system, requires that market conditions should not be biased and the

---

[45]Evans (1997), p. 231.

[46]Slotboom (2002), p. 518, also see Beseler and Williams (1986), p. 31.

"See, for differentiation between two notions after the entry into force of WTO Agreements T-55/99, CETM v. Commission [2000] ECR, II-3207, at s.50, where the Court of First Instance of the EC (the "ECFI") observed without any further explanation. The reference to the concept of 'Subsidy' within the meaning of the WTO Agreement on Subsidies and Countervailing Measures has, as the Commission submits, no relevance whatsoever to the classification of the measure in question as State-aid within the meaning of Community Law."

policy measures supporting state support need to be categorised on the basis of justifiable and non-justifiable use of subsidies.

Going into the specific details and to gain an understanding about how subsidies impact on the WTO trading system, it is necessary to differentiate between the export-subsidies and subsidies for domestic market.

It is also noteworthy that in several instances these subsidies (domestic and export) are either convergent or complement each other. "An *export subsidy* has a direct impact on the terms of cross-border trade because it counters, in whole or in part, the tariffs levied on the product by the importing nation and makes the like product relatively cheaper."[47] Subsequently, the cumulative effect of such support, can lead to the prevalence of the imported products on the domestic market of the importing countries.[48] A *domestic subsidy* or to be specific here, a subsidy for the infrastructure development, is on principle supposed to be granted to an industry or firm, mainly for infrastructure building of an industry or basic level development of an industry but not affecting the competition aspect of the market. In theory, this type of subsidy is for the welfare objectives and has less of an impact on international trade.[49] However, it is highly probable that these domestic subsidies reduce the factor cost, and in a way produces the ingredients and inputs that later help to increase the production of exports, so they may eventually converge, to attain the same objectives as export promotion. An explanation of this lies somewhere in the principal level approach towards subsidies. The interpretation of state aid and subsidies at the basic level still remains divergent. One can also find the difference of opinion while making interpretation about state support, between EU and US during the foundation stage of the WTO as well. As Sykes states "...absence of legal convergence hints that sound rules for the regulation of subsidies are not easily identified."[50] This is also due to the complexities of the market behaviour and the heterogeneous economic systems existing within the political system. In case any such state support is challenged, the focus finally is to bring changes in the governing policy, rather than trying to determine the difference of opinion at the principal level.[51]

Although subsidies have some justifications, as they support the infrastructure building for International trade, the main concern for regulation is the market distortion it causes, which challenges the working of free trade and needs regulation by fair trade measures. The two prominent distortions are, (1) for the country importing subsidised product, there is unfair competition of the like domestic products with the imports; such imports are cheaper due to the subsidies and the unsubsidised domestic products of the local producers are relatively expensive. Unfair competition due to subsidies may affect domestic producers and workers,

[47] Matsushita et al. (2003), p. 261.

[48] This can be termed as predatory pricing.

[49] Matsushita et al. (2003), p. 261.

[50] Sykes (2010), p. 474.

[51] Sykes (2010), p. 476.

which are the basic factor of an economy. So the effect of unregulated subsidy policy measures can be experienced along the vertical level. Resultantly, the economic principle of comparative advantage on the basis of which free trade system is presumed to progress gets challenged.

The relevance of comparative cost advantage, as a concept to develop the economy of a Member State in the WTO trading system was highlighted by the Appellate Body in the case of **United-States-Final Countervailing Duty Determination with respect to certain Softwood Lumber from Canada.**[52] Among the other issues, the matter before the A.B was also to review the Panel's findings concerning the benchmark applied by USDOC for applying countervailing duties.

The Appellate Body stated:

> "It is clear, in abstract that different factors can result in one country having comparative advantage over another with respect to the production of certain goods. In any event, any form of comparative advantage would be reflected in the market conditions prevailing in the country of provision and therefore, would have to be taken into account and reflected in the adjustments made to any method used for the determination of adequacy of remuneration, if it is to relate or refer to, or be connected with, prevailing market conditions in the market of provisions. This is because countervailing measures may be used only for the purpose of offsetting a subsidy bestowed upon a product, provided that it causes injury to the domestic industry producing the like product. They must not be used to offset differences in comparative advantage between the countries." The A.B acknowledging the relevance of comparative advantage in the free trading system tried to segregate the subsidy measures specifically applied for export, with the comparative advantage that is attained by a Member State in a production sector.

Further, it can be added that the A.B suggested an objective approach to be followed while interpreting the provisions for determining the subsidies as prohibited/actionable and for applying countervailing duties.

These aforementioned issues fall mainly within the subject area of microeconomics. We now take one macro-economic issue.

(2) The economic case for CVD (currency value devaluation) is an issue mainly related to macroeconomics. Although not discussed in the SCM Agreement, however was a matter of discussion during the formative stage of the WTO.[53] Economists have concluded that, "an undervalued currency has an effect similar to import tax or tariffs meant to restrict import alternatively that undervalued currency can also acts as export subsidies in the matter of the exportation of goods."[54] This is so

---

[52]WT/DS257/AB/R, para 109.

[53]See, p. no 9–10, Agreement Establishing the WTO. Coherence in global economic policymaking. The declaration states that globalization of the world economy has led to ever-growing interactions between the economic policies pursued by individual countries. Successful cooperation in each area of economic policy contributes to progress in other areas. The declaration cites links between exchange rate stability and the expansion of trade, sustainable growth and development, as well as the role of aid and investment flows and debt relief. Trade liberalization, it recalls is an increasingly important component in the success of adjustment programmes. (For details, see the document).

[54]Salvatore (1987), p. 13.

because the under-valuation of a currency or an artificially low currency makes exports cheaper, whereas the effect on imports of such policy measure is analogues to government imposing higher tariffs on imports, therefore imports becomes more costly. Persistent currency under-valuation induces import competition and encourages export industries. The example of the China-US trade relationship is relevant here. It is assumed by many researchers that China, has kept the value of its currency artificially low, thus indirectly subsidising its exports and taxing imports. "This line of argument gets substantiated by China's large accumulation of US dollar reserve."[55] In support of this viewpoint we analyse the trade situation of China. In the present-day context, exports from China have grown faster than imports, on the other hand in the US, Chinese imports have grown faster than exports, resulting in a US trade deficit.[56]

From the perspective of the WTO, devaluation can be assumed to be a policy measure adopted by any Member State that is likely to switch demand from foreign to home goods/products of a similar type.[57] "Such types of policies or policy measures that switch the supply of outputs from the domestic market to export promotion, then imposing tariffs, or tighter import quotas, or providing export subsidies, and so forth, all such adopted measures can be considered as substitutes for devaluation."[58]

Economic analysis of the subsidy practices based on this comparison also reveals another aspect of market distortion. The following is a comparison drawn between perfect competition and imperfect competition in the market.[59] The basic assumptions for perfect competition are;

1. In such a market system, there are number of suppliers of the goods, as each firm does not dominate the market and cannot individually affect the price.
2. A similar type of product/output, as substitute is available to the consumers in the market.

[55]On 21 July 2005, Chinese government announced that it would no longer peg the yuan to the US dollar. For reference see, Chad et al. (2005), p. 5.

[56]For reference see, United Nations Conference on Trade and Development. Dispute Settlement WTO 3.7 Subsidies and Countervailing Measure, p. 3, US merchandise trade deficit with China alone accounted for about $162 billion in 2004, or nearly one-quarter of the total US trade deficit, up from a negligible in mid 1980s.

[57]**Tradable goods** comprise all the goods and services produced in an economy which are actually or potentially imported or exported.

Non-tradable goods are goods and services which do not cross country borders, either because transport costs prohibit the export or import of the good or due to the non-tradable nature of the goods in question (e.g. public services, land, housing, construction, local specialties which cannot be traded in the market).

[58]Salvatore (1987), p. 48. For reference, also see Agreement Establishing the WTO. p. 9. "Coherence in global policymaking."

[59]The situation of perfect competition in the market is based on the Alfred Marshall's notion of market economies. Taylor (1960), pp. 450–453.

3. Consumers have information about the product, price of the product, therefore if a firm decides to charge higher price, there can be substitution.
4. The market system is based on the assumption that there are no barriers to entry and exists of the new firms in the long term. Consequently, the market is free for competition and there is free entry to the new suppliers.

Based on the above mentioned points, it would be reasonable to say that the framework for perfect competition (a situation based on the assumption) in the domestic market, makes it difficult for the undertakings engaged in international trade to respond strategically and seek favours in international trade that can have major market distortive consequences.

In the practical business world, markets finally yield to the conditions of imperfect competition in order to adopt the strategic mode and to face the day to day market challenges, the usual pattern that can be observed generally. Imperfect competition is characteristic both of industries in which there are only a few major producers, and of the industries in which each producer's product is seen by consumers as strongly differentiated from those of the rival firms. In imperfect competition then, firms and undertakings are aware of the possibilities that can influence the prices of their products and also that they can only sell more by reducing their price. Under these circumstances, each firm views itself as a price-setter, choosing the price of its product, rather than a price-taker (price automatically determined by the dynamics of the market system).[60] Usually, it is the imperfect competition that prevails in the market, and in that case, large firms usually have an advantage over smaller ones. Thus, finally the markets tend to be dominated either by one firm (monopoly) or by a few firms, i.e. oligopoly. When there are increasing returns to scale for a certain time period from any trade practice, this means market has become imperfectly competitive.

The issue of trade subsidies revolves around logical difficulties and dilemmas. The source of these dilemmas partially lies in the imperfect competition[61]; the system of market structure, that virtually works everywhere. Promoting criteria-based policy formation by the government, for giving subsidies or making policies in favour of industries that are highly profitable can also be an agenda of the governments due to political compulsions.[62] Comparing such policy measures with the objectives of the WTO, such policy framework of the Member States seems to deviate from the core objectives.

With the cost asymmetries as a result of imperfect competition, instead of a uniform support scheme, a selective export subsidy scheme that discriminates between firms that are more profitable is followed. Collie notes that if the

[60] Krugman and Obstfed (2009), p. 122.

[61] World Trade Report (2007), p. 60. www.wto.org.

[62] For instance, see Annex I and Annex II of the ASCM Agreement Annex I, Illustrative list of export subsidies and Annex II that deals with Guidelines on consumption of Inputs in the production process.

government could use a selective policy, then it would be optimal to subsidise the most efficient firm and impose a prohibitive tax on all the other firms.[63]

Discussing Monopoly as an Instance of Imperfect Competition Monopoly is a market situation in which there is a single producer of a commodity and there are no substitutes as such.[64] While discussing monopoly condition in the context of International trade, it can be explained that government favour is provided if the entry of the competitive firm is controlled by the government. The main examples for general explanation are banking services, airlines, TV channels, and several others services. *Free trade, from the perspective of WTO objectives means, large scale production, equitable resource distribution, fair chances of trade given to other Member States.* Monopoly supported by government intervention or any such policy measure is contrary to these commitments. An example from the recent past is the Russian military industry.[65] A major amount of subsidies were provided to military equipment and armaments industries. However, after the collapse of Soviet Union, the industrial sector could not support the consumer market with efficient products.[66]

Figure representing how a subsidy increases domestic monopoly profits.[67]

In the Fig. 2.1, D is foreign demand, MR (marginal revenue) from foreign sales, and the intersection between MC (marginal cost) and MR determines the profit-maximising quantity of the exports, Q. The price of the product is set at P, and monopoly profit per unit is the difference between P and MC along the price axis. The total monopoly profits extracted from the foreign market are represented by the shaded area. A specific export subsidy, government subsidy of X dollars per unit of output to the local monopoly firm lowers its marginal costs to (MC^s), reduces the export price from P to (P^s), and increases the quantity to (Q^s). Economic profit appropriated from foreign markets increases to the rectangular area bounded by points (MC^s), to (P^s), a, b. The subsidy cost to the government is the rectangular area bounded by MC, MC^s, a, c. It is smaller than the gain in monopoly profit

[63]Symmetric is used to refer to all firms within a country having identical costs of production. For details see, Collie (2006), p. 316. Also See, *The United States Tax Treatment for Foreign Sales Corporation,* WT/DS108/R, Para 2.1. FSC is a corporation created, organized and maintained in a qualified foreign country, a US possession outside the Custom territory of the United States under the specific requirements of section 921–927 of the US Internal Revenue Code. A, FSC obtains tax exemption on a portion of its earnings through "foreign trade income." E.C (the complainant, now EU) claimed that by applying tax exemption through the FSC scheme, the US violated 1) Article 3.1(a) of the SCM agreements by granting the subsidies contingent in law on export performance. 2) Article 3.1(b) of the SCM by granting subsidies contingent in law upon the use of domestic over imported goods.

[64]Blair and Kenny (1987), pp. 253–256.

[65]The Eighth Ministerial Conference formally approved the Accession Package of the Russian Federation on 16 December, 2011. On 22 August, 2012, the WTO welcomed the Russian Federation as its 156th member.

[66]Segal (1998), pp. 596–609.

[67]Salvatore (1987), p. 321.

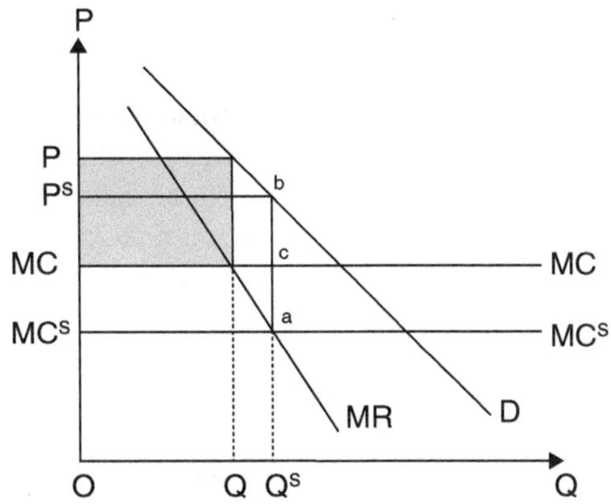

Fig. 2.1 Figure showing the effect of subsidies for export and profit relationship

(monopoly profit area M C, P^s, b, c). The difference between the gain in monopoly profit and the cost of the subsidy, is the net gain to the country. The size of the net gains depends on the shape of the demand curve. Again, information on the cost structure and the demand elasticity is needed to determine the optimal size of the subsidy required. The expectations in return are that any subsidies given would maximize an increase of appropriated profits over subsidy cost that government bears.

2.3.1 Subsidies in Relation to Production Function

As the differences between justifiable subsidies and non-justifiable subsidies are obscure, analysing the production function can help towards a better understanding of this practice. The production function would then be separated into two stages. In the first stage, intermediate inputs and primary composite of capital and labour would be used in fixed proportion to the output. In the second stage, capital and labour would be combined through a CES (Constant Elasticity of Substitution)[68] function to form the primary composite, depending upon the demand-based profit. With the support of a subsidy, these factors can be obtained at a cheaper price and this can subsequently help in export promotion. As long as the support is given for the production function to subsist, mainly in the case of Developing[69] and Less Developed countries and it can also be categorised under welfare or classified as non-profitable; thus, can be brought under the term "aid." Nevertheless, one has to analyse the intrusive character of this support.

[68]Spencer (1988), p. 327.

[69]Developing countries further subcategorized based on economic level.

2.3.2 Between Efficiency and Welfare

Defining and identifying a trade-distorting subsidy is, however, only the first step and the next would be to decide whether the trade-distorting subsidy should be removed. The criteria that can be used to determine if a subsidy is trade-distorting can primarily be based on the efficiency principle of economics.[70] The effect on the efficiency principle need to tested through, financial contribution, benefit, and the specific criteria applied.

[In the Fig. 2.1, it is assumed that export subsidies and import substitution subsidies are trade distorting. In fact, they are prohibited under Article 3 of the Subsidies Agreement.]

Although the issues related to subsidies are seen from the critical perspective in general, however, there are also certain welfare effects linked to the imposition of tariffs and support through subsidies, which can be beneficial to the Developing and Less-Developed countries. Under oligopoly, as Brander and Spencer (1984) have shown, tariffs can be used to extract rent from foreign firms and to shift profits from foreign to domestic firms.[71] A subsidy increases the welfare of a country by improving the terms of trade if it leads to a reduction in the price of the goods, both the imported and exported goods. A subsidy will increase the domestic country's welfare by shifting profits to the profit generating firms, so as to increase the domestic producer's surplus by increasing such output of the domestic industry. After a while, the investment can be shifted to other profit generating industries. Such investments can also be linked with comparative cost advantage theory. Basically, it improves the terms of trade by reducing the costs of production. Subsidies will enhance trade and welfare by shifting profits. This will induce the producer to increase production for export. A type of subsidy-effect of this kind is beneficial for Developing and the Less-developed countries.

However, the debate on subsidies and their removal is a slightly more complex process and it is necessary to put forward, the justification for subsidies from the perspective of welfare and development.

---

[70]Luca (2009), p. 42.

[71]Symmetric is used to refer to all firms within a country having identical costs of production. For details see, Collie (2006), p. 322. Also See, *The United States Tax Treatment for Foreign Sales Corporation,* WT/DS108/R, Para 2.1. FSC is a corporation created, organized and maintained in a qualified foreign country, a US possession outside the Custom territory of the United States under the specific requirements of section 921–927 of the US Internal Revenue Code. A, FSC obtains tax exemption on a portion of its earnings through "foreign trade income." E.C (the complainant, now EU) claimed that by applying tax exemption through the FSC scheme, the US violated 1) Article 3.1(a) of the SCM agreements by granting the subsidies contingent in law on export performance.

2) Article 3.1(b) of the SCM by granting subsidies contingent in law upon the use of domestic over imported goods.

2.4 Subsidies Under GATT/WTO

This section describes the discussion on subsidies from the establishment of GATT onwards. The sub-chapter is further divided into two main parts (1) dealing with subsidies from GATT onwards and (2) covering subsidies under the SCM Agreement, which is further divided into various sub topics.

2.4.1 Subsidies from GATT Onwards, a Brief Discussion

The issue of subsidy was given great significance in the WTO negotiations, although, it was not very widely discussed in the previous GATT organisation. Nowhere, in Article XVI of GATT 1947, is the term "subsidy" defined. Article XVI[72] of the GATT is divided into two sections. Section A, deals with subsidies in general. Section B of Article XVI, mainly deals with the elimination of export subsidies on non-primary products and also restricts the use of subsidies on the exportation of primary products. Additionally, it is worth noticing for the sake of comparison, that GATT started to work with dispute settlement provisions that were relatively basic, however, creating legal eligibility for challenging such acts that affected the parties.[73] Before the Tokyo Round, there remained ambiguity during the debates over the GATT, DRM[74] as there existed two divergent approaches, (1) Legalist and (2) Pragmatist. The legalist viewpoint was mainly followed by the US. It emphasised that the system should be more judicial and rely on the adjudication of disputes. The US also argued that such a rule oriented approach would promote resolution of disputes on merits and there would be objective effectiveness while implementation of the

[72]Article XVI of the GATT **Section A. Subsidies in General** Cl.1) If any Contracting Party grants or maintains any subsidy, including any form of income or price support, which operates directly or indirectly to increase exports of any product from, or to reduce imports of any product into its territory, it shall notify the *Contracting Parties* in writing of the extent and nature of the subsidization, and of the estimated effect. In case of the determination of serious prejudice, the contracting party shall upon request discuss the possibility of limiting subsidization. (For details, see GATT 1947 document).

Section B. Provision on Export-Subsidies Cl.2) The Contracting Parties recognize that the granting by a contracting party of a subsidy on the export of any product may cause undue disturbance to their normal commercial interests, and may hinder the achievement of the objectives of this Agreement(for details, see GATT 1947 document).

Cl.3) If, however, a Contracting Party grants directly or indirectly any form of subsidy to increase the export of any primary product from its territory, such subsidy shall not be applied in a manner which results in that Contracting Party having more than an equitable share of world export trade in that product (for details, see GATT 1947 document).

[73]Article XXIII of the GATT authorized the Contracting Parties in appropriate cases to suspend the application of tariff concessions or other GATT obligations to the party found to be acting in GATT-inconsistent manner.

[74]DRM: Dispute Resolving Mechanism.

decisions.[75] The other viewpoint was that of the pragmatists. The pragmatists suggested, that a Dispute Resolving Mechanism, should mainly be used to facilitate negotiated methods of resolving disputes. Their emphasis was on the process of consensus building and compromises and were rather flexible with the application of GATT rules. A major advocate of the pragmatist approach was the EU.[76] However, by the end of the Tokyo Round, Member States tried to revamp GATT's Dispute resolution procedure.

In the succeeding years, for regulation of international trade by dealing with the specific issue of subsidies, an attempt was made during the Tokyo Round of Subsidies code,[77] to broaden the scope of the term subsidy by adding more provisions. However, the members could not agree upon any uniform method to regulate subsidy. The two leading trade blocs within the GATT, the EC and the US, may serve here as an example, for explaining the reason of ambiguity while determining subsidies. Before taking into account the Tokyo round, some background is necessary on the political situations of the two main trading blocks, the EC and the US. The limitations of the US president, was a hurdle in the progress of the discussion on this topic and it cannot be ignored as it affected the progress of GATT. Under the existing circumstances of that period, it was not possible for the US to discuss many issues related to imports and exports at the GATT level.[78]

Following the formation of GATT, it was during the Nixon administration in 1971 that American economy faced great pressure, and therefore the Nixon government enacted DISC (Domestic International Sales Corporation) to enhance US exports through tax incentives. This was a sort of export subsidy scheme, however forbidden under GATT rules.[79] On the other hand, one of the leading economic blocs within GATT, which was also a main trading partner of the US, the EC, took initiatives to harmonise their tax system and relied on VAT (Value Added Tax) to raise public revenue. This scheme of taxation did not impose much on exporters[80]

---

[75]Litvak (1995), p. 571.

[76]Litvak (1995), pp. 571–572.

[77]Tokyo Round Subsidies Code, The signatories to this Agreement, noting that ministers on 12–14 September 1973, agreed that the Multilateral Trade Negotiations should, *inter alia,* reduce or eliminate the trade restricting or distorting effects of non-tariff measures, bring such measures under more effective international disciplines.

[78]The Truman administration negotiated under the authority of the 1945 Trade Agreements Extension Act, which authorized the president to enter into foreign trade agreements, but did not authorize entry into international organization. For reference see, Romano (2009), pp. 332–333.

[79]Brumbaugh (2004), pp. 1–3.

[80]Hart (1994), p. 4.The Treaty of Rome, signed in 1957, mandates that signatories harmonize indirect tax systems in order to achieve a free movement of goods and services within the common market The first step was taken in 1960 when the commission appointed three work groups (the Jansen Committee) and a Fiscal and Financial Committee (the Neumark Committee) to study the problems harmonization. Both reports recommended elimination of cascade-type tax systems and replacement with VAT-type systems. The VAT promotes a better balance of payments by allowing exporters to deduct the full amount indirect tax on products, something not possible with direct tax nor accurate with a cumulative tax. http://scholarship.law.berkeley.edu/bjil/vol 12/issl/1.

and this probably was like maintaining dual standards. At the background of varied trade policies followed by the Member States, the Tokyo Round negotiations began in 1973 and by the end of the negotiations, Member States agreed on the regulation of non-tariff barriers to trade through codification. This led to differences in the uniform opinion formation, as the EC questioned the US legislation concerning DISC, asserting that it was a US enactment in favour of export subsidies, violating Article XVI: 4 of GATT. The US retaliated this assertion of EC by arguing that income tax laws of France, Belgium and Netherlands also violated GATT rules.[81]

After the Tokyo Round, in the year 1980, the US went through an economic downturn. The US economy faced massive trade deficit, leading to growing resentment among the US citizens and politicians. The US politicians were gripped by pessimistic attitude during that period. They thought the GATT trade mechanism was not capable of protecting the US trade interests, which eventually forced the US trade leaders to think towards unilateralism. The US government that was in the grip of dilemma, finally in the year 1974, introduced Section 301, as an Amendment of the Trade Act.[82] This authorised the US president to respond in the cases of unfair practices by foreign firms.[83] The act was seen as a kind of shift by the US, towards unilateralism from multilateralism. The same mood remained until the formative discussions, before the formation of the WTO.[84]

Prior to the formation of SCM Agreement, proposals which reflect the difference of opinion between the EC and US can also be observed during the discussions. In December 1992, the European Community informally proposed changes in the subsidies draft, such as adding provisions for the broader use of green light category subsidies. Another significant issue of ambiguity between these parties was, whether civil aircraft agreement is required to be covered by a new code, exclusively for the aircraft industry or regulation of financial support to the aircraft industry would be possible under both the civil aircraft code and the general GATT subsidies code.[85]

---

[81]Litvak (1995), pp. 579–580.

[82]Section 301 of the Trade Act of 1974 was passed at a time of large and growing trade deficit, increasing flight of manufacturing activities abroad, the rise of Japan as an industrial giant, skyrocketing foreign debts and economic crises caused by dependency on foreign oil imports, all of which fueled a mood in US circles that was decidedly protectionist. US export industries attached considerable blame for the US economic woes on the weak enforcement regimes in the General Agreement on Tariffs and Trade (GATT), and the accompanying inability of US to enforce free trade commitments abroad. Section 301 authorised the President to impose economic sanctions on countries that 'burden or restrict US commerce.' For detail reference see, http://infojustice.org/archives/29465.

[83]Litvak (1995), p. 581.

[84]Senate Republican leader Robert Dole initially voiced concerns about whether the WTO posed a threat to US sovereignty. He struck a last minute deal with President Clinton, however, that provided for an "escape hatch" for the US to exist the WTO if congress were to believe that the WTO was treading on US rights. The compromise helped insure Senate approval. Litvak (1995), p. 608.

[85]Stewart (1999), pp. 221–223.

During the GATT period, the position of the law remained unclear in the case of matters concerning various forms of state support. The situation, in the absence of any specific definition of subsidies, remained such that the United States and the EC and other GATT contracting parties, rigidly maintained their divergent opinions on this multifaceted issue, requiring interpretation whether only government measures involving a charge on the public account were to be considered subsidies or it was any form of financial contribution.[86] An example of this can be seen in the case (US. C.C. P. Appeal) of **Zenith Radio Corp. V. United States,**[87] the Petitioner (an American manufacturer of consumer electronics) in this case contended that certain imported products got benefited from bounties or grants paid by Japan. Japan imposed a commodity tax,[88] an indirect tax on these products including the electronic products that are at issue here, when they were sold in the internal market, but remitted the tax when the products were exported. Moreover, any tax levied on the shipment of the product was refunded subsequent to exportation. Relying on the legal approach adopted in the case of **Downs. V. United States, 187 US 496,** the Customs Court ruled in the Petitioner's favour, i.e., agreed with the US argument, that Japan was promoting export by providing reductions in taxation. However, the Court of Customs and Patent Appeals, reversed the decision.[89] The judgment of the Court of Customs Patent and Appeal was affirmed by the US Supreme Court.[90]

Drawing parallels in the matters of subsidies, it can be observed that the approach followed by the EC\EU was different from that of the US. For this illustration, the opinion of an EC\EU case can be taken into account. In the case of **EEC Seed Crushers and Oil Processors Federation (applicant) v Commission of the European Communities,**[91] the application was lodged at the Court Registry with the declaration, that the Commission Decision 85/233 of 16th April 1985, terminating the anti-subsidy proceedings, concerning the imports of Soya,

---

[86]Slotboom (2002), p. 518.

[87]U.S. Supreme Court case 437 U.S. 443(1978).

[88]"Under the Commodity Tax Law of Japan," Law No. 48 of 1962, App. 44–48, a variety of consumer goods, including the electronic products at issue here, are subject to an indirect tax, a tax levied on the goods themselves, and computed as a percentage of the manufacturer's sales price, rather than as the income or wealth of the purchaser or seller. The Japanese tax applies both to products manufactured in Japan and to those imported into Japan. . . .Products shipped for exports are exempt, and any tax paid upon the shipment of a product is refunded if the product is subsequently exported.

[89]The Appeal Court held, that Japan does not confer a "bounty or grant" within the meaning of § 303 of the Tariff Act 1930 on the consumer electronic products by failing to impose a commodity tax when they are exported to this country, while imposing the tax when they are sold in Japan.

[90]Certiorari: 434 US 1060, 98 S.Ct. 1231, 55 L.Ed.2d 760 (1978). Opinion given by Justice Marshall.

[91]*Case 188/85, FEDIOL v Commission* [1988] ECR 4193.

originating from Brazil was void. The European Court of Justice observed,[92] "it should be pointed out that the concept of subsidy in Article 3 of the EEC Regulation No 2176/84[93] is not expressly defined, either in that regulation or in other Community measures." However, an illustrative list of export subsidies, referred to in Article 3(2) of the regulation, is annexed thereto. The last paragraph of that list defines a subsidy, *as constituting an export subsidy in the sense of Article XVI of the GATT, any other charge on the public account.* It follows both from the terms of that general provision and from the other examples mentioned in the list, that in the mind of the Community legislature, the export subsidies necessarily implied a '*financial burden*' borne directly or indirectly by the public bodies with the underlying concept of a charge. It also follows from Article 3(3) of the said regulation, which expressly excluded from the concept of subsidy, the exemption of a product from certain export charges or taxes. "The concept of charge, cover not merely cases in which the State advances funds, but also those in which it waives recovery of tax debts, thereby introducing an exception to a generally applicable rule of taxation."

Comparing the stance of the EC with that of the US, it is clear that the United States has employed a more objective approach to determine the practice of trade subsidies, rather than just opting for the types of *financial contribution, whether it is a charge on public money or not.* The legal position it has adopted is to ascertain the *benefits* obtained because of the subsidy. It disregarded the question of whether a charge on the public-account requirement was involved and focused on the *benefit* to the recipient provided by the disputed measure. It is noteworthy through the decision, that, "Government practice that cannot be characterized as export subsidies are countervail able under US law only if they fall within the statutory definition of a domestic subsidies."[94]

In other words, regardless of whether a government measure represented a charge on the public account, the United States considered a measure of other

[92]Case 188/85 Para 12 and 13 Para 12 (On 11th July 1988, the EEC Council adopted regulation EEC no 2423/88 which replaced Council Regulation EEC no 2176/84 as amended.) The concept of subsidy is not expressly defined, either in that regulation or in other Community measures. However, an illustrative list of export subsidies, referred to in Article 3(2) of the regulation, is annexed thereto. The last paragraph of that list defines as constituting an export subsidy in the sense of Article XVI of the GATT. The concept of export subsidy in the mind of the Community legislature necessarily implied a *financial burden* borne directly or indirectly by the public bodies. It also follows from Article 3(3) of the said regulation, which expressly excludes from the concept of subsidy the exemption of a product from certain export charges or taxes, that the concept of charge, covers not merely cases in which the State advances funds but also those in which it waives recovery of tax debts.

[93]Council regulation EEC no 2176/84 was amended by Council Regulation EEC no 1761/87. On 11th July 1988, the EEC Council adopted regulation EEC no 2423/88 which replaced Council Regulation EEC no 2176/84 as amended.

[94]U.S.C.A§ 1677(5) (West 1980 & Supp.4 Dec 1988) for further reference see, Sykes (1989), p. 203, note 26. The identification of export subsidies may prove quite troublesome in practice. www.jstor.org results.

GATT Member States, countervail able, if the measure conferred a *benefit* to a specific industry.[95] This must provide some advantage to the producer that was otherwise not available.

The inference that can be drawn from the approach followed in both the aforementioned cases is that there was a lack of specific definition and it was an inconsistent method of measuring the term 'state support'. This lack of consistency was further aggravated by gaps in the structure of GATT's provisions on subsidies and in the Tokyo Round of the Subsidies Code, the subsequent development.[96] Such an equivocal approach and the difference of opinion while making interpretation of the provision came into light also in the case of, **United States-Imposition of Countervailing Duties** on Certain Hot-Rolled Lead and Bismuth Carbon Steel Products originating in France Germany and the United Kingdom.[97] In this case, the EC complained before the Panel about subsidy determination and the methodology adopted by the US DOC for determining subsidies through grants, equity infusions, and loans.[98] Regarding the imposition of duties, the EC argued that there must be link between injury in the market and the subsidised import before imposing countervailing measures. Therefore, from the procedural aspect it primarily required establishing subsidies that provides competitive advantage to the exporting company.[99] In this case, the Panel concluded that imposition of countervailing duties by the US was inconsistent with its treaty obligations.[100]

[95]U.S.C.A§ 1677(5) (West 1980 & Supp.4 Dec 1988) for further reference see, Sykes (1989), p. 204, note 26. The identification of export subsidies may prove quite troublesome in practice. www.jstor.org results (The targeting criterion—commonly known as the "specificity test" or the "general availability test" ensures that many of the familiar activities of the governments are not characterized as "subsidies") For example, public education, government-financed highway and railway systems, national telecommunications networks, and even national defence activities provide economic benefits to domestic producers, but these benefits ordinarily accrue to a wide range of industries. Thus, such activities are usually not countervailing. In contrast, a special programme to educate workers in the semi-conductor industry or a special rail rate for the coal industry might well be countervailable.

[96]Tokyo Round of Subsidies Code from 1973–1979.

[97]SCM/185, Report of the Panel. Parties to the dispute European Community and United States.

[98]See para 6, SCM/185, Report of the Panel. US Department of Commerce initiated countervailing duty investigation with respect to certain hot-rolled lead and bismuth carbon steel products originating in France, Germany and United Kingdom.

[99]See para 33, The EC argued that the purpose for which countervailing measures were permitted under the Agreement was to offset trade distorting effects of subsidies resulting in material injury to the domestic producers. This required that a subsidy must at least be one of the causes of the injury. There must, therefore be a causal link between injury and the subsidised imports and this link must result from the distortion of competition brought about by the subsidy. In consequence, the determination that a subsidy may be countervailed had to be based on some competitive advantage accruing from the subsidy to the company whose products were countervailed.

[100]For reference see, the conclusion of the case. The Panel Concluded that to this extent the imposition by the United States of countervailing duties on imports of certain hot-rolled lead and bismuth carbon steel products from France, Germany, and the United Kingdom was inconsistent with the obligations of the United States under the Agreement.

From the different approaches and interpretations, applied by the parties concerning the issue of subsidies, it basically reflects the notion that at principal level subsidies cannot be defined accurately. Between the parties, i.e., the EC and US, there was a difference of opinion concerning the interpretation of the word 'subsidy' and the procedure adopted for imposing the countervailing duties.[101] The position taken by the EC regarding the state support to be considered as a subsidy was, that a financial contribution by a government was a necessary condition for the existence of a subsidy and for distinguishing it from other non-tariff barriers.[102] The EC further emphasised the rigid interpretation, stating that the word subsidy was used throughout the Agreement and in Article 4.2,[103] therefore it was based on some strict meaning, which cannot be modified by the parties at their will; nor could the panel have the possibility to decide on something between 'cost to the government' versus 'benefit to the recipient.'[104] On the other hand, the views forwarded by the US concerning subsidies, were focused on 'benefit,' rather than financial contribution.[105] For the purpose of interpretation, as to what constitute subsidy, the US accepted that it also relied upon Article 31 of the Vienna Convention, of the treaty agreement. The US stated the reason for their reliance on the Vienna Convention was based on the Tokyo Round Agreement, as the agreement contained no definition of subsidy, rather defined countervailing duty as a special duty levied for the purpose of offsetting any bounty or grant bestowed directly, or indirectly, upon the manufacturer, or for the production or export of any merchandise.[106]

---

[101] See para 46, The EC argued that if, as the EC believed, the Panel had to address the question of the determination of the existence of a subsidy, the Panel could not avoid the question of what were the constituent elements of a subsidy. There might not be a definition of the term subsidy in the Agreement but that did not mean that it was impossible to—glean from the Agreement some constituent elements of what subsidy was. If the term itself did not provide sufficient clarity, recourse to the rest of the text of the Agreement was normal under Article 31 of the Vienna Convention on the Law of Treaties.

[102] See para 47, The EC argued that the structure of the General Agreement provided further support for the view that a financial contribution by a government was a necessary condition for the existence of the subsidy. . .A financial contribution by the government was the crucial factor distinguishing subsidies from other non-tariff barriers.

[103] Subsidies and Countervailing Duties, Tokyo Round. Article 4.2. No countervailing duty shall be levied on any imported product in excess of the amount of the subsidy found to exist, calculated in terms of subsidization per unit of the subsidized and exported products.

[104] See para 48, The EC argued that given that the word 'subsidy' was being used throughout the Agreement and also in Article 4.2, it must have some definite meaning which could not be modified at will by the signatories. The Panel should therefore not let itself be put off from its task by the past and present theological disputes on "cost to the government" versus "benefit to the recipient." Rather, the Panel should simply have recourse to the natural meaning of the term subsidy as prescribed by Article 31.1 of the Vienna Convention. In doing so, the Panel ought to find that a subsidy cannot exist without some kind of financial contribution. . . .The EC submitted on the basis of these considerations that the determination of the existence of a subsidy in accordance with Article 4:2 of the Agreement required a financial contribution by the government and that some benefit was thereby bestowed on the recipient.

[105] See para 51.

[106] See para 50.

The Panel noted that the EC, in its specific claims has not raised the issue of financial contribution, however, it considered this issue in the context of the requirement of interpretation. The Panel, therefore held that for the proper determination of subsidies, all factors which were mandatory need to be considered.[107] Further to clarify the specific issues involved, the Panel stated that it is rather important to distinguish between the question of consideration of all relevant facts and the question of the weight to be accorded to certain facts as compared to other facts. If such a choice is made and certain facts have been outweighed, leading to disagreement between the parties, this cannot solely be the reason to find that not all the relevant facts have been considered.[108]

Leaving aside the US policy and the EC's approach on subsidies, practically speaking, any type of government programme can confer a domestic subsidy if it meets two criteria. It must first be sufficiently targeted "to a specific enterprise or industry, or group of enterprises or industries," and second, it must provide some opportunity or advantage to the targeted producers that would not otherwise be available to them in the marketplace. However, the EC (and other GATT contracting parties) took the position (in terms of international trade), that *so far as the subject of subsidy needs description, the determining characteristic is that it involves a financial contribution by the government.*

Despite several efforts, the stance of the nations on subsidies remained ambiguous until the formation of the WTO. It was during the Uruguay Round[109] that an, attempt was made to create detailed rules with provisions that can be applicable to all the WTO members in the light of their economic, political and social situations.[110]

The move from GATT to the WTO has raised the issue of competence as the perception has changed. However, the question of legal competence about the measures initiated, before the date of entry into force of the WTO Agreement, has put to test the possibility of the retrospective effect of the WTO SCM Agreement, provisions. In other words, whether it is possible for the WTO provisions to be applied for an act done prior to the formation of the WTO?

In the case of **Brazil–Measures Affecting Desiccated Coconut,**[111] Philippines claimed that even if Brazil's investigation had been concluded and countervailing measures imposed before the formation of the WTO, the continued implementation of the pre-existing measure need to be reviewed and re-examined in the light of new obligations.[112]

[107]See para 362.

[108]See para 364.

[109]Uruguay Round GATT conference 1986–1994.

[110]Hoda and Ahuja (2005), p. 1010.

[111]WT/DS22/R. Brazil failed to enter consultation within the stipulated period provided for in the Understanding on Rules and Procedures, Governing the settlement of disputes, therefore, Philippines requested for the establishment of the Panel.

[112]WT/DS22/R, para 26.

The dispute concerned, countervailing duties imposed by Brazil on the imports of desiccated coconut from Philippines. On 21st June 1994, based on a request for investigation by the domestic industry, Brazil initiated an investigation regarding the alleged subsidies.[113] The panel was established based on the terms of reference.

One of the main legal question was application of the SCM Agreement on this challenged issue, an issue which started prior to the formation of the WTO. The WTO Agreement came into force for Brazil, on 1st January 1995.The *investigations leading to imposition of duty was initiated on 21st June 1994* (prior to the entry into force of the WTO Agreement), and the countervailing duty on desiccated coconut from the Philippines was imposed on 18th August 1995.[114]

Brazil contended that neither GATT 1994 nor the Agreement on Agriculture were applicable to this dispute.[115]

The Panel's reply with regard to the Philippines assertion[116] whether the Panel could examine in the light of Article 32.3 of SCM Agreement the continued collection of a duty even where its imposition was prior to the entry into force of the WTO Agreement.[117]

> To this, Panel replied that specifically Article 32.3 SCM Agreement[118] applies to the reviews of 'existing measures' initiated pursuant to applications made on or after the date of entry into force of the WTO Agreement. It is thus through the mechanism of reviews provided for in the SCM Agreement, that the agreement becomes effective with respect to measures imposed pursuant to investigations to which SCM Agreement does not apply.... The panel further added that examination of the collection of duty extended to *the ground basis* on which the duty was imposed then in effect. The determinations on which those duties were based would be subject to standards that did not apply-and which, in the case of determinations made before the WTO Agreement was signed, did not yet even exist at the time determinations were made.[119]

[113]Brazil initiated an investigation regarding allegedly subsidized imports of desiccated coconut and coconut milk from the Philippines, Côte d'Ivoire, Indonesia, Malaysia, and Sri Lanka. On 18th August 1995, Brazil issued Inter-ministerial Ordinance No.11, pursuant to which it imposed a countervailing duty on the amount of 121.5% on imports from the Philippines. For detail see, the part, "factual aspects of the case." Pursuant to the Philippines request and with Brazil's acceptance, the DSB established a Panel to examine the matter.

[114]WT/DS22/R, para 13.

[115]Brazil argued that the Philippines may not invoke any provisions of GATT 1994 or the Agreement on Agriculture in this dispute. Brazil contended that only the provisions of the Tokyo Round SCM Code are applicable to this matter, and that the Philippines is entitled only to dispute settlement under the provisions of the Code. Accordingly, the Tokyo Round SCM Code was not covered under Article 1.1 of the DSU, and that the Panel may not apply it in this dispute. WT/DS22/R, see para 22.

[116]For detail references see, Section IV Main Arguments of the parties' p. 10.

[117]See para, 26 and 36.

[118]Article 32.3 Subject to paragraph 4, the provisions of this Agreement shall apply to investigations, and reviews of existing measures initiated pursuant to applications which have been made on or after the date of entry into force for a member of the WTO agreement.

[119]See, findings (a) of the Panel report WT/DS22/R, see para, 229–230. In para 231, Panel stated that the SCM Agreement does not constitute applicable law for the purpose of this dispute.

While assessing whether Article 32.3 of the SCM Agreement, as a rule cover the transactions during the transition period in the membership from the GATT to WTO, the Panel has clarified that Article 32.3 of the SCM Agreement is a rule to cover transactions during the transition period, enabling investigations on an issue that started on or after the date of entry into force of the WTO Agreement. However, for matters that started before the formation of the WTO, the issue may be reviewed,[120] but the WTO standards cannot be applied.[121] The Philippines argued that the Panel should examine the matter in the light of the SCM Agreement, the Panel stated that examining the continued collection of duty will be a shift from where it was not subject to, there by it will be a matter of applying the WTO standard. The Panel therefore denied the applicability of Article 32.3 of the SCM Agreement in this case.

Basically, the move from GATT to the WTO can be better seen as a transformation, reason being the WTO takes in more features and adopts broader perspectives while interpreting legal provisions. Nevertheless, the legal interpretations are made along the same lines and consistent with the primary objectives of the WTO.[122] The agreement establishing the World Trade Organization incorporates several annexes listing various agreements that are part of the WTO agreement. Annex 1A, encompasses the multilateral agreements on trade in goods. Of these agreements one is the "Agreement on Subsidies and Countervailing Measures."

---

[120]See Article 32.4 of the SCM Agreement.

[121]For reference, also see Appellate Body report, p. no 11. "With respect to the measure at issue in this appeal, we see a decision to impose a definitive countervailing duty as the culminating act of a domestic legal process which starts with the filing of an application by the domestic industry."

[122]From the Panel report, in the case of, *Brazil-Measures Affecting Desiccated Coconut*. WT/DS22/R, para 242. p. no 60:—explaining the object and purpose, panel stated that "In our view, one of the central objects and purposes of the WTO Agreement, as reflected in the preamble to the Agreement is to develop an integrated, more viable and durable multilateral trading system encompassing the General Agreement on Tariffs and Trade, the results of past liberalization efforts and all of the results of the Uruguay Round of Multilateral Trade Negotiations."

From the Appellate body report. (WT/DS22/AB/R,97-0695, p. no. 11)The WTO Agreement is fundamentally different from the GATT system which preceded it. The previous system was made up of several agreements, understanding and legal instruments, the most significant of which were the GATT 1947 and the nine Tokyo Round Agreements, including the Tokyo Round SCM code. Each of these major agreements was treaty with different membership, an independent governing body and a separate dispute settlement mechanism. Appellate Body further added that, "Unlike the GATT system, the WTO Agreement is a single treaty instrument which was accepted by the WTO members as a "single undertakings." Article II: 2 of the WTO Agreement provides that the Multilateral Trade Agreements in Annexes 1,2and 3 are "integral parts" of the WTO Agreements, binding on all Members." Annex 1A contains thirteen Multilateral Agreements relating to trade in goods, including the GATT 1994 which was incorporated by reference into that Annex. A general interpretive note was included in Annex 1A in order to clarify the legal relationship of the GATT 1994 which was incorporated by reference in to that Annex 1A. It provides that in the event of a conflict between provisions of GATT 1994 with the other agreements in Annex 1A, the later shall prevail to the extent of the conflict. Article II: 4 of the WTO Agreements provides that the GATT 1994 "as specified in Annex1A. . .is legally distinct from the General Agreement on Tariff and Trade dated 30 October 1947. . .."

(Herein, after ASCM). This agreement deals with the issue of subsidies very widely. The SCM Agreement introduced detailed rules on the procedures for investigations and imposition of countervailing duties.

Article XV, of Annex 1B[123] also makes a brief reference to subsidies and their distortive effects. This part is not taken into consideration for this book.[124]

As per the development of legal provisions on Subsidies, subsequent to the formation of the WTO, the exposition of the term subsidy seems to attain some level of standing as it is codified and categorically explained in the SCM Agreement.

2.4.2 Party to SCM Agreement and Subsidies in Relations to the WTO

There are two types of membership, original or by accession. After attaining membership of the WTO, members get automatically bound by the multilateral trade agreements, including the "Agreements on Subsidies and Countervailing Measures (ASCM)," as well as "Understanding on Rules and Procedures Governing the Settlement of Disputes (DSU)."[125] As a part of single trading system, Member States are expected to follow certain level of consistency, while framing domestic policies, ensuring that the WTO subsidy-provisions are not breached. In so doing, it is also obligatory for the WTO Members to bear in mind, the provisions of Article 31(1) of the Vienna Convention on the Law of Treaties.[126]

Furthermore, as a step towards coordination with the WTO trading system, Member States need to have the inclusion of conducive features in the policy

[123] Annex 1B is about the General Agreement on Trade in Services.

[124] Article XV of Annex 1B: General Agreement on Trade in Services, [(1) Members recognize that, in certain circumstances, subsidies may have distortive effects on trade in services. Members shall enter into negotiations with a view to developing the necessary multilateral disciplines to avoid such trade distortive effects.

(2) Any Member which shall considers that it is adversely affected by a subsidy of another Member may request consultations with that Member on such matters. Such requests shall be accorded sympathetic consideration.]

[125] Benitah (2001), p. 3.

[126] Article 31(1) of the Vienna Convention provides that "A treaty shall be interpreted in good faith with the ordinary meaning to be given to the terms of treaty in their context and in the light of its object and purpose."

mechanism. The possibility of consistent trade pattern gets established among the Member States, once there is adaptation of the WTO rules[127] and principles.[128]

Sustainability of the trade policies promoted by the WTO also demands flexibility at the normative level within the Member States, as discussed in the introductory chapter. The WTO promotes the principle of free trade market system by applying MFN principle, however, for the long term objectives, the feasibility of free trade also depends on political considerations, the general standard of rules for the markets of the Member States and the rules and procedures for compliance. Support of such market conditions requires certain level of value support through the established norms. In the absence of such conditions or if the existing norms are not supportive or they are not in line with the MFN clause, this means it requires a process of norm creation, norm promotion and implementation.[129]

As a starting point in the context of value analysis, the issue of subsidies in international trade attains value based legal characteristic at the point of domestic policies of the Member State's interface with market liberalisation policies created by the WTO. These market liberalisation policies created through the MFN principle are based on market efficiency, on high competition, free movement of goods, and efficient use of the resources; these are the primary concepts. Any form of trade promotion through subsidies derogates this conception. State sponsored support that is in the form of subsidies, the regulation of it, also attains significance in order to restrict a hierarchical set up in the market or monopolies in the market. To check such possibilities requires a set of policies that can act as regulatory mechanism at the broader level. These policies supported by provisions need to demarcate the limits of unchecked free trade. Moreover, it is to be noted here that the free movement of goods should be through a proper market set of policies from the respective countries. While promoting free trade, it cannot be ignored that the efficient use of resources as such is a concept of economics. Once trade liberalisation is followed in practice, without regulation, there is a high probability of it, affecting the rights of individuals, leading to the dominance of multinationals. In the overall set up, for the interest of individuals, a balanced approach between free trade and fair trade as regulatory measures seems a suitable alternative. This additionally requires, a standard legal set up based on assumed values "the underlying fair trade values" that can act as a regulatory mechanism.

Another issue of concern is how to meet the objectives of the WTO through free trade mechanism. The key objectives, of the WTO, as mentioned in the preamble

---

[127]"Legal systems include other different type of rules which do not directly relate to the way people should behave. These secondary rules are rules about rules which structure and regulate primary rules."

Hoecke (2002), p. 21.

[128]"A Legal principle may be defined as a norm which is worded in general terms, has a broad scope and translates a value which is more or less basic to the legal system or parts of it. A principle will often be worded in vague terms, such as "good faith," "legal security" which in their turn refer to prevailing moral values and world views." Hoecke (2002), p. 160.

[129]Footer (2006), p. 92.

are "raising standards of living," "ensuring full employment," "the maximum use of the resources," "expanding the production," "sustainable development" and the "exchange of goods." 'Recognising further that there is a need for the positive efforts designed to ensure that Developing countries and especially the Less Developing countries secure a share in the growth of international trade.'[130] The accomplishment of these objectives along with the promotion of free trade requires regulation of free trade with fair trade as an underlying principle.

Alternatively, it can be said that fair trade as a regulatory measures means, equitable market conditions and promoting opportunities for the Developing and Less-Developed countries for their development. Therefore, one can say in brief that *the constructive role of subsidies, such as for the welfare and development, along with the regulation of free trade can be the key for attaining objectives of the WTO in the market system based on liberalised trade policies.*

Studying subsidies from the perspective of the SCM Agreement has dual perspective. (1) To know the effect of subsidies on the WTO policies that are meant for the proliferation of free trade system and (2) framing policies for the accomplishment of the objectives of the WTO, demand the regulation of subsidies from the fair trade approach. In the second case i.e., for attaining the WTO objectives, subsidies can be divided into (a) justifiable and (b) non-justifiable state support.

2.4.2.1 The Key Features of the WTO Subsidy Agreement

The Subsidies and Countervailing Measures Agreement, provides detailed rules on various categories of subsidisation. The subsidies are mainly classified as prohibited and actionable subsidies. This agreement is very much in line with the basic objectives of the WTO and they can be mentioned in brief as,

1. Trade should be without discrimination.
2. Trade among the Member States should be free, and decrease in barriers through negotiations.
3. Foreign company investors and governments should be confident that the trade barriers would not be raised arbitrarily.
4. Trading should be beneficial for the Less-developed countries, giving them more time to adjust to the free market economy system, and also providing special privileges if so required.
5. Trading should be competitive, discouraging unfair practices, such as export subsidies and dumping products below the cost to gain a market-share.

   In pursuant to the above objectives of the WTO, the SCM Agreement is supportive for the Member States as,

[130] See Preamble of the WTO and the background discussions.

1. it tries to restrict the use of subsidies, so as to regulate the state control or state interference, while promoting the liberal trade policies across the borders,
2. the SCM Agreement gives legal competency to the Member States to counter the effects of subsidies by the use of prescribed procedures and
3. Member States are expected to form trade policies and the standards for the rules keeping in view the scope of the SCM Agreement.

Part 1, of the Agreement deals with general provisions, establishing the outlines for determining the practice of subsidies by introducing basic features such as "*financial-contribution*," and "*benefit*." The explanation of subsidies in Article 1 is mainly substantive and acquires procedural character after becoming linked with any specific policy objective. Thus the term "*specificity*" in the context of subsidies is described in Article 2[131] of the SCM Agreement.

2.4.2.1.1 Financial Contribution

While determining state support as subsidy, and for establishing initial level of qualifications, in order to test the state support, Article 1.1 of the Agreement starts with the term "financial contribution," one of the constituting factors considered for the purpose of a legally-determining subsidy.[132] The term financial contribution is not confined only to fiscal support, and for that reason is further classified to cover various forms of such measures as: (1) a transfer of funds by a government,[133] (2) revenue that was due, but is foregone by any government, (3) governments providing goods or services, other than for general infrastructure or the purchases of goods,[134] a government makes payments to a funding mechanism, or entrusts or directs a private party...[135] The first two explanatory provisions determine the financial contribution as described in Article 1.1(a) (1) of the Agreement:

[131]Specificity, Article 2.1, In order to determine whether a subsidy, as defined in paragraph 1 of Article 1, is specific to an enterprise or industry or group of enterprise or industries within the jurisdiction of the granting authority the mentioned principles shall apply. (for detail see Article 2 of the SCM Agreement)

[132]*United States-Tax Treatment for Foreign Sales Corporation*, WT/DS108/AB/RW, para 85. Appellate Body stated that, 'Article 1.1of the SCM Agreement sets out a definition of a "subsidy" Although, this definition is central to the applicability and operation of the remaining provisions of the agreement, Article 1.1 itself does not impose any obligations on members with respect to the subsidies it defines. It is the provision of the SCM Agreement which follow Article 1, such as Article 3 and 5, that imposes obligations on members with respect to subsides.'

[133]Direct transfer of funds involves (e.g. grants, loans, and equity infusion), potential direct transfers of funds or liabilities (e.g. loan guarantees).

[134]Sub-clause (iii) of Article 1.1 a (1) a government provides goods or services other than general infrastructure or purchases of goods.

[135]1.1(a)(1)(iv) a government makes payments to a funding mechanism, or entrusts or directs a private body to carry out one or more of the type of functions illustrated in (i) to (iii) above which would normally be vested in the government and the practice, in no real sense, differs from practices normally followed by governments.

i) a government practice that involves direct transfer of funds **ii)** a government revenue… By the inclusion of these two sub-clauses as outline measures, an attempt has been made at the general level to determine the various types of state support. However, while analysing the impact of state support, these first two explanatory provisions also need to be seen in the light of the country classifications Developed, Developing, and Less-Developed. The basis of the arguments, in support of state aid for development also has a historical perspective. Ministers during the Uruguay Round were trying to reach a general consensus for the global coherence of policies with regard to free trade, development, and co-operation, with some common objectives. The same reasoning for a flexible approach, with a wider scope through provisions is followed in the WTO trading system. The debate on all these issues, however gets focused on one main premises, whether trade liberalisation itself is sufficient for development.[136] This fact also sheds some light on the link between the WTO, as a trade regulatory institution, the IMF, as an institution taking account of monetary and financial stability, and the World Bank, being concerned for the development policies.[137]

As the discussion concerning the WTO objectives has been made in the introductory chapter, this section moves on to the role of the IMF. The role of IMF can be stated mainly, as to facilitate trade promotion among the nations by support through monetary stability.[138] The GATT trading system, the predecessor organisation of the WTO, also had a legal provision, supporting the link with the IMF through Article XV.[139] The following institution is the World Bank. The World Bank, through IBRD, works with the middle income and the Less-Developed countries in order to promote sustainable development, equitable distribution of resources, and job creating growth, reduction of poverty, and addresses several other issues of regional and global importance.[140] In addition to supporting these objectives, the IBRD also channels capital to the countries in need of reconstruction and development.

---

[136]Wouters and Coppens (2006), pp. 268, 273 and 278.

[137]Wouters and Coppens (2006), p. 267.

[138]Wouters and Coppens (2006), p. 268.

[139]Mentioning here the first two clauses of Article XV. Cl(1) The Contracting Parties shall seek co-operation with the International Monetary Fund to the end that the Contracting Parties and the fund may pursue a co-ordinated policy with regard to exchange questions within the jurisdiction of the Fund and questions of quantitative restrictions and other trade measures within the jurisdiction of the Contracting Parties. Cl (2) In all cases in which the Contracting Parties are called upon to consider or deal with problems concerning monetary reserves, balances of payments or foreign exchange arrangements, they shall consult fully with the International Monetary Fund. In such consultations, the Contracting Parties shall accept all findings of statistical and other facts presented by the fund relating to foreign exchange, monetary reserves and balances of payments, and shall accept the determination of the fund as to whether action by a contracting party in exchange matters is in accordance with the Articles of Agreement of the International Monetary Fund, or with the terms of a special exchange agreement between that contracting party and Contracting Parties.

[140]http://go.worldbank.org/D6IEM83I10.

In the background of the common economic and political objectives, supported by these institutions and along with it, the expected level of market efficiency and competition policies, state support also needs to be weighed in terms development and welfare objectives. The legal approach from the yardstick of the SCM Agreement for judging government support varies, hence cannot be bound by one rigid interpretation, because the classification of Member State has to be kept in mind and same scale cannot be applied to all. The necessity based state support can be illustrated, as follows;

(a) For the Less-Developed countries and some of the Developing countries, government support for basic infrastructure building.
(b) Government support for the initial phase of industrialisation
(c) The justification of support for capital formation, which may require additional categorisation 1) Between common individual and the trading class 2) The direct beneficiaries and indirect beneficiaries.

It is noteworthy; that provisions of the SCM Agreement, gives a relaxation, based on the general classification of the Developing countries, causing further issues and interests based disagreement. The probable cause of continuing disagreement is the lack of further categorisation of the Member States to cover the wide variance in the economic status of the Developing countries. Countries such as China, India, and Brazil are at different economic status in comparison to many other Developing countries and they do bargain to their advantage.

Another reason for the discontent that can be referred to, here is that for some of the Member States, the political reasons are crucial, and they are rigid while bargaining. Due to such a perception it seems to them that 'restricting state support' may be like shifting the concept of the role of the state and the formation of deregulation policies that will further reduce state support in the WTO context. Such issues are seen from the perspective of the limitations on sovereignty

iii) The third clause is the, "government providing goods or services other than general infrastructure, or purchases goods." This clause creates the scope for the basic level of state support for industrialisation, however, the level of support need to be tested by applying the regulatory provisions to see whether the support is contrary to the basic WTO objectives, such as a State itself purchasing goods as a supportive measure. It seems the intention of those who framed this agreement, was to give some concession to the Member States as long as the government support was at the basic level. For example, support to under-developed areas or for scientific development, infrastructure support for industries in the case of Developing and Less-Developed countries. Since, drawing a line between justifiable use of subsidy and non–justifiable use is a challenging task. The legal assumptions need to be focused on the objectives or the effects of the policies in such cases or every case needs to be seen according to its circumstances. For example, the case of subsidies for the fishing industries by the Developed countries (as discussed in another Chap. 6. The trade impact on environment). For this reason, the approach taken here is the same as that by the court when determining the term financial contribution for the purpose of declaring subsidy practices. In the case of the

United States-Final Countervailing duty determination with respect to certain softwood lumber from Canada,[141] the term "financial contribution" in the context of, Article 1.1(a)(1) (iii) of the SCM Agreement, is explained as follows:

> The A.B stated that the article contemplates two distinct types of transactions. The first is where a government provides goods or services other than general infrastructure. Such transactions have the potential to lower artificially the cost of producing a product by providing to an enterprise, inputs having a financial value. The second type of transaction falling within the sub-clause is where a government purchases goods from enterprises. This type of transaction has the potential to increase artificially the revenue gained from selling the product.

The A.B in this case has tried to outline the meaning of subsidy based on the effect of government support. This support by the government is in the form of 1) goods and services 2) government purchases of goods. The A.B has emphasised the effect to be seen of such government support measures, for the purpose of determining subsidies in the WTO context. (See Airbus case and the US export credit guarantee scheme also discussed in this chapter later)

Usually, (as per the WTO Agreement), a subsidy is deemed to exist if there is a financial contribution[142] by a government or any public body, or there is any form of income or price support and a benefit is thereby conferred.

Financial contribution, in the context of subsidies is a term that can be broadly interpreted to cover its effects. Sub-clause Article 1.1(a) (1) (iv), covers payment by governments to a funding mechanism. . .entrusts . . .or directs a private body. . ...[143] As the fundamental notion of subsidies to be tested by law is its relationship to state support, so it is a prerequisite to check the obligations followed or the actions taken by the government, or to find out if rules are by-passed by giving or delegating responsibility to someone or by directing them to private bodies. In order to determine whether a financial contribution exists by entrusting,[144] or by any form

---

[141] *United States-Final Countervailing Duty Determination with Respect to Certain Softwood Lumber from Canada,* WT/DS257/AB/R, para 53.

[142] The panel in *US-Export Restraint,* WT/DS194/R, para 8.74 concluded that export restraints did not constitute a subsidy, as they did not represent a financial contribution by the government.

[143] Article 1.1(a)(iv) a government makes payments to a funding mechanism, or entrusts or directs a private body to carry out one or more of the type of functions illustrated in (i) to (iii) which would normally be vested in the government and the practice, in no real sense, differs from practices normally followed by governments.

[144] *US-Countervailing Duty Investigation on DRAMS.* WT/DS296AB/R, para. 110, The term "entrusts" connotes the action of giving responsibility to someone for a task or an object. In the context of paragraph (iv) of Article 1.1(a) (1), the government gives responsibility to a private body 'to carry out' one of the types of functions listed in paragraphs (i) and (iii) of Article 1.1 (a) (1). As the United States acknowledges, delegation (the word used by the Panel) may be a means by which a government gives responsibility to a private body to carry out one of the functions listed in paragraph (i) through (iii).

of government direction,[145] the government action must be the focus of study, rather than just presuming the cause and effect relationship.[146] If the inclusion of the term financial contribution is analysed from the conceptual perspective, it seem the drafters, by specifically referring to this term, restricted the possibility of any general level government action to be the cause of the subsidy under investigation. Referring to the time of the negotiations, it was emphasised during the discussion stage that government measures that conferred economic advantages or a support of economic value can be deemed to be subsidies. The main reason for this specification was that prior to the Uruguay Round, the subsidy and countervailing measure provisions as mentioned in Article XVI and VI, of GATT 1947 and in the Tokyo Round Subsidies Code had no definition of subsidies as such, but was confined to mere explanation of the term subsidy.[147] The WTO SCM Agreement is specific and structured and the provisions are based on the objectives of the agreement, therefore by just emphasising the basis of the government action, any policy measure to be subsidies, rather than linking it with the effect, may lead to something outside the scope of the Agreement.[148] Nor is it possible to classify the use of subsidies as justifiable or the extent of its use as fair use, without such feature based reference to the explanation of subsidies. Although the SCM Agreement is upgraded and structured in comparison to the GATT subsidies code, however there is no proportionate ratio established to determine justifiable and non-justifiable subsidies,

---

[145] *US-Countervailing Duty Investigation on DRAMS*. WT/DS296AB/R, para 111. As for the term 'directs' we note that some of the definitions-such as 'give' authoritative instructions to and order (a person) to do—suggests that the person or entity that directs has authority over the person or entity that is directed. In contrast, some of the other definitions—such as 'inform or guide' do not necessarily convey this sense of authority. In our view, that the private body under paragraph (iv) is directed 'to carry out' a function underscores the notion of authority that is included in some of the definitions of the term direct.

Para 112.Paragraph (iv)of Article1.1(a)(1) further states that the private body must have been entrusted or directed to carry out one of the type of functions in paragraphs (i) through (iii). As the panel in *US-Export Restraints* explained, this means that the scope of the actions. . .covered by subparagraph (iv) must be the same as those covered by subparagraphs (i) (iii).

[146] *United States-Measures Treating Export Restraint as Subsidies*. WT/DS 194/R, para 8.42. The Appellate Body stated that[i]t does not suffice to demonstrate solely that a government granting a subsidy anticipated that exports would result, and elaborated. . ..anticipation of exportation. In other words, the Appellate Body found that a *cause and effect relationship* between the subsidy and actual or anticipated trends in exports was not sufficient to satisfy the 'tied to' standard of conditionality for export contingency to exist. Similarly, in the case before us, for the 'entrusts or directs' standards to be met, i.e., for there to be financial contribution in the sense of subparagraph (iv) the government's action must be the focus, rather than the possible effects of action on, or the reactions to it by, those affected, even if those affected, even if those effects or reactions are expected.

[147] *United States-Measures Treating Exports Restraint as Subsidies*. WT/DS 194/R, para 8.65 The negotiating history of Article 1 confirms our interpretation of the term "financial Contribution." This negotiating history demonstrates, in the first place, that the requirement of financial contribution from the outset was intended by its proponents precisely to ensure that not all government measures that conferred benefits could be deemed to be subsidies. Also See para 8.66.

[148] See para 8.38, WT/DS194/R.

through the provisions; this was probably left for economists or statistician. The issue nevertheless remains as a matter of debate and is often resolved on the basis of facts. Applying here the legal analogy from the Appellate Body's interpretation of the scope of Article 9.1(c) of the Agreement on Agriculture (see Chap. 3 Discussing agriculture subsidies from the WTO perspective….) "the phrase by 'virtue of' indicates that there must be a demonstrable link between governmental action and the financing of payments, whereby the payments are in some way, financed as a result of, or as a consequence of, the governmental action."[149]

The term 'financial contribution' also covers the continuing government support that started before the formation of the WTO. Article 1.1 (a) Clause (2) refers to any form of income or price support that falls within the definition of Article XVI[150] of the 1994 GATT agreement. The purpose of this provision seems to cover those cases related to subsidies or the ongoing policies if they remains uncovered by the above mentioned provisions, but are within the parameters of the previous GATT Agreement, to be covered under the present SCM Agreement.

Before applying a new set of provisions and in order for the procedural law to be applied, it is of relevance to determine whether previous provisions are replaced or carried forward. There remains a grey area of uncertainty for applying legal provisions for the transactions during the transition period. It is noteworthy that clause 1.1(a) (2) can be used to determine financial contributions for the purpose of subsidies but whether it fulfils the procedural requirement to initiate or continue investigations, is a matter for the Panel and the A.B to decide. It seems from the interpretation of the A.B, in the case of **Brazil–Measures Affecting Desiccated Coconut**[151] that before the formation of the WTO, there was a separate legal identity between GATT 1947 and the Tokyo Round SCM Code.[152] The Tokyo Round SCM code was administered by the Tokyo Round Committee on Subsidies and Countervailing Duty Measures, which comprised of the signatories to that code.[153] A complaining party could take the matter at issue under Article VI of the GATT 1947, and invoke the provisions of Article XXIII of the GATT 1947, or alternatively the provisions of Tokyo Round SCM Code before the formation of the WTO.[154]

---

[149]The words "by virtue of" therefore expresses the relationship between 'governmental action' and the 'financing' of payments for the purpose of Article 9.1(c).The essence of that relationship is between the 'nexus' or 'link' between 'action' and 'financing. See, *United States—Tax Treatment for Foreign Sales Corporations,* WT/DS108/AB/R, para 136. A "subsidy" within the meaning of Article 1.1 of the SCM Agreement, arises where the grantor makes a financial contribution which confers a benefit on the recipient, as compared with what would have been otherwise available to the recipient in the market place.

[150]Article XVI of the GATT Deals with Subsidies under GATT.

[151]WT/DS 22/R.

[152]Tokyo round subsidies code, 1973–1979.

[153]By the end of 1994, the GATT 1947 had 128 contracting parties, whereas the Tokyo Round SCM Code had 24 signatories.

[154]See p. no 12, WT/DS22/AB/R.

Unlike the previous GATT system, the WTO Agreement is a single treaty instrument accepted by the WTO Members as a single undertaking. There are indeed some basic differences between the two Agreements; however, there also exist a link between the two systems. The provisions and practices during the GATT period, as far as they are not contradictory with the SCM Agreement, are applicable. First, the procedural question here arises of what kind of rights and obligations a Member can imply out of this link.[155] A note of interpretation is added to Annex 1A for drawing some guidelines. In the case of conflict between the provisions of the GATT and a provision of another agreement in Annex 1A establishing the WTO, the provision of the other agreement should prevail. The second basic question is about the application of norms. In the case of a dispute, and if the issue demands to be referred back to the normative aspect, so for the purpose of interpretation, whether a normative basis during the GATT or Tokyo Round SCM code needs to be taken into consideration. Alternatively, the WTO needs to be seen as a treaty organisation distinct from GATT with its own aims and objectives,[156] these questions can be better resolved when the matter is referred to the D. S.B.

Therefore, the term financial contribution for the purpose of the SCM Agreement is not merely a monetary support, as within its ambit; any such support from the state which results in a direct or indirect financial gain is covered. On occasions, a question has arisen as to whether the subparagraphs/sub clauses, explaining financial contribution can be applied exclusively or whether they are mutually exclusive? As there is no scope or any such conditional relationship mentioned in Article 1.1(a)(1), therefore such an interpretation of the exclusive characteristics of the subparagraphs, precluding a transaction to be covered by more than one subparagraphs/sub clauses, while determining financial contribution is not valid.[157] After financial contribution, the following term is the benefit. When the outcome of

[155]See Article XVI: 1 of the WTO Agreement provides 'Except as otherwise provided under this Agreement or the Multilateral Trade Agreements, the WTO shall be guided by the decisions, procedures and customary practices followed by the Contracting parties to the GATT.'

[156]Article 28 of the Vienna Convention, "Unless a different intention appears from the treaty or is otherwise established, its provisions do not bind a party in relation to any act or fact which took place or any situation which ceased to exist before the date of the entry into force of the treaty with respect to that party."

[157]*United States-Measures Affecting Trade in Large Civil Aircraft (second complaint) Appellate Body Report,* WT/DS353/AB/R, AB stated in para 613. Beginning with the general architecture and structure of the provisions, we note that Article 1.1(a) (1) defines and identifies the government conduct that constitutes a financial contribution for purposes of the SCM Agreement. Subparagraphs (i)-(iv) exhaust the type of government conduct deemed to constitute a financial contribution. This is because the introductory chapeau to the subparagraphs states that "there is a financial contribution by a government. . .., i.e. where:" Some of the categories of conduct-for instance those specified in subparagraphs (i) and (ii)-are described in general terms with illustrative examples that provide an indication of the common features that characterize the conduct referred to more generally. Article 1.1(a) (1), however, does not explicitly spell out the intended relationship between the constituent subparagraphs. Finally, the subparagraphs focus primarily on the action taken by the government or a public body.

a financial contribution in any form is a benefit, the subsidy acquires a substantive legal identity.

2.4.2.1.2 Benefit

Article 1.1(b) of the agreement, deals with the term benefit, whether it is obtained by, or given to any business entity. In the description of the term "subsidy" under the ASCM, there are two basic elements as mentioned. "*A financial contribution by a government or any public body and a benefit is thereby conferred.*" The influence of the first element "financial contribution" is likely to be based on the objectives of policies framed by the government. That being so, it is logical to presume that the second element in Article 1.1 is concerned with the "benefit…conferred" on the recipient due to that government action. These two combined (financial contribution and benefit conferred) makes the substantive description of the practice of subsidy. Thus, subparagraphs (a) and (b) of Article 1.1 define the "giving of a subsidy" first, by performing an act either directly or through the policies of the granting authority, and second, the effect on the recipient.[158]

In the context of this study, and specifically for the scope of this chapter, the aim is to point out the comparable relationship of the state support in the form of justifiable subsidies and non-justifiable subsidies. The justifiable and non-justifiable limits are determined in terms of the market efficiency principles and the various objectives of the WTO.

When discussing 'benefit,' the general perception about the term is profit or obtaining profit, but in the context of the SCM Agreement, the effect of such profit need to be seen within the parameters of trade regulating provisions that are intertwined with the objectives of the WTO.[159] In order to determine the effect of subsidies, or to judge the trade distortive effects, requires an affirmative finding of the conferral of benefit in one form or the other, to a company. This relationship between 'financial contribution' and 'benefit' also needs to be tested in respect of the specific time period, as was upheld by the Appellate Body in the case of, the

[158]*Canada-Measures Affecting the Export of Civilian Aircraft, Appellate Body Report,* WT/DS70/AB/R, para. 156.

[159]*Case of the United States-Countervailing Measures Concerning Certain Products from the European Communities,* WT/DS212/AB/R, para 108. AB stated in para 108, that "…United States has misconstrued our findings in those two appeals. In *Canada-Aircraft,* we were asked whether the 'cost to government' was relevant to the interpretation of 'benefit' within the meaning of Article 1.1(b) of the SCM Agreement. In finding the 'cost to government' not to be the relevant benchmark for identifying the 'benefit', we said that Article 14 of the SCM Agreement prescribes the guidelines required to 'calculate the benefit' to the recipient conferred pursuant to paragraph 1 of Article 1. We concluded that this phrase in Article 14 necessarily provides relevant context for interpreting Article 1.1, and we found that[a] benefit does not exist in the abstract, but must be received and enjoyed by a beneficiary or a recipient."

United States-Imposition of Countervailing Duties on Certain Hot-Rolled Lead and Bismuth Carbon Steel Products Originating In The United kingdom.[160] It would be worth to add here that the general outlines settled by the DSB for judging market distortion, further helps to draw the inference that the term benefit can been seen from different aspects. In the context of this study, the term benefit is considered mainly to determine whether the subsidies questioned are justifiable or not-justifiable." Besides the above-mentioned effects of benefits, any state support assumed to be a benefit also needs to be seen from a broader perspective and tested in the light of its objectives. Any support more than direct financial support also needs to be examined in the light of particular social and economic conditions in Developing and Less-Developed countries. Although, these concessions and relaxations given to Developing and Less-Developed countries are justified, however, there is a need for certain restrictions. The scope of state support is wide and can be in various forms, therefore the term benefit also needs to be analysed from the aspect of regulatory measures. A profound discussion concerning the analysis of the term benefit, and the extent of its applicability to determine subsidies and the effect of subsidies, was made in the case of **Canada-Certain Measures Affecting the Renewable Energy Generation Sector and in Canada-Measures Relating to the Feed-In Tariff Program.**[161] Concerning the determination of benefits in the context of market distortion affecting free demand and supply, two significant points on which the legal discussion continued and can be considered as source for future reference were (1) that a financial contribution confers an advantage on its recipient and cannot be determined in absolute terms, but requires a comparison with a bench mark.[162] For the determination of this benchmark, reliance can be

[160] WT/DS138/AB/R, para 62. Therefore, we agree with the Panel that while an investigating authority may presume, in the context of an administrative review under Article 21.2, that a "benefit" continues to flow from a united, non-recurring "financial contribution", this presumption can never be irrebuttable. In this case, given the changes in ownership leading to the creation of UES and BSplc/BSES, the USDOC was required under Article 21.2 to examine; on the basis of the information before it relating to these changes, whether a benefit accrued to UES and BSplc/BSES. We thus agree with the Panel's finding that the changes in ownership leading to the creation of UES and BSplc/BSES should have caused the USDOC to examine whether the production of leaded bars by UES and BSplc/BSES respectively, and not BSC was subsidized. In particular, the USDOC should have examined the continued existence of "benefit" already deemed to have been conferred by the pre-1985/86 "financial contributions" to BSC, and it should have done so from the perspective of UES and BSplc/BSES respectively, and not BSC.

[161] WT/DS412/AB/R ● WT/DS426/AB/R.

[162] WT/DS 412/AB/R●WT/DS426/AB/R para 5.165. We thus consider that the Panel's interpretative approach to the question of benefit under Article 1.1(b) of the SCM Agreement, including the reliance on the context found in Article 14(d), is the correct one. We do not consider that the determination of the mere existence, as opposed to the amount, of subsidy calls for a different interpretation of how to determine benefit under Article 1.1(b), read in the context of Article 14 (d) of the SCM Agreement, requires comparison between actual remuneration and a market based benchmark or proxy, and thus between amounts, in order to determine the existence of a benefit.

placed on Article 14(d)[163] of the SCM Agreement. (2) The second issue concerned identification of legal standards that can be applied for the analysis of benefit, and eventually for the determination of subsidies, in different kinds of policy measures adopted by the governments with a corresponding sets of objectives. This primarily requires characterising the existence of benefit within such policies or measures, and subsequently identifying these with the subsidies questioned. Then comes the testing stage, whether such subsidies can be termed as justifiable or not, and this indeed is a complex issue. The A.B, giving less significance to the '*but for test*'[164] has suggested that in such instances, benefit analysis needs to be based on the relevant market or market conditions.[165] In this case, **Canada-Certain Measures Affecting the Renewable Energy Generation Sector and in Canada-Measures Relating to the Feed-In Tariff Program,**[166] the discussion concerning the policy issues continued further and the evaluation based on the market, for determining benefit vis-a-vis policy objectives was given consideration, rather than excluded by the A.B.[167]

As regards the test of the free market system, where the trade of goods is promoted without applying restrictions, there are occasions before the DSB that demands the analysis of market distortion issues, related to the effect of subsidies.

---

[163]Article 14(d) of the SCM Agreement. The provision of goods or services or purchase of goods by a government shall not be considered as conferring a benefit unless the provision is made for less than adequate remuneration, or the purchase is made for more than adequate remuneration. The adequacy of remuneration shall be determined in relation to prevailing market conditions for the good or service in question in the country of provision or purchase (including price, quality, availability, marketability, transportation and other conditions of purchase or sale).

[164]WT/DS 412/AB/R●WT/DS426/AB/R, para 5.197. We first observe that if, as the Panel acknowledged, wind power and solar PV energy generation would not occur in Ontario absent the government's definition of the energy supply-mix, a 'but for' approach would be inapposite, for establishing benefit, because such an approach would, by definition, not measure what the recipient could obtain in the market place for wind power and solar PV energy generation. . . .The fundamental question that needs to be answered is what market provides the appropriate benchmark.

[165]WT/DS 412/AB/R●WT/DS426/AB/R, para 5.169. The definition of the relevant market is central to, and a prerequisite for, a benefit analysis under Article 1.1(b) of the SCM Agreement. The existence of a benefit can properly be established only by comparing the prices of goods and services in the relevant market where they compete. It would seem logical for a panel that is tasked with a benefit determination to begin its analysis by defining the relevant market, which will be used for the purposes of undertaking the benefit analysis.

[166]WT/DS412/AB/R ● WT/DS426/AB/R.

[167]Nevertheless, while introducing legitimate policy considerations into the determination of benefit cannot be reconciled with Article 1.1(b) of the SCM Agreement, we do not think that a market-based approach to benefit benchmarks excludes taking into account situations where governments intervene to create markets that would otherwise not exist. For example, governments create electricity markets with constant and reliable supply. . . ..Although this type of intervention has an effect on market prices, as opposed to a situation where prices are determined by unconstrained forces of supply and demand, it does not exclude per se treating the resulting prices as market prices for the purpose of a benefit analysis under Article 1.1(b) of the SCM Agreement.

This requires that the term 'benefit' be correlated with the outcome of policies and trade practices, for example export-oriented practices or policies that can be presumed to be prohibited subsidies. Here the approach adopted by the DSB in applying the term benefit is taken, when determining whether subsidies are the reason for effect.

In the case of **Canada-Measures Affecting the Export of Civilian Aircraft,**[168] the legal dispute arose concerning Canadian measures, such as financing and loan guarantees provided by the Canadian Export Development Corporation to the civil aircraft industry, which Brazil alleged were export subsidies, contrary to the obligations under SCM Agreement.[169]

> Interpreting the term, "benefit" mentioned in Article 1.1 (b) of the SCM Agreement, the Appellate Body in this case affirmed the Panels view that, "the ordinary meaning of 'benefit' clearly encompasses some form of advantage . . ..In order to determine whether a financial contribution (in the sense of Article 1.1 (a) (i) confers a 'benefit', i.e., an advantage, it is necessary to determine whether the financial contributions places the recipient in a more advantageous positions than would have been the case but for the financial contribution."[170]

The A.B both from the substantive and procedural aspect of law, tried to develop the link between financial contribution and benefit stating that the two are separate legal elements in Article 1.1 of the SCM Agreement.[171] The A.B has attempted to formulate an objective outline by construing *that benefit means to put more advantage than otherwise it is available in the market.*[172] Despite this straight line approach followed by the A.B, every case needs to be seen from its own perspective as there can be several forms of advantages. Comparing this interpretation with the WTO objectives, such as promoting trade opportunities to the Developing and Less Developed countries, the link forged between financial contribution and benefit can require further elaboration based on the contextual approach.

---

[168]WT/DS70/AB/R.

[169]See para 1.1 and 2.1 of WT/DS 70/R.

[170]*Canada-Measures Affecting the Export of Civilian Aircraft (Canada-Aircraft), Appellate Body Report,* WT/DS 70/AB/R, para 149.para 153, 154.

[171]*Brazil-Export Financing Programme for Aircraft, Appellate Body Report,* WT/DS46/AB/R, para 157. Moreover, the Panel compounded its error in finding that the "financial contribution" in the case of PROEX subsidies is not a "potential direct transfer of funds" by reasoning that a letter of commitment does not confer a "benefit." In this way, in its interpretation of Article 1.1(a) (i), the Panel imported the notion of a "benefit" into the definition of a "financial contribution." This was a mistake. We see the issues—and the respective definitions of a "financial contribution" and a " benefit" as two separate legal elements in Article 1.1 of the SCM Agreement, which together determine whether subsidy exists, and not whether it is granted for the purpose of calculating the level of a developing country Member's export subsidies under Article 27.4 of that Agreement.

[172]WT/DS 70/AB, para 149.

2.4.2.1.3 The Recipients of Benefits or "the Question of Specificity"

Before the formation of the WTO, there was no such classification of subsidies as Actionable, Prohibited, and Non-Actionable. How subsidies are to be determined as prohibited or what type of subsidies could be categorised as prohibited became an ambiguous issue during the time of discussions concerning the formation of the WTO.[173] It was during Dunkel draft that 'specificity' was decided as a prerequisite for determining a subsidy as actionable. Article 2 of the SCM Agreement, draws the distinction between subsidies in general and subsidies for given specific objectives, by outlining that no policy or legislative measures will be considered as specific if its effects are general or they are just coincidental, rather than having a certain objective.

Whenever, a case is brought before the DSB, three basic features, "financial contribution," "benefit" and "specificity" and their consolidated effect is taken into consideration. Then subsequent to investigation, countervailing measures/duties are imposed. Any benefit, as a consequence of a financial contribution, should be directed to a specific industry. "A benefit does not exist in abstract. Logically, a benefit can be said to arise only if a person, natural or legal, or a group of persons has in fact received something as stated by A.B in the case of **Canada-Measures Affecting the Export of Civilian Aircraft.** "[174] What can be construed from this statement is that specificity is an inevitable procedural requirement, if a case concerning the issue of subsidy is to be brought before the WTO's Dispute Settlement Body, Article 2.1 sub-clause (a)[175] deals with the scope, the subject for which the subsidy is obtained, or to whom the resulting advantages of a subsidy are intended, either directly or implied by the legislation. Article 2 (b) demarcates what is specific and what is not specific. For challenging the use of subsidies, through the SCM Agreement provisions, the procedure requires that the claims should be linked to any benefitting industry, enterprise or any legal person. Despite the outline drawn in the provisions, the possibility of presumption remains in these cases brought under consideration. In principle, the application of Article 2.1

[173] For instance the US sought to apply the prohibited category to both the type, (1) support for export on non-primary products as well as to domestic subsidies. However, this restriction was not based on any strict classification or specification. In order to create scope for the justifiable use, some statute based determining criteria was needed. The Dunkel Draft took a middle course, prohibiting the export subsidies in the illustrative list, subsidies contingent upon export performance, and subsidies contingent on the use of domestic over imported goods. Many of the participants during Dunkel draft (e.g., India, Korea, Brazil, Canada, EC, Nordics, Japan, Switzerland) proposed that a subsidy must be specific before it may be countervailed. The Dunkel draft makes "specificity" a prerequisite to finding a subsidy as actionable. See, Stewart (1993), pp. 70–71.

[174] For detail reference, see WT/DS70/AB/R, para 154.

[175] Article 2.1(a) Where the granting authority, or the legislation pursuant to which the granting authority operates, explicitly limits access to a subsidy to certain enterprises, such a subsidy shall be specific.

sub-clause (b)[176] is based on criteria or conditions which are neutral, which do not favour certain enterprises over others, and which are economic in nature. Probably Article 2.1(b) is added to create distinction between *incidental affects and intentional measures*. However, when applying state support or aid for good reasons, not for market distortion, there still is a possibility of unexpected incidental affects in the market. In such cases, in order to determine, if the effects of the measures are likely to be incidental or intentional, one possibility for assessment is by applying a "private investor test."[177] This test is generally applied by EU courts to determine the use of State aids.[178] An analogical application of this test in the case of subsidies measures is possible, by establishing the relationship between benefit and specificity. In such cases the benefit primarily needs to be tested from the perspective of

[176]Article 2.1(b) Where the granting authority, or the legislation pursuant to which the granting authority operates, establishes objective criteria or conditions and provided that eligibility is automatic for the objective criteria (for details, see SCM Agreement).

[177]*C-234/84 Belgium v Commission* [1986] ECR 2263. para 14. 'An appropriate way of establishing whether such a measure is a State aid is to apply the criterion which was mentioned in the Commission's decision and, moreover, was not contested by the Belgian Government, of determining to what extent the undertaking would be able to obtain the sums in question on private capital markets. In the case of an undertaking whose capital is held by the public authorities, the test is, in particular, whether in similar circumstances a private shareholder, having regard to the foreseeability of obtaining a return and leaving aside all social, regional-policy and sectoral considerations, would have subscribed the capital in question. It is noteworthy that limitations of private investor test were debated by EC in the case of UNITED STATES-IMPOSITION OF COUNTERVAILING DUTIES ON CERTAIN HOT-ROLLED LEAD AND BISMUTH CARBON STEEL PRODUCTS ORIGINATING IN FRANCE; GERMANY AND UNITED KINGDOM. Report of the Panel SCM/185, para 200. The EC further argued that in the eyes of the DOC, a "reasonable private investor" was an outside investor. However, in the cases regarding products from France and the United Kingdom, the investor was the government which was an inside investor or owner-investor. The rationality of an outside investor was likely to differ considerably from the rationality of an inside investor and approach that did not take this economic reality into account was illogical and contrary to relevant facts and economic reality. For an inside investor who had a big stake in a company, it made commercial sense to continue to invest in such a company even whilst an outside investor would no longer do so. The inside investor would be concerned about safeguarding and recovering his existing stake in the company. He faced the risk of losing all or a substantial amount of his existing stake in an ailing company if that company was bankrupted or liquidated: the company would be worth more as a going concern, and therefore the inside investor (irrespective of whether he was a private or a public investor) would be motivated to help keep the company in operation and provide additional investments to that end without thereby acting in a commercially unsound manner. If the inside investor provided further investment and helped turn the company around, where an outside investor would not have done so, this could not be taken to mean that the capital infusion was unsound and, therefore, amounted to a subsidy. Moreover, an inside investor had greater expertise and knowledge about the company and the market in which it operated and therefore was usually better capable than an outside investor to assess the prospects for future profitability of the company. Also, the fact that an outside investor may be less well informed and less confident of his information about the firm's prospects, usually will make him demand a higher rate of return than the inside investor.

[178]Herdegen (2003), p. 246.

Article 14[179] of the SCM Agreement, or the respective market place can be the basis for such comparison.[180]

It can further be construed, that Article 2.1 sub-clause (b) emphasise that a subsidy will be considered as a general subsidy, unless there are certain prescribed conditions by the granting authority and its benefits are automatically directed to a certain enterprises. Nevertheless, Article 2 sub-clause (c) tends to attribute a certain level of discretion, mainly to the DSB in order to find the "specificity." The likely use of this sub-clause depends on the instances where the specific purpose is not deciphered after the application of clause (a) and (b). It can be said that this clause creates possibilities at a profound level, for detecting the purpose of policies.[181] Additionally, one cannot ignore the possibilities of several levels of policy interpretations, becoming established on the basis of this provision.

The debate on the issue of specificity became polarised between the parties, in the case of **United States-Final Countervailing Duty Determination with Respect to Certain Softwood Lumber from Canada.**[182]

As the US concluded, based on Article 2.1(c), the recipient under the provincial stumpage programmes were limited to a group of industries. In fact, the US-DOC'S finding was based on its definition of the term "group of industries," by which it meant those companies and individuals that used the programmes.[183]

---

[179]Article 14 of the SCM Agreement deals with Calculation of the Amount of a Subsidy in Terms of the Benefit to the Recipient.

[180]*Canada-Measures Affecting the Export of Civilian Aircraft*, WT/DS70/R, para 9.112 to para 9.116.

[181]Article 2.1(c) If, notwithstanding any appearance of non-specificity from the application of the principles laid down in sub-paragraphs (a) and (b), there are reasons to believe that the subsidy may in fact be specific, other factors may be considered. Such as use of a subsidy programme by a limited number of certain enterprises, predominant use by certain enterprises, the granting of disproportionately large amounts of subsidy to certain enterprises and the manner in which discretion has been exercised by the granting authority to grant a subsidy (for details, see SCM Agreement).

[182]WT/DS 257/R.

[183]*United States-Final Countervailing Duty Determination with Respect to Certain Softwood Lumber from Canada.* See Para 4.48. The legal point asserted by Canada was not accepted by the court.

para 4.50 The term "certain enterprise" is a defined term for the purpose of Article 2 "an enterprise, industry, or group of enterprises or industries." At issue in this case is the meaning of the terms "industry" and in particular "group of....industries." The meaning of "industry" is [a] particular form or branch of productive labour; a trade, a manufacture. In the context of the WTO agreement and the SCM agreement this requires an examination of product-based criteria. Part V of the SCM agreement provides that the term "domestic industry" shall be interpreted as referring to the domestic producers as a whole of the like products or to those of them whose collective output of the products constitute a major proportion of the total domestic production of those products. The term domestic industry thus refers to the producers on the basis of products. The logical inquiry to be undertaken by the investigating authority of an importing member is therefore whether the parallel foreign industry is subsidized on a specific basis.

Canada in its second written submission states para 4.230 The concept of "specificity" has been with the WTO and GATT for nearly two decades. It was first considered by the Committee on

> We note in this respect, that Article 2.1(c) of the SCM Agreement provides that if there are reasons to believe that the subsidy may in fact be specific, other factors may be considered. The use of the verb "may" rather than shall, in our view, indicates that if there are reasons to believe that the subsidy may in fact be specific, an authority may want to look at any of the four factors or indicators of specificity.[184]

In this case, the Panel body acknowledged that when determining a subsidy by virtue of Article 2.1(c), and if there is reason to believe so, the prescribed body may look to any of the four factors discussed in Article 2.1(c) The four factors are; (1) *the use of a subsidy programme by a limited or selected number of enterprises*, (2) *a predominant use of subsidies by certain enterprises*, (3) *granting of disproportionately large amounts of subsidies to certain enterprises* (4) *discretion for such use or subsidy being given out of proportion to a certain enterprise*. Besides these factors, there can be other indictors where support is specific, and makes the case for countervailing duties; for example, *in case, such an advantage is restricted for any geographical reason, or any such state support falls under Article 3 of the SCM Agreement or if there is a possibility to substantiate that such form of state support is a subsidy*. The panel body, it seems has attempted to put forward the view, that the application of the term specificity for the procedural purposes is given more flexibility and takes into account the practice of subsidies from various dimensions. Subsequent to determining either of these factors, the legislative provisions or policies can be compared for further consideration i.e., as to whether such measures can be considered as specific for an industry or group, and are thus promoting or providing the use of a subsidy.

There can be instances of covert support that cannot be directly covered through the provisions, but, based on facts and circumstances, presumptions, can be drawn. In such, cases, the intent of the parties needs to be ascertained[185] before final approval of the non-justifiable use of subsidies. Furthermore, in Article 2(c), specificity also needs to be seen in the context of prohibited subsidies as classified under 3.1(a) 'subsidies contingent in law or in fact', whether solely or as one of several other conditions, upon export performance, including those illustrated in Annex I. For determining what *can be contingent to the fact*, requires some level of standard setting, and based on that standard, it can be established that such support

---

Subsidies and Countervailing Measures (SCM Committee) in 1985, when the SCM group of experts provided it with draft guidelines for the application of the concept of specificity in the calculation of the amount of a subsidy other than an export subsidy. The draft guidelines set out a series of rules based on what government did to restrict the availability of a programme. Where access was restricted to certain enterprises based on non-neutral criteria, the programme was considered as de jure specific. On de facto specific, the lone paragraph (f) addressed government action affecting availability in terms of a "de facto" deliberate granting of an advantage to certain industries. The draft language de facto specificity evolved over the course of the Uruguay Round negotiations, but at all times remained concerned with the granting by government of selective access to a subsidy programme.

[184]Panel in para 7.123.

[185]Lester (2011), p. 17.

is linked to export promotion even without directly being related to a legal contingency as mentioned in Article 3.1(a) footnote 4.[186] This creates some level of discretion for standard setting. However, this discretion needs to be tested based on the factors mentioned in 2.1(c).

In the case of Actionable subsidies, as the scope of presumptions are higher, it is essential to use specific criteria to test if such support cause adverse effects, such as (a) injury to the domestic industry of another Member, (b) nullification or impairment of benefits accruing directly or indirectly to other Members under GATT 1994. In particular the benefits of concessions bound under Article II of GATT 1994, (c) serious prejudice to the interests of another Member.

The question then arises as to what standards can be applied for such a determination? An approach to this situation can be, that factors within Article 2(c) are included to establish some sort of standards to determine subsidies or to identify if any concession or support is given to the domestic industry in order to encourage protectionism or promote export.[187] In this regard, the A.B has followed a much more precise approach and tried to remove vagueness by stating that the inference is based on intent, and *whether the subsidy is to promote export*, can be construed as based on objective standards.[188]

[186] This standard is met when the facts demonstrate that the granting of a subsidy, without having been made legally contingent upon export performance, is in fact tied to actual or anticipated exportation or export earnings. The mere fact that a subsidy is granted to an enterprise which is for export should not for that reason alone be considered to be an export subsidy within the meaning of this provision.

[187] Lester (2011), p. 10.

[188] *European Communities And Certain Member-States-Measures Affecting Trade in Large Civil Aircraft*. WT/DS316/AB/R, para 1050. The standard for determining whether the granting of a subsidy is 'in fact tied to anticipated exportation' is an objective standard, to be established, on the basis of the total configuration of facts constituting and surrounding the granting of the subsidy, including the design, structure, and modalities of operation of the measure granting the subsidy. Indeed, the conditional relationship between the granting of the subsidy and export performance must be objectively observable on the basis of such evidence in order for the subsidy to be geared to induce the promotion of future export performance by the recipient. The standard for *de facto* export contingency is therefore not satisfied by the subjective motivation of the granting government to promote the future export performance of the recipient. In this respect, we note that the Appellate Body and panels have, on several occasions, cautioned against undue reliance on the intent of a government behind a measure to determine the WTO-consistency of that measure. The Appellate Body has found that 'the intent stated or otherwise, of the legislators is not conclusive as to whether a measure is consistent with the covered agreement. 'In our view, the same understanding applies in the context of a determination on export contingency, where the requisite conditionality between the subsidy and anticipated exportation under Article 3.1(a) and footnote 4 of the SCM Agreement must be established on the basis of objective evidence, rather than subjective intent. We note, however, that while the standard for *de facto* export contingency cannot be satisfied by the subjective motivation of the granting government, objectively reviewable expressions of government policy objectives for granting may, however, constitute relevant evidence in an inquiry into whether a subsidy is geared to induce the promotion of future export performance by the recipient.

The three basic elements/factors (financial contribution, benefit and specificity) are distinctly covered, from many aspects, in the Agreement for the interpretation of State Support as subsidies. The SCM Agreement for the substantive explanation of the subsidies uses two key elements "financial contribution" and "benefit" and the third one "specificity" for the procedural qualification. The term financial contribution and benefit are categorised in several provisions [Article 1.1(a) (1)... (a)(2) and Article 1.1(b)] for the broader coverage of the effects of subsidies or the implication of the policies supporting subsidies. The multi dimension approach for the interpretation of subsidies is necessary for the specific categorisation as, (1) prohibited (2) actionable (3) non-actionable. Further, this specific categorisation of subsidies can be applied to study wide range of subjects, such as, the relationship between trade and the environment, the cross border effect on trade due to the subsidies in the agriculture and industrial sector, transparency in trade by determining the real source of product, and by adopting the rules of origin. The study of subsidies, as categorised based on the WTO, also necessitates interpretation of the SCM Agreement provisions, in relation to country classification. The classification of countries as Developed, Developing and Less-Developed creates a comparative approach for the implementation of free market policies. From the outlines determining subsidies, it seems that the explanation of subsidies by discretely taking into account the three factors is an attempt to construct a harmonious relationship among the Member States, in order to meet the objectives of the WTO. However, to what extent it is successful is part of this study, in this chapter and the following chapters, based on the topic "**Subsidies in the Context of the WTO's Free Trade System-A Legal and Economic Analysis**"[189]

2.5 Classification of Subsidies

The SCM Agreement considering the WTO objectives classifies subsidies into three categories, so as to distinguish between the types and their effects on the objectives of the WTO.

According to the WTO, a subsidy is classified as;

1. Prohibited
2. Actionable
3. Non-actionable

[189]The title of this book.

2.5.1 Prohibited Subsidies

Prohibited subsidies are the kind of subsidies that directly induce export performance and also include subsidies contingent upon the use of domestic inputs. Article 3 of the ASCM therefore; prohibits two forms of subsidies, or any such measures adopted by any Member State to encourage such subsidies. These are subsidies for the promotion of exports and, subsidies on the use of domestic goods over imported goods.[190]

The inclusion of the MFN clause and the National Treatment Principle is to strengthen the market liberalisation policies among the Member States. State support in the form of prohibited categories of subsidies is contrary to trade liberalisation policies and causes distortion in the promotion of free trade. It creates unfair competition in the market, as the subsidy based products can be sold at a cheaper price. As a consequence of such policies, market efficiency, based on fair competition is affected. The continued practice of giving such support, affects the efficient use of resources, so the regulation through fair trade measures attains primary relevance.[191] Such policies, if adopted by the Developed countries, depress market opportunities and disallows the growth of a comparative cost advantage for the Developing and Less-Developed countries, thus hindering the main objectives of the WTO.

2.5.1.1 Export Promoting Subsidies

It is noteworthy that Article 3.1, expressly excludes from its scope any form of subsidies or support provided for the purpose of agriculture. Article 3 mainly covers the subsidies for the export of industrial goods. Any forms of subsidies for export performance are based on financial contribution[192] and benefit to any specific industry. Continuing the discussion on prohibited subsidies further, the provision Article 3.1(a), covers subsidies that are meant for export performance contingent both in law or in fact. Thus, the issue of contingency is based on two suppositions, *de jure* and *de facto* contingency. De jure contingency can be explained directly by the words of the legislative provisions, whereas de facto contingency needs to be ascertained by circumstances. For substantiating this view, paragraph 166 and

[190] Hoda and Ahuja (2005), p. 1012.

[191] The above mentioned are in reference to why fair trade regulatory measures are required to check subsidies.

[192] See *United States–Measure Treating Exports Restraints as Subsidies,* WT/DS194/R, para 8.71, para 8.75. The concept of subsidy is based on financial contribution; therefore financial contribution is essential element. Government entrustment or direction to any private body is very different from the situation in which the government intervenes in the market by means of export restraint and cannot be considered as financial contribution for subsidies.[The dispute concerns the treatment of export restraint under US countervailing duty law. Canada alleges that measures at issue include Section 771(5) of the Tariff act of 1930(19 U.S.C §1677(5), as amended by the Uruguay Round Agreements Act.].

167 are referred to from the case, **Canada-Measures Affecting the Export of Civilian Aircraft**[193] in which Brazil alleged some of the Canadian measures as subsidies. The measures alleged in this case, (TPC) as subsidies are based on such facts as the pre-condition requirement of Article 3.1(a) of the SCM Agreement.

> Para 167: "Article 3.1 (a) prohibits any subsidy that is contingent upon export performance, whether that subsidy is contingent 'in law or in fact.' The Uruguay Round negotiations have, through the prohibition against export subsidies, that are contingent in fact upon export performance, sought to prevent circumvention of the prohibition against subsidies contingent in law upon export performance. In our view the legal standard expressed by the word contingent is the same for *de jure* or *de facto* contingency."[194]

By laying emphasis on the term 'standard' as the determining basis for a fact, based on circumstances to be considered as subsidies, the A.B has tended to follow a rather objective approach in applying this provision. It has not based the application of the part of the provision, dealing with the contingency of fact, on any pre-determined criteria. Rather the A.B, clarifies, that facts can be linked with the granting of subsidies for export performance or contingent on such a manner, thus leading to the promotion of export. Further, to make things clear, the A.B agreed with the Panel body that facts depend upon the circumstance of the case and there cannot be a general rule. This probably means that the A.B kept in mind, the WTO objectives and also the fact that any party should not be able to take advantages of the gaps within the provisions. In the cases where export subsidies need to be established based on facts (*de facto*), the contingency, based on standards is established, when the facts demonstrate that the granting of a subsidy is either factually or in anticipation linked to export performance.[195]

2.5.1.1.1 Explaining Briefly the Illustrative List of Export Subsidies Under Annex I of the SCM Agreement

The Uruguay Round Agreement, on Subsidies and Countervailing measures indeed covered a detailed description of subsidies, based on financial contribution, and conferring benefit on any specific industry. Based on practical measures and to avoid confusion over different forms of state support, the basis of state support for legal and economic purposes was classified in different features. The inclusion of these basic elements was also done, in order to promote free trade objectives.[196]

---

[193]WT/DS70/AB/R, Canada appeals the Panel's findings that TPC (Technology Partnership Canada) assistance is contingent upon export performance. [WT/DS70/R… para 2.1,This dispute concerns some of the Canadian measures that Brazil alleges as subsidies and are inconsistent with the Canada's obligations under Article 3.1(a) and 3.2(b) of the SCM Agreement].

[194]WT/DS70/AB/R, para 167.

[195]Article 3.1(a) This standard is met when the facts demonstrate that the granting of a subsidy, without having been made legally contingent upon export performance, is in fact tied to actual or anticipated exportation or export earnings.

[196]World Trade Report (2006), Exploring the links between subsidies, trade and the WTO. p. xxxii. http://www.wto.org/english/res_e/publications_e/wtr06_e.htm.

Nevertheless, it often transpires to be a complex issue for determining, that to what extent subsidies should be provided. Subsidies can be given in many indirect forms to promote export, such as through the means of government financing, for transportation, by financing through a preferential exchange rate, tax concessions probably not available in the market, and through various other schemes.[197]

Export subsidies classified in Article 3.1(a)[198] are further elaborated as instance in Annex 1 of the ASCM, and listed as 'Illustrative list of export subsidies.' The provisions mentioned in Annex 1, covers a wide range of subjects that can be covered for analysing subsidies as the commercial policy of the Member States, influencing international trade. Additionally, for the purpose of applying legal procedures mentioned under SCM Agreement, this list is supportive of making interpretations and applying specific provisions on a case by case basis. The illustrative list may be used to determine whether the challenged measure is inconsistent with the obligations to follow trading rules and therefore falls under the criteria mentioned in Article 3. The first four clauses from (a) to (d), covers export subsidies mainly in a direct form, such as direct export subsidies to a firm, a currency-retention scheme, internal transport and reducing freight charges on exports, and other forms of legislative provisions, supporting export through agencies directly or indirectly.[199] This is in order to confirm a support measure to a private person as an export subsidy, under clause (c), (d), (j) and (k), and to prove that support is from the side of government. This was observed by the A.B in the case of **Canada-Measures Affecting the Importation of Milk and the Exportation of Dairy Products Second Recourse to Article 21.5 of the DSU by New Zealand and the United States.**[200]

---

[197]World Trade Report (2006), Exploring the links between subsidies, trade and the WTO. p. xxii. http://www.wto.org/english/res_e/publications_e/wtr06_e.htm.

[198]Article 3.1(a) of Subsidies and Countervailing Measures.

[199]Annex I

(a) The provisions by governments of direct subsidies to a firm or an industry contingent upon export performance;
(b) Currency-retention schemes or any similar practices which involve a bonus on exports;
(c) Internal transport and freight charges on export shipments, provided or mandated by governments, on terms more favourable than for domestic shipments;
(d) The provision by governments or their agencies either directly or in directly through government-mandated schemes, of imported or domestic products or services for use in the production of exported goods, on terms or conditions more favourable than for provisions of like or directly competitive products or services for use in the production of goods for domestic consumption, if (in the case of products) such terms or conditions are more favourable than those commercially available (for details, see SCM Agreement).

[200]WT/DS103/AB/RW2-WT/DS113/AB/RW2 (Footnote113) Article 9.1(c) of the Agreement on Agriculture may be contrasted with Article 9.1(e) of the Agreement on Agriculture, as well as with Article 1.1(a) (1) (iv) of the SCM Agreement, and items (c) (d) (j) and (k) of the Illustrative List of Export Subsidies (the Illustrative List) of the SCM Agreement. In these provisions, some kind of government mandate, direction, or control is an element of a subsidy provided through third party.

Furthermore, a special description is made about Clause (d) in the list, as it deals with discriminatory practices between government schemes. The double standards means for the products used in the production of goods on the one side for domestic consumption, and on the other hand, products used for the production of exported goods. This is broadly explained by the Panel Body in the case of **Canada Measure Affecting the Importation of Milk and the Exportation of Dairy Products.**[201] In Panel Body's view, paragraph (d) under the illustrative list requires the presence of three elements.

(a) the provision of 'imported or domestic products . . .for use in the production of exported goods,' on terms or conditions more favourable than for provision of likely or directly competitive products . . .for use in the production of goods for domestic consumption,
(b) such products for use in the production of exported goods, are included and supported by governments or their agencies either directly or indirectly through government-mandated schemes, and
(c) the more favourable terms or conditions for such products used in the production of exported goods are basically more supportive in comparison to than those commercially available on world markets

The next four clauses from (e) to (h) are related to the measures of fiscal policies of a Member State, mainly dealing with export promotion through direct and indirect taxes.[202] These clauses, try to illustrate the effect of fiscal policies on international trade. The case discussed below illustrates the tax exemption as

[201] WT/DS103/R, para 7128.

[202] (e) The full or partial exemption remission, or deferral specifically related to exports, of direct taxes (for details, see SCM Agreement) or social welfare charges paid or payable by industrial or commercial enterprises;

(f) The allowance of special deductions directly related to exports or export performance, over and above those granted in respect to production for domestic consumption, in the calculation of the basis on which direct taxes are charged;

(g) The exemption or remission, in respect of the production and distribution of the exported products, of indirect taxes in excess of those levied in respect of the production and distribution of like products when sold for domestic consumption;

(h) The exemption, remission or deferral of prior-stage cumulative indirect taxes on goods or services used in the production of exported products in excess of the exemption, remission or deferral of like prior-stage cumulative indirect taxes on goods or services used in the production of like products when sold for domestic consumption(for details, see SCM Agreement);

(i) The remission or drawback of import charges in excess of those levied on imported inputs that are consumed in the production of the exported (making normal allowance for waste) (for details, see SCM Agreement);

(j) The provision by governments (or special institutions controlled by governments) of export credit guarantee or insurance programmes, of insurance or guarantee programmes against increases in the cost of exported products or of exchange risk programmes, at premium rates which are inadequate to cover the long term operating costs and losses of the programmes;

(k)The grant by governments (or special institutions controlled by and or acting under the authority of governments) of export credit at rates below those which they actually have to pay for the funds so employed (or would have to pay if they borrowed on international capital markets in

subsidies. In the case of **US Foreign Sale Corporation Scheme,**[203] the European Communities requested the Panel to find that by maintaining, tax exemption, and by applying special administrative pricing rules, the US violates Article 3.1(a) of the SCM Agreement.[204]

The question is whether FSC is a corporation created, organised and maintained in a qualified foreign country, or a US possession outside the custom territory of the United States under the specific requirements. An FSC obtains tax exemption on a portion of its earnings, which means a portion of the foreign trade income or deemed to be foreign trade income is exempted from taxation in the US.[205] The EU contended before the panel that maintaining tax exemptions and special pricing rules violated Article 3.1(a) of the SCM Agreement.[206] In the original proceedings in this dispute the panel concluded that the FSC scheme, consisting of sections 921–927 of the United States Internal Revenue Code (IRC) and related measures establishing special tax treatment for foreign sale corporations was inconsistent with the obligations of the US under Article 3.1 (a) of the SCM Agreement and under Articles 3.3 and 8 of the Agreement on Agriculture.[207]

The act of tax exemption was inconsistent with Article 3.1(a) of the SCM Agreement as it involved subsidies contingent . . .upon export performance. The basic factors for the subsidy to be established, i.e., the financial contribution and benefit to a specific group of industries were quite apparent in this case. The support through policy measure was discriminatory, as the subsidy by means of a tax concession, was contingent upon export performance and was a circumvention of subsidy rules.[208]

Further to add here, within the scope of Annex I, Clauses (h) and (i) are based on the relative consideration of policy measures adopted by the legislative bodies.

---

order to obtain funds of the same maturity and other credit terms and denominated in the same currency as the export credit), (for details, see SCM Agreement).

(l) Any other charge on the public account constituting an export subsidy in the sense of Article XVI of GATT 1994.

[203] *United States–Tax Treatment for "Foreign Sale Corporation,"* WT/DS108/R.

[204] See WT/DS 108/R, para 3.1.

[205] See WT/DS 108/R, para 2.1.

[206] See WT/DS108/R, para 2.1.

[207] WT/DS 108/RW2, Annex A, page 3.

[208] 19 U.S.C§ 1303 (1976). The statute provides as follows: "Levy of countervailing duties (a) (1) Whenever any country, dependency, colony, province, or other political subdivision of government, person, partnership, association, cartel, or corporation, shall pay or bestow, directly or indirectly, any bounty or grant upon the manufacture or production or export of any article or merchandise manufactured or produced in such country, dependency, colony, province, or other political subdivision of government, person, partnership, association, cartel, or corporation, then upon the importation of such article or merchandise into the United States, whether the same shall be imported directly from the country of production or otherwise, and whether such article or merchandise is imported in the same condition as when exported from the country of production or has been changed in condition by remanufacture or otherwise imposed, a duty equal to the net amount of such bounty or grant, however the same be paid or bestowed."

Clause (h) deals with exemption, remission or deferral of the accumulation of indirect tax on the products for export, provided this type of relief is not granted in the general course for the products, when sold for domestic consumption and this indicates the discriminatory practices.

Another occasion of conditional support arises, if there is a possibility of remission or the drawing back of import charges on the imported inputs in excess of the normal rate, and these imported inputs are used for export promotion. Promotion of such government schemes, can be for the reason that a firm may use same type of home market inputs, or home market input supplemented by imported inputs of same characteristics for promoting exports. The reason for such schemes can be, along with export promotion, balancing the demand and supply with-in the domestic market, or to gain concessions while trading goods with other member nations under regional trade agreements. Such policies are applied to boost the exports of domestic inputs, either by using partly imported and partly domestic inputs. Giving financial support, in the form of reduction in import charges for the inputs used in a specific industry that, finally leads to exports, is discriminatory and contrary to the MFN and the objectives[209] adopted by the WTO. These issues are covered under clause (i) of Annex I and can be dealt with in detail, through Annex II and Annex III of the SCM Agreement. The following two clauses (j) and (k) are about export credits and other related programmes. Clause (j) covers, provisions formed by any government of the Member State that deals with some sort of security in the form of insurance or measures covering market risks. This provision is applicable, in the cases of policies with supporting financial feature in the form of insurance programmes, that in case the price of an exported product increases in the market of other Member State, thus affecting the demand or there is depreciation in the value of the currency in the Member State, that has imported the product, thus making it expensive. Such unexpected market turns creates financial burden, for the long term operating costs of the respective export industry. The point worth contesting here from the perspective of subsidies is, that premium rate charges are not enough to cover the long term cost of the programme, which means the government is a service provider at a discounted price, and therefore promotes to take risks for exports.[210]

[209]Part of the Preamble of the WTO "Resolved, therefore, to develop an integrated, more viable and durable multilateral trading system encompassing the General Agreement on Tariffs and Trade, the results of past liberalization efforts and all of the Uruguay Round of Multilateral Trade Negotiations." It covers the objective, that trading should be more competitive discouraging unfair practices such as export subsidies and dumping products below the cost to gain a market-share.

[210]Canada-Dairy (Article21.5-New Zealand and US), para 93, (WT/DS103/AB/RW, WT/DS113/AB/RW) 'Our approach is supported by the standards used in items (j) and (k) of the illustrative List of the SCM Agreement. Item (j) is concerned with export subsidies that arise through the provisions by the government of a variety of export credit guarantee and insurance programs. Under item (j), the provision of such services by the government involves export subsidies when the premium rates charged do not cover the long-term operating costs and losses of the programs. Thus, the measure of value under item (j) is the overall cost to the government, as the service provider, of providing the service. Likewise, in item (k), where the government provides export

Next in line is clause (k). Clause (k), covers government support measures in terms of credit, to promote exports at a rate below the international market rate. This is a form of giving material advantage.[211] Such supportive provisions affect fair competition in the market and indirectly create discriminatory effect in the context of free trade promotion. These supports include, financial support by a government, at a price lower than that which they would have to pay, if they borrowed from the International market. Another such possibility of undue support arise, if payment is sponsored by the government to an exporter or financial institution to obtain credits, and can be covered in this provision.[212]

From the procedural point of view, the interpreting terms, specific to the context is significant for determining any form of state support aims to subsidies for export. In the context of determining the promotion of export subsidies, one may face the possibility of semantic overlap between the terms "material advantage" as mentioned in clause (k) of Annex I and "benefit" as covered in Article 1.1(b) of the agreement. This matter of interpretation came before the Appellate Body in the case of **Brazil–Export Financing Programme for Aircraft**[213]

> The question before the Appellate Body was whether the term "material advantage" in clause (k) of the illustrative list in Annex I, was in effect the same as the term "benefit" in Article 1.1(b) of the SCM Agreement. The Appellate Body's reasoning differed from that of the Panel's. The A.B, tried to make distinction between the terms, and followed the approach that "benefit" is mainly associated with "financial contribution" as mentioned in Article 1.1(a) 1 to define subsidy as a substantive issue, whereas material advantage, as included in clause (k), is directly linked with the subsidies already having the

---

credits, the measure of the value of the service provided by the government is the amount "which [governments] actually have to pay for the funds so employed(or would have to pay if they borrowed on international capital markets..)". Again, the measure of value is by reference to the cost to the government, as the service provider, of providing the service. Therefore, items (j) and (k) give contextual support and rationale, for using the cost of production as a standard for determining whether there are "payment" under Article 9.1(c) of the Agreement on Agriculture in these proceedings.'

211 The Brazil-Export Financing Programme for Aircraft, the DSB recommended that Brazil should bring its export subsidies for regional aircraft under the *Programma de Financiamento às Exportações* ("PROEX") interest-rate equalization scheme, into conformity with its obligations under Article 3.1(a) and 3.2 of the Agreement on Subsidies and Countervailing Measures. See para 77,78 of the AB, WT/DS46/AB/RW.

212 Brazil-Aircraft, WT/DS46/AB/R, para 181. The issue here is whether the export subsidies for regional aircraft under PROEX "are used to secure" for Brazil a "a material advantage in the field of export credit terms" "...the OECD Arrangement can be appropriately viewed as one example of an international undertaking providing a specific market benchmark by which to assess whether payments by governments, coming within the provisions of item (k), are used to secure a material advantage in the field of export credit terms..." in our view, the appropriate comparison to be made in determining whether a payment is "used to secure a material advantage", within the meaning of item (k), is between the actual interest rate applicable in a particular export sales transaction after deduction of the government payment (the net interest rate) and the relevant CIRR [Commercial Interest Reference Rate].

213 WT/DS46/AB/R.

characteristics of prohibited export subsidies. Hence the two terms are distinct and are for different legal purpose.[214]

The list in Annex I, finally concludes with clause (L) covering any other form of state support to promote export, that is by means of a charge on a public account.

2.5.1.2 Subsidies Contingent upon the Use of Domestic over Imported Goods

This clause emphasises the need for regulatory fair trade values to check discriminatory practices. In relation to Article 3.1(a) it seems that article 3.1(b) is a complementary provision, which attempts to reach the scope of the WTO objectives. Article 3.1 (b) deals with the contingency, in which a subsidy is provided for the use of domestic goods in preference to the imported-goods, a market discriminatory practice also violating the MFN principle. This clause proposes a general prohibition without letting any explicit distinction between questions related to law or any such condition related to facts. Any member affected by such factors can bring claims under this provision and will be remedied. In the case of **Canada-Certain Measures Affecting the Automotive Industry,**[215] the main issue was the Canadian measure, providing duty free treatment for the imports of automobiles, buses, and specified commercial vehicles under Customs Tariff, Motor Vehicles Tariff Order, 1998 and the Special Remission Orders.[216] Claims were made by European Communities and Japan that the measures followed by Canada were inconsistent with the prohibition of subsidies contingent upon the use of domestic over imported goods, under Article 3.1(b) and in consistent with Article III:4[217] of the GATT Agreement.

The A.B stated that the Panel's analysis in this case was incomplete as it failed to take into account the object and purpose of the SCM Agreement.[218] The A.B by drawing these implications further stated that as there is nothing in the Article 3.1 (b) covering *subsidies contingent in fact,* as regards the use of domestic over

[214]See WT/DS46/AB/R, para 179, 180.

[215]WT/DS139/AB/R, WT/DS142/AB/R (request for consultation July 1998, Panel report on February 2000 and Appellate body report on May 2000). See para 1 of the Appellate Body. The EU and Japan were the appellants in this case. On the same line see *Certain Measures Adopted by China on Imports of Automobiles,* WT/DS339/R, para 7.633, para 7.634, para 7.635 for reference see, para 39, 45, 46 and 47 of the Appellate Body report.

[216]To qualify for the exemption, an eligible manufacturer's local production of motor vehicles had to achieve a minimum amount of Canadian value added (CVA), and its local production had to maintain a minimum ratio (production to sales ratio) with respect to its sales of motor vehicles in Canada.

[217]The products of the territory of any contracting party imported into the territory of any contracting party shall be accorded treatment no less favourable than that accorded to like products of national origin in respect of all laws, regulations and requirements affecting their internal sale.

[218]WT/DS139/AB/R, para 137 and para 138.

imported goods, this can be interpreted also to mean that there is nothing to imply that subsidies contingent in fact can be excluded from consideration.[219] It seems that the A.B by following such an interpretation, in *the lack of normative support to fair trade regulation rules and procedures* in several Member States has endeavoured to follow a broader prohibitive approach to the discriminatory practices. This approach is an attempt to promote the scope of free trade market policies by applying fair trade regulatory measures and to inculcate such values. Any such subsidy that promotes the use of a like domestic product is contrary to the MFN clause. Regulating any such measure requires a prohibitive provision against discriminatory trade practices, supported by fair trade market norms. In the lack of such norms, the A.B has attempted to suggest the limits of state support explicitly. However, to what extent the adjudicating bodies draw such limits or can create alternative explanations, not strictly in line with the previous interpretations, is a matter to be questioned as to whether the reasoning is reconcilable with the text and spirit of the relevant WTO rules?[220]

Basically, Article 3 of the SCM Agreement is a proposed outline covering prohibited subsidies. Prohibited subsidies are void-ab initio and are restricted at the initial stages. Thus, within the provisions of Article 3, there is less room for flexibility as regards classifying subsidies as justifiable and non-justifiable. The subject of subsidy is a matter of state support, so an important question arises for study, that what types of subsidies are justifiable and which are non-justifiable. The possibility to make such categorisations is in the case of actionable subsidies as classified under SCM Agreement. Article 5 and Article 6 covers state support, that is actionable and it demands further elaboration in the context of (1) development (2) basic infrastructure (3) fair policy measures.

2.6 Actionable Subsidies

Attaining the WTO objectives, demands a level of market system that establishes some kind of interlink between the objectives of WTO and the progress of free trade through MFN principle. Set of objectives, such as "*economic endeavour should be conducted with a view to raising the standard of living, ensuring maximum employment and expanding the production of trade in goods, additional efforts need to be made to ensure that Developing countries and Less-Developed countries among them get the share of growth in international trade for their economic development.*"[221] Adoption of solely prohibitive measures for using subsidies may be a hindrance to achieve these objectives and can transpires to be paradoxical. *The fair trade approach demand the need to maintain a balance between market efficiency*

[219] Para 139.

[220] Cosbey and Mavroidis (2014), p. 12.

[221] For detail reference see, the preamble of the WTO.

principles based on free competition and the objectives of the WTO. One cannot undermine the fact that the above mentioned objectives of the WTO does have the support of fair trade values. With all these set of criteria, and demand for the development of the market system based on comparative cost advantage requires flexibility. Thus, the state support classified within the context of actionable subsidies[222] can be divided into justifiable and non-justifiable subsidies.

Actionable subsidies can be defined as any form of subsidies other than those mentioned in Article 3 of the SCM Agreement. Article 5 and Article 6 of the SCM Agreement covers substantive obligations for the Member States to follow while adopting such policies. These subsidies are justifiable to the extent that they are not profit-making. Question arises, when do they take the form of non-justifiable state support and therefore are liable as actionable subsidies. Actionable subsidies can be objected to if they cause injury to the domestic industry[223] of another Member State country.[224] There is a negation clause added as a legal shield for the Member State alleged to practice such subsidies. When such an issue is alleged, then the State charged with such practices can prove that there is no effect on the market of the other Member State, because of its subsidy policies.[225] The inclusion of *de minimis* clause is also noteworthy, as it probably creates a purposeful flexibility for the use of state support.[226]

For the types of subsidies to be legally unacceptable, the determination of injury to the domestic industry must be based on positive evidence and involves an objective examination of:

1. the volume of the subsidised imports and the effects of the subsidised imports on prices of like products in the domestic market of the importing country
2. the consequent impact of these imports on the domestic producers of such a products.[227]

Subsidies under Article 5 are not void-*ab initio,* rather creates a possibility for the economic up-liftment of the Developing and mainly the Less–Developed

[222] Article 5 of the SCM Agreement

[223] The term domestic industry here should be seen in the light of Article 16 of the SCM Agreement.

(a) Domestic producers as a whole are producers of like products
(b) The collective output of the products constitutes a major proportion of the total output of the domestic production.

[224] Trebilock and Howse (2002), p. 196.

[225] Article 6.2 Notwithstanding the provisions of paragraph-1, serious prejudice shall not be found if the subsidising Member demonstrates that the subsidy in question has not resulted in any of the effects as enumerated in para 3.

[226] Article 11.9 There shall be immediate termination in cases where the amount of a subsidy is *de minimis*, or where the volume of subsidized imports, actual or potential, or the injury is negligible. For the purpose of this paragraph the amount of subsidy shall be considered to be *de minimis* if the subsidy is less than 1% ad valorem.

[227] Bossche (2008), p. 580.

countries. That is, if they are considered as a primarily level support to develop the market structure through comparative cost, Article 5, although restrictive on adverse effect, nevertheless creates the possibility for harmonious construction of development policies, in the wake of opportunities generated through free trade. Many of the Developing and Less developed countries lack the normative support for market liberalisation, and indeed requires flexibility at the normative level, which means shifting from the rigid sovereign principles. Perhaps, keeping in mind the development needs of the Member States, the drafters kept the provisions within Article 5 and Article 6 open ended. While assessing, any dispute on the issue of subsidies that comes before the court, these open-ended provision creates a possibility for the court to see each case independently and enhances the possibility for a balance between free trade market approach and fair trade regulatory measures.

Taking into account the objectives of the WTO as mentioned in its preamble, and the approach adopted by the Panel in the case of **Canada-Measures Affecting the Export of Civilian Aircraft,**[228] one can infer that the purpose of including separate provision for an actionable subsidy is to create a legal boundary between justifiable use and non-justifiable use of the subsidy. The justifiable use is for such purposes as social welfare or the development of infrastructure, etc. The non-justifiable use, is for such purposes as export promotion, encouraging the purchase of domestic goods in place of exported goods of the same type. There can be a harmonious[229] use of subsidies; nevertheless, the justifiable use of subsidies loses its validity once adverse effects are caused due to its continuance. Adverse effects are, such as (a) injury to the domestic industry of another Member (b) nullification and impairment of benefits and concessions, these bound under Article II GATT 1994.[230] The case taken as reference here is to see the contextual relevance of Article 5.

[228]WT/DS70/R, para, 9.119. We note that the SCM Agreement does not contain any express statement of its object and purpose. We therefore consider it unwise to attach due importance to arguments concerning the object and purpose of the SCM Agreement. In our view, however, the avoidance of net cost to government is not the object and purpose of the multilateral disciplines contained in the SCM Agreement. Rather, as suggested by Canada itself at para.96 of its first submission, we consider that the object and purpose of the SCM Agreement could more appropriately be summarized as the establishment of multilateral disciplines on the premise that some forms of government intervention distort international trade [or] have the potential to distort [international trade].

[229]Harmonious with the objectives of the WTO.

[230]Article II Schedule of concession

1) That the contracting party shall accord no less favourable treatment to the commerce of any other contracting parties 2) Products described in Part I of the Schedule relating to any contracting party shall on their importation be exempt from custom duties 3) Products described in Part II of the Schedule relating to any contracting party shall on their importation be exempt from all other duties or charges of any kind imposed on or in connection with importation. . ..

The Panel has interpreted Article 5 for application in the case of the **United States-Continued Dumping and Subsidy Offset Act of 2000.**[231]

> The Panel stated,[232] in order to examine Mexico's claim that the CDSOA is inconsistent with Article 5(b) of the SCM Agreement, we must determine whether or not the CDSOA is an actionable subsidy. A measure constitutes an actionable subsidy if it is a "subsidy", if it is "specific", and if its use causes "adverse effects."

The Panel body in this case tried to resolve Mexico's claim[233] by establishing the level of support that can be considered as subsidies according to the provisions of Article 5(b). It concluded, that a link should exist between the policy and the adverse effects caused. A further link can be established if any specific criteria or a pattern between policies and the outcome is found. Depending on a case to case situation, several other factors can be taken into account, such as:

1. the use of a subsidy programme by a limited number of enterprises,
2. creating discretion for certain enterprises and the manner in which the discretion is exercised,
3. the granting of disproportionately large amount of subsidy to certain enterprises. It is clear from the approach of the Panel that there ought to be some substantive evidence to establish the effect, and for the trade practice to be labelled an actionable subsidy rather than considering it by mere presumption.

2.6.1 Serious-Prejudice Article 6

Serious prejudice in the context of the SCM Agreement, can be described as the effect of policies and practices that impairs equal market opportunities of other Member States, for the purpose of export. Serious prejudice is in itself not a type of market affect; but like a presumption of cause to the consequence. The provisions

[231]On 21st December 2000, Australia, Brazil, Chile, the European Communities, India, Indonesia, Japan, Korea and Thailand made joint request for consultations with the United States of America. The complainants requested consultations with the US concerning the amendment of the **Tariff Act of 1930**, the act usually referred to as 'Byrd Amendment.' According to the complainant, the Act is inconsistent with the obligations of the United States, under certain provisions of the Act, the Anti-dumping agreement SCM Agreement and the WTO Agreement.

Mexico asserted that the use of the CDSOA had caused "adverse effects" within the meaning of Article 5(b) of the SCM Agreement, i.e., nullification or impairment of benefits accruing directly or indirectly to the other Members under GATT 1994 in particular, the benefits and concession bound under Article II of GATT 1994.

[232]See WT/DS217/R and WT/DS234/R, para 7.106, 7.107.

[233]See para 3.6 of the Panel Report. Furthermore, Mexico considers that the payments made under the Offset Act constitute specific subsidies within the meaning of Article1 of the SCM Agreement, which causes "adverse effects" to its interests, in the sense of Article 5 of the SCM Agreement, in the form of nullification and impairment of benefits accruing directly or in-directly to Mexico.

mentioned in Article 6 are appended to Article 5(c).[234] With the objective of determining whether the subsidy being given is actionable and to understand the cause and effect relationship in a comprehensive manner, Article 6 covers the explanatory provisions. Article 6.1,[235] Article 6.2 and Article 6.3 try to elaborate different aspects of "serious prejudice" in the context of Article 5(c). Clause 1 of Article 6 covers situations where it is likely that serious prejudice can exist and covers the aspects of such measures in relation to it.[236] As an illustration, Article 6.1 lays down the criteria for determining the sufficient grounds.

1. Serious prejudice must be deemed to exist if a proportion of the subsidisation is for more than 5% of the value of the product
2. It is to cover the operating losses.

Whereas, under Clause 3 of Article 6,[237] situations are covered where there is a possibility that serious prejudice because of subsidies may arise and within its provisions attempts are made to cover the likely effects due to it. Article 6.3 covers situations or practices, in which the possibility of serious prejudice arises if:

1. Member State, exporting a product by taking a subsidy, displaces or impedes (for the purpose of displacement or impeding of exports)[238] imports of the like product of another Member. The displacement can be either because of the product exported from the market of a subsidising Member or from any third-country market [Article 6.3(a) and (b)]

---

[234] Article 5 No Member should cause, through the use of any subsidy referred to in paragraphs 1 and 2 of Article 1, adverse effects to the interests of other Members, i.e. Clause (c) Serious prejudice to the interest of another member.

[235] Article 6.1 is obsolete nowadays. Article 31of the SCM Agreement states that the provisions of paragraph1 of Article 6 and the provisions of Article 8 and Article 9 shall apply for a period of 5 years.

[236] Article 6.1 lays down the criteria for determining sufficient grounds. (1) Serious prejudice shall be deemed to exist if proportion of subsidization is for more than 5%. (2) Subsidies are provided to cover the operating losses (3) Subsidies other than one time measures which are non-recurrent and cannot be repeated for that enterprise and are given for the development of long term solutions and other social problems.

[237] Article 6.3, the possibility of serious prejudice arises if (1) Export of a Member State, produced by taking a subsidy, displace or impede imports of the like products of another member. (2) the consequence of such subsidy is lowering of the price of like product (3) the effect of the subsidy is an increase in the share of the subsidised product in the market for detail see Article 6.3.

[238] Article 6.4 For the purpose of para 3(b) the displacement or impeding of exports shall include any case in which, subject to the provisions of paragraph 7, it has been demonstrated that there has been a change in relative shares of the market to the disadvantage of a non-subsidized like product. Change in relative shares of the market include (a) there has been an increase in the market-share of the subsidized product; (b) the market-share of the subsidized product remains constant in circumstances in which, in the absence of a subsidy, it would have declined; (c) the market share of the subsidized product declines, but at a slower rate than would have been the case in the absence of a subsidy. Exceptions to displacement or impediment are mentioned in Article 6.7 of the SCM Agreement.

2. The consequence of such form of subsidy is, lowering of the price, a significant price under cutting[239] of like products or, like products made in any third country or there is an increase in the market-share of the subsidised product [Article 6.3 (c) and (d)].

These affects as described, seems to be based on free trade system's interaction with market efficiency principles, the general market competition norms, the comparison with fair price standards, and the possibility of equitable market opportunities for others. An explanation from the economic point of view is, that such market effects occurs, if there is unregulated free trade. This naturally means that there is a need for fair trade regulatory mechanisms to create a balance between conflicting interests. The term *serious* along with *prejudice* is to cover those aspects and features that have high potential for causing market distortion based on certain presumptions.

The above mentioned conditions are the procedural requirements for the complaining member to show that a subsidy has caused negative effects in the markets of any importing country. Nevertheless, if a subsidising member can prove that subsidies do not produce any of these effects or a complaining member fails to finally prove any of the above-mentioned effects, the legal stance of serious prejudice will lose its validity as this is also emphasised by the court in the case referred to.

In the case of the, **United States-Subsidies on Upland Cotton,**[240] the question before the Panel and later before the Appellate Body was "whether the effect of subsidy in this case creates significant price suppression." A primary question of market efficiency, an effect based measure to determine serious prejudice is as.

> The Appellate Body stated[241]: "Turning to the question of relevant 'market,' we observe that Article 6.3(c) of the SCM Agreement addresses the situation where 'the effect of subsidy is significant price suppression[242] and to demonstrate that the subsidy has that effect within the meaning of article 6.3(c)."

---

[239]For the purpose of para 3(c) price undercutting shall include any case in which such price undercutting has been demonstrated through a comparison of prices of the subsidized product with prices of a non-subsidized like-product supplied to the same market.

[240]WT/DS267/AB/R. Brazil claimed that United States domestic support measures granted support to a specific commodity in excess of that decided during the 1992 marketing-year and therefore did not satisfy the conditions in paragraph (b) of Article13 of the Agreement on Agriculture and therefore were not exempt from actions based on paragraph I of the Article XVI of the GATT 1994 or Article 5 and 6 of the SCM Agreement.

[241]Para 400.

[242]Appellate Body, para 423, para 424. Although the Panel first identified "price suppression" and "price depression" as two separate concepts in paragraph 7.1277, footnote 1388 of the Panel Report, suggests that, for its analysis, the Panel used the term "price suppression" to refer to both price suppression and price depression. We recognize that "the situation where 'prices'. . .are prevented or inhibited from rising" and the situation where prices are pressed down, or reduced may overlap. Nevertheless, it would have been preferable, in our view, for the Panel to avoid using the term 'price suppression' as short-hand for both price suppression and price depression, given that Article 6.38(c) of the SCM Agreement refers to price suppression and depression as distinct

From this case, it can be inferred that whenever a matter is brought before the DSB to determine if the state support falls in the category of actionable subsidy, primarily, the DSB, will take into account that serious prejudice has led to the consequences. This can be in the form of its affects on the market, such as price suppression or depression. The Appellate Body in this case has defined the term price suppression and price depression as two different market effects, thus disagreeing with the Panel's interpretation.

The legal purpose for including these term in the SCM Agreement is to create an implied limit to justifiable subsidies. Additionally, the provisions help to test the effect of a support or aid given in any form by the government or body, whether it can be categorised as an actionable subsidy or not. "Serious prejudice" within the subsidies Agreement is a term that cannot be put into strict brackets: rather its exact affect is determined by circumstances. The term can also be applied in detecting the effects as a result of retrospective practices, and also for making a distinction based on the WTO objectives between support in the form of justifiable subsidies and non-justifiable subsidies.

After this description, the question arises whether a form of subsidy which cannot be considered under the category of prohibited or actionable, can be termed as non-actionable forms of subsidies.

2.7 Non-actionable Subsidies[243]

Referring to the debate mentioned in the introduction chapter,[244] concerning the fact that market concepts of productivity, efficiency, and wealth are interlinked with technological advancement. Improvement in productivity by technological advancement leads to efficient use of resources, better production methods, and the creation of more and new opportunities. Until recently, it was possible to obtain

concepts. We agree, however, that the Panel's description of price suppression in paragraphs 7.1277 of the Panel report reflects the ordinary meaning of that term, particularly when read in conjunction with the French and Spanish versions of Article 6.3(c), as required by Article 33(3) of the Vienna Convention on the Law of Treaties.

[243]Non-actionable subsidies are subject to the provisions of Article 31 of the SCM Agreement. (Article 31:—The provisions of paragraph 1 of Article 6 and of the provisions of Article 8 and 9 shall apply for a period of 5 years, beginning with the date of entry into force of the WTO Agreement.

[244]Beinhocker (2007), p. 294.

exemption for these kinds of subsidies from the WTO rules on prohibited and actionable subsidies, however, in the present times the exemptions are no longer valid.

Non-actionable subsidies are obsolete under the WTO[245] Agreement, but for the purpose of distinction between the types and to seek background information concerning various forms of subsidies, and its use as justifiable and non-justifiable, a description of non-actionable subsidies has relevance. Under the categorisation, when the present form of the SCM Agreement was accepted, subsidies are treated as non–actionable if they are neither prohibited nor subjected to any countervailing measures discussed under Article 10 to 23.[246] Any form of state support for the purpose of research and development, for higher education or for research-based connections with firms is usually accepted and hence justifiable.[247] Other general forms of state support that are usually exempted from the regulatory provisions of the WTO are:

1. Assistance to a disadvantaged region within the territory of the Member Country for the purpose of regional development.[248]
2. Assistance in adopting new environmental requirements for sustainable development, imposed by law or regulations with limitations.[249]

Usually, non-actionable subsidies are also termed green light subsidies and are covered under Article 8 of the SCM Agreement. Without outlining the basic features through legal provisions, these subsidies are specified briefly in the study.

Article 8 covers some specific kinds of subsidies such as, [Article 8.2(a)] assistance for research activities conducted by firms or by higher education or research establishments on a contract basis. First,[250] is assistance to the disadvantaged regions in the name of development. Second,[251] is assistance to promote the adaptation of existing facilities to new environmental requirements, which are also non-actionable when limited to 20% of the adaptation

[245]These expired on 31 December 1999.

[246]1) Actionable subsidies as mentioned in Part III of the SCM Agreement. 2) The assistance covers not more than 50-percent of the cost of pre-competitive research.

[247]This assistance covers no more than 75% of the cost of industrial research.

[248]Each disadvantaged region must be clearly designated.

[249](1) is a one-time non-recurring measure, (2) is limited to 20% of the cost of adoption, (3) does not cover the cost of replacing and other assistance, (4) is directly linked to firm's planned reduction of nuisances.

[250]Article 8.2(b).

[251]Article 8.2(c).

cost, but exclude the cost of replacement and are specifically limited to a planned reduction in a firm's pollution and do not cover any manufacturing cost-savings.

2.8 Subsidies for Development

The concept of subsidies for development is mainly associated with Developing countries and much more with Less Developed countries. The two main supportive provisions that forward the agenda of development for Developing and Less-Developed countries are: (1) concessions by the industrialised economies through the GSP, (2) Special and Differential treatment under Article 27 of the SCM agreement.

2.8.1 Commitments of the Industrialized Economies Under the GSP[252]

The concept of a Generalized System of Preference (GSP) was introduced by UNCTAD at its first conference held in 1964. Developing countries proposed that flexibilities for their exports in Developed countries' markets would be beneficial because:

1. A Developing country would increase their exports.
2. They would diversify their production sector into industries that produce and export higher value-added goods, which would help their economy to transform itself, from the rural based economy to industrial and the urban.
3. The GSP would reduce their dependence on foreign aid.[253]

In 1970, the GATT contracting parties adopted the GSP, through a mechanism by which the Developed countries gave tariff preferences to the imported products of the Developing countries. The concession through the GSP, made possible the implementation of a system of generalised, non-reciprocal, non-discriminatory preferences as agreed to at the UNCTAD conferences. Other provisions that

[252]The Generalised System of Preferences and Special and Differential Treatment for Developing countries in the GATT and WTO by Robert Read, www.lancs.ac.uk p. no 11.

[253]Macrory et al. (2005), p. 1538.

support the development agenda are Article XXXVI,[254] XXXVII[255] and XXXVIII[256] of the GATT agreement.[257]

This special provision (GSP) remains an integral part of the WTO obligations of the industrialised countries through part IV of the GATT agreement 1994. Its scope,

---

[254]The contracting parties, a) recalling that the basic objectives of this Agreement include that raising of standards of living and the progressive development of the economies of all contracting parties.

b) Considering that export earnings of the Less-Developed contracting parties can play a vital part in their economic development and that the extent of this contribution depends on the prices paid by the less-developed contracting parties for essential imports, the volume of their exports, and the prices received for these exports.

c) Noting, that there is a wide gap between standards of living in less-developed countries and in other countries.

[255]1. The Developed contracting party shall to the fullest extent possible-that is, except when compelling reasons, which may include legal reasons, make it impossible to give effect to the following provisions.

a) Accord high priority to the reduction and elimination of barriers to products currently or potentially goods of particular export interest to Less-Developed contracting parties, including custom duties and other restrictions.

b) Refrain from introducing, or increasing the incidence of, custom duties or non-tariff import barriers on products currently or potentially of particular export interest to Less—Developed contracting parties.

c) Refrain from imposing new fiscal measures.

3. The Developed contracting parties shall :

a) make every effort, in cases where a government directly or indirectly determines the resale price of products wholly or mainly produced in the territories of Less-Developed contracting parties to maintain trade margins at an equitable level.

b) give active consideration to the adoption of other measures designed to provide greater scope for the development of imports from Less-Developed contracting parties.

c) give special regard to the trade interest of Less-Developed contracting parties when considering the application of the other measures permitted under the agreement.

[256]Contracting party shall collaborate jointly, with the framework of this agreement and elsewhere, as appropriate, to set forth in Article XXXVIII.

2) In particular, the contracting parties shall a) where appropriate take action including action through international arrangements, to provide improved and acceptable conditions of access to world markets for primary products of particular interest to Less-Developed contracting parties and to devise measures designed to stabilize and improve conditions of world markets.

e) Collaborate in seeking feasible methods to expand trade for the purpose of economic development, through international harmonization and adjustment of national policies and regulations through technical and commercial standards affecting production, transportation and marketing and through export promotion by the establishment of facilities for the increased flow of trade information and development of market research.

[257]The contracting parties, a) recalling that the basic objective of this agreement including the raising of standards of living and progressive development of the economies of all contracting parties and considering that the attainment of this objective is urgent for Less-Developed contracting parties.

b) Considering that export earnings of the Less-Developed contracting parties can play a vital part in their economic development.

c) Noting that there is a wide gap between the standards of living in Less-Developed countries and in other countries.

however, is now reduced, as separate provisions are incorporated for S&D treatment. GATT Article XXXVII sets out the commitments and undertakings in support of the GSP on the part of the industrialised economies, which is to be given to the extent possible.

After the formation of the WTO, GSP have been reduced to concessionary measures of the Developed countries. However, along with GSP, other GATT Articles that support the WTO's agenda for development are also taken into consideration whenever so required.

In the light of the objectives of the WTO,[258] flexibilities for the Developing countries, within the SCM are expressed specifically in Article 27. Article 27 of the SCM Agreement deals with Special and Differential Treatment for the Developing countries and these special provisions are exclusive of the GSP. These provisions are *substantive efforts to create coherence between free trade and the WTO objectives, attainable through fair trade measures*.[259]

2.8.2 *Special and Differential Treatment, Article 27 of the SCM Agreement*

Article 27, of the SCM Agreement includes provisions giving concessions to the Developing-countries. Article 27 is divided into 15 clauses, but the focus here will be on the first five clauses as they cover the provisions drawing the general outlines of the concessions for the Developing nations. In the same context, and in addition to Article 27, Article 29 clause 1, 2 and 4, supplement the above mentioned clauses

---

e) Recognizing that international trade as a means of achieving economic and social advancement should be governed by such rules and procedures and measures in conformity with such rules and procedures.

[258]The objectives as taken from the preamble "that relation of the parties in the field of trade and economic endeavor should be conducted with a view to raising standard of living, ensuring full employment and large and steadily growing of income." Additionally, the preamble also recognizes the efforts designed to ensure that Developing countries and mainly the Less-Developed countries seek a share of growth in international trade, as one of the key objectives of the WTO's free trade policy.

[259]**From the preamble** i) Recognizing that their relations in the field of trade and economic endeavor should be conducted with a view to raising standards of living.

ii) Enhance the means for doing so in a manner consistent with their respective needs and concerns at different level of economic development.

ii) Recognizing further that there is a need for positive efforts designed to ensure that developing countries, and especially the least developed among them, secure a share in the growth of international trade commensurate with the needs of their development.

in attaining common goals by giving concessions to the nations that are at the stage of economic transformation.[260]

The distinction between Developing and Less-Developed countries, however, remains ambiguous despite the per capita threshold of $1000 fixed as a criterion to determine the status.[261]

The line of argument in support of subsidies is based on claims, that subsidies can also play an important role in the economic development of the Developing and Less-developed countries. In support of flexibilities for such state support, general rules have been formed through Special and Differential treatment measures created under Article 27. Article 27(2) makes a transition from the general discipline, mainly with regard to the prohibited subsidies, by explicitly mentioning that restrictions under Article 3.1(a) "Subsidies contingent, in law or in fact, whether solely or as one of several other conditions, upon export performance, including those illustrated in Annex I, shall not apply as such to the Developing countries." Exemption for the listed group of Developing countries remains for a certain time

---

[260]Article 27.1 Members recognize that subsidies may play an important role in economic development programmes of Developing country members.

Article 27.2 The prohibition of paragraph 1(a) of Article 3 shall not apply to

(a) Developing country Members referred to in Annex VII
(b) Other Developing country Members for a period of 8 years from the date of entry into force of the WTO Agreement, subject to compliance with the provisions in paragraph 4.

Article27.3 The prohibition of paragraph 1(b) of Article 3 shall not apply to Developing country Members for a period of 5 years, and shall not apply to at Less-Developed country Members for a period of 8 years (for detail reference, see the article).

Article 27.4 Any Developing country Member referred to in paragraph 2(b) shall phase out its export subsidies within the 8-year period, preferably in a progressive manner. However, a Developing country Member shall not increase the level of its export subsidies, and shall eliminate them within a period shorter than provided for in this paragraph when the use of such export subsidies is inconsistent with the development needs (for detail reference, see the article).

Article 27.5 A Developing country Member which has reached export competitiveness in any given product shall phase out its export subsidies for such product(s) over a period of 2 years. However, for a Developing country Member which is referred to in Annex VII and which has reached export competitiveness in one or more products, export subsidies on such products shall be gradually phased out over a period of 8 years.

Article 29.1 Members in the process of transformation from a centrally–planned economy into a market, free-enterprise economy may apply programmes and measures necessary for such a transformation.

Article 29.2 For such Members, a subsidy programmes falling within the scope of Article 3, and notified according to paragraph 3, shall be phased out or brought into conformity with Article 3 within a period of 7 years from the date of entry into force of the WTO Agreements. In such a case, Article 4 shall not apply and the scope of paragraph 1(d) of Article 6 shall not be actionable under Article 7.

Under Article 29.4 In exceptional circumstances Members referred to in paragraph 1 may be allowed departures from their notified programmes and measures and their time frame by the committee if such departures are deemed necessary for the process of transformation.

[261]The Generalised System of Preferences and Special and Differential Treatment for Developing countries in the GATT and WTO by Robert Read, www.lancs.ac.uk p. no 14.

period. In the case of these Developing countries, referred to in Annex VII, the prohibition of paragraph 1(a) of Article 3 does not apply. The exemption from the prohibited subsidies mentioned for the Less-Developed countries is not restricted by any time period either. This form of special consideration is not absolute, rather is specified for the purpose of development, as mentioned in Article 27.4.[262] Furthermore, a leeway is also available in the case of actionable subsidies, if the claims are against the Developing countries and can be covered under Article 27.7.[263] Additionally, in order to keep the legal position of the Developing countries at par with the Developed countries, and to cover the economic difference, the presumption of serious prejudice mentioned in Para 1 of Article 6 by virtue of Article 27.8 has been confined. The presumption is rather qualified and any such attempt to establish serious prejudice should be supported by concrete evidence. Weighing these concessionary measures from the perspective of free trade on the one side and fair trade as regulatory measures on the other, a new issue arises. The issue concerns how far these concessionary measures are justifiable or how to draw line between justifiable and non-justifiable subsidies.

The case is referred to below as an example where the panel and the A.B faces a dilemma while dealing with Special and Differential Treatment provisions. Accepting that Special and Differential Treatment provisions support economic development programmes in the Developing countries and Less-Developed countries, the court also emphasized that some conditions also need to be followed along with these special considerations.

In the case of **Brazil–Export Financing Programme for Aircraft,**[264] claims were made by Canada under Art 3 of the SCM Agreement, that export subsidies were granted by Brazil through a programme termed Programa de Financiamento ás Exportações (PROEX) on sales of aircraft to foreign buyers.[265]

---

[262]Article 27.4 Any Developing country member referred to in paragraph 2(b) shall phase out its export subsidies within the 8 year period, preferably in a progressive manner. However, a Developing Country Member shall not increase the level of its export subsidies, and shall eliminate them within a period shorter than that provided for in this paragraph when the use of such export subsidies is inconsistent with the development needs. If a Developing country Member deems it necessary to apply such subsidies beyond the 8 year period, it shall not later than 1 year before the expiry of this period enter into consultation with the Committee, which will determine whether the extension of this period is justified after examining all the relevant economic, financial and development needs of the Developing Country Member in question. If the Committee determines that the extension is justified, the Developing Country member concerned shall hold annual consultations with the Committee to determine the necessity of maintaining subsidies. If no such determination is made by the Committee, the Developing Country Member shall phase out the remaining export subsidies within 2 years from the end of the last authorized period.

[263]Article 27.7 The provision of Article 4 shall not apply to a Developing country Member in the case of export subsidies which are in conformity with the provisions of paragraphs 2 through 5.The relevant provisions in this case shall be those of Article 7.

[264]WT/DS46/AB/R.

[265]Para 6 Appellate Body Report, WT/DS46/AB/R. "PROEX interest rate equalization subsidies begin after the aircraft is exported and paid for by the purchaser. The payments are made in the form of bonds issued by PROEX to the financing institution. After each export transaction is

The Appellate Body decided that[266]

"Members recognize that subsidies may play an important role for the economic development programmes in the Developing country Members." Both from its title and terms, it is clear that Article 27 is intended to provide special and differential treatment for Developing country Members, under certain specified conditions. In our view too, Para 4 of Article 27[267] provides certain obligations that Developing country members must fulfil if they are to benefit from this special and differential treatment during the transition period. On reading paragraphs 2(b) and 4 of Article 27 together, it is clear that the conditions set forth in paragraph 4 are positive obligations for the Developing country members, not affirmative defences. If a Developing country member complies with the obligations in Article 27.4, the prohibition on export subsidies in Article 3.1(a) simply does not apply and otherwise, Article 3.1(a) does apply." The case was not decided in Brazil's favour.[268]

In effect, it seems that the orientation of Article 27 is to create support, to the Developing countries in the form of special treatment through provisions. Between the existing heterogeneity among the group of Developing countries, the Article also has some level of common goals and objectives based on consensus among the Member States. These are based on attempt to balance between free trade market concepts and the objectives of the WTO. Considering this as a premise, the approach of the A.B seems to suggest, that along with special relaxations there are certain obligations.

2.8.2.1 Other Opinion (Critical of the Approach Adopted by the Appellate Body)

The DSB as a court always has a discretion to apply the provisions of any act, either in the strictest possible manner or to adopt a liberal approach in the light of the

---

confirmed, the Bank of Brazil applies to the National Treasury of Brazil for the issuance of bonds designated as National Treasury Note–Series I (NTN-I) bonds. The National Treasury issues these bonds and transfers them to the Bank of Brazil, which in turn passes the bonds to the lending bank (or its agent bank). The lending bank can redeem the bonds on a semi-annual basis for the duration of the financing, or can sell them on the market at a discount immediately upon receipt. NTN-I bonds are denominated in Brazilian currency, indexed to the dollar as of the date the bonds are issued. The bonds can only be redeemed in Brazil, and only in Brazilian currency."

Para 65 Brazil did not argue that Article 27, entitled "Special and Differential Treatment of Developing country Members," is in no way subordinate to Article 3 or any other SCM Agreement, nor is it to be narrowly interpreted in favour of any other provision. Rather Article 27 was a transitional arrangement with its own terms. In Brazil's view, the temporary legitimacy of Developing country Member's export subsidies are presumed unless it is proven that a particular member is not in compliance with its obligations under Article 27.

[266] WT/DS46/AB/R, para 140.

[267] The Generalised System of Preferences and Special and Differential Treatment for Developing countries in the GATT and WTO by Robert Read, www.lancs.ac.uk p. no 14.

[268] Para 164, and for all these reasons, we uphold the overall conclusion of the Panel, in paragraph 7.76 of the Panel Report, that "Brazil has increased the level of its export subsidies, within the meaning of Article 27.4 of the SCM Agreement." And, thus, we find that Article 3.1(a) applies to Brazil in this case, because Brazil has not complied with the provisions of Article 27.4.

position of the parties or based on the distinct type of situations and circumstances, demanding some alternative application of the rules based on exceptions. The Appellate Body in this case seems to have applied the provisions dealing with subsidies in a strict manner.

In the case of **Brazil-Export Financing Programme for Aircraft,**[269] the claims were made by Canada under Article 3.1(a) of the SCM Agreement[270] based on the facts as stated specifically in Para 31, 32 and 37. Brazil tried to establish that PROEX payments were not used to secure any material advantage, a point contested by Canada. The second point Canada raised was that Brazil's increase of subsidies was, violation of Article 27(4).[271] Canada while bringing the matter before DSB, linked subsidies with "the high level of expenditure" and further contested it based on the object and purpose of the SCM Agreement. On the other hand, Brazil's view was that a "budgeted amount of appropriations made[272]"(through a budgetary process) should be considered for making comparisons, even if there was an increase in the level of export subsidies, as the PROEX payments were not provided on a per unit basis.[273]

---

[269] WT/DS46/AB/R.

[270] See para 7.

[271] See para 4.147 Panel report, Canada argues, however, that since Article 27 is an exception to Article 3, Brazil has to adduce evidence to prove that it has complied with the conditions set out by article 27.4. Canada further argues that it has to satisfy two conditions, (1) that it must phase out its export subsidies within 8 years after entry into force of the WTO Agreement. (2) that it must phase out export subsidies in shorter period than 8 years if the use are inconsistent with the development needs.

Para 4.148 Canada disagrees with Brazil's statement that Article 27 is *lex specialis* to Article 3 which is *lex generalis*. Canada argues that *lex specialis* is invoked where choice has to be made between conflicting treaty obligations interest.

[272] AB, para 146. Brazil argues that the Panel erred in using actual expenditure, rather than budgetary appropriations. Para 147, the Panel found that the level of a Member's export subsidies in its meaning refers to the level of subsidies actually provided not the level of subsidies which a member planned or authorized its government to provide through budgetary process. The Panel said the view was confirmed by footnote 55 to the SCM Agreement.

[273] Brazil taking here the instance of Article 25.3. "The content of notifications should be sufficiently specific to enable other members to evaluate the trade effects and to understand the operation of the notified subsidy programmes. In this connection, and without prejudice to the contents and form of questionnaire on subsidies, Member shall ensure that their notifications contain the following information:

i) form of a subsidy (i.e. grant, loan, tax concessions, etc);
ii) subsidy per unit or, in cases where this is not possible, the total amount or the annual amount budgeted for that subsidy (indicating, if possible, the average subsidy per unit in the previous year);"

The Appellate Body, while deciding this legal matter has given more weightage to footnote 55[274] of the ASCM and has added that they are not persuaded by Brazil's argument relating to the notification provisions of Article 25.[275]

The approach adopted by the A.B seems a little unexpected. Correlating it with the WTO objectives, the specific clauses of Article 27.7 and Article 27.8, creates alleviation within the Subsidies Agreement of the WTO, for the economic improvement of the Developing and Less-Developed countries and the A.B has not taken that into consideration.

In my opinion, the A.B could have followed a liberal approach considering that Brazil is a Developing country and the Aircraft industry requires considerable investment. Additionally, high risks factors are involved in the aircraft industry, therefore the state based support of various types is a necessity.

An additional crucial point before the Appellate Body was to assess whether the export credits, provided by Brazil are in the form of "*material advantage*" as mentioned in Para 1, clause (k) Annex I. The Appellate Body has noted that Brazil did not provide enough information to establish that an interest-rate equalisation by PROEX was not used to secure a material advantage.[276]

The scope of proceedings as outlined by provisions, through Article 6.1, covering the possibility of actionable subsidies that can create market distortion, refers to the total amount of ad valorem subsidisation of a product if exceeding 5%. However, footnote attached to it creates relaxation. It mentions "*...since it is anticipated that civil aircraft will be subject to specific multi-lateral rules, the threshold in this sub-paragraphs does not apply to civil-aircraft.*" The statement in the footnote makes it clear that some special consideration is possible for the financial support awarded by state to the aircraft industry. This creates a possibility for lenient approach to interpret the term material advantage. Ironically, the case has been decided in the light of Article 3.1(a) of the SCM Agreement as the restrictive parameters for state support. Article 3 covers the grounds for prohibited subsidies, therefore the application of this Article reflects the narrow lane adopted by the A.B while deciding the case.

Considering the above-mentioned provisions and, following the basic objectives of the WTO, which covers the creation of opportunities for Developing and Less-Developed countries, my opinion is that claims could have been made better specifically in the light of "Actionable subsidies," under Art 5 and Art 6. Additionally, a suggestion could have been added by the A.B as such in support of the development agenda for the Developing countries. The assumptions stands, that taking into account the increase in subsidies, the Appellate Body could have

---

[274]Footnote 55 of the ASCM, For a Developing country Member not granting export subsidies as of the date of entry into force of the WTO Agreement, this paragraph shall apply on the basis of the level of export subsidies granted in 1986.

[275]Article 25 refers to the notification and surveillance Clause 3, The content of notifications should be sufficiently specific to enable other Members to evaluate the trade effects and to understand the operation of notified subsidy programme.

[276]See para 179.

recommended that Brazil reduces the PROEX amount from 3.8% to a negotiable value between the parties or is this a decision influenced by the view Canada.

2.9 The North South Divides on "Subsidies"

During the time period, when the WTO began to function, most of the Developing and Less Developed country economies were based, by and large, on agriculture and cottage industries, which acted as structural challenge for rapid industrialisation. Promoting industrialisation in parity with the international market system requires strong policy support for a certain period of time.

The SCM Agreement however, recognises certain special considerations, such as, state support for the purpose of development, for developing the comparative cost advantage principle, for the growth of infant industries, for national security and other exigencies; nevertheless, there are still issues of contention between the Developed and Developing Member States of the WTO.

The domestic industry of a Developing nation faces an already-existing market domination, because of the economies of scale and other externalities, while competing with multinational firms of the Developed nations. The Developed countries on the other hand, try to solve their economic problems such as unemployment, lagging growth, industrial outsourcing, by imposing restrictions on imports and by subsidising exports.[277] Drawing a parallel between the Developed and Developing/Less-Developed countries concerning the use of subsidies, Member States seems to lose track of attaining the objectives, and rather follow the approach inspired by political considerations. The difference of opinion between the two sides is termed the North-South divide.

[277] The key elements are (a) to accord high priority to the reduction and elimination of barriers to products of currently or potentially of particular export interest, including customs duties and other restrictions which differentiate unreasonably;

(b) refrain from introducing, or increasing the incidence of customs duties or non-tariff import barriers on products currently or potentially of particular export interest;

(c) refrain from imposing new fiscal measures, and in any adjustments of fiscal policy accord high priority to the reduction and elimination of fiscal measures . . . which hamper, significantly the growth of consumption of primary products, in raw or processed form, wholly or mainly produced by Less-Developed contracting parties, and which are applied specifically to those products.

This consideration can also be observed in Article XVIII of the GATT. Specifically, Clause 2 of Article XVIII deals with policies and programmes of economic development designed to raise the general standard of living, Clause 3, creates a possibility for the circumstances where no measure consistent with those provisions is practicable to permit the contracting party in the process of economic development, and Clause 11, considers that contracting party can take into account a balance of payment situation for relaxing restrictions on imports.

2.9.1 The Practices Followed by the Developed Countries

Bonum necessarium extra terminos necessitatis non est bonum. Necessary good is no good beyond the bounds of necessity.

Developed countries often use for research and development, subsidies that fall under the heading of non-actionable subsidies. Article 8, (now obsolete) of the ASCM widely covered non-actionable subsidies that were also known as green-light subsidies. On a parallel basis, one may refer to Article 87(3) of the EC Treaty, Article 107 cl (2) cl (3).[278] These Articles supports aid for economic development, execution of an important project of common European interest, development of economic activities or of certain economic interests. Apart from these, state aid is partially given to instruments such as, for Common Agricultural Policy funds; aid granted by supranational organizations, such as the European Space Agency; and also for defence and public works. State support with such objectives, serves as an institutional support for infrastructure development and economic promotion. Even though these aids are meant for economic development, one cannot ignore their affects on the WTO market policies of trade liberalisation. As there is no strict line of demarcation between state aid and subsidies (justifiable and non-justifiable), such state-aid is also used as an instrument to support industries. In the EU, several forms of subsidies are used to promote directly-targeted economic activities, especially, regional development, since new EU members are at lower levels of development, initially when they join.

The most relevant subsidies from the EU structural funds are as mentioned. The European Commission (EC/EU) budgeted €196 billion to the structural Funds for 2000 to 2006, of which €26.2 billion was used in 2003.The Structural Funds reserved €13 billion for research infrastructure and networks, innovative business start-ups, and technical upgrading of SMEs.[279]

Another instance is referred to here, concerning the policy level approach followed by the US, the most Developed economy. The US has a long history of providing financial support for research development and energy sectors. This includes not only direct financial support, but also para-fiscal support through the provisions of legislative acts. Legislation very much reflects the objectives of the government, for example the Price Anderson Act.[280] The main purpose of the Price-Anderson Act is to ensure the availability of a large pool of funds, currently about $10 billion[281] for providing prompt and orderly compensation to the members of the public, in case they incur damages from nuclear or radiological incidents, no

[278]These clauses deals with aid granted compatible with internal market.

[279]Aguayo and Gallagher (2005), pp. 18–19.

[280]**The Price-Anderson Act** was enacted into law in 1957 and has been revised several times. It constitutes Section 170 of the Atomic Energy Act. The latest revision was enacted through the "Energy Policy Act of 2005" and which extended it through to December 31, 2025.

[281]For detail reference see, Price-Anderson Act November 2005, American Nuclear Society. Federal Affairs. www.ans.org.

matter who might be eventually held liable. This is a high degree of state support, as the Act provides dual coverage, that is, the same protection is available to a covered licensee or contractor, and also extends by virtue of indemnification, to any persons who suffer, regardless of their relationship to the licensed activity. Such a wide supportive coverage provided by the Act is a high incentive to the use of technology and the further advancement of technology. Additionally, there are several investment tax credits and production credits designed to benefit renewable technologies. These include the Investment Energy Tax Credit, established by the Energy Tax Act of 1978, and the Production Tax Credit (PTC), authorised the under-Energy Policy Act.[282] With such an existing disequilibrium it seems as if it is difficult to achieve the objectives of the WTO, if nations already in an advantageous position try to take further advantages under the heading of subsidies for research and development. The Developed nations already have an export surplus and these supports will place them in further advantageous situations.

Such situation of economic disequilibrium between the nations, raises two question, (1) why do governments use subsidies in the Developed countries? and (2) how do these subsidies impact international trade?[283] As the use of subsidies remains within the dilemma of justifiable and non-justifiable limits of use, so any state policy for technological advancement, even if it is supported by legal provisions, demands some level of demarcation between funding for research and innovation and the overlapping effects of such funding in the market system, from the perspective of free trade. A salient feature of such subsidies can be observed in the case of state support for infrastructure building and state investment in R&D, mainly used by the Developed countries in the case of the aircraft industry, both for civil and for defence purposes, and investment in the case of the pharmaceutical industry.[284] Putting things in terms of economics, one can say that the average costs of production are reduced because of such support. In legal terms, justification for such state support varies, based on the social set up, welfare schemes adopted, the extent of the economic development expected, and the underlying objectives for the advancement of technology. Any policy support for subsidies in order to achieve technological advancement necessitates some regulatory clauses also, in order to legally enable funding for research and innovation[285] on the one hand, but also to check the spill over effects in the market system on the other.

---

[282]Goldberg (2000), p. 14.

[283]World Trade Report (2006), p. 55. Exploring the links between subsidies, trade and the WTO. http://www.wto.org/english/res_e/publications_e/wtr06_e.htm.

[284]World Trade Report (2006), p. xxvi http://www.wto.org/english/res_e/publications_e/wtr06_e.htm.

[285]In many of the instances, rather than seeking ways of directly subsidizing R&D, the intellectual property rights system is usually relied upon by governments to encourage firms to invest in knowledge creation. A patent, for example, guarantees its owner the sole use of a patented invention during a specified period. This conferred monopoly right ensures higher returns on investments made in creating knowledge. Once the patent expires the underlying knowledge can be used by others. To a large extent, the length of the period of patent protection will determine

A salient economic feature of many modern industries is the heavy expenses at the primary stages. Such costs are also due to the significant investments in R&D and expenses in highly specialised capital equipment. Typical examples of such industries are, the aircraft industry and the pharmaceutical industries. In such a set-up, state support also reduces the average production costs. Additionally, as per the welfare schemes, if a government has reasons to believe that consumer welfare, which is not often reflected in the printed prices, exceeds the losses or the costs, and such producers would suffer without a subsidy, the government may wish to consider subsidising thus encouraging producers to supply the relevant goods.[286] Justification for such subsidies may also vary, based on social welfare measures, economic development, advancement of new technology, proper utilisation of the limited resources and widening the scope of commercial practices.[287] What is significant here is to demarcate between a justifiable threshold and a non-justifiable level, as the cross subsidisation effects because of such state support[288] to the free trade market system cannot be ignored. An another issue of concern arises as to whether such policy support measures are time bound or not, otherwise it may start effecting the free market principles of efficiency and eventually falls within the restricted categories of subsidies as it puts fiscal burden on the government exchequer. This can really be a 'catch 22' situation as reduction or removal of such subsidies may lead to the reversal of the achievements from midway, and the prolonged use of such subsidies effects the trends of the market competitiveness. The question then arises, as to whether it is possible to establish a global values, based on social, cultural, economic and scientific parameters for such subsidies, irrespective of the classification of the Member State, through the existing provisions and in the present classification of subsidies in various

---

whether an appropriate balance has been struck between encouraging investment in R&D and allowing society to benefit from R&D—generated knowledge spillovers. World Trade Report (2006), p. xxvi. http://www.wto.org/english/res_e/publications_e/wtr06_e.htm.

[286]World Trade Report (2006), p. 59. Exploring the links between subsidies, trade and the WTO. http://www.wto.org/english/res_e/publications_e/wtr06_e.htm.

[287]Subsidies in the Energy sector: An Overview Background Paper for the World Bank Group Energy Sector Strategy. July, (2010), p. 24. http://siteresources.worldbank.org/EXTESC/Resources/Subsidy_background_paper.pdf.

[288]Subsidies in the Energy sector: An Overview Background Paper for the World Bank Group Energy Sector Strategy. July, (2010), p. 23. http://siteresources.worldbank.org/EXTESC/Resources/Subsidy_background_paper.pdf.

A case of *cross subsidisation*:—involves a group of consumers paying more than the general cost of supply and the surplus is used to subsidise the provision to the other group at a price that is lower than the cost of supply to the subsidized group. This cross-subsidisation may be formulated with varying degree of transparency. A variation on this theme is where the cost of supply is higher to the targeted group (because of distance from main supply points or low local load density), but the price to both groups set the same. This has the result that one group pays above cost and the other pays below cost.

orders.[289] If we compare this position, with the economic situations in many of the Developing and Less-Developed countries, there are instances such as the fires that burnt a garment factory[290] and killed many people in Bangladesh. It seems like there exist wide contrast in the basics of the trading system and requires timely revision of the agreements.

Another crucial issue that adds to the North South divide is the question of Agricultural subsidies. So far as the discussions on agricultural subsidies are concerned, this question in terms of economic stability and infrastructure building is significant for the African nations. By providing subsidies to their own farmers, Developed nations try to dominate the agricultural market. This trading practice very much affects the African continent because agriculture, along with raw materials, is their main exports. The foreign exchange earned through those exports helps them to acquire technology. Such issues are crucial and are often raised at the conferences. Some midway solution agreeable to both sides needs to be evolved to resolve the crisis. (Agriculture subsidies in detail are discussed in chapter. . .no. 3)

2.9.2 The WTO Ministerial Conferences

The Ministerial conference is a forum to bring changes in the methods of working and to resolve the ambiguities among the Member States. The ministerial conference is the main decision making platform of the WTO and can initiate discussions and also take decisions concerning any of the trade agreements.[291] It is noteworthy that the formation of the rules of trade within the WTO is a dynamic process and therefore after meetings of the representative of the Member States, there can be possible changes in the scope or shifts in the existing rules, creating new sets of obligations or changes in the existing set of obligations.[292] This can be either to fulfil certain new set of obligations or altering the existing set of obligations. Ironically, the ministerial conferences often end up in polarisation or deadlock on certain issues, rather than forming any concrete opinion as the members are often unsure whether they are ascribing to legal, economic or political objectives on the matters during the discussions.[293]

[289]Subsidies in the Energy sector: An Overview Background Paper for the World Bank Group Energy Sector Strategy. July, (2010), p. 7. http://siteresources.worldbank.org/EXTESC/Resources/Subsidy_background_paper.pdf.

[290]Wednesday, January (22), (2014), NY Daily News.com/world.

[291]For detail reference see www.wto.org.

[292]The topmost decision making body of the WTO is the Ministerial Conference, which usually meets every 2 years. The Ministerial Conference can take decisions on all matters under any of the multilateral trade agreements.

[293]Footer (2006), p. 44.

2.9.2.1 The Doha Conference 2001

The fourth WTO ministerial-conference was held in Doha, Qatar from 9 to 14 November 2001.[294] WTO members remained deeply divided on subsidies and several other issues.[295] The subsidies given for the purpose of agriculture remained a major blockage between the Developed and Developing nations, as an attempt was made to bring on equal footing the regulation of agricultural subsidies and the subsidies in general.[296] The agendas forwarded by the Developing countries and the concession based demands were quite extensive. Developing nations demanded that Developed Member States, eliminate arbitrary access rules in their market and the GSP needs to be based on the economic history of a Member State, rather than applied on an arbitrary basis. Developing nations also emphasised, that the matter of food security is fundamental for them, hence they should be allowed to sustain a certain level of protection from farm imports in case so required.[297] Additionally, there was also a proposal that they should be exempted from the countervailing measures or other actions pertaining to subsidies, in order to promote basic development necessities. These can be described as subsidies with "legitimate development goals, which covers, support for regional growth, technology research and development, state support for diversification, development and implementation of an environmentally friendly method of production."

Serious concern was shown by the Developing nations regarding new commitments. However, they found these commitments increased the legal conditions, imposed on them by the WTO, such as under TRIPS[298] (Agreement on Trade-Related Aspects of Intellectual Property Rights). The emerging economies suggesting their economic conditions on the one hand, and the WTO system suggesting its own terms and conditions, on the other, often create dead-locks. This necessitates enough "policy space" for such economies according to their respective situation and circumstances to accommodate the WTO agenda. During the Doha conference, it was emphatically pointed out that the Developed nations had gone through several stages before reaching their present status. Developing nations proposed that subsidies, which were provided for technological improvement and for the eradication of poverty, social and environmental problems should be considered in line with sustainable development and, hence, should not be considered as trade distorting. The Conference finally ended by agreeing on some

---

[294] WT/MIN(01)/DEC/1.

[295] G/SCM/39, 20 November, 2001(01-5767) Committee on Subsidies and Countervailing Measures.

[296] Tangermann (2014), p. 5.

Also see, Annex VII of the Subsidies and Countervailing Measure Agreement allows some Developing nations to pay export subsidies to a certain extent. Among them is a group who are eligible so long as their GNP stays below US$1000 per capita. This is subject to the agreement among the Member States regarding the method of calculations. (See also footnote 68 of Annex VII of the Subsidies and Countervailing Agreement).

[297] Murphy and Chatterjee (2013), p. 1.

[298] WT/MIN (01)/DEC/2, 20 Nov, (2001), DOHA Ministerial conference.

concessions for Developing and Less-Developed countries. Ministers affirmed that the governments of the Less-Developed countries could be allowed to pay subsidies that are essential for basic industries. This concession can be covered under actionable subsidies, and consequently both Developing and Developed countries have flexibility for financing their exporters to a restricted extent, i.e., consistent with their specific development needs. Members also agreed that more time should be given to some countries to phase out their export-contingent subsidies. Finally, ministers instructed the Subsidies Committee to give some of the Developing countries more time to phase out subsidies. These were based on the requirement to export, according to the procedures in a committee document.

2.9.2.2 The Hong Kong Conference in 2005[299]

As a result of the failure of Cancun in 2003, several of the issues discussed during the DDA were dropped, such as the issue of investment, competition, and government procurement. The considerations that dominated the proceedings in Hong Kong were the theme of the Development Agenda, the interests of Developing and the Less-Developed countries, the controversial issue of agricultural subsidies, the effect of subsidies on fisheries.[300] Several new issues were also added, relating to non-agricultural market access (NAMA), trade in services (GATS) and certain IP related issues such as the finalisation of the TRIPS amendment on compulsory licences for pharmaceutical products.[301]

Besides discussing other issues, ministers affirmed the decisions and declarations adopted during the Doha conference. The issue of agricultural subsidies was again a primary matter of discussion. There were proposals by some of the Members that exemptions given, to the general prohibitions on the use of subsidies need to be phased out.[302] Member States agreed to eliminate most of the subsidies by the end of December 2013. The policy measures that were indirectly connected to export subsidies were also discussed in detail, e.g., export credits and insurance programmes.[303] One of the key suggestions was to define these policies strictly so as to avoid supporting export promotion indirectly.

Additionally, the discussions included the restrictive role of state trading enterprises. As the main policy-objective of the WTO is to promote free trade, therefore maintaining consistency between policy and practice is the primary reason for restricting the role of state-trading enterprises, which was pointed out during this conference.

---

[299]WT/MIN (05)/DEC, 22 Dec, (2005).

[300]The Rules Negotiations-Fisheries Subsidies. www.wto.org/english/tratop_e/rulesneg_e/fish_e/fish_e.htm.

[301]World Trade Organization 6th Ministerial Conference Hong Kong 13–18 December, (2005) by Esmé du Plessis p. 2,4,13.

[302]See as the continuation of the Doha Agenda.

[303]TN/RL/15, 30 November (2005). Negotiating Group on Rules.

State trading enterprises supported by government policies, such as tax concessions and other forms of aid, reduces the costs of the factors of production, cumulatively leading to export subsidies.[304]

Restricting the further increase in the quantity of subsidies, was a matter agreed on between the Member States, but providing special-aid for food in certain areas, or dealing with an emergency situation was supported overwhelmingly. Additionally, subsidies on cotton products were also discussed. This resulted in quota-free access to cotton exports from the Less-developed economies. Structural reforms for the African cotton producers and exporters were also widely supported.[305] Cotton exports is a source of special economic support to the farmers in Benin, Burkina Faso, Mali, Chad, and Senegal. These countries have protested against US cotton subsidies for years. During the Hong Kong conference, the US agreed to reduce export subsidies to its cotton farmers.[306]

As a continuing practice, the importance of special and differential treatment was recognised and reaffirmed. Flexibilities provided for small economies also received the support of the majority of the Member States during this conference. Basically, the S&D treatment provisions are included in order to optimise the use of the flexibilities and as alternatives in order to improve the position of Developing Member countries.[307]

Finally, ministers of the Member States, affirmed that the governments of the Less-developed countries would be permitted to continue paying subsidies in order to export goods that are otherwise prohibited for the Developed countries, which means giving them special consideration. The earnings through exports will help to meet their development needs. Members also agreed that more time should be given to some of Developing countries to phase out their export-contingent subsidies, where the economy is in a vulnerable situation, due to the transformation from the agricultural to the industrial sector.

2.9.2.3 Bali Conference 2013[308]

Following the agenda from the previous conferences, the discussion on subsidies between the Developed and Developing/Less-Developed continued during this negotiation round. In fact, there were some positive developments, as the Member States were able to relax the rigid stand adopted during the Doha Ministerial

---

[304]World Trade Organization 6th Ministerial Conference, Hong Kong 13–18 December, (2005) by Esmé du Plessis p. 4.

[305]TN/AG/21.Committee on Agriculture, Special Session.

[306]Das, Hong Kong Ministerial of Doha Round of Multilateral trade Negotiations: Achieving a Low-Level Equilibrium. p 6. http://www.cid.harvard.edu/cidtrade/Papers/das-lle.pdf.

[307]World Trade Organization 6th Ministerial Conference, Hong Kong 13–18 December, (2005) by Esmé du Plessis p. 13.

[308]Ninth Session. (The WTO's Tenth Ministerial Conference was held in Nairobi, Kenya from 15th to 19th December, 2015).

conference. The representatives of the Member States linked the ongoing discussions with the subjects already under consideration since the Doha Development Agenda and showed full support during the discussion, to fulfil these commitments and in order to give effects to the objectives.[309] Cited here are the key issues of the Doha Development Agenda; (1) trade facilitation, (2) agricultural subsidies (discussed in the Chap. 3, i.e., on agriculture subsidies) and (3) issues related to export competition.

Trade Facilitation
In this regard Member States reaffirmed that the non-discrimination principle of Article V of GATT 1994[310] remains valid.

Export Competition[311]
Further during the discussions, Member States recognised that all forms of export subsidies and export measures of the same effect are highly trade distorting and protectionist measures. In this regard Members drew the approach, from discussions at the Hong Kong Ministerial conference in 2005. During the Hong Kong conference, it was decided to use the utmost restraint with regard to all forms of export subsidies. As an outcome of the discussions there were no strict commitments, however the members agreed on maintaining the positive trend and to exercise restraint with regard to providing any new form of export subsidies and similar such measures.

Briefly mentioning here, it seems from the outcome of Bali conference, that there was some constructive progress concerning the Member State's approach towards bringing their domestic policies in line with the WTO objectives. However, political compromises between conflicting interests and goals opposing often complicates the situation. Often, a considerable extent of deviation from the assertions made during the conferences can be noticed when it comes to forming policies and the application of rules among the Member States.

2.10 The Airbus-Boeing Dispute (Raising New-Milestones)

2.10.1 The Issue of Trade Subsidies and Background Information About the Companies

The case of Airbus-Boeing[312] needs specific discussion, as the subsidy question in this case was determined in an unprecedented manner demanding new

[309] WT/MIN (13)/Dec.

[310] Article V deals with freedom of transit of goods, vessels and other means of transport.

[311] WT/MIN(13)/40 WT/L/915.

[312] Carbaugh and Olienyk (2004), p. 1.

Article 6, Boeing-Airbus Subsidy dispute: By the year 1960, three American firms Boeing, Lockheed and Mc-Donell Douglas, entered the aviation industry. Within a short span, these firms

interpretations. The facts and arguments that have emerged, in the light of technological changes used in the civil aircraft in order to sustain competition, gives the impression, that the terms, such as "financial contribution," "subsidy in the form of buying of goods and services"[313] and "benefit" need to be seen from a new perspective. In the civil aviation market, the two market-dominating aviation companies are Boeing[314] from the US and Airbus, an EU company from the EU economy.[315]

As a matter of fact, European companies were the first to produce commercial aero-planes for the international market. Subsequently, the American companies also tried to make their own impact in the international aviation sector.[316] The competition between the two companies Boeing and Airbus kept growing. Both the EU and the US tried to resolve this trade issues through negotiations based on the provisions of the agreements made in 1992. As the two sides could not reach any solution, the matter was brought before the WTO in the form of two cases.

---

established an upper hand in the market, raising serious concern for the governments of the European Union member countries about their market position. Consequently, four of the European governments pooled the resources to establish a single trans-national manufacturer, which finally led to the formation of Airbus in 1969. This newly formed "Airbus" company was a consortium owned by British, French, German and Spanish companies. Airbus was owned by just two firms, namely, European Aeronautic Defence and Space Company having 80% shares (EADS was formed by the merger of Aerospatiale Matra SA of France, Daimler Chrysler Aerospace AG of Germany and the Construcciones Aeronautics SA of Spain.) and British firm BAE system having the remaining 20%.

[313]Article 1.1(a) 1 (iii) "a government provides goods or services other than general infrastructure, or purchases goods."

[314]Presently, Boeing Company is a **Public Company** incorporated in 1934 as Boeing Airplane Company.

[315]The "European economy" term refers collectively, the market of the Member Countries.

[316]Carbaugh and Olienyk (2004), p. 1.

Article 6, Boeing-Airbus Subsidy dispute: By the year 1960, three American firms Boeing, Lockheed and Mc-Donell Douglas, entered the aviation industry. Within a short span, these firms established an upper hand in the market, raising serious concern for the governments of the European Union member countries about their market position. Consequently, four of the European governments pooled the resources to establish a single trans-national manufacturer, which finally led to the formation of Airbus in 1969. This newly formed "Airbus" company was a consortium owned by British, French, German and Spanish companies. Airbus was owned by just two firms, namely, European Aeronautic Defence and Space Company having 80% shares (EADS was formed by the merger of Aerospatiale Matra SA of France, Daimler Chrysler Aerospace AG of Germany and the Construcciones Aeronautics SA of Spain.) and British firm BAE system having the remaining 20%.

2.10.2 Case (i): European Communities and Certain Member States-Measures Affecting Trade in Large Civil Aircraft (WT/DS316/R)

The United States (complainant) contended that state support in the form of subsidies, which are the issue in this dispute, benefited the production and marketing of the full range of LCA[317] manufactured by Airbus, and therefore the Airbus LCA is a subsidised product distorting the free trade market principle.

The US alleged that the Member States of the European Communities (Germany, France, the United Kingdom and Spain), financially supported, large civil aircraft, first, by covering the below-market rates with financial support and later with a flexible repayment obligation after the sale of the aircraft.[318] Additionally, the debt cancellation and the equity infusions[319] by the EC and grants through government-controlled banks were also alleged to be non-justifiable support.[320] Hence, with such an extent of support, the US assumed that the "launch aid programme" provided to Airbus for the A380, the A340-500/600, and A330-200 models were export subsidies, violating the provisions of Articles 3.1(a) and 3.2 of the SCM Agreement. In addition to the above type of subsidy, the unprecedented level of "Launch aid programme,[321] as research aid" which the US also considered violated Article 5(a), 5(c), 6.3(a) 6.3(b) and 6.3(c) of the SCM Agreement, were provided by the EC.

[317]Para 2.1, the parties agree that the product at issue in this dispute is large civil aircraft, as distinguished from smaller (regional) aircraft and military aircraft. Large civil aircraft (LCA) can generally be described as weighing over (15,000 kg).

[318]This includes provision by the EC and the Member States, for financial contributions to develop, expand, and upgrade facilities and other infrastructure for Airbus companies. The instances are investments by German authorities in Hamburg, Nordenham, Bremen and Varel, by French authorities in the Toulouse region, by UK authorities at Broughton, Wales, and by Spanish authorities at numerous locations in Spain.

[319]The subsidy from government equity infusions is the savings to the firm from avoidance of market cost of equity. The subsidy, if any, is what the market requires before providing similar funds. If the government provides funds at a lower cost than the market demands, it bestows a subsidy.

[320]Para 2.5 (e) of the Panel Report. Examples are such as, equity investment by the French government into Aerospatiale in 1987 and 1988, an equity infusion of French state-owned Credit Lyonnais into Aerospatiale in 1992 and in 1994, the French government's 45.76% share of Dassault aviation's capital. The investment by the German government through the Kreditanstalt für Wiederaufbau (KfW) in Deutsche Airbus in 1989 and the return of the shares acquired through this transaction to Deutsche Airbus are also to be included.

[321]In May 2005, the European Commission defended the prospect of Launch aid because it was a part of the commercial landscape of aircraft development in Europe. The French foreign minister stated that the French state has given financial support to A380 programme and expected to continue it.

However, in response to the assertions made by the US, the EU pointed out that the Panel should dismiss the claims of the US. as the question of launch aid[322] subsidies was a matter of study in retrospect.[323]

The issue of subsidies also arose in the form of infrastructure support and the extent to which such a support can be considered justifiable The US submitted that the EC/EU governments also supported the Airbus by infrastructure facilities for the development of the A380 model of the Airbus,[324] which often distorted the balance between state support and regulatory mechanism, through provisions, meant for restricting the state support.

Arguments forwarded by the European Communities The EC\EU explained specifically that the investment did not constitute a subsidy, as it was not given under terms more favourable than the market terms. In its defence, the EC/EU further added that the investments by the German government and Daimler co., in the Deutsche Airbus were part of the 1989 restructuring of Deutsche Airbus.[325]

The EC/EU also submitted that in order to meet the requirements of Article 5 and 6.3 of the SCM Agreement, the US is supposed to establish the required relationship between the alleged subsidies and the specific forms of adverse effects. The EC argued that Article 5 needed to be applied in a non-retrospective manner.[326]

The Question of Continuity of Benefit
With regard to the question of "benefit," the EC asserted that the US bears the burden of proving the continuity of the benefit to the current manufacturer of LCA.

---

[322]In May 2005, the European Commission defended the prospect of Launch aid because it was a part of the commercial landscape of aircraft development in Europe. The French foreign minister stated that the French state has given financial support to A380 programme and expected to continue it.

[323]See from para 4.56. When tracing the roots of the **Launch aid**, reference must be made to the year 1969, when the government of France and Germany entered into an agreement to foster European cooperation in the field of aeronautics. On the basis of these reasons, the US asserted that "Launch aid" was a subsidy within the meaning of Article 1 of the SCM Agreement because it involved a financial contribution within the meaning of Article 1.1(a) of the SCM Agreement.

[324]The German authorities provided infrastructure support in the cities of Hamburg, Nordenham and Bremen, the French authorities in the city of Toulouse, the UK authorities in Broughton (Broughton in Wales) and the Spanish authorities in the several locations in Spain See Measures at issue Para 2.5 (a) (b) (c) *European Communities and certain Member States – Measures Affecting Trade in Large Civil Aircraft* WT/DS316/R.

[325]The EC argued that this conclusion was not undermined by the fact that the investments by the German government and Daimler Benz in Deutsche Airbus were part of the 1989 restructuring of Deutsche Airbus. While the US argued that the "separation of the alleged restructuring package from the KFW capital injection was artificial, the EC argued that it was an artificiality that the US had created by challenging only a particular aspect of the 1989 restructuring package." The EC submitted that the 1989 restructuring was consistent with the actions a private investor in the shoes of the German government would have undertaken to minimize its losses.

[326]This is the consistent way of interpreting Article 28 of the VCLT, which sets out the general rule that treaty provisions do not apply retroactively.

While making these claims, the EC further added that the identity of the recipient, or, if the benefit had *passed through*, it was a legal requirement that the operator benefiting from the subsidy need to be identified,[327] and according to EC, the US had failed to establish it.[328] Further referring the A.B's point of view, the EC asserted in its defence, a rebuttable presumption stating 'that an arm's length fair market value privatisation, excludes the pass through of benefit from seller to buyer of a state owned firm'.[329]

The Panel rejected the EC\EU's request that subsidies provided by the EC\EU's prior to 1995 be excluded from the proceedings. The Panel based this conclusion on the fact that Article 5 described a particular relationship between the antecedent *conduct of Member States and subsequent events.* It further described Article 5 as a situation rather than an act, which required an examination of a representative period for the purpose of establishing the effects of the subsidy.

Concerning the passing of benefit the EC in its defence referred to several transactions, which according to the EC had the effect of eliminating subsides. This was however, rebutted by the US. Claims made by the EC that benefits conferred initially had extinguished for the reasons of subsequent transactions

---

[327]The EC argues that by failing to demonstrate how the alleged subsidies to other companies provide benefit to Airbus SAS, the US had failed to make a prima facie case of violation of the SCM Agreement. The EC recalls the Appellate Body's observation that "a 'benefit' can be said to arise only if a person, natural or legal, or a group of persons has in fact received something." Put simply, subsidies paid to entities that simply no longer exist, much less manufacture and sell LCA, cannot be assumed to benefit Airbus SAS, which has not, in the Appellate Body's words, in fact received something. Whether it has "in fact received something" is for the United States to prove. The EC explains that the identity of recipient, extinction, extraction even 'pass through' are all different ways of expressing the same principle. The US calls it the "continuity of benefit." In reality, the EC explains that it is the requirement that the operator benefitting from the subsidy must be identified. The EC adds that in accordance with the jurisprudence, the US bears the burden of proving the "continuity of benefit" from alleged subsidies to entities other than Airbus SAS, the current manufacturer of European LCA, through to SAS. The EC submits that the US—as the complaining party bears the burden of proving its claims.

[328]*European Communities and Certain Member States-Measures Affecting Trade in Large Civil Aircraft,* WT/DS316/R, para 4.8. The EC argues that by failing to demonstrate how the alleged subsidies to other companies provide benefits to Airbus SAS, the US has failed to make prima case of violation of the SCM Agreement. The EC recalls the Appellate Body's observation that "a 'benefit' can be said to arise only if a person, natural or legal or a group of persons, has in fact received something. Put simply, subsidies paid to entities that no longer exist, much less manufacture and sell LCA, cannot be assumed to benefit Airbus SAS, which has not, in the Appellate Body's words, in fact received something." Whether it has "in fact received something" is for the United States to prove. The EC explains that identity of recipient, extinction, extraction even pass through are all different ways of expressing the same principle. The US calls it the "continuity of benefit." In reality, EC explains that it is the requirement that the operator benefitting from the subsidies must be identified.

[329]See WT/DS316/R Para 4.15.

were rejected by the Panel. The Panel considered that Airbus SAS to be the same producer of Airbus LCA as the Consortium Airbus Industrie.[330]

Appellate Body Decision (in Brief)

The Appellate Body agreed with the Panel's view that equity infusions by the French government constituted subsidies.[331] It further identified, that R&TD (Research and Technological Development) funding had came from the French government since 1986, for civil aeronautics-related to R&TD projects, in which the Airbus participated.[332] With regard to the issue of subsidies given prior to the formation of the WTO and its effects, the A.B also stated that "adverse effects "within the meaning of Article 5 could be caused by subsidies granted prior to 1st

[330]Para 7.286 In summary, for purposes of our assessment of the United States claims under Article 5 of the SCM Agreement, we consider Airbus SAS to be the same producer of Airbus LCA as the consortium Airbus Industry. We do not consider it necessary for the United States to affirmatively demonstrate the "pass-through" to Airbus SAS of the benefit conferred by financial contribution that had been provided to Airbus industry prior to 2001 in order to make out a prima facie case. Para 7.287 Nor do we consider it necessary for the United States to demonstrate the "continuity" of benefits conferred by prior financial contributions provided to Airbus industry or Airbus SAS as a prerequisite to establishing that European Communities has caused through the use of a subsidy . . .., adverse effects to the interests of the United States. para 7.288 We therefore reject the European Communities arguments (i) that the benefits conferred by certain financial contributions provided to Airbus Industry or Airbus SAS have been extinguished by the series of allegedly arm's-length, fair market value transactions set forth in Para 7.204 of this Report; and (ii) that the so called "extractions" of cash and cash equivalents of Dasa and of CASA, by Daimler Chrysler and SEPI, respectively, effectively extinguished a portion of the benefits previously conferred by financial contributions that had been provided to Dasa and CASA.

[331]*European Communities and Certain Member States-Measures Affecting Trade in Large Civil Aircraft*, WT/DS316/AB/R, para 1402. The Panel found that the following R&TD measures constituted specific subsidies that caused serious prejudice to the United States' interests under Article 5(c) and 6.3(a), (b) and (c) of the SCM Agreement. The grants to Airbus provided under the Second, Third, Fourth, Fifth and Sixth EC Framework Programmes. Appellate Body Report, para 1403. "The R&TD subsidies enabled Airbus to develop features and aspects of its LCA on a schedule that it would otherwise have been unable to accomplish. Even in the case of those R&TD subsidies directed to pre-competitive research, the ability to fund such efforts at a time when it would likely have been unable to do so in the light of other demands on its resources was in our view, significant in ensuring the launch of successive models of Airbus LCA."

[332]The A.B report, para 649. "For the foregoing reasons, we reverse the Panel's finding in para 7.1422 of the Panel Report, that the R&TD loans provided pursuant to Spanish PROFIT programme were within the Panel's terms of reference and we uphold the Panel's findings in of the Panel Report, para 7.158 that the French R&TD grants were within the Panel's terms of reference." The Appellate Body agrees with the Panel decision "that equity-infusions infrastructure supports that are at issue complemented and supplemented the product effect of LA/MSF and impacted on the Airbus's ability. On the other hand, it also considered that the Panel erred under Article 5(c) and 6.3(a) (b) and (c) of the SCM Agreement without establishing a link between R&TD subsidies and the Airbus Company's ability to launch the product, corroborated it with the final end of the product.

January 1995.[333] Disregarding the arguments advanced by the European Union concerning the withdrawal of subsidies, the A.B upheld the Panel's findings that cash extractions did not constitute withdrawal of subsidies.[334]

The Appellate Body Upheld the Panel's Findings Concerning the Benefit Analysis

The European Union appealed the Panel's findings arguing that there was no requirement to conduct a "pass-through" analysis between past subsidy recipients and current Airbus LCA producers for the benefit determination.[335] Therefore, the European Union requested the Appellate Body to reverse the findings as it was based on incorrect interpretations.

The A.B, disagreeing with the EU's point of view, upheld the Panel's findings. Furthermore, the A.B reasoned that 'the economic realities of the production of Airbus LCA demonstrated that the Airbus Industrie consortium (that is, each of the

[333]Para 665, Article 28 indicates that "subsidy programmes" continuing in force or maintained after1January 1995 were generally intended to fall within the temporal scope of Part II of the SCM Agreement (which prohibits the granting or maintaining of export and import substitution subsidies). By its terms, Article 28 does not refer to individual acts of subsidization, nor does it refer to obligations arising under Part III of the SCM Agreement. A.B report, para 666. The interpretation of Article 5 of the SCM Agreement in the light of the principle of Non-retroactivity reflected in Article 28 of the Vienna Convention. Para 672 (Logically it seems to us that Article 28 also necessarily implies that, without a contrary intention, treaty obligations do apply to any situations which has not ceased to exist-that is to any situation that arose in the past, but continues to exist under the new treaty.

[334]The EU argued that Panel erred in its interpretation and application of the term withdrawal in Article 4.7and 7.8 of the SCM Agreement. Appellate Body see para 759. Accordingly, we uphold the Panel's finding, in paragraphs 7.283, 7.284 and 7.289 of the Panel report that the "cash extractions" did not result in the "withdrawal of subsidies," within the meaning of Articles 4.7 and 7.8 of the SCM agreement. With respect to the sales transactions at issue, we have no basis to make the finding that they resulted in withdrawal of subsidies as we have not completed the analysis to determine whether they extinguished prior subsidies.

[335]WT/DS316/AB/R Para 75. The European Union argues that the Panel's findings that there was no requirement to conduct a "pass-through" analysis between past subsidy recipients and current Airbus LCA producers was premised on an erroneous interpretation and application of the requirement to demonstrate a "continuing benefit "that is based on Article 1, 5, and 6 of the SCM Agreement. In the European Union's view, contrary to the Panel's findings, a "pass-through" analysis is equally applicable to Part V as to Part III of the SCM Agreement given the common definition of subsidy in Article 1 of the SCM Agreement. WT/DS316/AB/R Para 77. In conclusion, the European Union requests the Appellate Body to reverse the findings of the Panel relating to "pass through," "extinction," and "extraction" and "withdrawal" of subsidies. Moreover, as a consequence of the Appellate Body reversing the Panel's finding that Article 5 of the SCM Agreement does not require an additional demonstration that all or parts of the benefit found to have been conferred by the provision of financial contribution continues to exist or presently exists, the European union requests a reversal of the Panel's analysis of the causal link between the alleged subsidies and present adverse effects. In the European Union's view, the Panel should have taken into account, inter alia, the passage of time in order to examine whether past subsidies were still capable of causing present adverse effects by, for instance, applying amortization rules.

Airbus partners, their respective affiliates and Airbus GIE) and Airbus SAS were the same producer of LCA(….)'

So far as the issue concerns restructuring of the existing company, oral discussion between the parties was suggested. The European Union did not contest the United States' assertion that the Airbus operation or production activities did not change as a result of the restructuring.[336] This led the A.B to infer that their existed a relationship between the predecessor companies and Airbus SAS. As a matter of fact, the predecessor companies and Airbus SAS were related, at least to some extent, through common ownership. Therefore the A.B concluded that they were not facing a situation where a predecessor and successor companies are unrelated and operate at arm's length and where a "pass through" analysis might therefore be required.[337]

2.10.3 Case (ii): United States-Measures Affecting Trade in Large Civil Aircraft (WT/DS353/R)

As the attempt to reach an amicable solution between the US and the EU failed for the second time, the EU requested the Panel to be established in pursuant to Article 6 of DSU, Article XXIII: 2 of the GATT 1994 and Article 4 and 30 of the SCM Agreement.

[336]Para 775 Based on these considerations, we do not consider that, as alleged by the European Union, the facts of the case give rise to a requirement to conduct an analysis of whether the benefit of subsidies provided to the Airbus Industrie consortium "passed through" to Airbus SAS. First, there is no suggestion here that subsidies were provided to a different input product that was separate or distinct from downstream "subsidized product," as was the case in US-Softwood Lumber IV. Second, although we do not exclude that there may be other circumstances, including ones involving the restricting of companies in which the receipt of a subsidy by a predecessor company may not mean that it is enjoyed by a successor company, we recall the Panel's findings that, despite the changes to their "legal organization," the economic realities of production of Airbus LCA demonstrated that the Airbus Industrie consortium (that is, each of the Airbus partners, their respective affiliates and Airbus GIE) and Airbus SAS were the same producer of LCA[. …] At the oral hearing, we engaged the participants in some discussion as to whether the restructuring of predecessor companies to form EDAS, and thereafter Airbus SAS, involved a change in LCA productive activities and corporate contractual relationships. The European Union did not contest the United States' assertion that Airbus operation or production activities did not change as a result of the restructuring.

[337]See Para 776. Finally, we do not consider that the relationship between the predecessor companies and Airbus SAS is one that can characterized as a relationship between unrelated companies operating at the "arm's length." Instead, the companies and Airbus SAS were related, at least to some extent, through common ownership. We conclude, therefore, that we are not faced with a situation where predecessor and successor companies are unrelated and operate at arm's length and where a "pass through" analysis might therefore be required.

Some Key Points

The crucial legal question was in the form of claims made by the EU, which NASA provided goods and services to Boeing, for LCA related research and charged less than the adequate remuneration. According, to the EU claims, this practice falls under the category of subsidies as mentioned under Article 1.1(a) (1) (iii) of the SCM Agreement.[338] The EU alleged that subsidies, both prohibited and actionable, were provided to the Boeing Company and other supporting companies prior to their merger with Boeing.[339]

EU further asserted, that the US Federal Government provided technological and infrastructural support through the NASA DOL (Department of Labor), DOD (Department of Defense) and DOC (Department of Commerce).[340]

The European Community alleged that Boeing and the US government had collaborated to advance aeronautical technology and to give it a competitive edge.[341] The European Communities also argued that the State of Washington and its municipalities were providing additional financial support to benefit the "project Olympus," i.e., the Boeing 787 assembly facility.[342]

As a result of these subsidies, there was a significant loss in sales and displacement with respect to the orders of Airbus A330, and the original A350, A320 and A340 series of LCA, within the meaning of Article 6.3(c) of the SCM Agreement.

However, the US, in its defence, further argued that to sustain the ground of "technology effect," in its allegations, the European Community had not presented

---

[338]Para 4.114 of the Panel report The European Communities claims that NASA provides goods and services, within the meaning of Article 1.1(a) (1) (iii) or the SCM Agreement, to Boeing for LCA-related research and that NASA receives less than adequate remuneration for the goods or services it provides, which results in a benefit to Boeing's LCA division within the meaning of article 1.1(b) of the SCM Agreement.

[339]WT/DS353/R, para 2.1 Panel report. This dispute concerns various **alleged prohibited and actionable subsidies** provided to and benefiting the United States producers of large civil aircraft (the U.S. LCA industry) including, in particular, the Boeing company and Mc-Donnell Douglas Corporation prior to its merger with Boeing.

[340]Para 2.1 (ii) Subsidies provided by the federal government. The European Communities allege that the US Federal Government transfers economic resources to the U.S. LCA, industry on terms more favourable than are available on the markets or not at arm's length through certain measures applied by NASA;DOD; DOC; DOL and through certain federal tax incentives.

[341]Para 3.1(b) (ii) *United States-Measures Affecting Trade in Large Civil Aircraft, WT*/DS353/R (report of the panel).

[342]See para 4.39 The European Communities also submits that, the Panel consider the road and port improvements themselves to be general infrastructure, in the alternative, the rights given to Boeing in connection with road and port improvements constitute the provision of goods and services other than general infrastructure within the meaning of Article 1.1(a) (1) (iii) of the SCM Agreement. These rights were provided only to Boeing, and they give Boeing legal certainty with respect to elements of the road and port improvements that are important to the operation of its production facility and that could otherwise result in economic losses. Thus they provide a benefit to Boeing that is not available on the market.

any convincing reason to believe that Boeing could not have developed the 787 model, in such a short time without the technological support of NASA.[343]

The Panel's Decision

In reply to the question of the purchase of services, the Panel fragmented the approach adopted by the EC/EU and stated that, as the Boeing was using NASA's R&D mainly for its own benefit, therefore, it was not a purchase of services by the government as claimed by the EC/EU. On the other hand, the panel also added that the use of facilities, equipment, and employees provided to Boeing through R&D contacts constituted goods or services within the meaning Article 1.1(a) (1) (iii) of the SCM Agreement.[344]

Appeal by the US (at Variance with Panel's Findings)

The US, in its appeal, stated that the Panel's findings seemed to violate Article 12.7 of the DSU as the discussion in this case was specific to financial contribution in the form of payments.[345] With regard to the issue of "government's purchase of services" the US was not fully in agreement with the Panel's interpretation and conclusions.

Moreover, apart from the above mentioned issue, the US was not in agreement with the Panel's findings that NASA R&D was principally for the benefit and use of Boeing. It rather perceived critically, the Panel's estimate of subsidy as too general to be specific.

In contrast to the US claims, the EU appealed against the Panel's findings that Article 1.1(a) (1) (iii) of the SCM excludes from its scope transactions properly characterized as "**purchase of services**" even if those transactions includes "**direct transfer of funds**."[346] The second question pertaining to the trade subsidies that the EU appealed was the Panel's non acceptance of the cumulative effect of the B&O

[343]Para 4.371 (The European Communities could not point to any evidence that any of the R&D programmes that it claimed benefitted the 787 were specific for 787). The European Communities argued that general research on technologies provided "learning" that Boeing drew upon in its applied research for the 787. Boeing explained that ....as a theoretical matter, foundational research such as the NASA conducts, does not create particular technologies or products because it is too far removed from the development stage. The United States submitted that BCA, (Boeing Commercial Aeroplanes) had ample cash to finance R&D, and Boeing had unconstrained access to capital markets. Therefore, United States did not need alleged subsidies to fund its commercial operations. The US further added that Boeing was able to bring 787 to the market sooner than Airbus's competitive version of A350 because it started manufacturing it earlier. Therefore, the alleged subsidy had nothing to do with its decision to move forward with the 787.

[344]See para 7.1027 of the Panel report for detail reference.

[345]Article 12.7 of the DSU Where the parties to the dispute have failed to develop a mutually satisfactory solution, (the Panel shall be the DSB) in such cases the report of the Panel shall set out the findings of fact, the applicability of relevant provisions and the basic rationale behind any findings and recommendations that it makes. Where a settlement of the matter among the parties to the dispute has been found, the report shall be confined to a brief description of the case and to reporting that a solution has been reached.

[346]For detail reference, see para 54 and 56 of the WT/DS353/AB/R.

tax rate reductions along with the effects of the aeronautical R&D subsidies in the 200–300 seat LCA market. The other related issue that the EU appealed for reversal, was the Panel's findings that the USDOD-RDT&E programmes were not causing the same effects as the other aeronautics R&D subsidies.[347]

Decision of the Appellate Body

With regard to the decision given by the Panel,[348] that NASA procurement contacts and USDOD assistance instruments were not purchase of services in the sense of making a financial contribution,[349] the Appellate Body differed and acknowledged that the question concerning "purchase of services" was an interpretative issue. Nevertheless, the A.B without giving any specific legal opinion declared the decision given by the Panel on this matter to be moot and of no legal effect.[350] Furthermore, the A.B attempted to draw a parallel between the NASA procurement contracts and USDOD assistance instruments. According to the findings of the A.B, the payment and access to facilities, equipment's and employees provided to Boeing under the NASA procurement contract constituted a financial contribution, in a similar way to the payments and access to facilities provided to Boeing, under the USDOD assistance instruments at issue, as these measures were part of a joint venture.[351] In relation to the tax issues, the A.B affirmed the Panel's findings that lowering of B&O tax rate, by the state of Washington was similar to the revenue foregone, hence, a form of financial contribution within the meaning of Article 1.1 (a)(1)(ii) of the SCM Agreement.[352] With regard to the claims made by the US, that

---

[347]For detail reference, see *United States-Measures Affecting Trade in Large Civil Aircraft*, WT/DS353/AB/R, para 68.

[348]See WT/DS353/R, para 7.1027. For the reasons given above, the Panel considers that the question of whether or not a transaction is properly characterized as a purchase of services depends upon whether or not the work performed was principally for the benefit or use of the government (or unrelated third parties), or rather principally for the benefit or use of the government (or unrelated third parties), or rather principally for the benefit or use of the 'service' 'seller' itself......While NASA's aeronautics R&D contracts take the form of a governmental procurement of services, the totality of the evidence before the Panel leads to the conclusion that the substance of these transactions cannot be properly characterized as a purchase of services for the purpose of Article 1.1(a)(1) of the SCM Agreement. Also see WT/DS353/R, para 7.1038.

[349]For detail reference, see WT/DS353/A.B/R, para 587.

[350]Para 620 The Panel in this dispute interpreted the omission of the term "services" from the second sub-clause of subparagraph (iii) as an indication that the drafters of the SCM Agreement did not intend measures constituting government purchase of services to be covered as financial contributions under Article 1.1(a)(1)(i). This interpretative issue does not need to be resolved by us because it is not relevant for purposes of resolving the disputes before us, that is, whether the NASA procurement contracts and USDOD assistance instruments, which we have found to resemble joint ventures constitute financial contributions within the meaning of Article 1.1(a)(1) of the SCM Agreement. We therefore declare the Panel's interpretation that "transaction properly characterized as purchases of services are excluded from the scope of Article 1.1 (a) (1) (i) of the SCM Agreement."

[351]For detail reference, see WT/DS353/A.B/R, para 625.

[352]See WT/DS353/AB/R, para 831.

the Panel had erred by quantifying the valuation of the total benefits conferred by NASA, covering not only LCA related research, but other transactions that the EC had not brought before, and considering the objectives of the SCM Agreement, the A.B stated that "a precise, definitive quantification of the subsidy was not required for the purpose of serious prejudice analysis",[353] and the amount stated by the Panel could be taken as an estimated amount only[354] On this ground, the A.B accepted the claims to review, on the findings made by the Panel, as those findings were based on erroneous amount.[355]

The Airbus Dispute and Stretching the Issue of Subsidy In this case, the question of subsidies is not confined to the general state support, but also includes the federal support intertwined with corresponding local support measures. Through comparative study, it gives the impression that such support measures are acting as subsidies in an ostensible manner. Based on the EU's above mentioned reasoning, it is quite fitting to estimate that the purchase of services is not excluded under Article 1.1(a) (1) (iii), although not mentioned explicitly. Further, based on the arguments put forward, it is not unreasonable to estimate that the direct transfer of funds, provisions of goods and services, pursuant to NASA R&D contracts for the Boeing company are *financial contributions* within the meaning of Article 1.1 (a)(1). As a legal mechanism in support of such aid, undoubtedly, there is an exception within the regulatory provisions, in favour of giving subsidies that makes the application of subsidies permissible for the civil aircraft industry, to a certain extent. The exemption clause makes the scope for royalty-based financing for civil aircrafts and further relaxations in the case of the inability to repay because of fewer sales than forecasted.[356]

However, the facts of the Airbus-Boeing dispute reveals new forms of subsidies and state support, which may not be coordinated but are in the form of multiple subsidies, apparently beyond the scope of the exemption clause. This raises questions concerning the justification for various forms of supports, relaxation and other potential forms of subsidies that are given exemption. In practice, providing a basic infrastructure is justified under the category of state-aid, ironically, to what extent it may be given remains an unresolved issue between the parties.

Finally, the A.B upholding the decision of the Panel affirmed that Launch-aid provided by the mentioned members of the E.U/EC countries were subsidies in a principal form, crossing the justifiable limits and affecting the basic free trade objectives of the WTO. After going through the detailed discussions, that were

[353]See WT/DS353/AB/R, para 697.

[354]See WT/DS353/AB/R, para 700.

[355]See WT/DS353/AB/R, para 700 and para 723.

[356]Article 6.1 (d) **deals with direct remission of debt, i.e., remission of government-held debt, and grants to cover debt repayment.** ***Footnote*** (Members recognize that where royalty-based financing for civil aircraft programme is not being fully repaid due to the level of actual sale falling below the level of forecast sales, this does not in itself constitute serious prejudice for the purpose of this paragraph).

made by the Panel and Appellate Body on this issue, the suggestion is that some new provisions in the ASCM may be added, from the market competition perspective, which may cover and regulate the state support in the form of Launch-aid.

2.11 Conclusions

Following the debate on the trading systems, from the times preceding the creation of the WTO to its formation and until today, it seems the categorical exclusion of subsidies in any form of trading system is a remote possibility. It is also clear that subsidies and state-aid in the lack of proper balance between fair trade and free trade objectives affects competition in international trade. On the other hand, one needs to take into account the facts that there are occasions when subsidies and state-aids may be necessary, such as for welfare and development. The regulatory limitations in the present SCM Agreement can be drawn based on the restrictive provisions. Probably, these provisions are the measures to create balance between free trade and the fair trade regulatory mechanism.

Justifiable subsidies and non-justifiable subsidies that are part of actionable subsidies as classified in this chapter, have some common features, as both are provided by the state. In the wake of common grounds and the policy supports, it is highly possible that justifiable subsidies, which later may take the form of non–justifiable subsidies, are used to promote exports that are objectionable under the SCM Agreement. Ironically, through the SCM Agreement in its present form, it is difficult to overcome the obscurity between justifiable subsidies and non-justifiable subsidies.

The issue of subsidies arises at various levels and it becomes even-more intriguing in the cases where provinces within a nation provide support to promote trade in one form or the other. This form of state support can be seen in the Airbus case.

The SCM Agreement classifies subsidies mainly into prohibited and actionable subsidies. Within these regulating provisions, there are flexibilities, so that every situation can be seen from its own perspective and the DSB can also apply some discretion. In order to avoid Member States taking advantage of the gaps existing in the provisions, some legal checks and balances are provided by the ASCM; for example, Annex VI, provides procedures for on the spot investigation. It is also obligatory for the legislative bodies of the Member States, to follow justifiable reasoning for the granting of flexibilities under the enacted provisions. The primary and secondary rules framed by the Member States should be in line with the of trade liberalisation policies.

The critics of the WTO raise their concern about the sovereign values of domestic policies, but one cannot ignore the treaty obligations under the WTO which is part of international law.

However, considering the fundamental economic realities, it cannot be denied that there is a need for subsidies, but they have to be allocated in a disciplinary manner and with the WTO as an institution acting as a control mechanism. Those favouring the idea of free trade, have always criticised subsidies as a means of government control that eventually affect fair competition. Certainly, there is some truth in this argument but the economic logic behind the government interference also cannot be ignored. When the market fails, policy instruments are deployed to correct the distortions. Therefore, subsidies can be considered as a tool to correct market distortions. Government intervention in the case of negative externalities is also justified, such as in the case of pollution, over-production, etc.

The main point of contention, i.e., export subsidies, still remains a matter of continuing discussion. As already mentioned in the text, subsidies improve the relative business position of the exporting nations. There is a need to think constructively and objectively about the reasons behind these relaxations, both in the case of Developing and Developed nations. A relevant point for this argument is that the WTO has not declared the criteria for determining the status of a nation as a Developing country. A Member State declares the status of its own free choice.

Another reason for unequal market possibilities is that the market size of some of the Developing countries is relatively large and some of them have attained significant industrial capability too. The subsidy for exports and for building the infrastructure has a different meaning in the Less-Developed countries than in the Developing countries such as China, India, Brazil, and several other states that are in the same line. The WTO lacks any strict criteria to keep evaluating the economic conditions, therefore, the relaxation provided in the WTO Agreements are manipulated for favourable terms of trade.

Comparing the WTO objectives of welfare and development with the free trade obligations, there is a possibility of strain between the two. In the light of these circumstances, one suggestion is that the principles of free trade along with fair trade should go together.

With the gradual adoption of globalisation as a trend, people have undoubtedly become outward-looking, but one cannot ignore the ethics and principles that have laid the foundation for the socio-economic and political structure of the nations.

Furthermore, within the WTO, there is no such term determining "state-aid" or any provision that creates a distinction between state-aid and a subsidy. Therefore, the issue of subsidies needs to be analysed based on the relative economic situation. Assessing the SCM Agreement, in the context of free trade and development objectives, one can say that it is an approach for prescribing trade guidelines, in order to create coherence between market efficiency and fair opportunities to trade to cover economic, political, social and several other types of objectives, for all types of Member States in the international trading system.

References

Barnard C (2010) The substantive law of the EU: the four freedoms. Oxford University Press, New York

Beinhocker E (2007) The origin of wealth: evolution complexity and radical remaking of economics. Harvard Business Press, Boston

Benitah M (2001) The law of subsidies under the GATT/WTO system. Kluwer Law International, London

Beseler JF, Williams AN (1986) Anti-dumping and anti-subsidy law: the European communities. Sweet & Maxwell, London
Biondi A, Eeckhout P, Flynn J (2004) The law of state aid in the European Union. Oxford University Press, New York
Blair RD, Kenny LW (1987) Microeconomics with business applicatioins. Willy, New York
Bossche PV (2008) The law and policy of the World Trade Organization. Cambridge University Press, Cambridge
Carbaugh RJ, Olienyk J (2004) Boeing-Airbus case, a sequel. Glob Econ J 4(2):1–5
Collie DR (2006) Tariffs and subsidies under asymmetric oligopoly, Ad valorem versus specific instruments. The Manchester School Blackwell Publishing Ltd, 74 (3), pp 314–333
Cosbey A, Mavroidis PC (2014) A Turquoise mess: green subsidies, blue industrial policy and renewable energy: the case for redrafting the subsidies agreement of the WTO. J Int Econ Law 17(1):11–47
Evans A (1997) European Community Law of state aid. Oxford University Press, New York
Footer ME (2006) An institutional and normative analysis of the World Trade Orgainization. Martinus Nijhoff, Leiden
Funta R (2009) EC law on state aid legal framework, case law and the story in the Alitalia State Loan Case. J Law Technol 3(2):311–323. http://mujlt.law.muni.cz/view
Hart CA (1994) The European Community's Value-Added Tax system: analysis of the new transition regime and prospects for further harmonization. Berkley J Int Law 12(1):3–40
Herdegen M (2003) Principles of international economic law. Oxford University Press, Oxford
Hoda A, Ahuja R (2005) Agreement on subsidies and countervailing measures: need for clarification and improvement. J World Trade 39(6):1012–1015
Hoecke MV (2002) Law as communication. Hart, Oregon
Lester S (2011) The problem of subsidies as a means of protectionism: lessons from the WTO EC-Aircraft Case. Melbourne J Int Law 12(1)
Litvak U (1995) Regional integration and the dispute resolution system of the World Trade Organization after the Uruguay Round: a proposal for the future. Univ Miami Inter-Am Law Rev 26(3/6):571–578
Macrory P, Appleton AE, Plummer MG (eds) (2005) The World Trade Organization: legal economic & political analysis, vol I. Springer, New York
Matsushita M, Schoenbaun TJ, Mavroidis PC (2003) The World Trade Organization: law practice and policy. Oxford University Press, Oxford
Krugman P, Obstfed M (2009) International economics: theory and policy. Pearson Addison Wesley, Boston
Romano PR (2009) The sword and the scales: the United States and International Courts and Tribunals. Cambridge University Press, New York
Luca R (2009) The definition of subsidy and state aid: WTO and EC law in comparative perspective. Oxford University Press, New York
Salvatore D (1987) The new protectionist threat to world welfare. Elsevier Science Publishing Co, Inc., New York
Segal IR (1998) Monopoly and soft budget constraint. RAND J Econ 29(3):596–609
Slotboom MM (2002) Subsidies in WTO and in EC law broad and narrow definitions. J World Trade 36(3):517–542
Spencer BJ (1988) Countervailing duty laws and subsidies to imperfectly competitive industries. University of Chicago Press. ISBN:0-226-03608-1. http://www.nber.org/books/bald88-1
Stewart TP (1993) The GATT Uruguay Round: a negotiating. History (1986–1992) Volume La: Commentary. The Kluwer Law and Taxation Publishers, Netherlands
Stewart TP (1999) The GATT Uruguay Round a negotiating history (1986-1994) Volume IV: The End Game (Part I). Kluwer Law International, The Hague
Sykes A (1989) Countervailing duty law, an economic perspective. Columbia Law Rev 89 (2):203–210
Sykes AO (2010) The questionable case for subsidies regulation: a comparative perspective. J Legal Anal 2(2):474–476
Taylor OH (1960) A history of economic thought. Mc Graw-Hill Book Co, INC, USA

Trebilock MJ, Howse R (2002) The regulation of international trade. Routledge, New York
Wouters J, Coppens D (2006) International economic policy-making: exploring the legal linkages between the World Trade Orgainization and the Bretton Woods Institutions. Int Organ Law Rev 3(2)

Cases

Banks v British Coal and Secretary of State [2001] ECR I-6117.C-390/98
Belgium v Commission [1986] ECR 2263. C-234/84
Brazil-Export Financing Programme for Aircraft WT/DS46/R
Brazil-Export Financing Programme for Aircraft WT/DS46/AB/R
Brazil-Measures Affecting Desiccated Coconut WT/DS22/R
Canada Measures Affecting the Export of Civilian Aircraft WT/DS70/AB/R
Canada-Certain Measures Affecting the Automative Industry WT/DS139/AB/R
Canada-Certain Measures Affecting the Renewable Energy Generation Sector WT/DS412/AB/R
Canada-M easures Relating to the Feed-In Tariff Program WT/DS426/AB/R
Canada-Measures Affecting the Export of Civilian Aircraft WT/DS70/R
Canada-Measures Affecting the Importation of Milk and the Exportation of Dairy Products WT/DS103/AB/RW2 WT/DS113/AB/RW2
EEC Seed Crushers and Oil Processors Federation v Commission of the European Communities Case 188/85
European Commission v EDFC 124/10[2012]ECR I-0000.EDF
European Communities and Certain Member States-Measures Affecting Trade in Large Civil Aircraft WT/DS316/R
European Communities And Certain Member-States-Measures Affecting Trade in Large Civil Aircraft WT/DS316/AB/R
Federation Nationale du Commerce Exterieur des Produits Alimentaires and Syndicat National des Negociants et Trsnsformateurs de Saumon v French Republic [1991] ECR1-5505. C-354/90, FNCE
FEDIOL v Commission [1988]ECR 4193
Italy v Commision [1999] ECR I-02981C-6/97
Preussen Elektra AG v Schhleswag AG [2001] EUECJ
United States Imposition of Countervailing Duties on Certain Hot-Rolled Lead and Bismuth Carbon Steel Products Originating in the United Kingdom WT/DS138/AB/R
United States-Subsidies on Upland Cotton WT/DS267/AB/R
United States-Countervailing Measures Concerning Certain Products from the European Communities WT/DS212/AB/R
United States-Final Countervailing Duty Determination with Respect to Certain Softwood Lumber from Canada WT/DS257/AB/R
United States-Imposition of Countervailing Duties on Certain Hot-Rolled Lead and Bismuth Carbon Steel Products Originating in France; Germany and United Kingdom SCM/185
United States-Measure Treating Exports Restraint as Subsidies WT/DS194/R
United States-Measures Affecting Trade In Large Civil Aircraft (second complaint) WT/DS353/AB/R
United States-Measures Affecting Trade in Large Civil Aircraft WT/DS353/R
United States-Measures Treating Exports Restraint as Subsidies WT/DS194/R
United States-Tax Treatment for Foreign Sales Corporation WT/DS108/AB/RW
United States-Tax Treatment for Foreign Sales Corporation WT/DS108/R
United States-Tax Treatment for Foreign Sales Corporations WT/DS108/AB/R
US-Countervailing Duty Investigation on DRAMS WT/DS296AB/R
US-Export Restraint WT/DS194/R

Reports and Electronic Sources

Aguayo F, Gallagher KP (2005, December) Preserving policy space for sustainable development. International Institute for Sustainable Development, Canada. www.iisd.ca

Blauberger M, Rike K (2010) European Competition vs Global Competitiveness: transferring EU rules on state aid and public procurement beyond Europe, Centre for Competition Policy. University of East Anglia

Brumbaugh DL (2004) A history of the Extraterritorial Income (ETI) and Foreign Sales Corporation (FSC) Export Tax benefit Controversy. CRS Report for Congress. http://www.taxhistory.org/thp/readings.nsfcf7

Chad PB, Crowley MA, McCulloch R, Nakajima DJ (2005) The U.S trade defecit made in China. www.chicagofed.org/.../2005/ep _4qtr2005_part1

Das DK., Hong Kong Ministerial of Doha Round of Multilateral Trade Negotiations: achieving a low-level equilibrium. http://www.cid.harvard.edu/cidtrade/Papers/das-Ile.pdf

Goldberg M (2000, July) Federal energy subsidies not all technologies created equal. REPP Research report. No. 11. https://earthtrack.net/content/federal-energy-subsidies-not-all-technologies-are-created-equal

Murphy S, Chatterjee B (2013, December) The issue of public stockholding in the WTO: Trade and Food Security CUTS International, Jaipur, International Food & Agricultural Trade. ICTSD.§. http://e15initiative.org/wp-content/uploads/2014/12/E15 Agriculture Chatterjee MurphyFINAL.pdf

Nanto D, Jackson JK, Morrision WM (2005, June 23) China and CNOOC Bid for Unocal. Foreign Affairs, Defense and Trade Congressial Research Service Library. CRS report for Congress. http://www.hsdl.org/?view&did=460852

Tangermann S (2014, December) Post Bali issues in agricultural trade: a synthesis. OECD Global Forum on Agriculture, Paris. https://www.oecd.org/tad/events/AL-Tangermann.pdf

Thomas JR (2001) Collusion and collective action in the patent system: a proposal for patent bounties. http://scholarship.law.georgetown.edu/facpub/306

Riess A (2006) EIB Papers European Investment Bank, vol 11, no 2. http://www.eib.org/attachements/efs/eibpapers/eibpapers_2006_v11_n02_en.pdf

World Trade Report (2006) Exploring the links between subsidies, trade and the WTO. http://www.wto.org/english/res_e/publications_e/wtr06_e.htm

World Trade Report (2007) www.wto.org

Chapter 3
Discussing Agriculture Subsidies; from the WTO Perspective

Abstract Subsidies in the agriculture sector, either from industrialised economies, or its unregulated use in the farm sector by the emerging economies, creates inconsistencies in the agreed trading approach to achieve the objectives of the WTO (Objectives as mentioned in the preamble of the WTO). These objectives, enshrined in the preamble of the WTO declaration are also supported by the underlying principles of fairness, equity, distribution of resources, and creating reasonable trading opportunities for all the Member States, classified as Developed, Developing and Less-Developed countries (The key objectives to promote welfare and development are as: 'economic endeavor should be conducted with a view to raising standards of living,' 'recognizing the need for positive efforts to secure the share of growth in international trade of the Developing and Less Developed countries' as inscribed in the preamble). Ironically, the promotion of free trade market policies, also concerned with the liberalisation of agricultural trade, on a phase by phase basis, for some reasons takes a narrow approach and often become restricted to trade bargains. The Agreement on Agriculture, (AoA, here after) in the context of the WTO's trading principles is an attempt to limit the use of agricultural subsidies, mainly by the industrially advanced countries of the WTO. Whenever, discussions from the trade liberalisation policy perspectives are held, usually they get interfaced with fair trade approach, and in this concern, agricultural subsidies provided by the Developed nation is contended as an issue of trade distortion. Such measures adopted by the developed countries indeed reduces the export opportunities of the Developing and Less-Developed countries, creating an opposing trend for the development of the comparative cost advantage and welfare of the Developing and Less-Developed countries.

The political economy approach towards free trade, also leads the discussion in the matters of agricultural subsidies from the view point out of the others, as a specific set of government obligations towards the farming class, irrespective of the Developed and Developing/Less-Developing countries. Therefore, taking into account the basic objectives expressed in the AoA, i.e., to establish a free market oriented agricultural trading system, in order to promote possibility for development and the creation of market opportunities in equitable way for the Member States, the study in this chapter tries to analyse the contradictions that emerges, when despite the promise to reduce subsidies, the Developed countries, on the contrary, maintain their agricultural support level. In comparison to this, the governments in the Less-Developed countries have meagre incentives to invest in

G. Singh, *Subsidies in the Context of the WTO's Free Trade System*,
DOI 10.1007/978-3-319-62422-8_3

their agriculture sector. This makes the case complex, as for the Less-Developed countries the agricultural subsidies are a matter of necessity, while, for the Developed countries; they are, a matter of trade advantage. The AoA attempts to promote the idea that free trade along with the objectives of welfare and development go side by side, but how far the balance between the two agendas can be maintained, is something to be examined in this study.

3.1 Free Trade Versus Subsidies for the Agricultural Sector

Nations turning to the system of free trade and through it searching for methods of technological advancement, and on a parallel basis also realising the need for economic stability, have brought the subject of agricultural trade within the domain of WTO framework. As an inclusive subject of the WTO system, farm products are modelled as part of the free trading system, mainly by applying two policy measures. (1) Reducing cross border restrictions on trade in agriculture products. The reduction of tariffs and market access commitments mentioned in Article 4,[1] of the Agreement on Agriculture and market access through tariff reduction by Member States, was discussed at length in the case of the **Chile-Price Band System and Safeguard Measures Relating to Certain Agricultural Products,**[2]

[1]AoA, Article 4 clause (1) Market access concessions, contained in Schedules relate to bindings and reductions of tariffs, and to other market access commitments as specified therein. (2) Members shall not maintain, resort to, or revert to any measures of the kind which have been required to be converted into ordinary custom duties, except as otherwise provided for in Article 5 and Annex 5.

[2]WT/DS207/AB/R, para 187.With these considerations in mind, we turn now to Chile's contention that Article 4.2 of the Agreement on Agriculture "is not a specific or more detailed way of addressing the prohibition against exceeding tariff bindings under Article II: 1(b) of the GATT. Our consideration of this argument requires a comparison of the two provisions in these two covered agreements. Article 4.1 of the Agreement on Agriculture explains that market access concessions for agricultural products relate to tariff bindings and to reduction of tariffs, as well as to other market access commitments that can be found in Member's Schedules. Article 4.2 requires Members not to maintain "any measure of the kind which have been required to be converted into ordinary custom duties," and provides an illustrative list of measures other than ordinary custom duties. Article 4.2 prevents WTO Members from circumventing their commitments on "ordinary customs duties" by prohibiting them from "maintaining, reverting to, or resorting to" measures other than "ordinary customs duties." The first sentence of Article II: 1(b) of the GATT 1994 also deals with ordinary customs duties, by requiring Members not to impose ordinary customs duties in excess of those recorded in their Schedules. Thus, the obligations in Article 4.2 of the Agreement on Agriculture and those in the first sentence of Article II: 1(b) of the GATT both deal with "ordinary customs duties" and market access for imported products. See para 200, we turn now to Article 4, the provision of Part III of the Agreement on Agriculture. Article 4 deals with "Market Access." During the course of the Uruguay Round, negotiators identified certain border measures which have in common that they restrict the volume or distort the price of imports of agricultural products. The negotiators decided that these border measures should be converted into ordinary custom duties. As ordinary customs duties are more transparent and more easily

and (2) reducing the domestic support, such as agricultural subsidies. Subsidies for the purpose of Agriculture are discussed under the AoA and are specific in terms of policy guidelines. In order to draw the limits between the SCM Agreement and the AoA, it is worth referring here to the fact that the emphasis through the scope of this Agreement, is at different levels, however, it has some common features. In the SCM Agreement, the prohibition on subsidies under Article 3,[3] are applied with exception to such state support covered under the AoA. With the objective of making trade in agricultural goods part of a global trading system, the AoA provision stipulates a reduction in such state support as mentioned in the Schedule of Commitments of the Member States.[4]

The AoA covers both, the subsidisation of sales in domestic markets and for exports. In the light of the WTO objectives and considering price volatility in the market and the need for food security, the use of subsidies in the agricultural sector can also be categorised as justifiable and non-justifiable, both for the Developed Member States and Developing Member States. The distinction between justifiable and non-justifiable state support can often be slim and while framing policies it is noteworthy to bear in mind the characteristics of such support, as a slight margin can lead to either side of legal parameter. The agricultural policies of the Developing nations are vastly different from those of the industrialised nations.[5]

The WTO has adopted AoA with the objectives such as *i) to establish a basis for initiating a process of reform in agricultural trade ii) a long term goal to reduce agricultural support and protection sustained over an agreed period of time iii) achieving binding commitments in the areas of market access,*[6] *domestic*

---

quantifiable than non-tariff barriers, they are also more easily compared between trading partners, and thus the maximum amount of such duties can be more easily reduced in future multilateral trade negotiations. The Uruguay Round negotiators agreed that market access would be improved-both in the short term and in the long term-through bindings and reductions of tariffs and minimum access requirements, which were to be recorded in Member's Schedule.

[3]SCM Agreement. Article 3.1 Except as provided in the Agreement on Agriculture, the following subsidies, within the meaning of Article 1 shall be prohibited.

[4]AoA, Article 3 Clause (1) The domestic support and export subsidy commitments in Part IV of each Member's Schedule constitute commitments limiting subsidization and are hereby made an integral part of GATT 1994.

Clause (2) Subject to the provision of Article 6, a Member shall not provide support in favour of domestic producers in excess of the commitments levels specified in Section I of Part IV of its Schedule.

Clause (3) Subject to the provisions of paragraphs 2(b) and 4 of Article 9, a Member Shall not provide export subsidies listed in paragraph 1 of Article 9 in respect of agricultural products or groups of products specified in Section II of Part IV of its Schedule in excess of the budgetary outlay and quantity commitment levels specified therein and shall not provide such subsidies in respect of any agricultural product not specified in that Section of its Schedule.

[5]Stewart (1993), p. 154.

[6]For reference, see www.wto.org. Market Access for goods in the WTO means, the conditions, tariff and non-tariff measures, agreed by members for the entry of specific goods into their markets. Tariff commitments for goods are set out in each member's schedule of concessions on

support,[7] *export competition.*[8] Member States expect, based on these objectives that the trading pattern in the agricultural goods among the Member States, will adopt and follow a market approach consistent with the free trade objectives of the WTO. With the objective of creating market opportunities for all the Member States, despite having diversity in economic system, market liberalisations policies for trade in agriculture products are complemented with the fair trade agendas as mentioned in the preamble of the AoA.[9] The main agendas are such as, *i) to establish a fair and market-oriented agricultural trading system, ii) in implementing their commitments on market access, Developed country Members would take fully into account the particular needs and conditions of Developing country, iii) that commitments under the reform programme should be made in an equitable way among all the Members, iv) Member States having regard to the agreement, that special and differential treatment for the Developing countries is an integral element of the negotiations, and shall, while adopting also take into account the possible negative effects of the implementation of the reform programme on Less-Developed and net food-importing countries.* While observing the discussions on agriculture trade, one can notice that there is a general level of consensus among the Developing nations that reform of the world agricultural trading system is essential. Paradoxically, agricultural exports from Developing to Developed countries are currently facing a multitude of tariff and non-barriers. Ironically, farming class everywhere seems to resist market liberalisation policies. Probably, this is due to the fact that the proliferation of free trade policies in the agricultural sector, on the same level as in the industrial sector, primarily checks state-support to a farming class, which however is quite often a necessity for the peasants and farmers.[10] The riddle for the WTO is that regulating state-support in the case of the industrial sector is presumed to promote efficiency and, fair-competition in the market, whereas the same measures when applied in the

---

goods. The schedules represent commitments not to apply tariffs above the listed rates-these rates are bound.

[7]For reference see, www.wto.org. The main conceptual consideration is that there are basically two categories of domestic support-support with no, or minimal, distortive effect on trade on the one hand (referred to as Green box) and trade distorting support on the other hand. (referred to as Amber box measures).

[8]For details see, the preamble of the Agreement on Agriculture, and Young. Issues papers 3 http://ageconsearch.umn.edu/handle/14573. The Export Competition Pillar of the agricultural negotiations includes direct export subsidies, export credits state trading enterprises and food aid.

[9]For details see, the preamble of the Agreement on Agriculture, and Young.

Issues papers 3. http://ageconsearch.umn.edu/handle/14573. The Export Competition Pillar of the agricultural negotiations includes direct export subsidies, export credits state trading enterprises and food aid.

[10]Since the Second World War, most governments even of the industrialized world have taken the view that agriculture is not like other areas of economic activity. It is special and merits special treatment to encourage, to assist and to protect it. For reference see, Nugent (1993), p. 337. First, if prices suddenly go up, inflation will be immediately fuelled. Second, if prices fall too low, farmers may not be able to make an adequate living and may be forced off the land.

agricultural sector are perceived as the denial of the necessary state support to farmers. Adoption and implementation of common free trade policies by the Member States, and on this basis, the regulation of internal market to attain the objectives of the WTO, also requires discrete analysis, based on social and political factors in addition to legal and economic factors. It is necessary to understand that the conceptual background for the development of agricultural and industrial sector differs. The trade liberalisation policy, in the case of the agricultural sector faces counterforces from the rudimentary level of any political system.

In the matters of the industrial sector, it is through competition and efficiency that market forces try to promote the qualities in production, which is complemented by enhancing the scope for efficient allocation of resources along with maximizing the benefits. With the promotion of a free trade market system, the outcome of such policies is manifested in the local market by a decrease in the prices of the products and a wide range of choices.

However, in matters concerning trade in agricultural products, between Developed countries and the other block consisting of the Developing and Less-Developed countries, one cannot expect the promised benefits. In most of the Developing and Less-Developed countries, the economic set up is such that it is mainly concerned with the transformation from an agricultural sector to an industrial sector on a phase by phase basis. The support through subsidy measures in this respect often helps in the development of the industrial sector and also maintaining some level of sustenance in the agriculture sector.[11]

3.1.1 Subsidies for Agriculture; A Crucial Issue for the Member States

Undoubtedly, the objectives of the Agreement on Agriculture are in line with the basic WTO objectives of free trade, however, they also demands normative flexibility from the Member States to adopt the new internal market set up. In the broader context, it can be said that scope needed to achieve the WTO objectives, through trade in agriculture goods, depends upon the extent of the consolidation of the free trade market system, meaning thereby the restrictive use of subsidies and also a balance being sustained between free trade market concepts and fair trade values.

Attaining a certain level of balance between free trade and fair trade objectives probably is a crucial issue and has remained a matter of discussion in the successive WTO conferences. Thus, in order to achieve this end, the Member States have agreed to work for attaining these long-term trade objectives, which are feasible through substantial progressive reductions in government support to agricultural

[11]Luca (2009), pp. 25–26.

trade,[12] such as price support[13] and equally to work for the reduction of protectionism, by reducing tariff measures over an agreed period of time.[14] The relevance of this approach for attaining the WTO objectives is explicable through the provisions of Article 20[15] of the WTO Agreement on Agriculture, which stipulates 'that the subsequent negotiations on trade in agricultural products will take into account inter alia, the experience to that date, from implementation of the reform programme agreed on in the Uruguay Round.'

The WTO in order to promote free trade, has outlined the objectives. *"The key to attaining this objective is substantial progressive reductions, in agricultural support and the sustained protection"* to both the farming and the industrial sector. However, it is noteworthy that the policy applications for the industrial sector and for the agricultural sector are seen from a different perspective by the Member States.

There are many substantive reasons for the state support in the area of agriculture that can be traced to the social and political structure of the Member States, and furthermore the choices concerning the factors. *The question of why state-support is necessary to the farmers, finally leads to the broader issues of farm subsidies.* The Agreement on Agriculture the 'AoA' concluded during the Uruguay Round, brought the discipline of agricultural subsidies into the WTO trading system, and eventually categorised the use of subsidies for agriculture as being, based on specific commitments.[16] Besides the commitments, two significant reasons that need to be explained for farm subsidies are (1) price volatility (2) food security.

---

[12]See Article 6 of the Agreement on Agriculture.

[13]AoA, Annex 2, clause 1(b), the support in question shall not have the effect of providing price support to producers. ***Price support:*** It is quite usual that governments of the nations intervene in one respect or the other in their agriculture market sector. The reasons they do so and the method adopted by them may vary. Governments of the Developing and Less-Developed country may intervene to keep the food prices artificially low. On the other hand, in the Developed countries because of the technological changes number of people working in farmland has decreased. Support from government allures people towards the farming sector. Another reason for government intervention is to sustain a confidence level in the market, in case of price volatility. There can be several other reasons also.

For details see, Agriculture Price Supports by Thompson (2nd edition). http://www.econlib.org/library/Enc1/AgriculturalPriceSupports.html.

[14]AoA Article 4 clause 1, Market Access concessions contained in Schedules relate to bindings and reductions of tariffs, and to other market access commitments as specified therein. Clause 2, Members shall not maintain, resort to or revert to any measures of kind which have been required to be converted into ordinary custom duties, except as otherwise provided for in Article 5 and Annex 5.

[15]Recognizing that the long-term objectives of the substantial progressive reductions in support and protection resulting in fundamental reform is an ongoing process, Members agree that negotiations for continuing the process will be initiated one year before the end of implementation period, taking into account (a) the experience to that date from implementing the reduction commitments, (b) the effects of the reduction commitments on world trade in agriculture, (c) - Non-trade concerns, special and differential treatment to Developing country Members and the objective to establish a fair and market-oriented agricultural trading system.

[16]Meléndez-Ortiz et al. (2009), p. 329.

3.1.1.1 Price Volatility

Volatility in a market, is a situation of a demand and supply dilemma and its affects on prices. In economic terms, volatility can be referred to as variations of market variables with the passage of time.[17] When talking about volatility in the context of trade in agricultural products, price volatility refers to fluctuations in prices of the agricultural products. Such fluctuations are a matter of serious concern when they cannot be anticipated, creating market uncertainty. Market uncertainty for a long duration creates unexpected risk for producers, traders, consumers, and governments. In order to check the negative consequences of such uncertainty, government interference through support can be necessary. Such government aid can be in the form of price support, subsidies or any administrative or legislative method for food security.[18] In terms of WTO free trade objectives, volatility in the global markets for agricultural products is more difficult to be projected precisely. Many governments as a remedial measure have a tendency to try and stabilise their domestic markets through various types of policy intervention measures, such as by export restrictions, or import restrictions. There is a possibility that such policies may create further instability in the international markets and restrict fluctuations of domestic markets from being absorbed in international markets. Adopting such like policies however shows the limitations to the free trade concept in handling the international trade of farm products through the WTO.[19]

3.1.1.2 Food Security

Free trade objectives also create responsibilities among the Member States to have better functioning agricultural markets and to create more opportunities, rather than trying to seclude oneself.[20] Member States acknowledged that if the challenge of food security is to be met, free trade can play a major part by marketing the production variables in an economical manner to producers. Whereas by adopting the means of insulation through tariff measures, it will reduce the efficiency and the production limit will remain dependent upon the confined sources. As a matter of constitutional responsibility,[21] Member States agree and often debate on the matter whether it is their right to protect their vulnerable populations from steep prices rise. In reality some countries lack the required measures to protect vulnerable populations from price fluctuations and the consequences. Food security is also a matter of constitutional responsibility, and some of the Member States have

---

[17]Wright (2011), pp. 44–52.

[18]PRICE VOLATILITY IN FOOD AND AGRICULTUE MARKETS: POLICY RESPONSES 2 June 2011. http://www.oecd.org/tad/agricultural-trade/48152638.pdf.

[19]Tangermann (2014), p. 6.

[20]Howse and Josling (2012), p. 2.

[21]Howse and Josling (2012), p. 7.

adopted schemes, such as cash transfer in lieu of subsidies[22] to support their populations living at the threshold level. However, these measures are often a matter of debate between subsidies and welfare measures, and the extent of limits for such policies.

3.2 The Agreement on Agriculture and the WTO Subsidies Agreement

The objectives of the WTO, such as welfare, development and creating market opportunity for trade among the Member States are based on common trading concepts, such as efficiency and fair trade regulatory measures, and these act as underlying concepts in most of the WTO Agreements.[23] When reading the AoA and in particular defining the scope of Agricultural subsidies, one inevitably needs to refer to the SCM Agreement, in order to link it with the broader contextual approach of the WTO objectives.

A subsidy as defined within the SCM Agreement is a general expression, of the various forms of state support in international trade, covering both the effects on private entrepreneurship and also on non-corporate economic groups and entities. The AoA does not define the term "subsidies" however; it states that export subsidies are those contingents upon export performance under Article 9.1 of the AoA.[24] In order to establish state support quantity, and the probable effects caused because of it, the AoA applies a general term, i.e., AMS, the Aggregate Measurement of Support.[25] As per the WTO trading system, Member States have different

[22](1) Japan has a large number of programmes to encourage and insure its domestic agricultural sector (agriculture insurance schemes) and also schemes to attract the youth to farming. (2) Brazil has the World's largest conditional cash-transfer scheme (Bolsa Familia) under the Zero Hunger Strategy. (3) India operates the largest public distribution system in the world. The government distributes subsidised food grains to a targeted population. On this basis India also operates large-scale employment scheme. For reference see, Chatterjee and Murphy (2013), p. 3.

[23]Trachtman (2008), p. 22.

[24]Article 9.1 The following export subsidies are subject to the reduction commitments (a) The provision by governments or their agencies of subsidies such as 'payments in kind,' to a firm, an industry, producers of an agricultural products, cooperative or other association of such producers, or marketing board. (for details, see the agreement) (b) The sale or disposal for export by governments or their agencies of non-commercial stocks of agricultural products at a price lower than comparable price charged for like product. (for details, see the agreement) (c) Payments on the export of an agricultural product financed by the virtue of governmental action, whether or not charge on public account is involved. (for details, see the agreement) (d) the provision of subsidies to reduce the costs of marketing exports of agricultural products. (for details, see the agreement) (e) Internal transport and freight charges on export shipments, provided or mandated by governments (for details see the agreement) (f) Subsidies on agriculture product contingent on their incorporation in exported products. (for details, see the agreement).

[25]For detail reference, see Article 1(a) and Article 6(1) of the AoA. Article 1(a) of the Agreement on Agriculture, 'Aggregate Measurement of Support' means the annual level of support, expressed

levels of concessions, the threshold level i.e., permissible/non-permissible levels, of state support. Further, the qualification limits are different for Developed, Developing/Less-Developed countries. Hence the calculations, for AMS are different for Developed and Developing/Less-Developed countries.

The main concern when including the Agreement on Agriculture was to considerably strengthen the free trade market rules, by restraining the use of subsidies for trade in agriculture, or agricultural products on a similar basis as the SCM Agreement does for the goods in general. The specific definition, of a subsidy, is mentioned in the SCM Agreement and in order to maintain consistency between the agreements is also applied in the case of trade in agricultural products.[26] Clarification has been made in this regard by the A.B in the case of the **US-FSC,**[27] that the basic interpretation of a subsidy is the same and a subsidy is mainly a matter of fiscal gains. For a discussion on this issue at the foundational level, and how the concept of agricultural subsidy is related to the main theme of subsidies dealing with international trade on a principle basis, the background discussions can also be referred to here. The description of subsidies as covered under the present SCM Agreement was introduced with the concept of 'specificity.' During the Uruguay Round, the inclusion of the term specificity, enabled financial contributions by governments to be linked with the benefits to the recipient and with the specific objectives, for which such measures were taken.

The term specificity mainly covers the procedural aspects with further conditions based classifications in order to make a distinction between (1) subsidy and subsidy like effect, (2) export based subsidies and subsidies for domestic markets (3) Industrial and Agricultural subsidies and further distinction, in case subsidies

in monetary terms, provided for an agricultural product in favour of the producers of basic agricultural product or non-product specific approach. (for details, see the agreement) (1) With respect to support provided during the base period (2) with respect to support provided during any year of the implementation period and thereafter, calculated in accordance with Annex 3.

[26]Article 21, Clause 1 of the Agreement on Agriculture "The provisions of GATT 1994 and of other Multilateral Trade Agreements in Annex 1A to the WTO Agreement shall apply subject to the provisions of this Agreement."

Article 3.1 of the SCM Agreement, dealing with the Prohibited subsidy, begins with a clause creating scope of exception for the Agreement on Agriculture. It states "Except as provided in the Agreement on Agriculture, the following subsidies within the meaning of Article 1, shall be prohibited."

[27]WT/DS108/AB/RW, para 194. We have rejected the United States appeal regarding the proper characterization of the measure under Article 3.1 (a) of the SCM Agreement. The Panel held, and we have upheld, that the measure involves the foregoing of revenues that are otherwise due under Article 1.1 (a) (ii) of the SCM Agreement. As we have indicated in *US-FSC*, where a government foregoes revenues that are otherwise due in relation to agricultural products, a subsidy may arise under the Agreement on Agriculture. The fiscal treatment of agricultural products, under the measure, is not materially different from the fiscal treatment of products falling within the scope of the SCM Agreement. Accordingly, we see no reason to reach any conclusion under the Agreement on Agriculture that differs from our conclusion under the SCM Agreement.

are intertwined.[28] Despite sharing a common ground of free trade with the SCM Agreement, there are some special features that distinguish the AoA. It is probably the difference in the specific concerns between the two agreements that has led to the further classification of subsidies for agriculture in- to three sub-categories.

3.3 The Approach for Agriculture Subsidies During GATT and the Need for Classification

The division of international trade into two criteria, industrial and agricultural products occurred during the GATT period itself. However, there was no specific definition of subsidies included in the GATT. A general description about subsidies was made in Article XVI of the GATT. Furthermore, subsidies for the purpose of agriculture lacked any specific reference, however a, rather loose description was made within the context of primary products.[29] The use of subsidies was permissible but there was a limit to it based on the extent of proportionate share to the world trade. The concept of proportionate share cannot be put into clear terms or in relation to the different objectives of the Member States. Member States, during the formative discussions of the WTO kept note of this lacunae, which eventually lead to the broad exposition of the specific objectives in the preamble of the AoA. Different approaches for both industrial market policy and agricultural trade policy were adopted by the two leading economies, the US and the EU/EC, both insisting on following two different policy lines.

[28]For reference see, World Trade Report (2006), Exploring the links between subsidies, trade and the WTO. p. xxxviii, www.wto.org.

[29]In the year 1955, GATT Article XVI paragraph 3 was added to create an exception for agricultural products. The provision states as follows: [T]he contracting parties should seek to avoid the use of subsidies on the export of **primary products**. If, however, a contracting party grants directly or indirectly any form of subsidy which operates to increase the export of any primary product from its territory, such subsidy shall not be applied in a manner which results in that contracting party having more than an equitable share of world export trade in that product, account being taken for the shares of the contracting parties in such trade in the products during a previous representative period, and any special factors which may have affected or be affecting such trade in products. The term **'primary product'** has the same definition as defined under Article 56 of the Havana Charter. Article 56 states **Primary and Related Commodities** (1) For the purposes of this Charter, the term 'primary commodity' means any product of farm, forest or fishery or any mineral, in its natural form or which has undergone such processing as is customarily required to prepare it for marketing in substantial volume in international trade. (2) The term shall also, for the purposes of this Chapter, cover a group of commodities of which one is primary commodity as defined in paragraph 1 and the others are commodities, which are so closely related, as regards the conditions of production or utilisation, for the other commodities in the group, that it is appropriate to deal with them in a single agreement.

US Agriculture Policy and GATT

When GATT was formed, the working party from the US, argued to gain for the US domestic agricultural support. The basis of such support was protection, an alternative to restrict an increase of imports into the US market.[30] The aim of this measure was to safeguard against the forthcoming challenges. In order to legally validate such possibility, the US insisted on including a provision that permitted the retention of quantitative import restrictions and finally such provision was added. Therefore, GATT Article XI: 2(c)[31] legalised the retention of Section 22 of the US Agriculture Adjustment Act of 1933 allowing quotas to be imposed.

EU/EC Agriculture Policy and GATT

The Treaty of Rome establishing the European Union[32] singled out the need for an agricultural policy.[33] The EEC with memories of wartime shortages of food grains needed to avoid such a vulnerable situation again and, decided on common responsibility, via CAP, among its Members. In order to put this into effect, policy framing or decision making guidelines were issued, such as (1) Major policy framing and decision making in the matters of agriculture should be made through CAP (2) There should be a consistent approach in the issues of the common market among the Members. GATT agreement was signed on 30th October 1947, with the market objectives that Member States would lower customs tariffs on a number of items. For testing the level of consistency with GATT objectives, the treaty establishing the EEC was submitted to GATT before its entry into force. In this regard a GATT working party was established in 1956 to examine the compatibility of the Treaty of Rome establishing the EEC, with Article XXIV[34] of the GATT.

Finally, after the approval from the working party, the Common Agriculture Policy was adopted by the EU based on the common market and the financial

---

[30]Macrory et al. (2005), p. 191.

[31]Article XI 2(c), Import restrictions on any agricultural or fisheries product, imported in any form, necessary to the enforcement of governmental measures which operate (1) to restrict the quantities of the like domestic product permitted to be marketed or produced (for detail reference, see the Article) (2) to remove a temporary surplus of the like domestic product (for detail reference, see the Article) (3) to restrict the quantities permitted to be produced of any animal product the production of which is directly dependent, wholly or mainly, on the imported commodity. (for detail reference, see the Article).

[32]By the Maastricht Treaty (formally known as the Treaty on European Union; 1991), which went into force on November1, 1993, the European Economic Community was renamed the European Community and was embedded into the EU as the first of its three pillars. The treaty also provided the foundation for an economic and monetary union which included the creation of a single currency, the Euro.

[33]The signing of the Treaties establishing the European Economic Community (EEC) and the European Atomic Energy Community (EAEC or Euratom) in Rome on 25th March 1957 marked a key stage in the history of European Integration.

[34]Article XXIV of the GATT creates some sort of relaxation, according to which parties are able to reduce their tariffs below the MFN level afforded to the other WTO members, even though such an action technically violates Article I of the GATT. Saggi and Yildiz. *Art XXIV of the GATT: Good, Bad, or Both*? *economics.ca/2004/papers/0241.pdf.*

commitments of the Member States. Along the same lines, the overall set-up of common prices, currency stability, and harmonisation of administrative, health and sanitary regulations were structured.[35] This created a system of its own, regulating industrial and agricultural trade. Later in 1958, the Conference of Stresa was held and some more substance was added[36] to strengthen the CAP objectives. In brief, it can be said that main pillar behind the strong CAP system is the variable import levy[37]and the export restitution payment.[38] These measures applied together, are intended to ensure market stability in the EU.

3.3.1 Agriculture Subsidies Can Be Classified in Three Categories Amber, Blue and Green Boxes: A General Discussion

During the early stages of GATT, the subject of agricultural subsidies was excluded from the restrictive provisions. The general opinion among the Member States was that agriculture was a unique sector of the economy and for the reasons of food security and market volatility could not be treated like other subject matters. Because of the underlying public interest, it also created a considerable political pressure concerning the fact that the agriculture sector needs to be protected from the system of international market that cover trade in industrial market. The probable reason for such an attitude can be that the agricultural producer is both the seller of his produce, as well as a buyer for further cultivation. Further, it is noteworthy, that the buying of the farmer's produce usually depends upon various dynamic market factors, which often requires internal regulations. An emerging change in attitude among the majority of nations was seen during the Dillon round (1960–1961).[39] It was during this round that as a preliminary measures, tariffs on

---

[35]Seaton, Nia. "EU Policy Update (EU 2013.04): Reform of Common Agricultural Policy (CAP)" National Assembly of Wales. p. 1. http://www.assemblywales.org/13-069.pdf.

[36]In July 1958, participants at the Stresa conference agreed three objectives for CAP. (1) to increase farm incomes. . .by a price support policy. (2) to contribute to overall growth by allowing specialization within the Community and eliminating market distortions, (3) preserving family farming and ensuring that structural and price policies go hand in hand.

[37]The variable levy is an import duty that varies based on the difference between the import price and administered threshold price. It limits the price suppressing effects, and, indirectly, the quantity, of imported commodities. An export levy applies to certain commodities if the world price is higher than the price in the European Community, ensuring that domestic stocks are not sold on the world market to the detriment of European consumers.

[38]The restitution payment is in effect an export subsidy, based on the difference between the world price and market price. Restitution payments ensure that Community farmers receive roughly the same proceeds from export sales as they would if they had sold the products within the Community.

For reference see, Stewart (1993), p. 147.

[39]Tancu (2010), p.7. http://pure.au.dk/portal/files/12176/mt84715_thesis.pdf.

products like Soya beans, cotton, vegetables and canned fruits were reduced. Finally, during the Uruguay Round (1986–1994), the agriculture sector was eventually brought to the GATT negotiation table. As a matter of fact, agricultural trade was accorded 'special treatment 'and was exempted from GATT general rules. On the basis of special treatment, special measures were allowed, such as quantitative import restrictions, otherwise not permissible for other commodities. In addition to creating scope for relaxations, the relevance of subsidies for agricultural purposes was also emphasized. The term equitable way included in the preamble to the AoA is also noteworthy for this discussion.

Noting that commitments under the reform programme should be made in an equitable way among all Member. . .countries.[40] The term *equitable way* imbibed in the AoA is used in the context of reform measures among all the Member States, whereas in the GATT agreement, the term was used for the application of subsidies by the Member States.

Finally, after the discussion rounds, when the WTO was formed, it enshrined the Agreement on Agriculture (AOA), with specific provisions, flexibly demarcating between exempt and non-exempt[41] use of agricultural subsidies for the multilateral trading system. The justifiable and non-justifiable uses of subsidies for the agricultural purposes are categorised based on national perspectives for establishing market structure in line with free trade objectives and simultaneously for applying fair trade measures in order to sustain some level of balance between the conflicting interests among the Member States. It is an agreed fact that excess of subsidies,

---

[40]See Preamble of the Agreement on Agriculture (1) Recalling that long term objective is to establish a fair and market-oriented agricultural trading system.... (2) Recalling that the above mentioned long-term objective is to provide for substantial progressive reductions in agricultural support and protection.... (3) Committed to achieving specific binding commitments in the areas: market access; domestic support; export competition.... (4) In implementing their commitments on market access, Developed country Members would take fully into account the needs and conditions of Developing country Members by providing for a greater improvement of opportunities and terms of access for agricultural products.... (5) Noting that commitments under the reform should be made in an equitable way among the Members, due regard shall be given to the non-trade concerns such as (a) food security (b) environment protection (c) special and deferential treatment for Developing countries (d) and considering the effects of reform on Least Developed countries. **Special Proposal has been forwarded by SIDS with respect to the present AoA** For reference see, G/Ag/NG/W/97 Proposal By Small Island Developing States, 'In the letter and spirit of this preamble, countries co-sponsoring this submission stress the need to draw specific attention to the constraints which impact negatively on Members capacities to achieve an equitable share in new market opportunities arising from the Uruguay Round. This submission highlight, in particular, the structural weakness that small island Developing countries face in their efforts to ensure that multilateral liberalization of the agricultural sector would improve their small share of international trade.'

[41]The term AMS [Aggregate Measurement of Support] is defined under Article 1clause (a) which covers exempt and non-exempt level of support. Aggregate Measurement of Support means the annual level of support, expressed in monetary terms, provided for an agricultural product in favour of the producers of the basic agricultural product or non-product specific support provided in favour of agricultural producers in general, other than support provided under programmes that qualify as exempt from reduction under Annex 2 to this Agreement.

even for agricultural purposes create trade distortion, so the accepted approach is allowing market access measures and market competition in order to promote efficiency. State support in the form of subsidies for agricultural purpose, is formally covered in the Agreement on Agriculture, and the scope for the justification of subsidies, and its ambit is substantially structured in the form of set rules and provisions.

Subsidies to the agriculture sector, cannot be classified into a singular type of objective, considering the classification of the Member States of the WTO. While talking about subsidies for the agricultural purposes, one need to keep in mind more specific needs and differences of purposes for their use such as, redistribution, income support, protection of the environment, and several other things that are unique to the agricultural sector, such as food security and rural development.[42] Objectives of the Member States may also vary based on the level of development. In several Developing countries, agricultural policy issues still revolves around the basic concerns, like food security, poverty alleviation, rural development, and stabilization of export revenues. In the Developed countries, the question of food self-sufficiency does exist, but increasing attention is being shown to food safety and environmentally sustainable farming.[43]

The AoA refers to the long term objectives of substantial progressive reductions, (1) in continuing agricultural support and (2) protection sustained over an agreed period of time. It is expected that the accomplishment of these objectives will result in correcting and preventing restrictions and distortions in world agriculture market.

What is crucial in the WTO context is the distinction between support that is considered less or non-trade distorting and distorting. Under the AoA, the most trade-distorting support, covered under 'Amber Box category' is subject to reduction commitment.[44]

How are agricultural subsidies market distorting? With respect to the promotion of a free trade market system, it is necessary to focus on three policy areas, (1) market access, (2) domestic support and (3) export competition.[45] Further, in order to obtain a natural equilibrium between demand and supply, reduction in tariffs for cross border trade is also essential in agricultural products. This naturally means that the domestic producers have to lower their prices/sell at a minimum profit, their agricultural products so as to compete with imported products. Such practices may cause temporary loss to the domestic producers. The possibility to cover the loss that domestic producers have to bear as a result of a surge in imports,

[42]For reference see, World Trade Report (2006). Exploring the links between subsidies, trade and the WTO. p.120,. www.wto.org.

[43]For reference see, World Trade Report (2006). Exploring the links between subsidies, trade and the WTO. p. 120, www.wto.org.

[44]For reference see, World Trade Report (2006). Exploring the links between subsidies, trade and the WTO. p. 123, www.wto.org.

[45]For reference see, World Trade Report (2006). Exploring the links between subsidies, trade and the WTO. p. 123, www.wto.org.

is in fact a redress by the government, either through the policy measures or by the means of monetary compensation to the farmers. In support of farmers and to compensate for the cost of production, governments organizes price support schemes through public and co-operative agencies.[46] Cases where there is a need for intervention in the market regulations due to the seriousness of the matter or in cases of urgency, governments can intervene on special requests by farmer's societies or any such bodies. As a government backing measure, the price support can be in the form of the minimum support prices and can also be given through procurement policies[47] in some countries. In the case of minimum support price, this is the price fixed by the government to protect the producer. It is often possible that the market price for an agricultural commodity falls below the declared price due to a bumper harvest or because of depression in the market, in that situation, according to the policy of minimum support price, government agencies purchases the entire quantity offered by the farmers at the declared minimum price.[48] This responding government support, compared from the perspective of the WTO objectives promoting free trade, can in a way turn out to be undue interference in the market. Such factors, if uncalled for, are inconsistent with the values of free trade, and are trade distorting.[49] A well-known maxim for this is *Bonum necessarium extra terminos necessitates non est bonum.* 'Necessary good is not good, beyond the bounds of necessity.'

Subsidies basically having an intangible character, their affects cannot be exactly assessed on the prospective basis; hence, attempting a substantive determination of subsidies, on the basis of provisions in the agreement, cannot cover all its features and objectives. Therefore, in order to establish the impact of farm subsidies on the basic objectives of the WTO, it is for the DSB to decide whether that form of state support fulfills the welfare and development criteria and provides reasonable support to the farmers or not. However, with the aim of achieving the WTO objectives, state support in the form of subsidies for the agricultural sector is classified into Amber, Blue, and Green boxes.[50] This is a general classification to draw a level of legal certainty, and is not based on any basic conceptual distinction.

---

[46]http://mospi.nic.in/mospi_new/upload/Manual-on-Agricultural-Prices-and-Marketing.pdf. p. 2.

[47]Procurement price of a commodity refers to the price at which government procures the commodity from producers/manufacturers for maintaining the buffer stock or the public distribution system. Procurement prices are fixed generally at a level which is somewhat higher than the level of minimum support prices but lower than the prevailing market prices. http://www.indiaagronet.com/indiaagronet/Agri_marketing/contents.

[48]http://www.indiaagronet.com/indiaagronet/Agri_marketing/contents.

[49]Khor (2003), p. 7.

[50]See, The WTO Agriculture Negotiations, "The issues, and where we are now" p.50. www.wto.org.

3.3.1.1 Amber Box[51]

With the promotion of trade liberalisation policies in the agricultural sector, the market factors and competing interests took a new form. The already existing all non-tariff barriers, that were an impediment for any import opportunity were to be eliminated or converted to the tariff measures. With an attempt to gradually undermine the scope of such protectionist measures, one of the methods adopted was introducing new policies, based on the free trade concepts. Further, progressing in the same line, a system of tariff-rate quotas was created. Introducing this new regulatory measure had the primary aim of broadening the market scope by increasing the existing import access levels in some products, and on the other hand providing certain level of access opportunities, by flexible tariffs that were not available earlier. This means lower tariffs within the quotas, and provision for higher rates for quantities outside the quotas.[52] Within the provisions, the scope was also created for defining the level between the two set of policies (free trade and restriction based quotas) by the judicial bodies, whenever so required.

In pursuance of the regulation of trade in agricultural products, and for the reduction of government support, through the parameters of the AoA, a quantified declaration of the existing support was required. With this aim, a provision requiring the declaration of support by a Member State is mentioned in Article 1(a)[53] and Article 1(h)[54] of the AoA. Declaration on the basis of the AMS[55] is an exposition of the existing level of support i.e., given before the formation of the WTO by any Member States. Included as provisions for the policy guidelines of the Member States, the introductory provision of Article 6 cl (1) emphasises the reduction of state support. "*The domestic support reduction commitments of each Member contained in Part IV of its Schedule shall apply to all of its domestic support*

[51] All domestic support measures considered to distort production and trade (with some exceptions) fall into the Amber box, defined in Article 6 of the Agriculture Agreement as do all domestic supports except those in the Blue and Green box.

[52] WTO Agriculture Negotiations. The issues, and where we are now. (Briefing document), p. 31. http://www.wto.org/english/tratop_e/agric_e/agnegs_bkgrnd_e.pdf.

[53] Article 1(a) "Aggregate Measurement of Support" and 'AMS' mean the annual level of support, expressed in monetary terms, provided for an agricultural product in favour of the producers of the basic agricultural product or non-product specific support provided in favour of agricultural producers in general other than support provided under programmes that qualify as exempt from reduction under Annex 2 to this Agreement (for details, see the Article).

[54] Article 1(h) Total Aggregate Measurement of Support, means the sum of all domestic support provided in favour of agricultural producers, calculated as the sum of all aggregate measurements of support for basic agricultural products, all non-product specific aggregate measurements of support and all equivalent measurements of support for agricultural products (for details , see the article).

[55] Current Total AMS is the sum of: All product-specific AMS and Non-product specific AMS. All product-specific AMS can be further categorized as (1) Market price support (2) Non-exempt direct payments (3) Other non-exempt measure. If the value of product-specific support or non-product-specific support does not exceed *de minimis* no need to cover it. Article 6.4.

measures in favour of agricultural producers, with the exception of the measures which are not subject to reduction in terms of criteria set out in this Article and in Annex 2 of this Agreement." This creates a substantive guideline, limiting access to state of support by implicitly classifying it as market distorting.[56] For the categorisation of state support, AMS is based on two features. (1) AMS is mainly linked with respect to the support provided during the base period.[57] (2) The calculation of AMS includes the support, subject to reduction commitments, on an annual basis and final amount provided during any year of the implementation period.[58] After making comparisons and the relevant data obtained, the subsidies leading to the trade distorting level can be classified as "Amber box" subsidies.[59] The AMS estimates also allow some assessment of the distribution of support, on specific commodity basis.[60]

Considering the core objectives of the WTO, Member States are expected to make a declaration of the existing level of support, first, in order to maintain transparency, a feature of fair trade value and secondly, also to check market distortion because of the state support and third for the purpose of promoting trade liberalisation policies for agriculture products. These trade distorting Amber

---

[56]Ingco and Nash (2004), p. 119.

[57]The data at the base period is an indicator for attaining knowledge with regards to trends in agricultural support and the extent of consistency followed by the Member States, with the set of obligations that are set through the WTO Agreement. Article1(a)(i) With respect to support provided during the base period, specified in the relevant tables of supporting material in-corporated by reference in Part IV of a Member's Schedule.

Member's commitments. The WTO negotiations produce general rules that apply to all Members, and specific commitments made by individual Member governments. The specific commitments are listed in documents called 'schedules of concessions,' which reflect specific tariff concessions and other commitments that they have given in the context trade negotiations, such as the Uruguay Round. For trade in goods in general, these usually consist of maximum tariff levels which are often referred to as 'bound tariffs' or bindings. (GATT Article II) In the case of agricultural products, these concessions and commitments also relate to tariff rate quotas, limits on export subsidies, and some kinds of domestic support. All WTO Members have a schedule of concessions which is either annexed to the Marrakesh Protocol to the GATT 1994 or to a Protocol of Accession. For detail reference see www.wto.org schedules of concessions on goods.

[58]Article1(a)(ii) With respect to support provided during any year of the implementation period and thereafter, calculated in accordance with the provisions of Annex 3 of this Agreement (Annex 3 of this agreement deals with Domestic Support: Calculation of Aggregate Measurement of Support).

[59]The Cairns Group's objective is to bring about liberalisation of global trade in agricultural produce. In particular, its members aim to abolish export subsidies and trade-distorting ("amber box") domestic support measures for agricultural products and seek to improve market access for exported agricultural goods. The coalition attempts to present a common front in multilateral trade negotiations at the World Trade Organization (WTO), tabling joint proposals and occasionally working with like-minded groups such as the G20 group of developing nations.

[60]For reference see, World Trade Report (2006). Exploring the links between subsidies, trade and the WTO. p. xxxii, www.wto.org.

box subsidies are subject to the reduction commitment under the schedule of commitments.[61]

During the GATT period and afterwards, the discussions on the reduction of agricultural subsidies has been going around, covering the issues from both the Developed and the Developing countries. The nexus of the existing level of state support can be seen in the Members Schedule of Accession to the WTO. However, based on the declaration by the Members in Member's schedule part IV, of the existing level of support it is feasible to create some sort of exemption ratio.

In response to this and to accommodate the justifiable use of subsidies, the *de-minimis* limit was included in the AoA. *De-minimis support can be either product specific or non-product specific*[62] *and* is applied in the non-exempt category measures.

Beyond the *de-minimis* limits,[63] subsidies, which are trade distorting, are not exempt and are liable to be challenged. Despite this categorization unresolved issues arises as to what instances justifiable subsidies can become trade distorting.[64] Such instances are resolved by the DSB in the respective cases.

All domestic support measures considered to distort trade and production, generally fall into the Amber box, with some exceptions. The ratios cannot be fixed strictly for compliance, but can be defined based on the characteristics of state support and with the assurance that Member States will keep on reducing the support on a phase by phase basis with the binding guidance of the policy makers.

---

[61]To determine AMS, the World prices are based on 1986–1988, base period and as a result, the AMS does not vary with world prices, but instead with the changes in domestic production and support prices. Editors Ingco and Nash (2004), p. 119.

[62]De-minimis support can be either product specific, for example, subsidy given to a particular crop wheat or rice or any other crop either for trade or at the initial stages to a crop which can at the later stage be used for the purpose of trade or non-product specific subsidies such as subsidies given for the use of fertilizers in general or loans being given to the farmers at a subsidized rate irrespective of any particular crops. To calculate the AMS support both the specific and non-specific subsidies can be calculated if so required.

[63]*Korea-Measures Affecting Imports of Fresh Chilled and Frozen Beef,* WT/DS161/R The issue in dispute, raised by the US was concerning the Korea's regulatory scheme, the extent of the Aggregate Measurement of Support provided by Korea, was in excess of the *de-minimis* level as prescribed under the Agreement on Agriculture.

[64]Anderson and Martin (2005), pp. 245–271. AoA (Domestic Support Commitments) Article 6 Clause 4(a) A Member shall not be required to include in the calculation of its Current Total AMS and shall not be required to reduce (1) product-specific domestic support which would otherwise be required to be included in a Member's calculation of its current AMS where such support does exceed 5% of that Member's total value of production of a basic agricultural product during the relevant year and (2) non-product-specific domestic support which would otherwise be required to be included in a Member's calculation of its Current AMS where such support does not exceed 5% of the value of that member's total agricultural production.

Clause (b) For Developing country Members, the *de minimis* percentage under this paragraph shall be 10%.

3.3.1.2 Blue Box[65]

Subsidy categorisation also enables acknowledging the use of subsidies for justifiable purposes. State support, classified as Blue box, and a necessary support measures are a kind of exemption from the general rule of prohibition on subsidies. In the context of the WTO free trade objective, it can be articulated that subsidies linked to the production must be kept within a defined limit so that their effects are not trade distorting. Blue box subsidies are of such a kind that they are linked to a specific product, but are not provided in order to increase the production level and affecting the genuine costs. Blue box categorisation rather covers aid linked to production limiting programmes, and such aid is calculated according to production data from the previous years. Some countries suggest maintaining state support by the blue box category, as they perceive it as a crucial means of keeping away from the Amber box.[66] Subsidies under the Blue box category can be considered decoupled,[67] in cases where payment to the producers is based on the area or yield. These specific provision, are covered under Article 6.5 of the AoA,[68] which states that direct payments under production-limiting programmes should not be subject to a commitment to reduce domestic support if,

1. such payments are based on fixed area and yields; or
2. such payments are made on 85% or less of the base level of production or
3. livestock payments are made on a fixed number of heads.[69]

However, such payment should not exceed the limits as prescribed. As an example of the practical application of this sort of policy measures, can be seen in the EU. The EU area compensatory payments for farmers are based on an aggregate base area across countries or regions, and individual farmers' decisions on the allocation of land for commodities. With such corresponding measures allowed for state support, it can be said that the Blue box provisions have excluded price support or input payments for variables that are of a price fluctuating nature, however it exempts the permitted area payments.[70]

---

[65]Details concerning the blue box are set in para 5, Art 6.

[66]http://indianec.wordpress.com/2010/12/06/the-three-boxes-of-wto/.

[67]*United States-Subsidies on Upland Cotton*, WT/DS267/AB/R, para 321, '[d]coupled income support' applies to one type of 'direct payment' to producers that may benefit from exemption from reduction commitments and protection under peace clause. Paragraph 6(a) Annex 2, AoA, sets forth that eligibility for payments under a decoupled income support program must be determined by reference to certain 'clearly-defined criteria' in a defined and fixed base period. Paragraph 6(b) requires the serving of any link between the amount of payments under such a program and the type or volume of production undertaken by recipients of payments under that program in any year after the base period. Paragraphs 6(c) (d) serve to require that payments from prices and factors of production employed after the base period. Paragraph 6(e) makes it clear that [n]o production shall be required in order to receive payments under a decoupled income support.

[68]Meléndez-Ortiz et al. (2009), p. 140.

[69]For detail reference, see Article 6 cl.5 (a) AoA.

[70]Meléndez-Ortiz et al. (2009), p. 147.

Subsidies permitted through these provisions are probably a means to safeguard the farming community. The farming occupation involves many risks, such as the weather conditions, crop diseases, side effects due to the use of fertilizers, etc., which may require support from the government from time to time. As the Blue box subsidies are predisposed to be compensatory by nature, therefore are not subject to the reduction agreement like Amber box. With the objectives of keeping the subsidies in this box as distinct and separate from influencing the trade, the limit to such payment is quantified on fixed acreage yields or livestock numbers as the baseline. However, a more liberal approach concerning the use of state support is followed in the case of green box subsidies.

3.3.1.3 Green Box[71]

State supports given to the farmers in this category are exempt from reduction obligations. Therefore, to be awarded the exemption through this box, state support should not be trade distorting or have even a minimum distorting effect. Basically, there is no fixed limit in this category. The main considerations is the characteristics on which subsidies can be classified as Green box, and these are:

1. such state support need not be trade distortive and therefore not contrary to free trade objectives of the WTO,
2. these subsidies need to be funded by the government and that also not by charging extra prices from the consumers.[72]

Subsidies under this category are covered mainly in Annex 2 of the AoA. Policy measures adopted in this category involves expenditures or revenue foregone in relation to programmes, which provide services or benefit to agriculture or the rural community. The state support from the policy perspective, which falls under the exemption category from the reduction Commitments are as follows.[73]

In Annex 2, Clause 2, some of the subjects covered are:

(a) Research, including general research and for particular products, also in connection with environmental programmes
(b) Pest- and disease-control measures
(c) Training services including general and specific matters
(d) Extension and advisory services, transfer of information, and the results of research
(e) Services for the inspection of particular health safety measures

[71]The Green Box is defined in Annex 2 of the Agreement on Agriculture.

[72]For detail reference, see http://www.wto.org/english/tratop_e/agric_e/agric_e.htm 1, October, 2002.

[73]The introductory statement is "Domestic support measures for which exemption from the reduction commitments is claimed shall meet the fundamental requirement that they have no, or at most minimal, trade-distorting effects on production."

(f) Marketing and promotion services
(g) Infrastructural services, including electricity reticulation, roads and other means of transport.

The other measures additionally permitted mainly for the Developing countries are, state support for public stockholding (mentioned under clause 3 of Annex 2),[74] meant for food security and certain types of domestic food aid, (mentioned under clause 4 of Annex 2).[75] The second form of state support is through direct payment methods. The amount of direct payment to the producer is based on the set of commitments; the discussions on these payments is made at the committee level. These direct payments include

1. Decoupled income support.[76]
2. Income insurance and income safety net programmes.[77]
3. Payments made directly or indirectly for relief from natural disasters.[78]
4. Structural adjustments.[79]
5. Environmental programmes[80] and Regional assistance programmes.[81]

Green box measures need to conform to the fundamental requirement mentioned in Para 1 of Annex 2 also.[82] These types of subsidies are considered essential and

---

[74]Clause 3, Annex 2, Public stockholding for food security purposes. "Expenditure (or revenue foregone) in relation to the accumulation and holding of stocks of products which form an integral part of a food security programme identified in national legislation. This may include government aid to private storage of products as part of such programme. The volume and accumulation of such stocks shall correspond to predetermined targets related solely to food security."

[75]Clause 4, Annex 3, Domestic food aid, "Expenditures (or revenue foregone) in relation to the provision of domestic food aid to sections of the population in need. Eligibility to receive the food aid shall be subject to clearly-defined criteria related to nutritional objectives."

[76]Clause 6, Annex 2, Eligibility and the amount of payment defined Decoupled income support: Decoupling has become one of the key issues in agricultural policy both at the national level and international level. The need to minimize international trade distortions associated with the support to the agricultural sector was a key element in the principles for agricultural policy reforms adopted by OECD ministers in 1987. This analysis of decoupling focuses on the production impacts of policy instruments or policy packages. Decoupling: a conceptual overview. OECD 2001. www.**oecd**.org/data**oecd**/23/51/25481500.

[77]Clause 7, Annex 2, Government financial participation in income insurance and income safety-net programmes.

[78]Clause 8, Annex 2.

[79]Clause 9, Annex 2, Structural adjustment assistance provided through producer retirement programme, Clause 10, Annex 2, Structural adjustment assistance provided through resource retirement programme, Clause 11, Annex2, Structural adjustment assistance provided through investment aids.

[80]Clause 12, Annex 2, Payments under environmental programmes.

[81]Clause 13, Annex 2, Payments under regional assistance programmes.

[82]Support measure shall have no, or only minimal, trade-distorting effects or effects on production and should confirm to the following basic criteria. (a) the support in question shall be provided through a publicly-funded programme not involving transfers from consumers. (b) the support in question shall not have the effect of providing price support to the producers.

hence permitted considering the ongoing reforms based on the objectives of the WTO. A general interpretation for creating a distinction with other categories of subsidies can be, that green box subsidies are supportive measures for covering specific policies such as environment programmes, research and development, food aid, regional development programme, crop insurance and so forth. Perhaps, realising the essential requirement of the farming community, the progenitors of this institution made a separate class for such a necessary state support. Furthermore, in order to test a subsidy through the yardstick of green box, one expects, an approach different from industrial sectors will be followed by the Member States at the policy level also, for the issues classified exclusively for the farming class.

Despite the existing level of relaxations, the approach of the Member States during the WTO discussions often reflects some new forms of demands. It was observed that some of the Member States wanted to alter the subjects in the box categorisation. As per the existing practice, it is such that when governments buy food stocks from the farmers at the support price, this allocation falls within the category of the Amber box.[83] However, there is some concession for the Developing countries and the Less-Developed countries in this regard. The exemption limit is 10% of the domestic support expressed in terms of current total AMS as specified in part IV of the Member's Schedule.[84] As a matter of recent development, during the Bali conference, Member States agreed that food security is a vital issue. A group of Member States termed as G-33, proposed some changes in the current AoA. Referring here in the context of the exemption criteria, it was proposed that buying of food stock from farmers by the state should be considered as support to low income farmers and classified under the Green box. Further, the G-33 also emphasised that such support needs to be without restrictions limits.[85]

From the outcome of the discussions, on the issue of agricultural subsidies, it seems there is a mixed opinion of the Member States on the issue of providing special exemptions to some class of subsidies. Some of the Developing countries, often propose that several other kinds of subsidies should be included in the Green box criteria whereas, others are critical of the existing limits of subsidies often suggesting that existing subsidies influence the factor costs.[86] This equivocal stand can be seen in the various conferences which often creates ambiguity among the Member States of the WTO.

From the WTO's free trade perspective, it can be said that the purpose of agriculture subsidies classification, as Amber, Blue and Green box, is also to

---

[83]WTO Ninth-Ministerial Conferences Bali, (2013). *Briefing note: Agriculture negotiations—the bid to harvest some low hanging fruit.* www.wto.org/english/thewto_e/minist_e/mc9_ebrief-agneg.

[84]For detail reference, see Article 6 cl 2 of the AoA.

[85]WTO Ninth-Ministerial conferences Bali, (2013). *Briefing note: Agriculture negotiations—the bid to harvest some low hanging fruit.* www.wto.org/english/thewto_e/minist_e/mc9_ebrief-agneg.

[86]The WTO Agriculture Negotiations, "The issues, and where we are now", pp. 50–54. www.wto.org.

generate trading values within the Members States, which is an aspect of fair trade policies. As regards the fair trade objectives based on the equity principle, such as creating equal trading opportunity, for Developed, Developing and Less-Developed countries, the distribution of resources and also for the development of comparative cost advantage, through trade in agricultural products, the classification between the three types, Amber, Blue or Green also enables to demarcate between the justifiable and non-justifiable use of subsidies for attaining the objectives by a Member State. However, finally it is the context, which can determine whether the support given is justifiable for attaining the objectives.

Despite the fact that subsidies as so defined, in the present form of classification do indeed creates at least a minimum set of standards for the use of subsidies however, lacks the concrete conceptual approach to state support for agriculture. The basic factors that provide the outline to the subsidies in principle are mentioned in the SCM Agreement.

3.4 The Agreement on Agriculture with "lex specialis" Status

The binding provisions restricting the use of subsidies for the exports, one of the key aspects of the WTO trading system, in order to promote free trade, are laid in the SCM Agreement. The substantive part of the subsidy definition are based on factors, such as 'financial contribution' and 'benefit'. In the case of subsidies for agricultural purposes, the financial contribution and benefit is linked to the farm sectors as regards both for the domestic production and export trade.

Despite the common approach being pursued by the WTO, through various agreements to promote free trade and meeting free trade objectives, the Agreement on Agriculture, however, seems to have a special status. Article 21[87] of the AoA explicitly creates the *lex specialis* status for this Agreement. This special status to the Agreement is with regard to the application of regulatory provisions for maintaining trade in agricultural products, in comparison to goods in general.[88] While, acknowledging such a status, the question for judicial interpretation naturally arises, "whether the term subsidy mentioned in the AoA has the same interpretative approach as in the SCM Agreement." For the purpose of resolving ambiguity in interpretation, when the issue raised is related to subsidies used in either form, and that also for promoting trade, it is pertinent to determine for

[87]The provisions of GATT 1994 and of other Multilateral Trade Agreements in Annex 1A to the WTO Agreement shall apply subject to the provisions of this Agreement.

[88]*Lex Specialis*, in legal theory and practice, is a doctrine relating to the interpretation of laws, and can be applied both in domestic and international law contexts. The doctrine states that where two laws govern the same factual situation, a law governing a specific subject matter (*lex specialis*) overrides a law which only govern general matters (*lex generalis*).

distinction, whether the term subsidy in AoA and in the SCM Agreement are with the common objectives and have same connotation or not.[89]

Recalling the statement, that the discussion on agricultural subsidies is based on "trade-subsidies" defined under the SCM Agreement as the conceptual parameters, that also cover export subsidies in international trade, nevertheless, a specific discussion on subsidies for the purpose of agriculture trade is made under the "Agreement on Agriculture." Accordingly, one can argue that "benefit," is an inseparable aspect of the subsidy definition. Despite the fact, that "benefit" is significant factor for determining subsidy, the SCM Agreement does not postulate any strict criteria to be followed when state support in any form is considered as the benefit conferred.

Probably, the interpretation of the term benefit has been considered more of a technical matter to be determined based on the background facts, resolved on a case by case basis. Whenever, the occasion arises to determine the subsidies by applying the parameters from the SCM Agreement and the AoA, the possibility of semantic overlap between these two terms "benefit"[90] and "payment"[91] cannot be denied.

The issue concerning the relationship between the two agreements and the also about common characteristics between the term 'benefit' and 'payment' arose in the following case. In the case of **Canada Measure Affecting the Importation of Milk and the Exportation of Dairy Products,**[92] the issue in this case was raised against Canada, by two Member States, New Zealand and United States. Both New Zealand and the United States claimed that the government of Canada was providing export subsidies on dairy products by a Special Milk Classes Scheme.[93] This support was in contravention of its export subsidy commitments as recommended by the Agreement on Agriculture under Article 9.1(a) '*the provision by governments or their agencies of direct subsidies*' and 9.1(c) '*payment on the export of an agricultural product that are financed by virtue of governmental action.'* The United States, in its claim, also stated that consequently this was violation of Article 3 of the SCM Agreement.[94] Canada in this concern stated,

[89]For reference, see Puyana et al. (2007), pp. 209–264. ISSN 1692–8156.

[90]"Benefit" as defined under Article 1.1 (a) the SCM Agreement.

[91]AoA Article 9.1(c) Payments on the export of an agricultural product that are financed by virtue of governmental action, whether or not a charge on the public account is involved, including payments that are financed from the proceeds of a levy imposed on the agricultural products concerned or on an agricultural product from which the exported products is derived.

[92]*Canada-Measure Affecting the Importation of Milk and the Exportation of Diary Products*, WT/DS103/R.

[93]See para 1.5 of the Panel report "The Government of Canada is providing subsidies, and in particular export subsidies, on dairy products through its national and provincial pricing arrangements for milk and other dairy products without regard to the export subsidy reduction and other WTO commitments undertaken by Canada."

[94]See para 3.4, 3.5, 3.7 of the WT/DS103/R.Para4.96, WT/DS103/R. Nevertheless, New Zealand emphasized that focusing attention on whether a producer produced in-quota or over quota milk, ignored what was really at issue in this case. That was whether providing exporters with access to lowered–priced milk for products destined for exports-as occurred with special class5(e) in-and over-quota, as well as with special Class 5(e) in and—over quota as well as with special class 5(d)—constituted a subsidy within the meaning of the Agreement on Agriculture.

that the sale of milk at differing prices does not constitute subsidy within the meaning of Article 1 of the SCM Agreement.[95]

The matter raised before the Panel body by the complaining parties, challenging the Canadian scheme, required interpretation of the related provisions of both the Agreements, SCM and the AoA. The legal questions at issue were, whether the sale of milk at differing prices falls within the ambit of subsidy as defined under Article 1 of the SCM Agreement and secondly, whether the payment of subsidy was contingent upon export performance as mentioned under Article 9 of the AoA.

Panel body: The complaint invoked the provision of both the Agreements, SCM Agreement & the AoA so the Panel body followed the sequence and first took the matter from the perspective of AoA. It is worth noting that Article 21 of the AoA explicitly prioritises, the application of the provision of AoA in comparison to the provision of other Agreements.

Regarding the issue of export subsidies[96] to be determined through Article 9.1(a) of the AoA, the Panel body tried to determine the scope of the term payment in Article 9.1(a) in the broader context and co-relate it with subsidies. Relating the term 'payment' with the objectives of this Agreement and with the SCM Agreement, the Panel body stated that the term payment cannot be applied as a term in contract law. *It rather connotes a gratuitous act, a bounty or benefit provided, for example in the pursuit of policy objectives. Further the Panel Body added, a payment for the purpose of export, exist only if a benefit is granted. This is further mandated by the general context of this provision, which includes Article 1 of the SCM Agreement.* The Panel body finally held that, the explanation of subsidy under Article 1, requires that benefit be conferred for there to be subsidy under the SCM Agreement.[97]

On appeal, the A.B overruled this interpretation given by the Panel body and in lieu, expressed the view that the Panel had not adopted a consistent approach in interpreting the term "subsidy". According to the A.B, the Panel followed the interpretation, with the rationality that where there is existence of payment, there is benefit, and therefore a subsidy also exists whenever there is payment. This was actually a flawed interpretation.[98] The panel could not create a distinction by which

[95]See para 3.12.

[96]Para 7.37. The Canadian Dairy Commission and the provincial milk marketing boards acting under delegated authority make milk available to exporters under clause 5(d) and (e) at prices lower than the prevailing domestic price.

[97]See para7.44. WT/DS103/R, WT/DS113/R [Concerning the action under Article 3 of the SCM Agreement, Panel Body stated that it has been found that Canadian scheme is inconsistent with i) Canada's obligations under both Article 3.3 and Article 8].

[98]See para 91 and 92 of the Appellate Body. The conferral of benefit does not necessarily constitute a "payment-in-kind" and a "payment-in-kind" is not necessarily a direct subsidy. Para 91"Thus, on our reading of the Panel Report, the Panel equated a "Payment-in-kind" with a direct subsidy, and then equated a payment-in-kind with a benefit. For the Panel, it followed logically from the existence of a benefit that a direct subsidy also existed. If the benefit was provided by the governments or their agencies, it followed, furthermore that there was an export subsidy as listed in Article 9.1(a) of the Agreement on Agriculture.

it can be clarified that the conferral of a "benefit" did not necessarily constitute a "payment-in-kind" and "payment-in-kind" was not likely to be a "direct subsidy."[99] Moreover, the scope of the term "payment-in-kind" could not be equated with the term "benefit" as mentioned in the SCM Agreement.

From the reasoning followed in the analysis, it seems that the A.B has an inclination to create a distinction between the term 'payment' and 'benefit,' with the emphasis on the fact that all kinds of 'payments in kind' cannot be considered as benefit. The A.B tried to make the interpretation that subsidies in terms of AoA can be established, first by linking payments to benefits as defined under the SCM Agreement and subsequent to this, subsidy need to be ascertained. The main emphasis of the A.B here is that the word 'payment' as mentioned in the provision of the AoA, can be both for state support in the form of monetary payments and payments-in-kind.[100] It is noteworthy here that the term 'benefit' as mentioned in the SCM Agreement is in the form of a general reference, and an interpretation can be drawn without strict limits. The A.B has tried to establish the distinction between the terms in this case, in what can be said that there exist the narrow margin of difference in terms of features depending upon the policy objectives.

Regarding the issue of the relationship between the SCM Agreement and AoA, the A.B further clarified that 'relationship between the Agreement on Agriculture and the SCM Agreement is defined as a link formed by Article 3.1 of the SCM Agreement. Article 3.1 of the SCM Agreement states that certain subsidies are prohibited except as provided in the Agreement on Agriculture, which clearly means based on the WTO guidelines that export subsidies for agricultural products has to be examined in the first place under the Agreement on Agriculture, thus justifying the *lex-specialis* status.[101]

Within the AoA, there is a specific reference that export subsidies that are contingents upon export performance are subject to reduction in the light of export competition commitments through the WTO objectives.[102] In parallel to this

[99]In the second recourse to Article 21.5, para 155. The Appellate Body upheld the compliance Panel's findings that the measure at issue—the supply of "commercial export milk" by Canadian dairy processors—involves export subsidies in the form of "payments" on the export of milk financed by virtue of government action.

[100]See para 91 and 92 of the Appellate Body The conferral of benefit does not necessarily constitute a "payment-in-kind" and a "payment in kind" is not necessarily a direct subsidy. Para 91Thus, on our reading of the Panel Report, the Panel equated a "Payment-in-kind" with a direct subsidy, and then equated a payment in kind with a benefit. For the Panel, it followed logically from the existence of a benefit that a direct subsidy also existed. If the benefit was provided by the governments or their agencies, it followed, furthermore that there was an export subsidy as listed in Article 9.1(a) of the Agreement on Agriculture.

[101]Also see the case *United States-Subsidies on Upland Cotton,* WT/DS267/R related to the same issue.

[102]For details see, Article 8 and Article 9 of the Agreement on Agriculture. Article 8 Each member undertakes not to provide export subsidies otherwise than in conformity with this Agreement and with the commitments as specified in that Member's Schedule. Article 9 The following export subsidies are subject to reduction commitments. (a) the provision by government or their agencies

provision regarding export subsidies, the SCM Agreement states that those subsidies "contingent in law or contingent to fact," whether solely or as one of several other conditions, upon export performance, are considered to be prohibited. This is a strict interpretation given in the SCM Agreement. In addition to the prohibited subsidies there are classifications such as actionable subsidies, within the SCM Agreement, that are flexible in terms of support for infrastructure building and for several other measures.[103] Comparing the objectives of both the agreements,[104] it seems that the AoA and the SCM Agreement, for the purpose of applying restrictions on the export subsidies are not at great variance, and are consistent with the objective of the WTO, i.e., market liberalization with certain regulations.

Despite the fact that both agreements follow similar approach on free trade, however, when the situation arises and one has to make presumptions easily, whether an act will lead to a subsidy and create market distortion, the possibility is higher in the cases that falls under the SCM Agreement. Whereas, for a situation to be established as a market distorting export subsidy, under the AoA, it may take much of the preliminary legal work, as the instances for examination brought under the provisions of the AoA are based on the calculation, for determining the AMS.[105] The concept of export subsidy under the AoA is confined to the extent of the ratio of

---

of direct subsidies, including payments-in-kind (b) the sale or disposal for export by governments or their agencies of non-commercial stocks of agricultural products at a price lower than comparable price (c) payments on the export of an agriculture product that are financed by virtue of governmental action (d) the provision of subsidies to reduce the costs of marketing exports of agricultural products (e) internal transport and freight charges on export shipments (f) subsidies on agricultural products contingent on their incorporation in exported products.

[103]PROHIBITED SUBSIDIES Article 3.1(a) Subsidies contingent, in law or in fact, whether solely or as one of the several other conditions, upon export performance, including those illustrated in Annex I.

Article 3.1 (b) Subsidies contingent, whether solely or as one of several conditions, upon the use of domestic over imported goods.

[104]*US-Upland Cotton,* WT/DS267/AB/R, para 549. We recall that the Agreement on Agriculture and the SCM Agreement are both Multilateral Agreements on Trade in Goods contained in Annex 1A of the Marrakesh Agreement Establishing the World Trade Organization and, as, such, are both 'integral parts' of the same treaty, the WTO Agreement, that are binding on all Members. Furthermore, as the Appellate Body has explained, a treaty interpreter must read all applicable provisions of a treaty in a way that gives meaning to all of them, harmoniously. We agree with the Panel that Article 3.1(b) of the *SCM Agreement* can be read together with the *Agreement on Agriculture* provisions relating to domestic support in a coherent and consistent manner which gives full and effective meaning to all of their terms.

WT/DS267/AB/R, para 571. Although an export subsidy granted to agricultural products must be examined, in the first place, under the *Agreement on Agriculture*, we find it appropriate, as has the Appellate Body in previous disputes, to rely on the *SCM Agreement* for guidance in interpreting provisions of the *Agreement on Agriculture*. Thus, we consider-export contingency requirement in article 1(e) of the *Agreement on Agriculture* having regard to that same requirement contained in article 3.1(a) of the *SCM Agreement*.

[105]Article 1(a) Aggregate Measurement of Support (AMS) means the annual level of support, expressed in monetary terms, provided for an agricultural product in favour of producers of the basic agricultural product or non-product specific support provided in favour of agricultural producers in general, other than support provided under programmes that qualify as exempt from reduction under Annex 2 of this Agreement.

state support, as is expressed in budgetary terms or in terms of quantity or both, under which a Member may grant export subsidies to agricultural products, which is finally covered by the term "Aggregate Measurement of Support." defined under Article 1 clause.

3.5 Farm Subsidies as a Tug of War Between Developed and Developing Economies

Prior to the formation of WTO, i.e., during the GATT period, Member States attempted to bring the subject of Agricultural trade into the disciplinary framework of international trade norms, similar to all the other disciplines of trade. However, the institutional set up could not attain much success in this regard due to the differences of opinion and because of the rigid individualistic approach being followed by the Member States.

This led to the demand for some commitment based programme. As a result of such a growing demand, in 1963, a committee was appointed by the GATT parties, so as to create a responsible understanding for the needs of the Developing countries. The inclusion of these programmes, as framed by the committee, led to further amendments, which were approved in 1964, and became part IV of the GATT, entitled as "Trade and Development."[106] The inclusion of "Trade and Development" as a specific agenda, created some serious responsibilities towards the economic advancement of both the Less-Developed and the Developing countries.[107] In order to create special measures for the economic advancement of the Developing countries, the Developing countries were granted a waiver for a 10 year period from the MFN clause. Later on, the GSP was included under the enabling clause of the Tokyo Round forming more favourable treatment for the Developing countries. Unfortunately, the GSP, a provision for the special consideration of the Developing countries was not very successful as some of the Developing countries benefitted much more in comparison to others, and therefore, the main objectives of the economic advancement and welfare of the people could not be achieved.[108]

---

[106]Srinivasan (2000), p. 0.24.

[107]**Part IV Trade and Development Article** XXXVI: *Principles and Objectives* Clause 1) The contracting parties, (a) recalling that the basic objectives of this Agreement include the raising of standards of living and the progressive development of the economics of all contracting parties, and considering that the attainment of these objectives is particularly urgent for less-developed contracting parties; (b) considering that export earnings of the less-developed contracting parties can play a vital part in their economic development and that the extent of this contribution depends on the prices paid by the less-developed contracting parties for essential imports, the volume of their exports, and the prices received for these exports. (c) noting, that there is a wide gap between standards of living in less-developed countries and other countries.

[108]Srinivasan (2000), p. 0.24.

Since the subject of agriculture remained unregulated also during the GATT period, individual Member States, such as the US, the EC and also many other Developing nations formed their own policy towards agricultural support, leading to a complex system for the import and export of agricultural items.[109] Among the Developed nations group, the governments started following the policy of transferring financial support to rural sectors after making gains from the industrial sectors. However, this led to the disproportionate increase in fiscal support to the farm sectors. On the other hand, the Developing nations faced different types of challenges. As a matter of fact, the Developing countries' agricultural sector, overall in budgetary terms represented a larger proportion of their national output. For the Developing countries, gains from their agricultural sector were a means of valuable export earnings. When exporting agriculture goods to the Developed countries, the complex mechanism of quotas, subsidies, and tariff and non-tariff barriers imposed by the Developed countries, in a way acted as a means of restricting imports from the Developing countries.[110]

Realising the complexities, a new set of rules and provisions were created, for trade in agricultural products, consistent, with the objectives of the WTO. When the Agreement on Agriculture was introduced into the WTO system, Member States committed themselves to regulate their existing level of state support in order to meet the objectives, as mentioned in the preamble of this agreement.

While framing the market rules in coherence with the WTO objectives, Developed countries agreed to the flexibility for Developing and Less-Developed countries taking into consideration the objective of development and welfare, enshrined in the preamble. These flexibilities as such are like systemic tools, so as to ensure the accomplishment of such objectives. An additional purpose of adopting these regulatory measures and applying them to the free trade of agricultural products, is to avoid market distortion. These measures are also applied to maintain certain level of balance between free trade policies and the underlying fair trade principles in order to achieve the objectives of welfare and development. Acknowledging the fact that the free trade system promoted by the WTO creates a competitive market set up among the Member States, a question arises as to, whether the market efficiency concepts based on free competition, are the correct market approaches for countries, where a large proportion of their population is struggling for food sufficiency.

While considering subsidies for agriculture, in the context of trade between the Developed countries and Developing/Less Developed countries, it can be observed that the cause and effect relationship is vital, and is based on the comparative

[109] Stewart (1993), p. 131.

[110] Stewart (1993), pp. 131–132.

approach adopted.[111] In order to justify the essential support in the matters of Developing and Less-Developed countries, the policy objectives of these Member States needs to outline the constructive role of subsidies for welfare and development that are based on the concepts of equity and distributive justice. This will further generate the values and standards for welfare and social advancement. The normative support also required for the policies of welfare and development which are newly added as a result of the WTO membership are on a principle basis more or less based on fair trade values for the advancement of weaker sections. However, the impact of such objectives on the concepts of free trade may create stress; the stress between the two doctrines can also be described as a free trade and fair trade dichotomy. This dichotomy, from the perspective of agriculture issues, between the Developed country on one side and Developing and Less-Developed countries on the other, can be termed as North South divide.

The North-South divide is not confined to agriculture import/export policies but also to the range of political issues. Given the fact that the issue of Agricultural subsidies has often raised political questions, this inherently sets up a test as to whether the economic development of several Developing and Less-Developed countries, based on agricultural reform is possible by adopting the basic principles of free trade.

The construction of two different premises, based on free trade objectives and fair trade objectives is a preliminary step, but creating the scope to achieve these objectives, still remains an open question. This issue, probably needs to be decided by each Member State also at the individual level. As the market liberalisation policies are in the progress and the market competition among the Member States is increasing, the issue of agricultural subsidies from a mere policy subject at a national level, now has attained a large questionable issue from the WTO perspective, as the Developing and Less-Developed countries' are transforming their economic set up from agrarian to industrial mode.

Agricultural sector in the Developing and Less-Developed countries makes major contribution in an economic set up; a description below:

1. Provides the native people with adequate, affordable, and culturally-appropriate food.[112]

[111]Article 13 of the AoA is known as the Peace clause. Article 13 of the AoA deals with "Due restraint" in initiating the actions to counter the subsidies. After reading Article 13, it can be concluded that Article 13 can be applied as the defence provision, in the case of prohibited subsidy claims. This defence provisions is not an open ended or without any restrictive limits, it is rather that Article 13 by including Annex 2 of the AoA assert that the total quantity of support granted through all non-green box domestic support measures (i.e. the measures that do not fully comply with the AoA Annex 2) to a specific commodity in any marketing year from 1995 to 2003 does not exceed the quantity of non-green box domestic support decided to be granted in the marketing year 1992. See. AoA Article 13 clause b (iii). The Peace clause is obsolete from December 31, 2003.

[112]For reference, see Pravin et al. (2010), p. 4. TRADE, POVERTY AND THE LAGGING REGIONS OF SOUTH ASIA, Working Paper 16322. http://www.nber.org/papers/w16322, and also Stewart (1993), p. 192.

2. Offers rural people the opportunity to earn and remain settled in rural areas.
3. Promotes economic development in agricultural sector and linked to it at the rural sector, which supports the set up at the local and the regional level.
4. State support in rural sector reduces the financial burden, helps in the protection of the rural environment, preservation of rural-based culture, traditional biodiversity and many other related matters.
5. The farming sector is still one of the main sources of employment for the people in the Developing and Less-Developed countries and is quite essential for their basic needs.

Considering the social and economic structure of the Developing and Less-Developed countries, the state support in the form of subsidies is essential, as justifiable support that can promote gradual industrial growth and sustain a certain level of an agriculture base. The merit of such subsidies is also acknowledged as in many of the Less-Developed countries, farmers are at a threshold level and the agricultural system to date plays a significant role in the economic, social and political development of the Developing and Less-Developed countries. With such background situation, the point of criticism that emerges considering the overall perspective of the Developing and Less-Developed countries, is that financial institutions and multinationals companies promote inconsistency and an unbalanced approach, in the agricultural sector trade.

Further in this context, it can be added that the perception of the Developing and Less-Developed countries towards state support given by Developed countries for the agricultural sector differs, which complicates the possibility of solution finding for the long-term market settlements among the Member States. The notion carried by the Developing and Less-Developed countries is, that the domestic market of the Developed countries cannot absorb the whole of the production and, therefore, they need access to the markets of Developing and Less-Developed countries. This notion may be partly true and can be observed in the case of trade practices followed by the multinationals. In order to counter such tendencies, the Less-Developing and the Developing economies often resort to protectionism. Therefore, using protectionism as a deterrent measure, they try to prevent market domination by the Developed economies and by this practice also restrain the surge in debts, which they might face in the case of excess of imports from the Developed countries.[113] Second, and of important concern for the Developing and Less-Developed nations is saving their economies from the market uncertainties, such as those that occurred in 2008.[114] Markets of the Developing and Less-Developed

[113] *India-Quantitative Restrictions on the Import of Agricultural, Textile and Industrial Products referred in the initial chapter* WT/DS90/R.

[114] For reference, see Howse and Josling (2012), p. 6. At the time of the 2008 price spike, the number of Developing countries both importers and exporters, which reacted with price insulating measures was significant. Among 60 low-income countries surveyed by the FAO in 2008, around one quarter had some form of export restriction in place on food-related agricultural products. East Asia and South Asia led in terms of export restrictions with around 40% of the countries surveyed

countries are vulnerable and due to the promotion of free trade, the back-and forth-market shift creates uncertainties. One such consequence of uncertainty can be, the capital flight from these countries.[115] In order to be shielded from such like negative impacts of uncertainties, these countries need to have foreign exchange in reserve. A further pressure on the economy is added by increase in the demand for foreign exchange, because of the ongoing changes in the pattern of market system of the Developing and Less-Developed countries.

The market system of these countries, which was earlier driven by agriculture and related matters primarily, now also has some aspects of the industrial segments, varying from intermediate to finished products. Furthermore, in order to achieve economic advancement and for buying technology-based goods, Developing and Less-Developed countries need foreign exchange, which they can obtain essentially by exporting agricultural products. Therefore, their claim for agriculture subsidies has reasonable grounds. By earning foreign money, they can buy technological goods or invest in building their industrial infrastructure.

Comparing this with the subsidies given by the Developed countries, it can be observed that the state support in these countries is mainly for different objectives, such as to advance their own production, and the quality elevation of the technology-based goods either for exporting to the Developing and Less-Developed countries or because of the competitive system they face from the parallel economies. Taking into account the pre-conditions mentioned for the use of subsidies, and based on the categorisation of the Member States, it seems that there exits some kind of contradiction when it comes to the implementation of the objectives of the

implementing these measures, but Europe and Central Asia were not far behind at close to 35 percent. Africa, Latin America and Caribbean, the Middle East and North Africa exhibited more or less similar values of close to 20%. The most significant of these interventions was in August 2010, when Russia announced an export ban on grains in the light of a disastrous harvest caused by hot dry weather and wide spread fires Ukraine introduced shipment quotas on exports at that time. These events combined with poor harvests in Canada and in Eastern Europe to cause wheat prices to double in 2010.

[115]Capital outflow should be considered as capital flight only if it limits the resources available for either servicing the country's external debt or the financing of development programs. For detail references see, Kant (1996), pp. 5–6. From the mid-1970s through the early 1980s, Mexico faced persistent balance-of-payments problems resulting from the government's efforts to defend the overvalued peso while incurring massive external debts. By the late 1970s, oil prices had begun to fall, and international interest rates rose sharply, throwing Mexico's external payments so far out of balance that by mid-1982 the country could no longer service its external debt. Throughout the early and mid-1980s, Mexico suffered a net capital outflow as a result of external debt service, high domestic capital flight, and weak foreign investment.

WTO, or there are complexities because of the previously existing legal standards set up for the policy formation.[116]

Notwithstanding the above mentioned facts, some positive aspects of the WTO can also be recognised. The Developing countries, such as Brazil, China, India and South Korea, have also started making a significant impact on international trade both from the agricultural and industrial perspective.

In theory, it seems that the WTO system follows the direction towards an equitable approach, however, the point yet to be analysed is which party is the beneficiary in practice of such concessionary policies.

3.5.1 Developed Countries

In the business of farm trade, Developed countries remain in an advantageous position, as the farmers of the Developed countries applying scientific methods and using technology based infrastructure have the opportunity to overproduce and export their farm products at a cheaper price. Additionally, the Developed countries try to establish their own quality and health standards and apply it in the form of non-tariff barriers. Such measures are often portrayed as a means of protecting plants, animals and human health in the importing countries. These quality standards, many a times can be of high order and sometime can create difficulties for the foreign producers to compete.[117]

On the other hand, the farmers of the Less Developed countries can barely support their population to a subsistence level. They can hardly afford to export their product at a competitive price. Additionally, the amount of money that is being spent on research in the Developed countries on food and food product exports is relatively higher compared to Developing countries and Less-Developed countries.

---

[116] The basic objectives of the WTO are mentioned briefly as:

1. trade should be without discrimination
2. trade should be free, and decrease in barriers through negotiations
3. foreign company investors and government should be confident that the trade barriers would not be raised arbitrarily
4. trading should be beneficial for Less-Developed countries, giving them more time to adjust to the free-market economy system, and also providing special privileges if so required
5. trading should be more competitive discouraging unfair practices such as export subsidies and dumping products below the cost to gain a market-share.

The general idea behind these objectives is to raise the standards of living, ensuring full employment and a growing real income of the people at large by promoting free-trade in goods and services.

[117] Josling and Roberts. 'Measuring the Impact of SPS Standards on Market Access.' *International Food& Agricultural Trade Policy Council*. http://www.oecd.org/tad/ntm/48632882.pdf.

3.5.1.1 A Brief Note on EU Agriculture Policy

As an example of the Developed economy, the situation of the EU/EC, can be discussed here as regards the extent of policy based support to its farmers. Within the EU/EC, Member States, follow the CAP, the Common Agriculture Policy.[118] Primarily, the CAP's principal policy instruments are the internal market support measures, such as the intervention price/purchases[119] and export subsidies for agriculture.[120] How far these measures are consistent with the free trade concepts of the WTO is a debatable question? It was during July 2004, that the CAP was altered to bifurcate subsidies at the two levels: a basic level of set payments provided by the EU; and an added amount provided at a devolved level by the national governments of the Member States. The affect of such policies as adopted by EU/EC, on the WTO free trade objectives became a matter of discussion in the following case.

In the case of the **European Communities-Export Subsidies for Sugar**[121] Australia, Brazil and Thailand were the complainants and requested the establishment of a Panel as the matter at issue was the subsidies provided by the European

---

[118]What is CAP? The EU/EC CAP should be seen in comparison to the WTO Free Trade policies and the objectives, which the WTO expects to achieve by promoting free-trade market approach.

CAP is based on the important objective of supporting the agriculture programme of the Member States so as to stabilize their internal market. The CAP also allows government intervention in the case of market failure which is also linked with the political aspect of the EU agriculture policy. This has also led to the over production of the food crops within the EU. (See section 3.3, 3.3(a) and 4, later in the text).

[119]The intervention price provides a support below which market prices should not fall. Intervention agencies buy agricultural commodities at the intervention price.

[120]For reference, see Weyerbrock (1998), p. 376.

[121]WT/DS265/R and WT/DS265/AB/R. Para 3.1, The European Communities established, in 1968, a Common Organization (CMO) for sugar, the main rules of which are today set out in "Council Regulation (EC) No. 1260/2001 on the common organization of the markets in the sugar sector." The Regulation was valid for marketing years 2001/2002 to 2005/2006. Para 3.3, The EC regime applied *inter-alia* to cane and beet sugar, sugar beet, and sugar cane as well as to iso-glucose. The sugar cane and sugar beet were primarily transformed into raw sugar and/or white sugar. [Within the EU, sugar production quotas are allocated to the Member States on the basis of the production based on any reference period. On the grounds of these quotas, quantities for A and B type of sugar are set for the Member States. Member States can transfer quotas between undertakings, taking into consideration the interest of the parties concerned, between sugar beet and cane production. The sugar produced in excess of A and B quantities are termed as C sugar and C type is not subject to any quota. Type C sugar is not eligible for domestic support and must be exported. If no proofs are supplied, that type C has been exported within the required period of time, a charge is levied on that sugar].

Para 3.7 To achieve the objectives of the Common Agricultural Policy and in order to stabilize the EC sugar market, the EC Regulation provides for intervention agencies to buy sugar. An intervention price is established for this purpose at a level which will ensure a fair income for sugar-beet and sugar cane producers.

Communities to its sugar industry,[122] which they considered contrary to the WTO objectives.

The sugar regime of the EC/EU established two categories of production quotas, one for A sugar and the other for B sugar. This quota system does not put limits on the quantities of sugar that may be produced or exported, however it fixed the quantity eligible for domestic price support and direct export subsidies based on A and B category. Additionally, the sugar produced in excess of the A and B category-quantities, called C sugar, while not subject to a quota, is not eligible for the domestic price support or direct export subsidies but must be exported.[123]

The legal issues raised were[124]

1. Type C sugar produced under the EC regime is provided with an export subsidy within the terms of Article 9.1(c) of the Agreement on Agriculture.
2. The export subsidy provided for type C sugar is in excess of the quantity outlay commitment levels. Therefore, the EC is acting inconsistently with regard to the provisions of Article 3.3 of the Agreement on Agriculture.
3. Additionally, the EC is providing export subsidies to Type C sugar and that is also inconsistent as far as the provisions of Article 3.1(a) and 3.2 of the SCM Agreement are concerned.
4. The EC violates Article 9.1(a) of the Agreement on Agriculture, since it does not reduces export subsidies.

With regard to the claims made, the European Community responded that exports of C sugar did not receive any benefit from export subsidies in the form of low price sale of C beet to C type sugar producers.[125] Concerning the issue of the intervention price,[126] the EC stated that the intervention price and production quotas were domestic support mechanisms and were subject to reduction commitments under AoA.[127] The EC further added that beet farmers were free to decide whether or not to produce C beet for exports. Further, the EC argued that a system of price or income support which "operate so as to increase subsidy was not contingent upon export performance and could not be considered as an export subsidy for the purpose of Agreement of Agriculture."[128]

---

[122]See para 1.1, 1.3 and 1.4 of the WT/DS 265/R.

[123]See para 3.4 WT/DS265/R.

[124]See para 4.2 WT/DS265/R.

[125]See WT/DS265/R, para 4.109.

[126]See para 4.72 WT/DS265/R The Complainants asserted that the instruments of the regime provided a strong incentive to EC quota holders to defend their quotas through surplus C sugar production, whether or not, the production of C sugar would be below the costs of its production. The intervention price provided a guaranteed price some three times greater than world price, but due to the domestic supply restrictions, quota holders secured market prices substantially in excess of the intervention price.

[127]See para 4.79.

[128]See para 4.118.

The Panel rejected the EC's defence claim and stated that the European Community was exporting sugar C in excess of the European Communities commitment level.

The Panel found that the EC administered a domestic market price above the intervention price under CAP, for A and B type sugar, by allowing a recovery of the deficit by exporting type C sugar below the total average cost.[129]

On Appeal, the EC argued that the Panel's finding was an error because "payments at issue are an internal allocation of resources." The Appellate Body accepted the Panel's reasoning and dismissed the EC's plea. The A.B stated "that as type C sugar cannot be disposed of in the internal market and must be exported without further processing, therefore, due to this legal requirement, any such advantages or payments or subsidies to C type sugar are subsidies on export which give advantage to the EC."[130]

From the broader perspective of free trade and its regulation through fair trade values, it is worth also discussing the connecting issue of dumping. The issue of dumping was not raised in this case, but the cross-subsidies[131] provided through by supporting provisions had resulted in dumping. Whether the market effect of dumping was premeditated by the EC or not is however, an another issue. The support given to sugar export was through the CAP, the farm policy adopted by the EU/EC. There was distortion to the free trade objectives of the WTO. In such instances, it is clear that the distortive consequences were as a result of subsidies, although the effect of dumping might be coincidental.

The EU CAP is also influenced by political considerations. In this context referring here an instance, followed by an intensive discussion, a political agreement on the reform of CAP was reached in June 2013. As a major progress, the UK government was able to secure an amendment enabling the regional governments within the Member States to take their own approach, for the implementation of CAP.[132] One probability cannot be discounted here, that this step was taken for some political reasons, probably to increase the members in the EU. This reform was also essential for securing the French farming community's support and French political support for the entry of Poland into the EU/EC. The French concerns were that if subsidy payment sources were not split between supra-national and national

[129]See para 7.310 WT/DS265/R.

[130]See para 274, WT DS265/AB/R.

[131]WT/DS265/R, para 4.39(a). The payment from the beet grower to the sugar processor was in the form of beet sold below its proper value to the grower, i.e., beet sold below its costs of production. As set out in the evidence presented by Australia, 'C' beet was categorized into C1 and C2 beet in the main C sugar-producing countries, with C2 beet being priced on the basis of an approximately split revenue from C sugar sales. Over the 11 years to 2002–2003 the payment for C2 beet was estimated to have averaged percent of the average total cost of producing beet in France and in Germany. Therefore, for sugar produced from C2 beet, Australia submitted that there was a payment-in kind, in the form of beet sold below its proper value by the growers to the processors.

[132]Seaton, "EU Policy Update (EU 2013.04): Reform of Common Agricultural Policy (CAP)" *National Assembly of Wales*. http://www.assemblywales.org/13-069.pdf.

levels within the EU, then the EU would be forced to cut subsidies because membership enlargement would stretch its budget.[133]

Farm subsidies provided by EU/EC has added to the complexities. With the objectives of bringing harmony to the global trends in trade, some changes were proposed during the Lisbon treaty. Intending to reform the present policy focus with regard to agriculture, the Commission has emphasised the need to bring more transparency with regard to individual beneficiaries of the agricultural funds.[134] The Commission has presently adopted a proposal on the reform of the EU farm subsidies for a period post 2013. However, with the Brexit new guidelines are expected to be formed.

During WTO discussions, many questions were raised by the Member countries about the EU/EC's CAP. This was mainly to promote the fair trade objectives of the WTO. The situation is unbalanced in financial terms, as only 5% of the European population work on farms and the contribution of the farm sector is only 1–2% of the European GDP. Based on these facts, it can be construed that large proportion of farm subsidies serves the purpose of only a small percentage of the Europeans.[135] There is often a difference of opinion among the political parties of the EU Members concerning Agricultural subsidies. After the Lisbon Treaty, leaders have tried to make some kind of policy shift with regard to agricultural subsidies. They want farmers and the farming industry to focus on:

1. Encouraging innovation
2. Increasing farmers competitiveness
3. Managing the risk factors
4. Encouraging the effective use of resources
5. Preserving eco-systems and
6. Promoting social inclusion.

In line with the changes proposed by the Lisbon Treaty, the European Parliament and the council have proposed changes in the regulations and some of the-relevant changes are mentioned in subsequent lines.[136] These changes are so as to be more in line with the WTO objectives.

---

[133]See, Bhala (2007), p. 976.

[134]New legislation [COM (2012)551]: amendment to proposal COM (2011) 628 final/2 for a Regulation of the European Parliament and of the Council on the financing, management and monitoring of the common agriculture policy. Issues concerning Agriculture were discussed in the Lisbon Treaty under Article 38, Article 39, Article 40 and Article 41.

[135]Dejaegher, Sarah. "The New Federalist, Webzine of the young European Federalist. EU Reforms Farm Aid: One Big Budget, Many interests." (2012). http://www.thenewfederalist.eu/EU-Reforms-Farm-Aid-One-Big-Budget-Many-Interests,04820.

[136]1. Proposal for Regulation on support for rural development by the European Agricultural Fund for Rural Development, COM(2011)627 final/2.

2. Proposal for establishing rules for direct payments to farmers under support schemes within the framework of the Common Agriculture Policy, COM(2011) 625 final/2.

3. Proposal for establishing a common organization of the markets in agricultural products. COM (2011) 626 final/2.

The CAP reform started in about 2010 and it covered the overall EU budgetary framework for 2014–2020. The Multiannual Financial Framework (MFF), provides the funds at the disposal of EU, including the CAP. A deal was secured both on the CAP and the MFF. The new CAP 2014–2020 agreed by the council and the EU parliament retains the essential characteristics proposed by the Commission.[137] The amounts allocated for the CAP, agreed under the new EU multinational financial framework, are outlined. The commission has proposed the amount for both the subjects in nominal terms.

(1) for direct payments and (2) for market related expenditure.

Expenditure for rural development, would be frozen at the level of 2013.In real terms it has been brought upto 2011 price levels. Additionally, it was one of the objectives before the reformed new CAP, that from 2014 onwards, the allocation of direct payment dedicated to the coupled support, to young farmers and small farmer will depend upon choices made by Member States.[138] It is expected that new CAP design is more efficient, specifically targeted and coherent.

Furthermore, due to the pressure on natural resources, the agricultural sector needs to take care of the effects on environment. It should be a matter of priority to use sustainable production methods. If the environment objectives are to be kept parallel with free trade, the Agrarian community needs to adapt to challenges stemming from changes in the climatic conditions. Therefore a basic requirements has been established that Members need to meet requirements in order to receive CAP funding.[139] From 2015 onwards, the CAP has introduced a new policy instrument for green direct payment which probably corresponds to the WTO, green box subsidies. This accounts for 30% of the national direct payment and rewards to the farmers for respecting three agricultural practices.

1. maintenance of permanent grasslands,
2. focusing on Ecological areas for environmental sustainability and
3. following patterns on crop diversification.

Expectations are that the CAP will advance a more balanced, transparent and more equitable distribution of direct payment among the Member states and among the farmers by 2020.[140]

There are proposals to remove disparities in the matters of direct payment to the agricultural workers. The reduction in disparities among the Member State is known as external convergence. In this respect a reformed measure has been

[137]European Commission, *Agricultural Policy Perspectives Brief*, Overview of CAP Reform (2014–2020). No5/ December 2013. p. 2.

[138]European Commission, *Agricultural Policy Perspectives Brief*, Overview of CAP Reform (2014–2020). No5/ December 2013. p. 3.

[139]European Commission, *Agricultural Policy Perspectives Brief*, Overview of CAP Reform (2014–2020). No5/ December 2013. p. 6. D.G Agriculture and Rural Development, Unit for agriculture policy.

[140]European Commission, *Agricultural Policy Perspectives Brief*, Overview of CAP Reform (2014–2020). No5/ December 2013. p. 8.

adopted. The level of direct payment per hectare is currently based on a minimum national average direct payment per hectare across all Member States of the EU. Another issue that has been put forward during the meeting, concerns internal convergence. Internal convergence is mainly to bring at the same level of the subsidies being provided within countries or regions.[141] Member states of the EU, until recently, allocated payments on the basis of past references, but now they have to follow a uniform payment per hectare approach from 2015 onwards. Members can take a national approach or a regional approach based on the administrative criteria.[142] What is remarkable that for the first time a coherent policy framework is possible for the European structural and for the investment funds. It seems also that Member States have agreed to improve their co-ordination in order to achieve the common EU aims and objectives. However, once Britain formally exists from the EU, it is expected that the new guidelines will be formed.

3.5.2 Developing Countries

In the context of WTO economic categorisation, Developing countries can also be termed as upcoming economies as they are in the transformation stage.

During the preliminary WTO discussions on agricultural-trade, the key issues that were involved were "the export subsidies and high tariffs of the industrialized nations, undermining the Developing countries and Less-Developed countries' efforts to build up their economies through free trade." The fulfillment of the objectives such as gradual economic advancement and the concerns for food security justifies subsidies by the Developing countries in general and by the Less Developed countries more specifically.[143] An issue of concern for the Developing countries is that they face difficulties in the form of quality restrictions and tariff measures in the markets of the Developed countries.[144] Such policies can also be because the countries they see as potential export markets intend to impose higher duties on processed imports than on the raw materials, as an alternative to tariff escalation-in order to protect their own processing industries.

[141]Those Member States that currently maintain allocations based on historic references must move towards more similar levels of payment per hectare. They may choose from different options: to take a national approach, or a regional approach (based on administrative or agronomic criteria); to achieve a regional/national rate by 2019, or to ensure that those farms getting less than 90% of the regional/national average rate see a gradual increase—with additional guarantee that every farmer reaches a minimum payment of 60% of the national regional average by 2019.

See European press release. http://europa.eu/rapid/press-release.

[142]Matthews (2012), p. 18.

[143]Cheng (2007), pp. 1–4.

[144]WTO Agriculture Negotiations. The issues, and where we are now. (Briefing document) p. 32. http://www.wto.org/english/tratop_e/agric_e/agnegs_bkgrnd_e.pdf.

Reforms in the agriculture segment of the economy along with other sectors are important for the Developing countries, as the vast majority of their rural population is engaged in farm activities directly or indirectly. Taking into account the diversity among the Developing countries, different sub-groups can be formed. Most of these countries have different social economic and political situations and the agriculture patterns also differ a lot. The so called box shifting can be observed in their development programmes. The possibility of the box shifting within the premises of AoA, from an Amber to Blue and Green box, as also discussed during the Bali conference, is undoubtedly a favourable option for the Developing and the Less-Developed economies. Because of this flexibility for using state support, the Developing nations, in order to establish a stable agricultural base, can give financial support decoupled from the trade benefits[145] in pursuance of the development and welfare objectives. The decoupled income support in pursuance of the development and welfare goals is exempt from the WTO reduction commitments and also get exempted when calculating AMS values.[146]

With regard to the further sub-categorisation of the Developing countries and in this context referring to the effect of development policies, the example of the phase by phase advancement of the emerging economies can be referred to here i.e., those that have first consolidated their agriculture sector and then moved forward to the industrial sector. For the emerging economies such as China and India, developing their infrastructure in the agricultural sector was primarily fundamental, for attaining comparative advantages subsequently in other sectors. After this stage, these Member States followed a course shifting, from the production of farming products to industrial and technology based products. It can also be mentioned here that in order to attain the targets, the Developing Member States referred to, followed planned agriculture-based economic policies. The success of China is one example of how planned agricultural policies supported the development of the industrial sector. After agriculture self-sufficiency, China, has come forward with an outward looking development model; one that is not shared by many of the Developing countries. It is worth considering, that adopting a similar type of model may be beneficial for other Member States, although these policies may be based on a socialistic pattern.

Another instance of achievements in farming economy based on a different model (non-socialistic) is also referred here. Three Developing countries taken as an examples, India, Indonesia, and the Philippines. These countries have adopted farm policies based on the Green revolution. The Green revolution was based on the

[145]Decoupling is the characteristic of any policy measure. In many countries government support to agriculture has traditionally relied heavily on market price support, provided either through border measures such as tariffs and export subsidies sometimes combined with domestic market interventions. Therefore, practically 'decoupling' should be seen as a matter of degree, rather than absolute concept. Some policies are more and other are less decoupled. Tangermann (2014), p. 23.

[146]An Index that measures the monetary value of support to the Agriculture sector. *Decoupled Income Support: The Case of United States, Direct Payment*. Sept, (2005). p. 9. http://economics.stanford.edu/files/Theses/Theses_2005/Somers.pdf.

understanding of the economic, social and political aspects of the societies respectively. The agriculture reform policies enabled public investment in the agricultural sector, investment in agriculture research, the establishment of an irrigation infrastructure, subsidised access to inputs, agricultural credit, as well as price guarantees.[147] In the terms of subsidies classification these policies can be termed Green box subsidies and are in line with Annex 2 clause 2 (f)[148] and (g).[149]

While making a comparison between the Developed and Developing countries agricultural policy, one can assess that the structural adjustment policies for attaining higher economic objectives are not substantially strong in the case of Developing and Less-Developed countries. This has also resulted in several new types of problems such as the agricultural workers becoming landless, a rise in unemployment, and other social problems such as drug abuse. The Developing and Less-Developing countries then also fall back into establishing industrial and farming policies as part of a single economic programme, in the light of free trade objectives, thus loosing the balanced approach.

3.5.3 Less-Developed Countries

From the perspective of trade in agricultural products, the Less-Developed economies are facing challenges of different types and many among them are struggling to provide basic facilities to a large number of their people. This further leads to the debate as to whether free trade policies, in the current form are suitable for the Less-Developed countries. Governments in many of the Less-developed countries interfere in the agricultural market and state also try to impose price controls to keep food prices artificially low. Subsequent to this measure, market boards buy agricultural products as they are authorised to buy and resell to the domestic consumers. With this trend farmers cannot earn much, thus resulting to the decline in per capita of food production as the farmers shifts to cash crop.[150] In view of the present food-crisis, it is of particular significance that, agricultural development agencies working in Africa, need to focus on the basic requirements before taking the second step towards industrialisation.

The primary objectives of the Less-Developed countries are:

---

[147] See Birner and Resnick (2010), p. 1443.

[148] Marketing and promotion services, including market information, advice and promotion relating to particular products but excluding expenditure for unspecified purposes that could be used by sellers to reduce their selling price or confer a direct economic benefit to purchasers.

[149] Infrastructural services including: electricity reticulation, roads and other means of transport, market and port facilities, water supply facilities, dams and drainage schemes and infrastructural works associated with environmental programmes.

[150] Thompson, Robert L. "Agricultural Price Supports." *The Concise Encyclopedia of Economics*, www.econlib.org/library/Enc1/AgriculturalPriceSupports.html.

1. Achieving food security by a reduction in food dependency through import and making their own agricultural markets operational
2. Increase in the net agriculture production in a sustainable manner
3. Improve the living conditions of producers through the enhancement of their income and their social-development.

3.5.3.1 Taking the Case of Africa Specifically

The priority of the African countries is to meet the above-mentioned objectives that require a focused policy framework, both at the WTO level and through the channels of African development agencies. What the basic requirement are for development and progress, needs to be clearly established in the lack of such support from the norms. At the foundation level, due consideration should be given to the formulation of rural and agricultural development strategies in a coordinated manner.[151]

It is during the later stage, that coordinated efforts need to be made on a broader scale, in which the East, West, North and South of Africa can be classed together. Once the objectives are decided on a collective basis, the message can be send up to the rural level, making the African people aware of both the challenges and advantages of free trade.

Some of the African countries have shown progress in the farm sector even to the extent of producing up to the level of exports. However, this does not remain consistent and has led to the inflation in the domestic markets because of the disequilibrium in the demand and supply. For example, in Senegal, there was an increase in horticulture production. As of 2005, the export of fruits and vegetables, french beans, tomatoes, and mangoes totalled 16,000 tons, mostly produced by Agro based companies.[152] The gain in export should have been in tune with the domestic demand and supply, rather than an attempt to obtain a market opportunity through the measures of unregulated free trade. As a consequence, in 2008, in Dakar, the capital city of Senegal, food riots occurred. Price hikes reverberated more strongly in Senegal and Mauritania, where there was a high dependence on imported wheat and rice. Ironically, in Dakar, European vegetables and Thai rice were cheaper than their own nationally produced counterparts.[153] The reason for the resentment shown by the people was also because the imported food products were sold at a cheaper price in comparison to their home grown food stuffs. It seems something was lacking with regard to market stabilisation policies. The stabilisation of agricultural prices and the support to farm sectors, are two of the principal objectives that requires co-ordination in the case of transforming

[151]Resnick and Birner (2010), p. 98.

[152]Resnick and Birner (2010), p. 101.

[153]Busch and Reinhardt (2006), pp. 119–129.

economies. In order to prevent such market occurrences, there are provisions in the AoA for the Member States to adopt policies, such as,

1. direct payment to the farmers as determined by the relation between the guaranteed and market price,
2. maintenance of public stocks of storable commodities,
3. direct control of supply and
4. disposal of output in a foreign market.[154]

Since, the norms to support free trade are not firmly in existence nor any similar normative construction has been attempted before adopting these new types of market policies, then as a consequence, in many of the Developing and Less-Developed countries there is a possibility of such market tensions in the wake of the existing, age old social set up and the external imposition of these market concepts.

Understandably, several of the African states are engaged in protectionist measures in the wake of the food price crises of 2008 and 2009.These incidences also depicts the lack of a balanced approach between the indigenous market system and the one promoted through free trade. As a result of unregulated and unbalanced approach to free trade, the perception has been encouraged to continue earning foreign exchange by exporting cash crops, consequently leading to a disequilibrium in the domestic markets.[155] During the 10th WTO Ministerial Conference, held at Nairobi on December 2015, specific attention was given to the agriculture issues mainly of the Less-Developed countries. Series of decisions were taken by the ministers, specifically on the subjects, such as agriculture, cotton trade, commitment to abolish export subsidies, preferential treatment for Less-Developed countries. These discussions got special reference in the form of 'Nairobi Package.' It is expected that Member States will give due consideration to fulfill the commitments.[156]

[154]Arzac and Wilkinson (1979), pp. 39–40.

[155]The level of rice import recorded between Nigeria, Ghana and Senegal, imports surges occurred 5 times for Ghana, 6 times for Nigeria and 3 times for Senegal. For reference see Rice imports in West Africa: trade regimes and food policy formulation by Lançon and Recherche MOISA presentation at 106th seminar of the EAAE Montpellier, France. www.*ageconsearch.umn.edu/bit stream/.../1/pp07la02.pdf.*

[156]For reference, see WT/MIN(15)/45.

3.6 Discussion on Agricultural Subsidies Under the Doha Development Agenda and Further Consultations During the Bali

In the matters of agricultural subsidies, the negotiations between the Developed countries and the other block consisting of the Developing and Less-Developed countries often remain inconclusive, because of the diverse views and conflict of interest among the Member's governments. This has also led to an incoherent approach, as regards the objectives mentioned in the preamble of the WTO. The WTO's promotion of free trade concept in the agriculture sector, aims to a further liberalisation of agricultural trade. Nevertheless, the free trade market policies need to be consistent with the development and welfare objectives, and support fair trade principles. By and large, it seems free trade is in favour of the Developed countries as their economy depends on the export of a diverse range of industrial and processed agricultural products. It is conceivable that such policies will benefit those countries that can compete on quality and price.

The discussion since the Uruguay Round has focused broadly on two issues: (1) the high levels of tariffs outside the quotas with some countries pressing for larger cuts on the higher tariffs, and (2) the quotas themselves, the way they have been administered.[157]

After the successive WTO round of conferences, the Doha development round of negotiations[158] provided a crucial ground, by which the future of the extent of the legitimacy of the agricultural subsidies for the Developed, Developing and Less-Developed nations can be assessed. Significantly, the Doha development round, revealed the bargaining power of many of the Developing countries by presenting their development-focused agenda. What transpired to be crucial at the Conference was that the Developing countries formed a negotiating coalition and their demands played a great role in causing a stalemate in the Doha round.

Developing countries alleged that the national agricultural policies of the Developed countries were the cause of the problems both at the domestic and international level as they intend to be protectionist, their tendency to isolate domestic markets from international agriculture markets. Discussion concerning the tariffs imposed as special safeguard measures were also held, i.e., the Special Safeguard Measure provisions of the Article 5 of the AoA. With regard to diluting the safeguard measures, the Developing countries were concerned that future tariff cuts, from their side, would increase the vulnerability of some of their newly-developed agro-industries to the external market. It was emphasised during the discussions that the continuation of special safeguard mechanism for some

[157]WTO Agriculture Negotiations. The issues, and where we are now. (Briefing document), p. 31. http://www.wto.org/english/tratop_e/agric_e/agnegs_bkgrnd_e.pdf.

[158]November 2001.

extended time favours Developing countries and Less-Developed countries. This was discussed with a proposal similar to the current SSG provisions.[159]

Based on the development and welfare objectives, the Developing countries also obtained special exemption on the basis of Special and Differential treatment.[160] So far as these provisions are concerned, the Doha Declaration recognised that *special and differential treatment* for the Developing countries should be an integral part of all the agreements including the Agreement on Agriculture. These concessions were to remain operationally effective so as to enable the Developing countries, to effectively take account of their development needs, including food security and rural development. The emphasis to continue with the special concessions for the Developing and Less-Developed countries created a stalemate-like situation.

The deadlock was broken after the Developed countries agreed on the gradual phase-out of the subsidies from their side. The EU agreed to the elimination of a large extent of the export subsidies by 2013, and also the disciplining of the export credits. Nevertheless, considering the current political scenario and after the Brexit, it seems that a full elimination may not be possible. However, a noticeable factor during this Conference was the bargaining power of the Developing countries, which offers hopes and the prospects for the reduction of the agricultural subsidies of the Developed countries.

Further it can be added, about this conference that Member States accepted the proposition, that the extent of farm subsidies being practiced by the Developed countries was critical for the African countries. As agriculture is central to Africa's economic construction, so Africa's key concern was the massive export subsidies provided by the EU governments to its farmers. Subsidies given by the Developed nations to their farmers, reduce the farm costs, and relatively, creates more demand for the imported agricultural goods in the African countries as the imported products are relatively cheaper. This leads to the gradual annihilation of the indigenous cultivation.

In the matters of international trade, the import demand can grossly effect the exchange rate movements or internal market developments in the importing country such as creating reduced domestic output or decline in the growth in the domestic farm sector (as discussed in Chaps. 1 and 2). This means need for more loans and foreign aid for the construction of the industrial side of the economy, and finally economy getting trapped in a cycle of debt or under the grip of powerful economies. The growing influence of China in the African countries is an example.[161]

---

[159] Harris and Harris Associates (2008), p. 4. www.apec.org.au/docs/08-SSG_Dh.pdf.

Member countries can invoke SSG's through a price-based-Formula and a quantity based formula. Safeguards only be invoked for products that were nominated for SSG status and only one type of safeguard action can operate at any time.

[160] Special and Differential treatment as mentioned in Article 27 of the SCM Agreement.

[161] For detail reference see, Dr Asche and Dr. Schüller, "China's Engagement in Africa- Opportunities and Risks for Development." *GTZ Partner of the Future Worldwide*, p. 46. Eschborn/Germany. www.gtz.de/de/dokumente/gtz2008-de-china-afrika-lang.pdf.

Despite difference in opinion on several issues, there were some constructive discussions too at Doha, such as the safeguard measures that need to be activated in exceptional circumstances when industrial adjustment pressures in the importing country.[162]

The declaration made during the conference was inadequate on the issue of disciplining the subsidies of the Developed countries. Although, there was a proposal for phasing out all forms of "export subsidies," no strict time frame for phasing out subsidies or for reducing them was committed to by either of the party. As a matter of positive advancement, a commitment to substantial reductions on a gradual basis, in the case of trade-distorting domestic support was agreed.

3.6.1 Bali Conference[163]

During the Bali conference, Subsidies for Agriculture, was also a key issue on the discussion table. Both the Developed and Developing/Less Developed countries provide subsidies to their farmers in one form or the other. In this regard, the Developing countries raised the issue that expectations from them to make commitments for maintaining trade liberalisation in the agriculture sector are higher than the Developed countries willingness to reduce subsidies for export.[164] In the course of discussions, the Developing/Less-Developed countries emphasised that for them giving subsidies to farmers is a necessity. Their justification for state support is based on the need for food security which is based on the fact that a large number of their people lives at a threshold level. It is often the case that the market liberalization agenda is heavily supported by the Developed countries. The interface between the normative aspects, multilateral free trade based and the domestic agenda based, often create complexities, as the domestic issues are compelled to a bargain, such as the matters of food security, subsidies for development, product standards, and several others. The complexities formed because of the different normative characteristics is one of the key reasons leading to the stalemate during several rounds of WTO ministerial conferences. Authors have different perspective on this issue. 'Regan'[165] as referred to by Prof. Mavroidis, in his book *Trade in Goods*, argued that the very purpose of GATT and the WTO was to counter market protectionism. Regan is right in stating that without the GATT trading system, the nations will have chances to protect the domestic industry. On the other hand, 'Bagwell and Staiger'[166] referred for comparison, in Prof. Mavroidis's book, states, that the role of trade agreement is essentially to *address a domestic problem and not*

[162]WT/MIN (01)/DEC/2, 20Nov (2001), DOHA Ministerial conference.

[163]WT/MIN (13)/38 Ministerial Conference, Ninth Session Bali, 3–6 December 2013.

[164]www.wto.org see, 9th WTO Ministerial Conference, Bali 2013.

[165]Regan (2006) (referred in) Mavroidis, *Trade in Goods* (2007), p. 14.

[166]Bagwell and Staiger (referred in) Mavroidis, *Trade in Goods* (2007), p. 14.

international externality. This view point also has reasonable justification, since the bigger economies influence the terms of trade and have strong incentives to set up the tariff measures. In order to maintain a balance between the domestic system and the international legal system, it is essential that the Governments of the Member States, *need to safeguard their sovereign interests rather than becoming subdued into multilateralism*.[167]

It seems the reason for protectionism is because of "the role expected from the trade agreement& forum, which is essentially to address a domestic problem and not an international externality. The dilemma with this explanation for the GATT &WTO is that it remains unclear why governments would negotiate such an agreement in the first place, unless their true aim was to maximize social welfare." The emphasis is also from the side of political pressure that a Member State has to deal with when he discusses the reasons for the protectionist policy.[168]This also revolves around the constitutional responsibilities. Necessity based protection or providing subsidies do have some analogous relationships with this reasoning's.

The issue of food security: The purchase of farm products by the government from the farmers, at a supported price to build up the stocks, is covered within the definition of subsidies. This type of support is classified as Amber Box subsidies.[169] During the recent WTO discussions the Developing countries put forward the issue that concerned them i.e., the permissible limit of storage is basically at the *de minimis* level, i.e., up to 10% of the value of production. Some of the Developing countries consider such a measure as a paradox in the WTO objectives of the welfare and development opportunities for the Developing countries. A group of Developing countries proposed that this clause requires flexibility as it is important for them to stockpile in order to supply the stocked produce to low income consumers also categorised under food security measures.[170]

One significant reason for stock piling instead of buying from the international market is that the economy of the Developing and Less-Developed countries is vulnerable, and additionally, the terms of trade concepts in practical terms do differ. Larger economies can influence the terms of trade by setting the tariffs in their favour and therefore influencing the market price.[171] This issue can again generate a

---

[167]Mavroidis, *Trade in Goods* (2007), p. 14.

[168]Mavroidis, *Trade in Goods* (2007), pp. 14–15.

[169]Amber Box "When government buy food from farmers at supported prices to build up stocks, that count as Amber Box, domestic support-the type that can distort trade by affecting the market prices."

[170]For details see www.wto.org Bali conference. One group, the G-33, circulated a proposal in November 2012 to amend the Agriculture Agreement, so that support of this type by the Developing countries- to benefit low income farmers or those who lack resources would be considered Green Box and therefore be allowed without limits. However there are contrary opinions to this proposal also. A group of members agree that food security is a vital issue but providing unconditional relaxations might lead to weakening the disciplines that apply to state support.

[171]Mavroidis, *Trade in Goods*. (2007), pp. 14–15.

debate as to whether trade liberalisation can be the best possibility for all type of economies.

Considering the existing scenario, Members have agreed to an interim mechanism on the issue of public stockholding, meant for food security purposes, until an agreement on a permanent solution is reached.

Furthermore, it was also agreed by the Member States to have an interim period allowing subsidies with the condition of gradual reduction. Additionally, it was agreed that until a permanent solution is reached, all Members should refrain from challenging, through the DSB mechanism, the compliance by the Developing member of its obligations under Article 6.3 and 7.2(b) of the Agreement on Agriculture, in relation to the support provided for traditional staple food crops in pursuance of public stockholding programmes for food security.

Additionally, during the conference, it was also agreed that a Developing Member benefitting from this decision must notify the committee if they exceed or were at risk of exceeding, the limits of AMS or the *de minimis* level.

A significant concern and in order to check circumvention, the proposal was presented that Developing Members should ensure that the stocks procured do not distort trade or adversely affect the food security of other Members. From the discussions held during the Bali conference, it seems the Developing Member States have put forward their concern regarding the agriculture market and the reasons for the need of the domestic level support. Such support seems to be for welfare and in order to provide a sense of security to their farming class. It is expected that income support and the stabilisation programmes that are put forward by the Developing countries will, probably also help in the redistribution of income.

3.7 Market Socialism as an Alternative for the Developing and Less-Developed Countries

Conflict between the ideologies supporting capitalism and socialism. Is the socialist model based on a fair trade approach?

If the economic concepts of free trade, are not the viable solutions for bringing improvement in living standards because of the complexities, due to the differences in the political, social and economic situations of the Member States, the question then arises, what is the alternative?

Can market socialism be an alternative to free trade; for the purpose of trade in agriculture? Market socialism is a derivative of Marxian theory. Its principles can be applied as an approach for attaining some level of social equality and distribution of resources. In this type of economic model, the farming structure is partly or completely owned and regulated by the government. Following this model of an economic approach at the foundation level can be supportive for bringing a certain level of equality, to the development of a market structure. First attaining self-sufficiency, then at the later stages, Member States can export their products to the competitive market economies.[172] This type of transformation can be seen mainly in the Eastern European countries. Prior to their joining the E.U, they followed a strict socialist economy seeking guidance from the USSR and COMECON,[173] however, with the disintegration of Russia, this has now changed.

Referred to here is the example of China, an economy that at its initial phase and until recently, followed a socialist pattern. In China, the collective farming movement began in 1950. The logic in this case was that small farms and individual households would not be able to cope with natural disasters.[174] After the land reforms based on a socialistic pattern, China showed an impressive agricultural growth. China's agricultural economy from 1978 to 1984, noted a grain production increase of 4.7% per year,[175] a fact which indicates success based on the socialistic pattern adopted by China. Moreover, at the second stage of development, the strong farming sector became the backbone for industrialisation. After forming a strong market base, the Chinese system began transforming to a capitalist mode.

On the other hand, one can see that those lobbying for capitalism, in the Western bloc, have also shed some of the elements of capitalist ideologies with regard to the question of the agricultural sector. This can be seen in the form of government intervention in the farming sector. Government's intervention in the agricultural arena cannot be denied and is in various forms, such as loan guarantees to large firms and deposit guarantees to savings and support through government financial institutions.[176]

The economic reasons as well, that have emerged due to the promotion of free trade, variance in socio-political structure also need to be taken into account when providing subsidies in Developed, Developing and Less-Developed countries.

In terms of academic and non-political discussions, and in order to understand the link between the social, economic, and political aspects of the problems of agriculture sector, from the level of generality, the views of Karl Marx cannot be ignored as some of his sayings seem to be of fundamental significance. His ideas on this issue seem to be similar to a natural law thinker.[177]

---

[172]Shleifer and Vishny (1994), p. 165.

[173]COMECON was the Council for Mutual Economic Assistance, (CMEA) established in January 1949 to facilitate and coordinate the economic development of the Eastern European countries belonging to the Soviet bloc. COMECON was formed under the aegis of the Soviet Union 1949 in response to the formation of the Committee of European Economic Cooperation in Western Europe.

[174]Zhang, L.X. *Agriculture and rural development in China*. Chinese Academy of Sciences. p. 1. www.worldfish centre.org China./China_agriculture.

[175]Zhang, L.X. *Agriculture and rural development in China*. Chinese Academy of Sciences. p. 4. www.worldfish centre.org China./China_agriculture.

[176]Penson et al. (2010), p. 6.

[177]According to Karl Marx, "The form of landed property with which we are dealing is a specific historical form, a form transformed by the intervention of capital and the capitalist mode of production. The original form was that of feudal landed property or of small peasant agriculture, pursued as a livelihood; In this latter case possession of the land and soil appeared as a condition of production for the immediate producer, with his ownership of the land being the most advantageous condition, the condition for his mode of production to flourish." For reference see, Marx (trans: Fernbach D) (1991), p. 751. Karl Marx outlined that the model of production with which we

The crucial statement (by Karl Marx), that profoundly challenges the capitalist mode of market system for agricultural products is the following:

> This is a determination by a market value brought about by competition on the basis of the capitalist mode of production; it is the competition that produces a false social value. This results from the law of market value to which agricultural products are subjected. The determination of the market value of products, i.e., also of products of the soil, is a social act, even if performed by society unconsciously and unintentionally, and it is based necessarily on the exchange-value of the product and not on the soil and the differences in its fertility.[178]

In the Capitalist mode it is the "Free market" economic system, in which an individual can employ resources according to their free will, with the primary purpose of profit making, whereas, in the socialist pattern resources are considered as collective property, and the government can intervene and make decisions as regards the welfare of the maximum number of the people. It is significant to note here, that the economy of the emerging nations rely very much on the checks and balances on free trade. However, what seems to be un-fateful was that the Soviet system was challenged from within. This was because of an ongoing over-investment in the military industry and meagre consideration was given to investment in agriculture. Therefore, a disequilibrium emerged in reforms and was moreover accelerated during the time of Gorbachev, which eventually led to the weakening of the soviet economic structure.[179]

In another way round, it can be said that the issue of agricultural subsidy sometime is a midway economic alternative in order to pacify the conflict between capitalism and socialism. Furthermore, it may not be incorrect to say that if Marxism means price fixing, then subsidies are semi-price fixing.[180] Considering the positive instances of the socialistic approach, one cannot deny it as a viable option, and that similar sorts of measure are required mainly in the case of transforming economies.

---

are dealing today, is a process that has gone through historical ages before the capitalist mode was adopted. It is noteworthy, that in the capitalist mode of production, he considers agricultural product, as the objects with a potential form of economic values, and which has the characteristic of being converted into an exchange value through money as a medium. Further, he explains that agriculture production was based on two general causes that are independent of capital.

(1) Fertility of the land with which he meant natural fertility and (2) The location of the land with which he meant the distance of the land from the basic resources such as, water sources of market etc. Here capital formation can be seen as unfair intervention which has led to the unregulated free trade practices.

[178]Marx (trans: Fernbach D) (1991), pp. 518, 799.

[179]Maude (2010), p. 276.

[180]Penson et al. (2010), p. 6.

3.8 The Relationship Between Subsidies for Biofuels and Agricultural Subsidies

The lure of renewable fuels has created an urge for bio fuels among the Member States, from those concerned about the reliance on fossil fuels and for the global environmental consequences, to those who perceive that renewable fuels can be used for economic reasons. With the rise in fuel prices, and because of the environmental concerns, a large number of countries have emphasised the development of renewable energy sources.[181] One such alternative is the commercial production of biofuels. However, with the growing demand for biofuels, new challenges are emerging.[182] Challenges such as, the fact that the use of corn for oil and vegetable oil from soya-beans, and palm oil for ethanol, appears to be escalating the pressure on food prices. Drawing conclusions based on facts and presumption, it can be said that if biofuels are to make a constructive contribution to sustainable development, the public policy and market policy of the Member States needs to be evolved both on the basis of an assessment of their contribution to sustainable development as well as through the various types of adverse implications.[183]

Discussing here, from the free trade policy concerns, on the one side and also from the constitutional objectives of the Member States, it is necessary to analyse the nature of the biofuel subsidies provided by the Member States and evaluate for making comparison with the constraints on the use of agricultural subsidies through the provisions mentioned in the AoA. The primary question arises, in which category, state support for biofuel research and its market production is to be classified. For the purpose of general differentiation and for the convenience in understanding, state support is classified in AoA under three categories, Amber box, Blue box and Green box. (as explained previously). If the biofuel subsidies are counted as restrictive agricultural subsidies, the point to be evaluated is, whether they should be notified as trade distorting either under the Amber or Blue box. If they are subsidies for the purpose of research and for the conservation of the environment, then they are exempted through the provisions of Annex 2 and can be considered as Green box subsidies. [Annex 2,(DOMESTIC SUPPORT: THE BASIS FOR EXEMPTION FROM THE REDUCTION COMMITMENTS) Clause 2(a) *research, including general research, research in connection with environmental programmes and research programmes relating to particular products.*] Ironically, the area of subsidies is so vast that the differentiations based on legal provisions do not cover all type of subsidy practices. Therefore, there often remains a dilemma about the justifiable and non-justifiable use of subsidies.

---

[181]World Energy Outlook 2012. International Energy Agency. Paris, 2012. p. 1. http://www.worldenergyoutlook.org/publications/weo-2012/.

[182]For reference, see Tangermann (2014), p. 41.

[183]Melendez-Ortiz et al. (2009), p. 530.

Generally, basic agricultural products transformed into other products can be minimally trade-distorting, for example, if a feedstock is a waste product or cellulosic material, then it is not a "marketable agricultural product" and can be used for the production of biofuels.[184] In such cases, biofuel subsidies could fit within the Green box, as defined.

While analysing the issue of trade distortion, another interpretation for the subsidies provided for bio-fuel production can be to consider them as an indirect support to the producers of feedstock; for example, corn, sugarcane, and oilseeds. Such support can be either in the form of basic support given to the farmers or support intertwined with the motive for the production of bio crops for the commercial purposes. Either of these interpretations could be advocated, without much differentiation between justifiable and non-justifiable use of subsidies. This is, due to the lack of provisions with differential scales to separate and determine if subsidies are provided with a profit motive or for nonprofit motives.

The AoA in this context seems to have an unclear foundation for a threshold requirement to be set up as a starting point, in order to classify trade distorting subsidies in the context of biofuels. The discussion nevertheless is specific and cover the horizontal plane, considering the subsidies to farm crops for biofuels and their further implications.

3.8.1 *Downsides of Biofuels Cropping*

Biofuels may be defined simply as "liquid or gaseous fuel produced from biomass and is used as a fuel for the purpose of transport." Biomass can be described as the raw material for the biofuel, which may come from agriculture, forestry or can be waste based.[185] The two main biofuels are Ethanol and Biodiesel.[186] Ethanol is usually produced from sugar and starchy crops such as cereals, whereas biodiesel is processed from oil seed crops.[187] With the rise in market demand for biofuel, leading to unregulated free trade, the planting of biofuel crops has increased, ironically resulting to the detriment of the cereal crops. This unregulated biofuels cropping can have implications beyond the balancing capacity of the WTO in the context of accomplishing its objectives based on fair and free trade under the present working position.

So far as the application of the AoA provisions are concerned, there seems to be a divide between the Developed and Developing countries, as it is in the case of

---

[184] Issue Brief: Converting Cellulose into Ethanol and Other Biofuels. A publication of Ethanol A cross America. 2010 Edition. p. 3. http://www.cleanfuelsdc.org/pubs/documents/CellulosicEthanolIssueBrief11109.pdf.

[185] Echols (2009), p. 6.

[186] Wright (2011), p. 49.

[187] Sorda et al. (2010), p. 6977.

subsidies for industrial goods. It seems that the domestic policies of the Developed nations concerning the market-use of biofuels are framed without taking into account the fundamental needs of those economies which are still at the early stages of industrialization. Following such a policy approach is like thrusting the Developed countries business concepts or business model, without enduring the social needs of the emerging economies as a priority basis. As also mentioned previously, such one-sided consideration goes contrary to the objectives of the WTO[188] and objectives of the AoA[189] as mentioned in the preamble.

3.8.1.1 Example of Biofuels in Malaysia

In Malaysia, the conventional method of producing biofuel is through trans-esterification which produces Palm-Methyl Esters (PME), primarily for the export market.[190] Of the total production, large amount of Malaysia's biodiesel production is exported to the EU and US. Thus, it can be concluded that the profitability of the Malaysian biodiesel export depends upon the production-cost of the palm-oil prices and the petroleum-prices. In order to attain more profit, the production of the biofuel is supported by government subsidies. As an outcome of these developments, palm-oil cultivation has relatively increased and there is a steep decline in the production of other crops. With the exception of paddy (rice), whose land conversion to other uses is regulated, other commodities, for example; rubber, cocoa, coconut, pepper, pineapple, tobacco, coffee, tea, and sugarcane are experiencing a decline in their areas of cultivation.[191]

Adding here in this regard excerpts from the report published. In the Helsingin Sanomat dated 25.5.2012, the article reported that the RSPO, Roundtable Sustainable Palm Oil, had suspended the granting of certificates to the Malaysian Company IOI,[192] an important supplier of palm for the Finnish Neste Oil. The basic objectives

[188]From the WTO preamble. "Recognizing that their relations in the field of trade and economic endeavor should be conducted with a view to raising standards of living, ensuring full employment and a large and steadily growing volume of real income and effective demand, and expanding the production of and trade in goods and services, while allowing for the optimal use of world's resources."

[189]From the AoA preamble. "Having regard to the agreement that special and differential treatment for developing countries is an integral element of the negotiations, and taking into account the possible negative effects of the implementation of the reform programme on least-developed and net food importing developing countries."

[190]Lopez and Laan (2008), p. 4.

[191]Lopez and Laan (2008), p. 13.

[192]IOI Corporation Berhad commonly referred to as **IOI**, was incorporated on 31 October 1969 as **Industrial Oxygen Incorporated Sdn Bhd**. IOI is one of Malaysia's biggest conglomerates that started off from industrial gas manufacturing.

of the RSPO was to certify that palm oil is being produced in a manner that does not harm people or nature.[193]

Bio crops cultivation on a commercial basis is creating a price-rise in cereal crops. In this regard, one can say, that the WTO Agreement seems a treaty based contract between the Member States, which is probably a regime creating exercise[194] by the Developed countries. With the multinationals promoting biofuel crops in Less-Developed and also in some of the Developing countries because of the conducive weather conditions, the interests of the small farmers has become subjugated to the wishes of the multinationals.

The social and economic implications for the Developing countries because of the commercial production of biofuels by the multinationals, demands an analysis based on the long term effects. Arguing here from the perspective of the WTO objectives, the question arises as to who is bearing the final burden of the Biofuel experiment? One may reach the conclusion that it is the small peasants mainly from the Developing and Less-Developed economies.

The provision of Green box subsidies, as included in the AoA, although designed to promote research, do not clarify the quantitative basis of the concession being given to the Member States. Although, a general set of restrictive provisions are mentioned in Article 6[195] of the AoA, but they do not create a specific set of obligations for the multinationals. In the lack of such specific provisions to disentangle whether the objectives are for the welfare of the farmers or for commercial purposes, the legal position remains feeble for the purpose of attaining a balance between the two different objectives, i.e., the promotion of free trade and the welfare and development measures supported by fair trade values set up in the AoA.

Within the framework of the WTO, there is no possibility for an individual to make claims in cases where his rights are affected. From the perspective of free trade and subsidies for biofuels, it seems that the economic aspects such as market efficiency, is promoting competition through experimentation and finally it is the survival of the most efficient that applies. However, as the Member States are categorised as Developed, Developing, and Less-Developed, the degree of institutional harmony within the Member states and meeting the common objectives through horizontal cooperation among the Member States also becomes a testing issue.

---

[193] As mentioned in the Helsingin Sanomat, dated 25.5.2012, the RSPO announced on its website that the IOI had not been following the ethics of trade, but engaged in illegal destruction of forests and the draining of wetlands that are important habitats for endangered species.

[194] Footer (2006), p. 3.

[195] Article 6 of the AoA. Decoupled income support. (a) Eligibility for such payments shall be determined by clearly-defined criteria such as income, status as a producer or landowner, factor use or production level in a defined and fixed base period. (b) The amount of such payments in any given year shall not be related to or based on type or volume of production, (c) not related to or based on the prices domestic or international (d) not related to or based on factors of production employed.

Comparing this, with the objectives supporting the welfare and development of the Developing and Less-Developed countries on a priority basis, as mentioned in the preamble of the AoA, this example about the effect of commercial biofuel cropping, illustrates the contradictions in the practices of the advanced economies and those of the Developing countries. These Developing countries follow trade practices without following the basic welfare objectives.

3.8.1.2 As an Instance of Developed Country the US Is Taken Here as an Example

There is indeed an attempt to reduce subsidies, however, state support is also provided for the commercial use of the new technologies and new methods. Referring here the example of the US, where state support is being provided to promote the use of biofuels. Several states in the US[196] established lower tax rates for gasohol than for gasoline. Additionally, one can notice the previous Acts, Volumetric Ethanol Excise Tax Credit Act, which is in the committee stage for renewal, as its term has expired.[197] Moreover, currently the US has introduced a bill entitled "Biofuels Market Expansion Act of 2011" which require automobile manufacturers to ensure that at least 50% of the models from the year, 2014–2015 and afterwards of the automobiles and light duty trucks manufactured for sale in the United States need to function with blended fuel.[198] These bills and several other ancillary acts heavily support the biofuel-based industry. Keeping in view the WTO objectives as a guiding principles while framing domestic policies, the Developed nations are expected to reduce the AMS, categorised under Amber Box. However, with the increase in such adopted policies, the burden seems finally to fall again on Developing and Less-Developed countries. The exemptions under the Green box need to be used for the welfare and other development purposes mentioned in the provisions. Member States used to consider that these exemptions need not be applied solely for the promotion of the trade.

---

[196]Biofuels Overview: Centre for Climate and Energy Solutions. p. 3. http://www.c2es.org/technology/overview/biofuels.

[197]Volumetric Ethanol Excise Tax Credit Repeal Act-Amends the Internal Revenue Code to provide for the immediate repeal (the current expiration date is December 31, 2011) of the income and excise tax credits for alcohol fuel mixtures (ethanol).

[198]**See Bill text** S.187-Biofuels Market Expansion Act of 2011 (introduced in the Senate) Sec 2, Clause 6. Authorization of Appropriations. There are authorized to be appropriated to the secretary to carry out this section, to remain available until spent

A) $50,000,000 for fiscal year 2012,
B) $100,000,000 for fiscal year 2013,
C) $200,000,000 for fiscal year 2014,
D) $300,000,000 for fiscal year 2015 and
E) $350, 000,000 for fiscal year 2016.

3.8.1.3 The Effect of Bio-Fuel in Africa

Biomass in the tropical countries is higher in terms of photosynthesis efficiency. With the growing demand for bio crops, this can lead to a shift in the agricultural pattern, from food-based crops to bio-crops. Hundreds of African people depend upon the wetlands for their livelihood. These wetlands are also the potential places for the growth of biofuels. Mozambique and Tanzania, two of the African nations taken here as examples are both well-suited for growing a range of feedstock crops, including sugarcane and cassava for ethanol and oilseeds for biodiesel.[199] Of all the bio crops, the cultivation of sugarcane poses heavy burden.[200] It requires large amounts of water and is therefore often grown in wetlands. Most of the bio-crop so produced is bought by the EU and the US, because of its availability at a cheaper price. On the other hand, the African economy remains in deficit of its basic food crops. The native people depend on the availability of fresh and clean water for the domestic uses and for the purpose of irrigation. This area is also used for seasonal grazing for agricultural purposes and for fishing at small scale. As a consequence of more of their land being used for the cultivation of bio crops, traditional economic system seems affected. Therefore, one cannot deny that the rise in the demand for biofuel can be both an opportunity and a threat to the African people. This issue from the perspective of the WTO initiates the debate, between public and private law, as the role of multinationals is seen a subject of private law and constitutional rights of the individuals as a matter of public law conception.

Analysed in relation to free trade, subsidies are not inconsistent unless used in a circumvented manner by distorting the WTO-based objectives of trade. As Article 8[201] of the SCM Agreement is no longer in function, whenever issues of public benefits are before adjudicating bodies, exceptions may be created by interpretations of the existing provisions that regulate subsidies.[202] In order to define the status of subsidies in agricultural products, there are specific provisions in the Agreement on Agriculture, but these provisions do not cover Bio fuel subsidies and their effects. When there are new emerging issues, the role of the Ministerial Conference holds significance for detailed discussions about the effects. The primary task of the ministerial conference is to discuss and carry out the functions of the WTO and take actions accordingly.[203] New programmes and agendas that are connected with the trade issues are dedicated to the specialized committees.

---

[199] Arndt, Channing, et al. *Are Biofuels Good for African Development?" An Analytical Framework with evidence from Mozambique with Tanzania,*" UN, wider institute. Working papers no. 210/110. p. 2.

[200] Sielhorst et al. (2008), pp. 20, 49.

[201] Article 8 was the temporary provision subject to renewal. In the aftermath of the 1999 Seattle Ministerial conference, this provision was allowed to lapse.

[202] Cosbey and Mavroidis (2014), p. 46.

[203] www.wto.org.

Remarkably, it was during the Doha Round of multilateral trade talks, that some of the issues concerning ethanol were addressed. This was not only for the improvement in market access, but also to make changes in the Agreement on Agriculture. A proposal was presented by Brazil to include the term environmental goods for Bio-fuel cropping and sale. This move was welcomed by many of the Developing countries. Brazil emphasised that a definition of environmental goods can help to encourage discussion on high tech products, which on many occasions may not be the priority for the Developing countries, but can be of interest to the Developed nations. Probably this can have an impact on the use of subsidies on the necessity basis, and with the economic distinction among the Member States.[204]

3.9 Conclusions

The farming occupation in every country is the source of food, the basis for life, therefore it is un-pragmatic to put on trial the whole issue of farm subsidies, but for the purpose of promoting free trade principles as the fundamental market values.[205] What ironical here is, the linking of the development agenda and welfare, with the trade in agricultural products.

The Agreement on Agriculture in the WTO was included with the idea of creating a comprehensive working system based on the concepts of free trade and accomplishing fair trade objectives. The profound objectives of the WTO were established to meet equitable aspirations such as, raising living standards, ensuring maximum employment and increasing the income level of the nations where the living standard of the majority of the citizens is too low to meet their basic needs. However, the way things have developed after the practical application of the WTO policies has resulted in a debate with mixed opinions. The extent of the commitments of the Member States to meet the WTO objectives, in the existing hierarchical order among the Member States, has raised new doubts. Developing nations that have reduced their domestic support measures also need to assess whether such a reduction is creating any new type of challenge to their farmers, particularly small and marginal farmers. The stress between free trade and fair trade concepts exists at various levels, with regard to implementing the provisions of the Agreement on Agriculture, and this rather creates hindrances in breaking down the cycle of poverty, inequality, and under-development. Undoubtedly, this is also due to the political pressure on the issue of the domestic-support measures. It is suggested that economic, political, and social consistency is required while following any policy approach to attain the WTO objectives.

[204]TN/TE/W/59 July, (2005) "Environmental Goods for Development" Committee on Trade and Environment Special Session. ENVIRONMENTAL GOODS FOR DEVELOPMENT Submission by Brazil.

[205]Fundamental market value means fundamental market values for the WTO.

The economic situation of Africa has been discussed as a reference; It seems the WTO has gone detracted from the objective of improving the standard of living and is fast moving with its agenda for liberalisation, also in this matter. On the other hand the lack of political responsibility of the African leaders is also a crucial factor. Therefore, the internal political system of the Member States also needs to include the realization of the development and welfare objectives.

Can free trade be referred to as an economic fiction, so far as the trade in agricultural products is concerned? On the one hand, Developed countries promote the concepts of free trade in Developing and Less-Developed countries and on the other hand also give extensive support to their farm sector. This seems like practicing market socialism, in the garb of capitalism.

Even with the inclusion of an exclusive Agreement on Agriculture in the WTO trading system, the issues related to trade in agricultural products are still unresolved. The market liberalisation concepts propagated by the WTO are meant to create opportunities for the transforming economies and as a welfare measure to solve the food crisis existing in several countries. However, the situation of Senegal, referred to in the text, shows the paradox of the free trade aspirations. Considering the situation of the African countries from the social and technological perspective, the present economic concepts supporting the free trade policies do not seem to intrinsically cover the social position and the system of several Less-Developed countries. What seems required is the normative base for the support of free trade market structure. Normative structures for the support of free trade, are also essential to meet development and welfare objectives and for creating a pre-requisite social base that can sustain a consistent, established, and trustworthy market system.

The way social effects have developed as a consequence of free trade policies, raises doubts as to whether the economic concepts applied for trade in industrial goods can also be the right approach for the purpose of trade in agricultural products.

Market liberalisation policies demands normative flexibilities from the Member States and in the lack of these, there is a possibility of a backlash. Social, political and economic aspects have been intertwined in societies for a long time. The WTO as an institution, is promoting concepts from its perspectives, so there is often a possibility of reactionary consequences, because of the social political and economic inconsistencies, that follow from the existing patterns in the society.

Who are the real beneficiaries of the subsidy?

From the experience it can be is said that implementing policies to support the economic development of small farmers has proved to be successful in some of the countries such as China, India, Malaysia and several others. Undoubtedly, this strategy has proved to reduce rural poverty and as a next step, the benefits from agriculture sector are used to complement the growth for industrialisation. The second group of beneficiaries includes the multinational agribusiness corporations, as they benefit from access to cheap inputs from the Developing and Less-Developed countries and also they provide the new markets to be served. The local markets and customary activities of rural societies are under the threat of destruction because of the multinationals sale of processed food in the markets. What further seems lacking within the AoA and that can save the basic rights of individuals, is the established basis for individual claims, in the form of provisions.

The development objectives are based on the comparative cost advantage theories. In the line with these objectives, the AoA acts as a mechanism for promoting export-oriented trade liberalisation. However, with the extent of the existing gap, between the large economies and the small market systems, it seems that however, egalitarian the WTO objectives are, trade liberalisation is inevitably creating market situation, where prices for agricultural products fluctuate in response to changes in aggregate supply and demand in markets, thus creating a short fall in the development programme. A short-term, adverse, exchange-rate movement can potentially lead to ad-hoc price based reactions across a number of imported farm products, and consequently will affect the economies of the Less-Developed countries.

The conventional wisdom as is preached by the free trade economists, is that a country should import food if it is cheap, rather than invest in the costly process of producing food within the country. Nevertheless, how far this economic concepts fits in with respect to essential items, seems to be a different question altogether.

Subsidies for research and development are high on agenda in the Developed economies. The initiatives to develop biofuels rest on the growing concerns over global warming and the demand for rapid economic growth. Developing biofuels is a noble idea but its implications on the small farmers and food crops cannot be ignored. It is suggested, that any such policy recommendations must be economically and socially consistent. This level of consistency requires a specification of the relationship between short-term economic development, together with an appraisal of long term social and political effects.

Considering the existing gap between the mentioned objectives and achievements, it is needful to strike a balance between agricultural trade liberalisation and the policy objectives of welfare and development. The justifiable use of subsidies requires that Member States weigh the costs of social, economic political and cultural basis on the one side and the objectives based on market efficiency and development on the other. This would also help to regulate both economic and non-economic values.

References

Arzac ER, Wilkinson M (1979) Stabilization policies for United States feed grain and livestock markets. J Econ Dyn Control (1):39–40

Bhala R (2007) Empathizing with France and Pakistan on agricultural subsidy issues in the Doha Round. Vanderbilt J Transnational Law (40):949–976

Birner R, Resnick D (2010) The political economy of policies for smallholder agriculture. World Dev 38(10):1442–1526

Busch ML, Reinhardt E (2006) Three is a crowd. World Polit 58(3). https://muse.jhu.edu/journals/world_politics/v058/58.3busch.html

Cosbey A, Mavroidis PC (2014) A turquoise mess: green subsidies, blue industrial policy and renewable energy: the case for redrafting the subsidies agreement of the WTO. J Int Econ Law 17(1):46–50

Footer ME (2006) An institutional and normative analysis of the World Trade Organization. Martinus Nijhoff Publishers, Leiden

Penson Jr. JB, Capps Jr. O, Parr Rosson III C, Woodward RT (2010) Introduction to agricultural economics. Prentice Hall, New Jersy

Luca R (2009) The definition of subsidy and state aid: WTO and EC law in comparative perspective. Oxford University Press, New York

Thompson LR (1993) The concise encyclopedia of economics. http://www.econlib.org/libraryEnc1/AgriculturalPriceSupports.html

Macrory P, Appleton AE, Plummer MG (eds) (2005) The World Trade Organization: legal economic and political analysis, vol I. Springer, New York

Fernbach D (trans) (1991) Marx K: the capital Vol-III. Penguin Classics, London

Maude G (2010) The aspects of the governing of the Finns. Peter Lang Publishing, New York

Mavroidis PC (2007) Trade in goods. Oxford University Press, New York

Melendez-Ortiz R, Bellmann C, Hepburn J (2009) Agricultural subsidies in the WTO green box, ensuring coherence with sustainable developments goals. Cambridge University Press, New York

Nugent N (1993) The government and politics of the European community. The Mac Millan Press LTD, New York

Puyana JFP, Pinilla FS, Ordonez RJR (2007) The cumulative application of the agreement on agriculture and subsidies and countervailing agreement. Int Law Rev 209–264. ISSN 1692–8156

Resnick D, Birner R (2010) Agricultural strategy development in West Africa: the false promise of participation ? Dev Policy Rev 28(1):97–115

Shleifer A, Vishny RW (1994) The politics of market socialism. J Econ Perspect 8(2):165–176

Srinivasan TN (2000) Developing countries and the multilateral trading system: from the GATT to the Uruguay Round and the future. Westview Press, Colarado

Stewart TP (1993) The GATT Uruguay Round: a negotiating. history (1986–1992) Volume La: commentary. Kluwer Law and Taxation Publishers, Deventer

Trachtman JP (2008) The economic structure of international law. Harvard University Press, p 22

Weyerbrock S (1998) Reform of the European Union's common agricultural policy: how to reach GATT-compatibility. Eur Econ Rev (42):374–377

Wright BD (2011) The economics of grain price volatility. Appl Econ Perspect Policy 33(1):44–52

Cases

Canada-Measure Affecting the Importation of Milk and the Exportation of Diary Products WT/DS103/R

Chile-Price Band System and Safegurd Measures Relating to Certain Agricultural Products WT/DS207/AB/R

European Communities-Export Subsidies for Sugar WT/DS265/AB/R

India-Quantitative Restrictions on the Import of Agricultural, Textile and Industrial Products WT/DS90/R

United States-Subsidies on Upland Cotton WT/DS267/AB/R

Reports and Electronic Sources

Echols MA (2009) Biofuels certification and the law of the World Trade Organization. Issue Paper No. 19. International Centre for Trade and Sustainable Developments. Geneva. www.ictsd.org

Arndt C, Msangi S, Thurlow J (2010) Are biofuels good for African development ? An analytical framework with evidence from Mozambique with Tanzania. UN, wider institute. Working papers no 2010/110. https://www.wider.unu.edu/sites/default/files/wp2010-110.pdf

Anderson K, Martin W (2005) Agriculture trade reform and the Doha Development Agenda. http://onlinelibrary.wiley.com/doi/10.1111/j.1467-9701.2005.00735.x/abstract

Chatterjee B, Murphy S (2013) Dhaka Roundtable on reviving the multilateral trading post-Bali issues: trade and food security. International Centre for Trade and Sustainable Development. http://cpd.org.bd/index.php/doha-round-ldc-wto-centre-for-policy-dialogue-cpd-multilateraltrading-bali

Cheng F (2007) Tariff escalation in World Agricultural Trade Case Study#10–11 of the Program. Cornell University, New York. http://cip.cornell.edu/handledns.gfs/1200428210

Dejaegher S (2012) The new federalist, webzine of the young European Federalist. EU Reforms Farm Aid: one big budget, many interests. http://www.thenewfederalists.eu/EU-Reforms-Farm-Aid-One-Big-Budget-Many-Interests,04820

Asche H, Schuller M (2008) China's engagement in Africa-opportunities and risk for development. GTZ Partner of the Future Worldwide. Eschborn, Germany www.gtz.de/de/dokumente/gtz2008-de-china-africa-lang.pdf

Harris D, D N Harris & Associates (2008) Special Safeguards and Agriculture Trade Liberlisation. RIRDC publication, no 8/125. www.apec.org.au/docs/08-SSG_Dh.pdf

Howse R, Josling T (2012) Agricultural export restrictions and international trade law: a way forward. International Food & Agricultural Trade Policy Council, Washington. http://www.agritrade.org/Publications/ExportRestrictionsandTradeLaw.html

Ingco MD, Nash JD (eds) (2004) Agriculture and the WTO, creating a trading system for development. The International Bank for the Reconstruction and Development. The World Bank, Washington DC. http://documents.worldbank.org/curated/en/2004/03/5050854/agriculture-wto-creating-trading-system-development

Kant C (1996) Foreign direct investment and capital flight, Princeton studies in international finance. Princeton University, New Jersey. http://www.princeton.edu/ies/IES_Studies/S80.pdf

Burl H, Durante D (2010) Issue brief: converting cellulose into ethanol and other biofuels. A publication of Ethanol Across America. http://www.cleanfuelsdc.org/pubs/documents/CellulosicEthanolIssueBrief1109.pdf

Jostling T, Roberts D (2011) Measuring the impact of SPS Standards on Market Access International Food & Agricultural Trade Policy Council. http://www.oecd.org/tad/ntm/48632882.pdf

Khor M (2003) WTO Agriculture Agreement: what is at stake? *Seatini Bulletin* Southern and Eastern African Trade Information and Negotiations Institute. http://www.seatiniuganda.org/support-our-work/whatson

Lopez GP, Laan T (2008) Biofuels at what cost? Government support for biodiesel in Malaysia. International Institute for Sustainable Development. Geneva. http://www.iisd.org/pdf/2008/biofuels_subsidies_malaysia.pdf

Matthew A (2012) Agricultural council continues CAP debate. http://capreform.eu/october-agricultural-council-continues-cap-debate/

The WTO Agriculture Negotiations. The Issues and Where we are now. www.wto.org

Price volatility in food and agriculture markets: policy responses (2 June 2011)

FAO, IFAD, OECD; UNCTAD; WFP the World Bank, the WTO, IFPRI and the UN HLTF. http://www.oecd.org/tad/agricultural-trade/48152638.pdf

Pravin K, Mitra D, Sundram A (2010) Trade, poverty and the lagging regions of South Asia. National Bureau of Economic Research, Cambridge. http://www.nber.org/papers/w16322

Recherche FL & Helene (2007) Rice imports in West Africa: trade regimes and food policy formulation. MOISA presentation at 106th seminar of the EAAE. Montpellier, France. www.ageconsearch.umn.edu/bitstream/.../1/pp07la02.pdf
Saggi K, Yildiz HM. Art XXIV of the GATT: good, bad, or both? http://economics.ca/2004/papers/0241.pdf
Seaton N (2013) EU Policy Update: Reform of Common Agricultural Policy (CAP) National Assembly of Wales. http://www.assemblywales.org/13-069.pdf
Sielhorst S, Molenaar JW, Offermans D (2008) Bio fuels in Africa: an assessment of risks and benefits for African wetlands. Wetlands International. www.wetlands.org
Solutions (2009) Biofuels overview: centre for climate and energy. http://www.c2es.org/technology/overview/biofuels
Sorda G, Banse M, Kemfert C (2010) An overview of biofuel policies across the world. Energy Policy. 38(11):6977–6988. http://www.sciencedirect.com/science/article/pii/S0301421510005434
Tancu M-D (2010) US and EU's agricultural policies in the context of the GATT/WTO. Åarhus University. http://pure.au.dk/portal/files/12176/mt84715_thesis.pdf
Tangermann S (2014) Post Bali issues in agricultural trade: a synthesis. OECD Global Forum on Agriculture, Paris. http://www.oecd.org/tad/events/AL-Tangermann.pdf
Young LM (2005) Export competition disciplines in the Doha Round, Trade Policy Issues. Paper 3. http://ageconsearch.umn.edu/handle/14573
Zhang LX. Agriculture and rural development in China. Chinease Academy of Sciences. http://pubs.worldfishcentre.org/Pubs/china/pdf/china_agricultural.pdf
TN/TE/W/59, (July 2005) "ENVIRONMENTAL GOODS FOR DEVELOPMENT"
WT/MIN(01)/DEC/2, (20 Nov 2001) DOHA Ministerial Conference
World Energy Outlook (2012) International Energy Agency, Paris. http://www.worldenergyoutlook.org/publications/weo-2012
WT/MIN(13)/38 Ministerial Conference, Bali. (2013)
World Trade Report (2006) www.wto.org
www.wto.org. schedules of cocessions on goods
www.wto.org. 9th Ministerial Conference, (3–6 December 2013) Bali
WTO Ninth-Ministerial Conferences. Bali, (2013) Briefing note: agriculture negotiations - the bid to harvest some low hanging fruit. www.wto.org/english/thewto_e/minist_e/mc9_ebrief-agneg

Chapter 4
Subsidies for Dumping

Abstract With the promotion of free trade, by the WTO, the Member States have started reducing the trade barriers, both in the agriculture and industrial sectors. As a natural consequence of phasing out of these trade barriers, consumer's access to the imported products has indeed become easier; the choices for the products have increased and because of the market competitiveness, the prices of the products have become relatively lower. Despite the promotion of these free trade objectives, the market system of the Member States have to face new forms of challenges, such as unfair use of trade-subsidies, strategic use of subsidies as a background support for predatory-pricing and also for dumping the products in the market of other countries. What further seems incompatible with the principles of free trade, is that Member States, by discarding the WTO objectives, have started reacting in an over-competitive manner in order to prevail in the market. Taking into consideration the trade statistics, it is evident that the business firms from both the Developed and Developing nations, in order to maximize profits try to out-manoeuvre in the free trading system, by resorting to the trade practice of dumping or using subsidies for dumping. Such practices have raised the issue of connection between Subsidies and Dumping for financial objectives. The issue of interrelationship between Dumping and Subsidies was raised in the case of United States-Definitive Anti-Dumping and Countervailing Duties on Certain Products from China, WT/DS379/R and in the case of China—Countervailing and Anti-Dumping Duties On Grain Oriented Flat-Rolled Electrical Steel from the United States, WT/DS414/R. Trade practices with such characteristics and strategy base, can be an abrogation of the WTO objectives, and are considered as unfair trade practices. Such like practices are apparent both in industrial and agricultural sector. Discussing the trade practice of dumping in general, it can be stated that dumping is a strategic business practice through which products are exported at a cheaper price than their ordinary price in the domestic market or exported at less than the fair value. Now the question arises of how such types of practices are feasible. Such business objective, seems feasible as a result of well-considered measures, for instance by the means of predatory pricing policies of the firms or alternatively, it can be said, the companies being supported to cover the market risks through one or the other form of subsidies.

This chapter is part of an ongoing debate, and attempts to cover the direct and indirect forms of subsidies being provided, with the strategic-market objective of dumping the products in foreign markets. The suggestion, as an alternative, is the adoption of competition policy measures, promoting efficiency, complemented

G. Singh, *Subsidies in the Context of the WTO's Free Trade System*,
DOI 10.1007/978-3-319-62422-8_4

with market regulations by the Member States. The objectives of the Competition policy in effect will naturally create checks and balances in the market system. Further, it can be added that it may be a one sided opinion to say that only the Developed countries play such market games, because Developing countries also use opportunities to dominate foreign markets. This eventually forms a part of the broader discussions, about balancing free trade and fair trade objectives, for the economic advancement of the Developing and Less-Developed countries.

4.1 Subsidies for Dumping: A Market Domination Strategy in the Free Trade System

The issue of free trade versus protection remains the broad theme of discussion. Within the levels of these discussions, the use of subsidies for dumping is a specific subject, demanding a test for the application of subsidies, through the parameters of justifiable or non-justifiable use. This indeed is with the underlying objective of checking the unregulated free trade that leads to market distortion.

Construing the discussion further from the WTO free trade perspective, promoting market efficiency and also advancing to achieve the goal of welfare and development of the Developing and Less Developed countries, mainly by adopting the market concepts of comparative advantage, however seems losing the track. In relation to the objectives of the WTO, it is worth recalling that the attainment of a comparative advantage gets hindered by providing subsidies for exports with the intention of dumping practices. As a result, in such market system, those industries with a comparative advantage eventually replaces those with comparative disadvantage.[1]

Despite the existence of well-founded trade distorting effects, there are several justifiable reasons for providing subsidies, such as for building infrastructures, providing state-aid for the purpose of research, state support for education and several other matters, which creates a wide area of legal discretion for the policy-makers to provide state-support. Practically such like policies may not have strict limitations. Within the SCM Agreement, subsidies classified as 'prohibited subsidies' are restricted under Article 3 of the SCM Agreement. However, subsidies having justifications based on primary or secondary objectives such as those of a welfare and development agenda, can be qualified, on the basis of Article 5, and, Article 6 of the SCM Agreement, that are dealing with actionable subsidies. The provisions covered in these Articles of the Agreement are based on a flexible approach for the interpretation of the provisions, allowing the justifiable use of subsidies. From the expression used in Article 5,[2] it seems that state support is

[1]Bentley and Silberston (2007), p. 35.

[2]Article 5 of the SCM Agreement No Member should cause, through the use of any subsidy referred to in paragraph 1 and 2 of Article 1, adverse effects on the interests of other Members, i.e., (a) injury to the domestic industry of another Member, (b) nullification or impairment of benefits

acceptable, except under conditions that can cause an adverse effect on the domestic industry of the other country. As there are no strict regulatory measures within the provisions, the possibility therefore remains that such forms of subsidies can subsequently lead to the promotion of export by exporting products at a cheaper price and later dumping these products.[3]

What encourages such a type of trade practices and how it escapes the legal regulation is probably the question for the overall trading environment created by institutional set up. With the proliferation of free trade, Member States, irrespective of the economic difference, such as GDP and, currency values of the Member States, are keen to promote trade practices and policies for their benefits and often may adopt practices such as "dumping" thus creating a hindrance to the objectives expected to be attained by free trade. Therefore, in order to check such practices, the WTO has adopted the Agreement on Anti-Dumping entitled "Agreement on the Implementation of Article VI of the General Agreement on Tariffs and Trade 1994." The basic idea behind Anti-dumping action is that an exporter should not be allowed to charge a lower price for his exports than that for domestic sales of the same product by the same exporter. If an exporter was allowed to charge lower prices for exports, than for the domestic sales of the same product, he would then attempt to cover these costs by sales at higher price or by attaining subsidies in the domestic market. Such business attempts will create effects that can be compared with unfair business practices, firstly, in the domestic economy and secondly in the foreign market. This is basically trade distortion and contrary to the key WTO objectives. Further in this regard, it can be added, that such trade practices also reduces the market opportunities for the other Member States. To prevent such practices, thus from causing injury to the domestic industry of an importing country, the importing country is entitled to impose anti-dumping duties, through the provisions of this Act.[4]

4.1.1 The Trade Practice of Dumping and Subsidies. Causing Price Suppression and Price Depression

"Dumping in general" can be defined,[5] as the practice of selling goods, in a foreign market, at a price below their domestic selling-price, after allowing for differences due to transportation expenses, tariffs, and other cost justifications. Such an export,

---

accruing directly or indirectly to another Members under GATT 1994, in particular the benefits of concessions bound under Article II of GATT 1994, (c) Serious prejudice to the interests of another Member.

[3]Cottier and Oesch (2005), p. 1013.

[4]AGREEMENT ON IMPLEMENTATION OF ARTICLE VI OF THE GENERAL AGREEMENT ON TARIFFS AND TRADE 1994.

[5]Douglas (1981), pp. 256–258.

at a lesser price, affects the sale of like products in the market of the importing country.[6] In the case of **CHINA-Countervailing and Anti-Dumping Duties on Grain Oriented Flat-Rolled Electrical Steel From the United States,**[7] the United States complained before the Panel Body, that the measures imposed by Ministry of Commerce of the People's Republic of China, were countervailing duties and anti-dumping duties on GOES (Grain Oriented Flat-Rolled Electrical Steel) imported from the United States.

The background to the complaint by the United States, before the Panel Body, in brief are as such. The issue of both subsidies and anti-dumping, was filed with MOFCOM[8] by the two Chinese steel producers, WISCO (Wuhan Iron and Steel Corporation) and Baosteel (Baosteel Group Corporation).

As regards the complaint, it was alleged that the United States producers of GOES,[9] in particular AK Steel and ATI, had engaged in injurious dumping and in support they were benefitting from subsidies.[10] These two firms alleged that 27 of the US state laws provided subsidies of the countervailing characteristics to the US GOES producers and as a result, the imports from the United States caused and threatened for further damage to the Chinese domestic industry.[11]

The US claims[12] referred to here in brief, was that China acted inconsistently with the provisions of the Anti-Dumping Agreement and of the SCM Agreement because its causation analysis[13] was not supported by positive evidence or based on an objective examination of the evidence.

---

[6]Article 3 of the Agreement on Implementation of Article VI of the General Agreement on Tariffs and Trade 1994. "A determination of injury for the purposes of Article VI of GATT 1994 shall be based on positive evidence and involve an objective examination of both (a) the volume of the dumped imports and the effect of the dumped imports on prices in the domestic market for like product, and (b) the consequent impact of these imports on domestic producers of such products."

[7]WT/DS414/R, Panel Report under appeal on 20 July, 2012.

[8]**MOFCOM,** Ministry of Commerce China through (Memorandum Regarding the Factual Disclosure on the Dumping Margin and Ad Valorem Subsidy Rate for Grain Oriented Flat-Rolled Electrical Steel Antidumping and Countervailing Cases.) See Para 7.7 of WT/DS414/R.

[9]**GOES**, Grain Oriented flat-rolled Electrical Steel. See para 7.7 of WT/DS414/R.

[10]See WT/DS414/R, para 7.7.

[11]See WT/DS414/R, para 2.2.

[12]See WT/DS414/R, para 45, At its outset, the United States argues that Article 3.1 of the Anti-Dumping Agreement and Article 15.1 of the SCM Agreement provide important context for the interpretation of Articles 3.2 and 15.2. Pursuant to Article 3.1 and 15.1 an investigating authority must base its injury determination on positive evidence and conduct an objective examination of the volume of dumped or subsidized imports and their effects on the prices in the domestic market for the like products.

[13]WT/DS414/R, para 9. At the outset, China submits that Article 3.1 of the Anti-Dumping and Article 15.1 of the SCM Agreement are Chapeau provisions that place the issue of the effect [of the dumped or subsidized] on prices in the broader context of Article 3 and 15 respectively. Para 10 China maintains that Article 3.2 and 15.2 impose "only a limited obligations on authorities" to consider the price effects of the subject imports that is, top examine, look at attentively, and think carefully about such price effects.

The A.B, discarding the claims made by China, stated as its reasons, that Article 3.2 and 15.2 require the investigating authority to understand, whether the imports are the cause of significant price suppression and depression in the domestic prices.[14] The Appellate Body, by applying the market rationality, affirmed the decision given by the Panel.[15] It emphasised that Article 3.2[16] and 15.2 of the SCM Agreement,[17] expressly postulated an inquiry into the relationship between subject's imports and the domestic prices of the product. Consideration was taken of, whether the effect of the items imported was to depress or suppress the domestic prices of the like product in the market of the importing country.[18] From the outcome of the case, it can be inferred that there are indeed complexities faced by the DSB, while measuring the economic values, and determining the gains and losses because of such imports. This probably is because of the competing interests. It is noteworthy that the promotion of competitive market policies is based upon the efficiency objectives adopted by the WTO free trade policies. A.B in this case gave the decision keeping in mind the central aspect of free trade and the extent of the scope of the protection justified, in the case of Subsidies and Dumping being practiced. Furthermore, it can be noticed that A.B has attempted, by the use of expression, "the casual relationship between subject imports and injury to the domestic industry" and "whether the effects of such imports or exports is to depress or supress domestic prices to a significant degree." This is to draw a line between

[14]See Para 169. As summarized in Para 154 above, we consider Article 3.2 and 15.2 require an investigating authority to consider the relationship between subject imports and prices of like domestic product, so as to understand whether subject imports provide explanatory force for the occurrence of significant price suppression or depression of domestic prices We are therefore not persuaded by the interpretations advanced by China.

[15]See WT/DS414/AB/R, para 139.

[16]Article 3.2 of the Agreement on Implementation of Article VI of the General Agreement on Tariffs and Trade 1994. With regard to the volume of the dumped imports, the investigating authorities shall consider whether there has been a significant increase in dumped imports, either in absolute terms or relative to production or consumption in the importing Member.... With regard to the effect of the dumped imports on prices, the investigating authorities shall consider whether there has been a significant price undercutting by the dumped imports as compared with the price of a like product of the importing Member or whether the effect of such imports is otherwise to depress prices to a significant degree or prevent price increase.

[17]With regard to the effect of the subsidized imports, the investigating authorities shall consider whether there has been a significant price under cutting by the subsidized imports as compared with the price of a like product of the importing Member, or whether the effect of such imports is otherwise to depress prices to a significant degree or to prevent price increase, which otherwise would have occurred to a significant degree.

[18]See para 140, Appellate Body further added "the word 'affect', which means to have an effect on" does not refer to the status quo but rather is concerned with how the status quo came to be. Contrary to China's argument, Articles 3.2 (of the-Agreement on Implementation of Article VI Of the General Agreement on Tariffs and Trade 1994) and 15.2 of the (SCM Agreement) link the effect on domestic prices with the particular prior event leading to it, that is the subject imports, by specifically requiring the investigating authority to consider whether the effect of subject import is to depress prices or to prevent price increase.

the free trade objectives and applying the regulatory measures based on the effect on the material conditions in the market.

By virtue of the WTO trading objectives, the practice of dumping can be considered as an outcome of *unethical* trade practices adopted by the nations. The use of subsidies for the purpose of dumping exports is unjustifiable and hence unethical in terms of WTO trading concepts.[19] This discriminatory practice, if adopted by a Member State is incompatible with the principles of *fair trade values*.[20]

4.2 The Background Conditions for Dumping

The practice of dumping means selling a product in a foreign market at less than its fair market value and there exists a price discrimination between the home and export market.[21] Additionally, it is significant to note that
while measuring the affects of dumping, the primary procedural condition to be satisfied is, that the measurement of the effect of sale, of a product in a domestic market is to be taken from a like imported products.[22]

Dumping affects market position in situations such as these,

1. When the home and foreign markets are separated by the domestic tariff protection, and there is very little knowledge to the foreign buyers of the actual price of the product in the producer's markets.
2. As there are no uniform set of rules on competition policies among the Member States and many of the Member States have not adopted such trade guidelines, so it is possible that there exists less competition in the home market[23] than the

[19]Within the framework of the SCM Agreement, the classification of subsidies as actionable; for the purpose of this research further classified as justifiable and non-justifiable. Justifiable subsidies and non-justifiable subsidies, or the instances the justifiable subsidies will take the form of non-justifiable, depends very much on the cause and effect relationships on the market.

[20]Significant features of fair trade that are specified for the purpose of study and applied in this chapter are as: Fair trade for promoting market transparency, creating efficiency based on fair competition, and the efficient use of resources. The unregulated use of subsidies is at odds with these concepts. The key objective to follow fair trade concepts is to promote equitable market conditions. Equitable market conditions mean, creating trade opportunities for the Developing and Less-Developed countries. There are provisions in support promoting equitable market condition. These provisions give relaxations, to provide subsidies for the Development in the case of Developing and Less-Developed countries.

[21]Brown and McCulloh (2012), p. 2.

[22]Article 2.6 Throughout this Agreement the term 'like product' (produit similaire) shall be interpreted to mean a product which is identical, i.e. alike in all respects to the product under consideration, or in the absence of such a product, another product which, although not alike in all respects has characteristics closely resembling those of the product under consideration.

[23]Because of the less competition in the home market, the firm can charge higher price from the consumers.

foreign market. The lack of free competition in the domestic market can also be because of the protectionist policies of that Member State.

3. There is a high possibility of exporting at a cheaper price, when a government favours, directly or indirectly, the export industries by favourable economic policies, for example, by providing soft loans or subsidies, etc. so that such industries can compete in the international market.
4. Another reason for the development of such market situations is the unwillingness and equivocalness of the WTO Member States in adopting a uniform set of rules for the legal instruments on competition policies.

In order to find out whether dumping has been practised, or is being practised, it is a legal requirement that the industry making the claims has suffered or the industry at issue has suffered or there are such possibilities rather than the accusations based on hollow presumptions.[24] This procedural issue was discussed in the case of **United States–Continued Dumping and Subsidy Offset Act of 2000,**[25] the dispute between the parties[26] arose concerning Continued Dumping and Subsidy Offset Act of 2000 (the CDSOA or the Offset Act also known as the Byrd Amendment).[27]

The Byrd Amendment, formally known as Continued Dumping and Subsidy Offset Act (CDSOA) was enacted by the US, in October 2000. According to the act, the proceeds from anti-dumping and countervailing duties were to be awarded to US companies that bring the dumping cases.[28]

Main Legal Issue

In this case, the complaining parties stated that the objectives of the (CDSOA) enabled US custom authorities, to distribute on an annual basis, the duties assessed and collected pursuant to the "countervailing duty order, and anti-dumping order" to the affected domestic producers.

Brazil, one of the complaining parties, requested before the Panel body to find that the Byrd Amendment is inconsistent with the US obligations under the various provisions of the AD Agreement, and the SCM Agreement.[29] As per the complaint

[24]Article 3.5 of the Agreement on Implementation of Article VI of the General Agreement on Tariffs and Trade 1994. (It must be demonstrated that the dumped imports are, through the effects of dumping as set forth in paragraphs 2 and 4, causing injury within the meaning of this Agreement. The demonstration of a causal relationship between the dumped imports and the injury to the domestic industry shall be based on an examination of all relevant evidence before the authorities. The authorities shall also examine any known factors other than the dumped imports which at the same time are injuring the domestic industry).

[25]WT/DS217/R, WT/DS234/R, also known as Byrd Amendment case.

[26]Complaining Parties are; Australia, Brazil, Canada, Chile, the European Union, India, Indonesia, Japan, Korea, Mexico and Thailand.

[27]See WT/DS 217/R, para 2.1 of The CDSOA was enacted on 28th October 2000 as part of the Agricultural, Rural Development, Food and Drug Administration and Related Agencies Appropriations Act, 2001.

[28]For detail reference, see WT/DS 217/R, para 2.2.

[29]For detail reference, see WT/DS 217/R, para 4.39.

made, the legal actions through this act, addressing the dumping and subsidization, do not fulfill the procedural criteria, and were contrary to Article 5.4,[30] 18.1,[31] of the AD Agreement, and Articles 10,[32] 11.4, 4, 7.9 and 32.1 of the SCM Agreement.[33]

The parties challenging this enactment also claimed that such benefits were a kind of subsidy, because complaints against the dumping practices through this act were not for the purpose of remedy, rather to encourage the business interest of the domestic firms in a non-competitive manner.[34] The US firm bringing such suit was given an extra advantage that was considered to be a subsidy in a disguised form by the complaining parties.

The Panel decided that although the CDSOA had created an adverse effect on the dumping, it was nonetheless non compatible with Article 18.1[35] of the A.D agreement.[36]

The Appellate Body affirmed the legal reasoning of the Panel Body and decided that the US had acted inconsistently with Article 18.1 of the Anti-Dumping Agreement and Article 32.1 of the SCM Agreement.[37] A.B further added that the US had infringed the obligations that are assumed under the agreement.

---

[30] Article 5.4 of the Anti-Dumping Agreement. An investigation shall not be initiated pursuant to paragraph I unless the authorities have determined, on the basis of an examination of the degree of support for, or opposition to, the application expressed by the domestic producer of the like domestic product. . .if it is supported by those domestic producers whose collective output constitutes more than 50% of the total production of the like product and no investigation shall be initiated when domestic producers expressly supporting the application account for less than 25% of the total production of the like product.

[31] Article 18.1. No specific action against dumping of exports from another Member can be taken except in accordance with the provisions of GATT 1994, as interpreted by this Agreement.

[32] Article 10 of the SCM Agreement. Members shall take all necessary steps to ensure that the imposition of a countervailing duty on any product of the territory of any Member imported into the territory of another Member is in accordance with the provisions of Article VI of GATT 1994 and the terms of this Agreement.

[33] See WT/DS217/R, para 4.39 (a), (b) (c).

[34] See Panel Report, WT/DS217/R, para 3.1, and para 4.30. According to Brazil, the remedies available under the Anti-Dumping Act of 1916 are not as easily obtained as the remedies under the Byrd Amendment. As discussed in the Report of the Appellate Body, the 1916 Act imposes certain requirements, in addition to showing the existence of injurious dumping, on parties seeking damages and on the government in order to obtain the requested civil or criminal remedy.

[35] No specific action against the dumping of exports from another Member can be taken except in accordance with the provisions of GATT 1994, as interpreted by this A.D Agreement.

[36] Para 7.51 of the Panel Report. In the light of the above, we conclude that the CDSOA constitutes a specific action taken in response to the situations presenting the constituent elements of dumping. We therefore conclude that the CDSOA is a non-permissible "specific action against dumping," contrary to AD Article 18.1. We also conclude that the CDSOA is a non-permissible "specific action against subsidy," contrary to SCM Article 32.1. Since the CDSOA is inconsistent with AD18.1 and SCM Article 32.1, the CDSOA is also in violation of paragraphs 2 and 3 of Article VI of the GATT 1994."

[37] See, WT/DS217/AB/R, para 302 and para 303 of the A.B.

It seems that the Appellate Body, taking the clue from the Panel's approach, stated that it was the competitive aspect of the market and fair chance to trade, which the free market concepts were trying to promote and that would become distorted by the application of the Byrd Amendment Act. The A.B made it clear that Article VI of the GATT 1994 and the Anti-Dumping Agreement, identified three responses to dumping, namely, definitive anti-dumping duties, provisional measures and price under takings and no other response is envisaged in the text of Article VI of the GATT 1994, or in the text of Anti-Dumping agreement. A.B further added that similar reasoning should apply to subsidisation. The GATT 1994 and the SCM Agreement provide four responses to a countervailing subsidy and they are (1) definitive countervailing duties (2) provisional measures (3) price undertakings and (4) multilaterally-sanctioned countermeasures.[38] Additionally, A.B stated that as the CDSOA is not in line with the four remedial measures envisaged by GATT 1994 and the SCM Agreement, therefore the CDSOA is inconsistent with Article 32.1 of the SCM Agreement.[39]

Based on the facts, it seems that the statute enacted by the US is more inward & protectionist in effect. In assessing the relevance of US enactment from the WTO perspective, the A.B has tried to give interpretations based on the objectives of the free movement of goods and the justifiable regulatory measures adopted. As a matter of legal construction, for the effectiveness of the WTO objectives, in the Member State's policy making, the A.B has attempted to shape the scope and engage with the changing stand of the Member States, through the WTO parameters. In the WTO context, the approach adopted by the A.B in this case is also to promote legal certainty,[40] and to create a balance between restrictive trade provisions and the free movement of goods. In this case, the uneven approach followed by the US government can well be seen as a departure from the main frame objectives of the WTO. By resolving the issue, the A.B has given substantive content, for the policy directions, in the matters of legal rules to be framed by a Member State.

Considering the background objectives, that a free trade market notion is based on efficiency, market transparency, and promoting equitable opportunity for other Member States, Companies/Member States, if following such a type of trade disposition as in this case, creates distortive market affects.

[38]See, WT/DS217/AB/R, para 269.

[39]See WT/DS217/AB/R, para273, para 274.

[40]Legal certainty is a principle in national and international law which holds that the law must provide those subject to it with the ability to regulate their conduct. Legal certainty is internationally recognized as a central requirement for the rule of law.

4.2.1 The Role of Subsidies in Predatory-Dumping and Strategic Dumping

Predatory dumping is a strategic form of trading practices. The dumping practices, termed as predatory dumping aims to drive foreign competitors or other forms of competitors from the importing country out of the competition. Such trade practices are often adopted with the intention of subsequently raising prices of the concerned product in the foreign market, assuming that barriers to entry for the new firms of like product exist in the home market.[41] Predatory dumping is the outcome of predatory pricing.

From the WTO perspective, it can be said that the practice of predatory pricing mainly covers the reduction of the price of a product for a short interval, so as to drive away the competing firms out of the market. The second market distortive affect of the predatory pricing can occur if in the long run, because of market domination of the firms by low cost production, it also prevents the entry of new firms. In the later stages, this also introduces an opportunity to form monopoly or monopoly like situation, for firms following the predatory prices, and gaining higher profits, as there are less risk factors left. What usually happens is that in order to attain monopoly situation, the firm or industry seeks support from the government either in the form of direct subsidies, or financial support through policy measures. This creates favourable business opportunities for such firms or industries and they can continue with exports at a lower price. It can be noticed that the use of subsidies if unregulated, also creates a threat of predatory pricing, by a foreign competitors to any importing country.

Strategic Dumping is a form of business practice which has some similarity with predatory dumping, but is also different in some respects. In order to attain business advantages through strategic dumping, foreign producers must have a strong business base in its home market as a primary set up, as is the case in predatory dumping. A confirmed business position at home can support short term losses, which a firm will sustain because of exporting at a low price in the foreign market. Furthermore, in the case of strategic dumping, the economies of scale[42] are used as a means to attain business gains in the long run.[43] Exports are made at a price less than the price of the product in the exporters home market with the strategic motive, (1) to increase the firm's or industries size (2) to enhance the quality of the product after establishing in the foreign market, (3) sales in the country of import shifts towards the imported product, thus helping to attain the market gain by the firm following strategic dumping practices. It is relevant to note here that the real intention in the case of strategic dumping is not to oust the internal competitor of

[41]William and Gaisford (2006), p. 340.

[42]The reduction in long-run average and marginal costs arising from an increase in the size of an operating unit in a factory, for example. Economies of scale can be internal to an organisation and the cost reduction can be due to the effect of technology in an industry.

[43]Araujo et al. (2011), p. 14.

the importing market, as it is in the case of predatory dumping, but rather the main objective is to gain the economies of scale in the long run.[44]

4.2.2 *EU Law Safeguard Measures in Comparison to the WTO System*

Drawing the parallel between the EU and the WTO system, the legal regulations to check these kinds of business practices are relatively structured in the EU trading system. In order to regulate imports into the European Union from outside the EU, Regulation 260/2009 (repealing and codifying Regulation 3285/94) incorporates the Uruguay Round Agreement on Safeguards, into EU Legal system.[45] The Safeguard measures designed to prevent market disruption are one of the three types of commercial policy instruments to protect the market of the Union from the excess of imports. The other two are (1) anti-dumping measures designed to protect the market from unfair import practices, (2) countervailing duties designed to protect the market from subsidised measures.[46] The EU market policies with regard to dumping measures or any such trade measures, internal (pertaining to its own members) and external (with respect to products from outside the EU) are based on the test of fairness and standards. As an overarching measure to maintain consistency with the WTO free trade system, the market policies of the EU try to co-ordinate between the internal and external market directives. At the principal level, the coherence between the internal and external trade policy measures is established with the objective of promoting the economic exchange, so that some level of openness needs to be maintained in order to take due care of the development efforts of the Developing countries and to additionally maintain standards of competitiveness in the European economy.[47] Furthermore, mentioning here with regard to the justification for the anti-dumping measure, the justification is based on the fact that international market in practical terms is imperfectly competitive and

---

[44]Brown and McCulloh (2012), p. 9.

[45]Barnard (2010), p. 213.

[46]Barnard (2010), p. 215.

[47]Free movement of goods within the EU is guaranteed in the Article 30 of the TEFU (prohibits all kinds of restrictions on trade between the Member States), Article 34–36 (prohibition of quantitative restrictions on imports and exports) and Article 110 (prohibition of discriminatory taxes on goods). Legislation in the EU and the member states might complicate market access for third countries, but basically once a third country good has been imported into an EU member state, it can freely circulate between the member states without further restrictions. For reference see "The Internal Market in a Global Context. Externalizing the four freedoms." Komerskollegium, National Board of Trade. January 20, 2012 p. 7 (36). 14(36). http://www.kommers.se/Documents/dokumentarkiv/Om%20oss/the-internal-market-in-a-global-context-externalising-the-four-freedoms.pdf.

there is no competition regulatory authority at the international level.[48] In comparison to this, within the EU internal market, price under cutting or reduction in price is critically evaluated if the offender is using its dominant position in the market. Usually the dominant market position is practiced with the intention to oust the competitors from the market or to create a monopoly like situation and disallow new firms to enter.[49]

Reference in this regard is made to the ECJ case, for understanding the abuse of a dominant position. The interpretation given by the court also needs to be seen in the light of EU competition policy.[50]

In the case of **AKZO Chemie BV v Commission of the European Communities,**[51] AKZO Chemie filed an application for the annulment of the Commission's decision of 14th December 1985. Before the application for annulment, the background facts are that the complaint was made by Engineering and Chemical Supplies (Epsom and Gloucester) Ltd., to the Commission, (see 85/609/EEC) in pursuant to Article 3 of the Regulation 17.[52] It alleged in the complaint, that AKZO Chemie BV, part of the large AKZO group, had abused the dominant position that it holds in the market. The business behavior of AKZO was based on the policy of selective and below costs-price cutting, designed to damage the business of the ECS, and hence was challenged.[53]

The European Court of Justice deciding the matter in the dispute, adopted two criteria to determine predatory pricing.

1. The existence of an abuse of a dominant position, "if prices are below average cost and through which a dominant undertaking tries to eliminate a competitor, this must be regarded as abusive."[54]

---

[48]Hindley No. 03(2007). ISSN 1653-8994.

[49]For reference, see "The Internal Market in a Global Context. Externalising the four freedoms." Komerskollegium, *National Board of Trade*. January 20, 2012, p. 15 (36). http://trade.ec.europa.eu/doclib/docs/2012/february/tradoc_149055.pdf.

[50]European Union competition law is an outcome of the need of the governments of the Member States to gradually follow one market policy and to see that the companies/corporations do not abuse their market power. Therefore, the trade policies are framed with restrictive provisions, (1) so as not to allow Cartels and other anti-competitive practices that affect the EU. This is covered under Article 101 of the Treaty on the Functioning of the European Union (TEFU) monopolies (2) not to allow the formation of monopolies, and preventing the abuse of the firm's dominant market position. This is governed by Article 102 TEFU. (3) State-aid, control of direct and indirect aid given by Member States of the European Union to companies. Covered under Article 107 of the Treaty on the Functioning of the European Union.

[51]*Akzo Chemie BV v Commission* [1991] ECR I-3359 ***Case C-62/86.***

[52]Council Regulation No 17 (EEC): First Regulation implementing Articles 85 and 86 of the Treaty *(at present Articles 81 and 82)* Articles 101 and 102 TFEU.

[53]See Para 1 of the Case details. 85/609/EEC: Commissions decisions of 14 December 1985 relating to proceeding under Article 86 of the EEC treaty.

[54]See AKZO v. Commission, [1991] ECR I-3359, Case ***C-62/86***, para. 71. Judgment of the court (Fifth Chamber).

2. If prices are below the average total cost i.e., the fixed cost + variable cost, but above the average variable costs, this must be regarded as abusive—if these prices are determined as a part of a plan to eliminate a competitor.[55] The criterion adopted is based on the costs and the market strategy followed by the dominant undertaking. Further, in this concern the basis of court's stance is mentioned. Citing reference to Article 86 of the EEC treaty,[56] the dominant position under Article 86 has been defined by the Court of Justice as "a position of economic strength enjoyed by an undertaking which enables it to prevent effective competition being maintained on the relevant market by affording it the power to behave to an appreciable extent independently of its competitors, its customers and ultimately of the consumers."[57]

Although this is not a WTO case, however a legal analogy can be derived, for conceptual understanding of predatory pricing and the judicial body's rationality for elaborating the dominant position in the market. After going through the details of the matter, the European Court of Justice (Fifth Chamber) decided that the Commission was right in finding that AKZO had offered and supplied flour additives to the customers of ECS [Engineering and Chemical Supplies (Epsom and Gloucester) Ltd] at unreasonably low prices, with the aim of damaging the ECS's business potential. This shows the market strategy adopted to oust rival firms. It seems by maintaining prices below their average total cost for a long period, without any justification, AKZO was able to damage the ECS business position.[58]

From the approach adopted, in this legal interpretation it is clear that pricing below the total cost/production cost with the intention of eliminating competitor does not fit in with the free trade market policies, neither it supports accomplishing the objectives of welfare and development. In order to continue in the long run, with below-production cost sale, some sort of support is required, which is often in the form of state-aid or subsidies. Comparing with the WTO system, it seems there is certain level of functional harmony between the EU market system and the WTO, although the objectives are different. It is reflected in both the trading systems, that such aid or subsidies, given with the intention of predatory pricing which subsequently can lead to dumping, can have no legal-bearing under the existing

---

[55] See para 72.

[56] Previous Article 86 of the EEC treaty, now Article 102 of the Treaty on the Functioning of the EU.

[57] For detail reference, see para 67 of the Case C85/609/EEC.

[58] Also see ***Tetra Pak International SA v Commission of the European Communities.*** (Competition) [1990] EUECJ T-51/89 (10 July 1990), case C-62/86. See Para 109, para 140. The court (fifth chamber) reiterated its stance by referring to the legal rationality adopted in AKZO case and stated "in AKZO this court did indeed sanction the existence of two different methods of analyzing predatory pricing. First, prices below average variable costs must always be considered abusive. Secondly, prices below average total costs but above average total costs but above average variable costs are only to be considered abusive if the intention is to eliminate the rival firm."

provisions of the SCM Agreement and of the Anti-Dumping Agreement of the WTO and EU market system.

4.2.3 Subsidies for Predatory Pricing, Beyond the Scope of Justifiable Limits

The subsidies classified as actionable subsidies, mentioned under Article 5 of the SCM Agreement, also illustrate the market consequences, due to the unjustifiable use of subsidies on the basis of which legal action can be initiated. These market consequences are:

a) Injury to the domestic industry, b) nullification or impairment of benefits accruing directly or indirectly to other Members under GATT 1994, in particular the benefits of concessions bound under Article II of GATT 1994, c) Serious prejudice to the interests of other Members.[59] These three impacts can be attributed to some form of financial contribution and certain level of benefit obtained by the exporting firm of the respective Member State.[60]

The use of a subsidy is debated between justifiable and non-justifiable use. State support that takes the form of subsidies for the purpose of predatory pricing and for dumping exports cannot be considered as justified. Within the WTO, the provisions dealing with actionable subsidies create the scope for the use of a justifiable form of subsidies. However, these provisions do not define the strict limits for the use of subsidies and there is a considerable possibility of the Member State crossing the limits. In the instances where justifiable limits are crossed, the effects are on the distortive side as already discussed.

Highlighting the regulatory role of the SCM Agreement, based on the fair trade concepts from the WTO perspective, it characteristically establishes positive criteria to regulate state support, that can otherwise be contrary to the WTO's aims and objectives. One of the basic purposes of both the WTO Agreement's, the Agreement on Implementation of Article VI of the General Agreement on Tariffs and Trade 1994 and the Agreement on Subsidies and Countervailing Measures, is to restrain the indiscriminate use of state support mainly for the purpose of export.[61] This also covers trade practice of predatory pricing. Predatory

[59] Article 5 of the SCM Agreement.

[60] Financial contribution and benefit as defined under Article 1 of the SCM Agreement.

[61] Article 3.1 (a) of the SCM Agreement. Subsidies contingent in law or in fact, whether solely or as one of several other conditions, upon export performance, including those illustrated in Annex I,

Article 6.3 of the SCM Agreement. Serious prejudice in the sense of paragraph (c) of Article 5 may in any case where one or several of the following apply: (a) the effect of the subsidy is to displace or impede the imports of another Member, (b) Such displacement can be from third country market (c) because of such subsidy there is significant price undercutting by the subsidised product, or significant price suppression, or price depression.

dumping or dumping by means of predatory pricing are contrary to the WTO market guidelines such as, for the opportunities to promote comparative cost advantage in the production sector, creating market opportunities for the other Member States, thus it can be challenged at the primary stage of the practice itself.

Once the trade practice is challenged at the initial stages, the adjudicating body needs to take a legal standpoint to, determine whether such a price set up is justifiable or non-justifiable. It can be said that the scope of such a justifiable and non-justifiable price set up, besides other factors, may also lie in the justifiable and non-justifiable use of subsidies.

Firms following such trade practices suffer losses and the loss they suffers on foreign markets is compensated by the profits at home or by subsidies or other forms of state support. This consequently leads to dumping with state support or subsidies.[62] Hence, it can be said that in the case of "predatory pricing strategies" different sorts of below cost pricing strategies are applied that have no-legal support base. Such market strategies with these characteristics act to eliminate a competitor, which is contrary to the WTO fair trade objectives and free trade efficiency principles.

There can be instances where the same firm practicing the predatory pricing is selling goods, even in the home country, below the actual cost, with the intention to eliminate the competitors in the home country. So while calculating the normal price in order to know the extent of the dumping, in accordance with the WTO/GATT code, *it is essential to observe whether the domestic price is the actual domestic price, or whether there is a sale below cost in the domestic market.*[63]

---

[62]Carbaugh (2011), p. 170.

[63]Agreement on Implementation of Article VI of The General Agreement on Tariffs and Trade 1994, Article 2.2 When there are no sales of a like product in the ordinary course of trade in the domestic market of the exporting country or when, because of the particular market situation or the low volume of sales in the domestic market of the exporting country, such sales do not permit a proper comparison, the margin of dumping shall be determined by comparison with a comparable price of a like product when exported to the third country, provided that this price is representative of the cost of production in the country of origin. Article 2.3 In cases where there is no export price or where it appears to the authorities concerned that the export price is unreliable because of association or a compensatory arrangement between the exporter and the importer or a third party, the export price may be construed on the basis of the price at which the imported products are first resold to an independent buyer.

4.3 Adoption of Competition Policy as an Alternative to Restrict Unfair Trade Practices

Within the WTO, there is no agreement on Competition policy as such, parallel to the agreement for regulating subsidies, and also an agreement to restrict dumping practices. The probable reason for the lack of such a policy-measure seems to be the wide economic, political, and market policy differences among the Member States, as well as, the three tier categorisation into Developed, Developing and Less-Developed countries. Despite the three tier classification of the Member States, and keeping in view the agenda to promote efficiency in the production sector and its promotion in the common market system, the WTO supports and encourages legislative measures and the formation of a policy framework for the enactment of Competition Law.

This was quite obvious during the Doha Ministerial conference in 2001,[64] where the essential points regarding competition policies were discussed. Despite, the equivocal stance adopted by the Members, in applying the General Agreement on Competition policy from the WTO level, in order to, achieve the objectives of free trade three subjective issues of primary significance were discussed.

(1) Core principles, including transparency, non-discrimination, and procedural fairness (2) provisions on hard-core cartels (3) support for the progressive reinforcement of the institutions of competition in the Developing countries. It is noteworthy that the term competition policy from the WTO perspective is used to promote competition based efficiency in the market structure, and is not just limited to the general features of the competition law dealing with anti-competitive practices of enterprises.[65] In the private sector, quality control also depends upon the level of competition. Until now the legal position on the competition policy is such that there is no strictly classified jurisprudence that can cover the issues of international trade, from the testing limits and also in relation to the application of competition law provisions at the multilateral level for the respective policies. However, it is of prime significance that in most of the WTO conferences, the discussions held tried to co-relate the relationship of trade and Competition Policy with the development and economic growth of the Developing and Less Developed Member States, taking into account the transformation of agricultural society into an industrial mode. The adoption of a competition policy instrument enables efficient allocation of resources. The key area of the impacts are (1) keeping the price closer to marginal cost (2) inducing firms to produce at the lowest possible

[64]For details see, www.wto.org. At the WTO Ministerial Conference in Doha (2001), the ministers recognized the case for a multilateral framework to enhance the contribution of competition policy for international trade and development, and the need for enhanced technical assistance and capacity-building in this area. During the Cancún Ministerial Conference (2003) Ministers re-affirmed all these Doha Declarations and Decisions and recommitted themselves to working to implement them fully and faithfully.

[65]For detail references, see WT/WGTCP/W/127.

cost (3) competition policy encouraging firms and industries to undertake research and development in order to sustain in the market.[66]

Some of the Developing countries in order to promote trade liberalisation policies have already adopted the competition policy aspects in their legal system for regulating their markets. Within a Developing country's economic system, the introduction of a competition policy instrument will help in removing measures such as bureaucratic regulations, licensing requirements for the foreign direct investments based on unnecessary conditions etc. India as a Developing country is referred here as an example.[67] The "Dominant position and its abuse by an enterprise have been defined under-section 4[68] of the Indian Competition Act 2002."It is expected that inclusion of a competition policy in the legal system will bring fairness in internal market system as well.

Further, for comparison, the example of the EU as a Developed Member Economy bloc and, for the instance of contemporary market practices with substantive competition law aspects are referred. Within the EU, i.e., among its Member States, there is no Anti-Dumping law to regulate their internal market system.[69] The market system of a Member States works as a free trading system, and is partially regulated by a common Competition Policy.[70] The provisions of the EU competition-policy keeps a check on the predatory pricing within the EU, through Article 102[71] (ex-Article 82 TEC) of the TEFU and EC regulation no 1225/2009. There is a possibility of new treaty after Brexit. The predatory pricing

---

[66]Whish (2001), pp. 3–5.

[67]**Competition Act 2002 has come into force to replace the Monopolies and Restrictive Trade Practices Act, 1969**. As after the economic reforms of 1990, it was felt that MRTP no longer suited the changing situation as India after adopting the policy of liberalisation, saw a substantial increase in the volume of international trade. (A change in the line of the WTO's approach). **For reference see, Competition Laws in India-Analysis & Comparison. p. 2.** www.indiajuris.com.

[68]Section 4 Abuse of dominant position (1) No enterprise shall abuse its dominant position. (2) There shall be an abuse of dominant position under sub-section (1), if an enterprise (a) directly or indirectly, imposes unfair or discriminatory (i) condition (ii) price in purchase or sale (including predatory price) of goods or services.

[69]Article 207 TEFU ex Article 133 TEC (Treaty Establishing European Community)

1. The common commercial policy shall be based on uniform principles, particularly with regard to changes in tariff rates, the conclusion of tariff and trade agreements relating to trade in goods and services, and the commercial aspects of intellectual property, foreign direct investment, the achievement of uniformity in measures of liberalization, export policy and measures to protect trade such as those to be taken in the event of dumping or subsidies. The common commercial policies shall be conducted in the context of the principles and objectives of the Union's external action.

[70]Motta (2004), p. 412.

[71]Any abuse by one or more undertakings of a dominant position within the internal market or in a substantial part of it shall be prohibited as incompatible with the internal market in so far as it may affect trade between Member States. Such abuse may, in particular, consist in:

(a) directly or indirectly imposing unfair purchase or selling prices or other unfair trading conditions,
(b) limiting production, markets or technical development to the prejudice of consumers,

practices in countries outside the EU, but that are otherwise Member States of the WTO, is checked by the legal provisions on Anti-Dumping. It can be argued that the EU, in its common market system has adopted a Competition Policy for trade with the Member of the EU and Anti-Dumping policies with regard to trade with countries outside the Union. As a matter of fact, the EU had to formulate a common market system in addition to its WTO Membership, which meant a free-movement of goods, labor, and capital system and a common monetary policy. Hence a common competition policy among the member states was a preferable option. The effect of subsidies/state aid on competition policy is discussed in Chap. 2, see the case of **Italy v. Commission,**[72] nevertheless, the EU retains the right to initiate anti-dumping investigations for imports from countries in agreements with Eastern European and Mediterranean countries.[73]

However, what cannot be ignored here are the differences in Anti-Dumping instruments and the Competition policy measures. Competition policy measures try to use the maximum of the market potential; where as Anti-dumping policies enables the government of the importing country to impose duties if the imported goods in the market are sold at less than the actual domestic price. Therefore, an approach, which does not create a contradiction between Competition Policies and Anti-dumping Measure needs to be adopted.

4.4 Subsidies for the Promotion of Export by the Developing Countries: Does This Constitute Dumping?

The WTO Subsidies Code covering various features of state support, enshrines a broad definition of what constitutes a subsidy, including strict provisions that would automatically or approximately give rise to countermeasures. The SCM Agreement, despite the inclusion of strict provisions to locate limits for the use of subsidies, also covers flexible provisions allowing for the justifiable use of subsidies. Inclusion of such supportive provision is basically an allocation of discretion, to enable Less-Developed and Developing countries certain level of flexibility to apply subsidies in order to promote development. However, it is worth mentioning here, that the lack of consistency of the domestic policies of the Member States in support of the WTO objectives, and because of the inadequate normative support

---

(c) applying dissimilar conditions to equivalent transactions with other trading parties, thereby placing them at the competitive disadvantage,
(d) making the conclusion of contracts subject to acceptance by the other parties of supplementary obligations which, by their nature or according to commercial usage, have no connection with the subject of such contracts.

[72] *Italy v Commission* [1999] 1 CMLR 1357, *C-6/97*, paragraph 61. (Common Market Law Reports).

[73] Wootan and Zanardi (2012), p. 9.

for the WTO based market concepts; these relaxations can be on the slippery edge of interpretations and may have the affect of defying the basic objectives of the WTO; The promotion of dumping practices is one such instance.

By virtue of Article 15 of the Anti-Dumping Agreement,[74] Developing countries expect special considerations from the Developed countries. It is worth referring here that such considerations for allowing special concessions are rather a matter of fact finding, and should be substantiated with the facts. After analysing the facts, interpretation can be applied as to how far such considerations can be availed. This matter of interpretation to determine the scope of Article 15 arose in the case of **United States-Anti-Dumping and Countervailing Measures on Steel Plate from India.**[75]

The complaint in this case was made by India, before the DSB, contesting the US's affirmative determination of the dumping of cut to length carbon quality steel plate products from India.[76] The dumping investigation was conducted by the US Department of Commerce under the US anti-dumping statute and related USDOC regulations.[77]

Main Legal Issue

The Indian Company as respondent, in this case was SAIL (Steel Authority of India Ltd), SAIL challenged the decision of the USDOC by stating that the decision was based on incorrect interpretation of the statute and the regulations. Moreover, SAIL pointed out that the USDOC had not accepted the data supplied by them and made inferences based on its own evaluations.[78] India also pointed out before the Panel Body, that the USDOC decision to reject all of the SAIL's information and to rely on the facts available by the US law, was inconsistent with the procedural provisions of the AD Agreement that implied reliance on the facts available.[79] India, in its defence plea also claimed that the United States violated Article 15[80] of the AD Agreement, by failing to give special regard to India's status as a Developing country, which means permissible concessions given to its industries. According to India, the US could have taken into account the special situation of SAIL as a Developing Country respondent, while considering the application of the AD

[74]Article 15 of the Anti-Dumping agreement. It is recognized that special regard must be given by Developed country Members to the special situation of Developing country Members when considering the application of anti-dumping measures under this Agreement. Possibilities of constructive remedies provided for by this Agreement shall be explored before applying anti-dumping duties where they would affect the essential interest of Developing country Members.

[75]WT/DS206/R.

[76]See Para 2.2 of the Panel Report.

[77]WT/DS206/R.

[78]See WT/DS206/R, para 2.7.

[79]See para 7.32.

[80]Article 15 of the A.D Agreement "it is recognized that special regard must be given by developed country members to the special situation of the Developing country members when considering the application of the anti-dumping measures under this agreement."

duties. Further, it added that US had failed to explore the possibilities of constructive remedies.[81]

The Panel, in this case, concerning India's claim for the special regard being given under Article 15 of the Anti-Dumping Act, emphasised that the consideration, according to the provision, is meant for final measures and not throughout the course of investigation or for procedural or substantive legal issues.[82] From the decision of the Panel, it seems the Panel body highlighted the approach that concessionary provisions to be availed of by the Developing countries, are linked relatively with the WTO objectives of development, rather than for intermediate and procedural measures, such as investigative procedures and the choice of methodology during the course of investigations. The concessions otherwise would be too general and would lose the point of an analysis on case by case. According to the Panel Body, simply because a company is operating in a Developing Country does not mean that it somehow shares the "special situation" of the Developing country member.[83]

From the respective approach followed by the Panel Body, it further leads to the question of, how far the relaxations in the form of subsidies are justifiable for the Developing Countries. The statement by US in its defence seems to be based on a balanced approach that a Member seeking the application of Article 15 must first demonstrate that some essential interest, as involved would be affected by applying anti-dumping measures.[84] It cannot be denied that state aid or subsidies used by the Developing Countries can also be used for the promotion of dumping products in the Developed Countries.[85] Therefore, in order to maintain a level of coherence in the WTO system, it can be suggested that along with the flexibilities provided, there

[81]See para 7.33 and para 7.104. India argues that USDOC violated the first sentence of Article 15 of the AD Agreement by failing to give special regard to India's status as a developing country when considering the application of AD duties. Para 7.105. India asserts that the United States violated the second sentence of Article 15 of the AD Agreement by failing to explore the possibilities of constructive remedies provided for the Agreement before applying the duties in this case.

[82]WT/DS206/R, para 7.111. In our view, the phrase "when considering the application of anti-dumping measures under this Agreement refers to the final decision whether to apply a final measure, and not intermediate decisions concerning such matters as investigative procedures and choices of methodology during the course of investigation."

[83]See para 7.110 and 7.111 "Members cannot be expected to comply with an obligation whose parameters are entirely undefined."

[84]See para 7.107.

[85]A particular form of export support is the use of export processing zones. Export processing zones (EPZs) have been established over decades and today significant shares of developing countries' manufactured exports originate in EPZs. An EPZ refers to one or more areas of a country where barriers to trade are reduced and other incentives are created in order to attract foreign investors. The incentives provided differ in nature and can change over time, but many or most take the form of fiscal measures—tax reductions or exemptions rather than cash. Whether EPZs represent a cost-efficient policy instrument to pursue industrial development is highly questionable. While many observers agree that some examples of successful EPZs exist, there are certainly also examples of EPZs creating distortions that are harmful to an economy. p. xxv.

also comes the need for the legal regulation. The regulatory provision also plays its role in order to sustain the opportunities for growth and the possible opportunities for free trade with the other Members of the WTO. Considering the WTO objectives and in order to create the equitable trading opportunities for all the Members of the WTO, there are implied limitations and legal bindings to define the limits of state support by applying the provisions of the SCM Agreement. Such restrictions, despite the lack of precise legal measures, are possible to be derived by analysing the facts on a case by case basis by the DSB.

Furthermore, with reference here to the classification of subsidies, for estimating the scope of state support, actionable subsidies, as classified within the SCM Agreement, are so defined that it creates the scope for the justifiable subsidies. Therefore, there is a possibility for each Member State to accommodate its own level of support. In the case of the Developing and Less-Developed countries, there is a possibility for additional concessions.[86] The lawful restrictive measures if adopted by the importing country are also based upon their own perspective on free trade market system. Usually, such perspectives of the importing country, on import restrictions, can be in order to maintain the fair level of competitive aspects in the market and to prevent importations bearing the possibilities of dumping. It would be fair to say that based on the WTO objectives, Article 15, creates the scope of concession for the Developing and Less-Developed countries, and is not a matter of statutory bias but rather an opportunity for development. With the promotion of free trade among the Member States as a background objectives, subsidies for welfare and development also requires searching for the limits, that need to be applied between the development objectives and competing interests. Basically, this requires proportionate balance between the competing interests. It is more of a question of practical limits rather than the induced limits made by the provisions. So far as a case by case consideration is concerned, the Panel body and Appellate Body are guided by the WTO objectives and purposes, i.e., for creating fair opportunities to trade among the Member States.

World Trade Report (2006) Exploring the links between subsidies, trade and the WTO. http://www.wto.org/english/res_e/publications_e/wtr06_e.htm.

[86]For reference, see Article 27.7 of the SCM Agreement "The provisions of Article 4 shall not apply to a Developing country Member in the case of export subsidies which are inconformity with the provisions of para 2 through 5 and the relevant provisions shall be those of Article 7. Additionally, Article 27.9 of the SCM Agreement. Regarding actionable subsidies granted or maintained by a Developing country Member other than those referred to in paragraph 1of Article 6, action may not be authorized or taken under Article 7 unless nullified or impairment of tariff concessions or other obligations under GATT 1994 is found to exist as a result of subsidy, in such a way as to impede or displace the like product of another member."

4.5 Subsidies for Dumping Agricultural Products

The WTO free trade system covers both trade in agricultural and industrial goods. This further extends the question as to how far free trade concepts, promoted by the WTO, are favourable to the farmers from the Developing and Less-Developed countries; or is it so that 'farmers stand to lose the most from the reductions in tariff protection.' The question becomes complex, because the expectations of the consumers are often different from the objectives. The welfare benefit, a key WTO objective, and the expectations of the consumers are based on lowering the prices of the goods whereas, the reduction in dumping exports is more of a fair trade regulatory objectives.

The issue of agricultural subsidies and dumping agricultural products remains an unresolved issue, and is contextually connected with the welfare and development objectives of the WTO. This controversial aspect lies with the use of farm subsidies by the Developed countries even for the purpose of the export of agriculture products. In order to define the limits for using subsidies based on the WTO objectives, it necessities making comparisons based on the Member State categorisation. Many of the Less-Developed countries and several of the Developing countries are at the stage of the transition from an agrarian model for their economy to an industrial model, but the cost of the displacement of agricultural livelihoods from such reforms is not being taken into account. The use of subsidies by this group of Member State is based on necessity. In contrast, there is a high level of farm support in the Developed countries, such as Japan, Europe, and the US, which is mainly used to sustain the price level in their market and to provide a safety net to the farm sector. It is also noteworthy that that US and the other Developed countries are in an advantageous position to gain market opportunities in the Developing and Less-Developed Countries. This however needs to be reduced dramatically under the assumed reforms.[87]

Brazil has questioned several measures adopted by the US as violating the Agreement on Agriculture. The effects of such a measure can be seen in (through price fluctuation of cotton) the prices in the African countries that are growing cotton,[88] as discussed in the chapter on agriculture subsidies. In the case of the **United States-Subsidies on Upland Cotton,**[89] the considerable price suppression of cotton in the international market was considered because of the subsidies by the US.[90] The A.B in this case upheld the Panel's finding that the GSM 102 export

---

[87]Discussed in the Chapter on Agricultural subsidies.

[88]See in WT/DS267/AB/R, para 214 of the Appellate Body.

[89]WT/DS267/AB/R.

[90]The Panel was established on 18 March 2003 to consider claims by Brazil regarding various United States measures that Brazil alleged constituted actionable subsidies within the meaning of Part III of the Agreement on subsidies and Countervailing Measures, prohibited subsidies within the meaning of Part II of the SCM Agreement, export subsidies within the scope of the Agreement on Agriculture, and subsidies actionable under Article XVI of the General Agreement on Tariffs

credit guarantees issued after 1st July 2005 were export subsidies within the meaning of Article 3.1 (a) of the SCM Agreement and Article 10.1 of the Agreement on Agriculture.[91]

Arguing in the context of trade regulatory measures based on various WTO Agreements, it can be said that the practice of agricultural dumping significantly affects Less-Developed countries and also Developing Countries agricultural trade. In the Less-Developed countries, export of agriculture products is vital for food, rural livelihood, and poverty reduction. Their economic base is pushed into the risk level, if the Developed nations continue dumping food products.[92]

Although it is quite vital to promote free trade objectives, GATT/WTO have not emphatically mentioned Agriculture Dumping and this seems as if they are missing the relevant point in global trade. The relevance of the definition mentioned in GATT Article VI has rather less of a regulatory effect, as it does not include enforcement measures in the case of agricultural dumping. It is effectually weak, because it lacks the characteristics to judge into detail as to, whether the domestic price actually reflects the cost of production of the products and that is a matter of high relevance in agriculture trade.

Steps to check agricultural dumping can be similar to those of restricting the dumping of industrial goods. The initial proceedings starts based on:

1. The extent of dumping
2. The percentage of export price that is below the cost of production.

If there are instances of dumping agricultural products, the dumping alleged by the parties can be determined, first by taking the "normal value/or price at which they are sold in the domestic market" of the exporting nation. (Article 2.1 of the Anti-Dumping Agreement permits the determination of the normal value). If the dumping has been practiced in the trade deal, then in order to calculate the percentage, "the comparison is made between the export price and the normal value."[93] A situation may arise that the price-value difference or the volume is fairly small as regards creating material injury on the market (known as the *de minimis*) level. Therefore it cannot be challenged, or if it is challenged but after investigation found that the price difference or the volume of the product is within *de minimis* level, the complaint will be set aside.[94] In order to calculate the extent of

---

and Trade 1994. The question before the Panel and later before the Appellate Body was whether the effect of subsidy in this case creates significant price suppression. A.B.

[91]For detail reference, see www.wto.org summary of the case.

[92]Preventing Dumping of Surplus (Meat-Parts) on Vulnerable Developing Country Markets, Association of World Council of Churches related Development Organisations in Europe, May 2008. http://trade.ec.europa.eu/doclib/html/138972.htm.

[93]Van Den Bossche (2008), p. 520.

[94]Article 5.8 There shall be immediate termination in cases where the authorities determine that the margin of dumping is *de minimis*, or that the volume of dumped imports, actual or potential, or the injury, is negligible. The margin of dumping shall be considered to be *de minimis* if this margin is less than 2%, expressed as a percentage of the export price. The volume of dumped imports shall

dumping, and after finding the differences between the export price and its normal value, the value attained can be multiplied by the quantity of goods imported either on a weighted average or on a transaction to transaction basis, and subsequently the value which shows the existing dumping margin can be counted for the affirmative dumping consideration.[95]

4.6 Conclusions

The Uruguay Round, that established the World Trade Organisation to strengthen free trade principles made a significant contribution, by introducing an Anti-dumping Agreement and the Subsidies and Countervailing Measures Agreement.

In determining the scope of free trade and attaining the development and welfare objectives, there has been a positive contribution by these instruments to regulate International Trade. The main idea behind the Anti-Dumping Agreement is that exporters should not be allowed to use the profits, they make in their domestic market, to subsidise the export prices. On similar basis, exporters should not be allowed to subsidise their exports price, from benefits provided by its government. As the present Anti-Dumping Agreement lacks provisions to cover several forms of non-competitive practices, so in order to broaden the regulatory scope, to cover the changing aspects of cross border trade practices, and for several other additional issues that remain uncovered, addition of provisions that can cover comprehensively the new subject area, such as dumping of agriculture goods is suggested.

Apart from such initiatives taken by the WTO, it is proposed that nations while trading, establish coordination among themselves, as there exist differences at the economic levels of every nation and such difference is one of the reasons for the trade practice of dumping. Free trade promotes market efficiency, which is a positive aspect in the market. However, in contrast, several multinationals practices, unethical market strategy, such as predatory pricing in the present free trade market structure. The trade practice of dumping as currently practised has significant anti-competitive effects, distorting the market efficiency. If anti-dumping policies are to guard against such affects, antidumping rules need to shift towards competition policy criteria for promoting market efficiency and to attain the other WTO objectives.

Nowadays, it can be observed during the WTO conferences, that the issue of subsidies to promote exports by the Developing countries has received mixed reactions. The Developed Member States often raise the issue that to what extent low-priced exports from the Developing countries can be allowed, as they have to bear the consequences like dumping, which affects their economy by shift in the

normally be regarded as negligible if the volume of dumped imports from a particular country is found to account for less than 3% of the imports of the like product in the importing Member.

[95]Macrory et al. (2005), p. 507.

production centres because of the cheaper production cost in the Developing countries. The legal framework through the DSB of the WTO institution tries, to maintain consistency with the WTO objectives and then apply provisions for flexibilities, however, it would be worth including in the Anti-dumping and Subsidies Agreement, provisions that supports flexibilities based on the factual market situation of the Member State.

In pursuance of fair trade policy perspective, it can be further suggested that antidumping rules, through the WTO Agreement can influence the respective policy making institutions of the Member States. This can be by countering such policies, framing such rules or restricting private business practices that adopt a protectionist attitude towards the competing foreign firms.

As a down side, anti-dumping measures are also prone to be used as an instruments of protectionism. Threat to impose such measures, without determining the facts means substantial procedural costs and forcing small companies to compromise. While establishing link between dumping and subsidies, Member States need to consider objectively, when it comes to imposing anti-dumping duties. It should be clarified whether the use of subsidies is justifiable or not or the subsidies are used to attain the WTO objectives.

In both countervailing and anti-dumping action, it is necessary to demonstrate that the subsidisation or dumping is causing injury to the domestic industry of the importing country. Considering the regulatory objectives, there is also a need for a flexible approach, in the cases, where relatively reduced export prices, based on price differences, might be a result of depressed demand. The state support in such cases is of compensatory nature rather than distortive.

Finally, despite the promotion of market liberalisation policies by the WTO, it is still accepted by many Members, that the State has to assume an active and positive role in assisting the industrial sector of its country and to be far more active in the case of agriculture. Therefore, policy reforms within the WTO should also focus on checking the agricultural dumping that is promoted due to un-regulated subsidies. However, so challenging, a balanced approach between industrial and agricultural trade is required, since the economic structure, mainly of the Less-Developed countries is at the transforming stage. Their industrial progress requires development based on a comparative advantage, which is possible by checking both the dumping practices and the use of unregulated subsidies. It is only after such aspirations, primarily getting accomplished it can be expected that the benefits of trade liberalisation through the WTO objectives will, reach every quarters.

References

Barnard C (2010) The substantive law of the EU: the four freedoms. Oxford University Press, New York

Bentley P, Silberston A (2007) Anti-dumping and countervailing action: limits imposed by economic and legal theory. Edward Elgar Press, Cornwall

Carbaugh J (2011) International economics. R.R Donnelley Printers, Crawfordsville
Cottier T, Oesch M (2005) International Trade Regulation: law and policy in the WTO: the European Union and Switzerland, cases, materials and comments. Cameron May Ltd, London
Douglas G (1981) Encyclopedia of economics. McGraw-Hill Inc, New York
Hindley B (2007) Antidumping policy in the EU, European Centre for International Political Economy. European Centre For International Political Economy, no. 03. ISSN 1653-8994
Macrory P, Appleton AE, Plummer MG (eds) (2005) The World Trade Organization, legal, economic and political analysis, vol I. Springer, New York
Motta M (2004) Competition policy theory and practice. Cambridge University Press, New York
Van Den Bossche P (2008) The law and policy of the World Trade Organization text, cases and materials. Cambridge University Press, New York
William AK, Gaisford JD (2006) Handbook on International Trade Policy. Edward Elgar, Bodmin
Whish R (2001) Competition law. Butterworths, Bath

Cases

Akzo v Commission 1991 ECR I-3359
China-Countervailing and Anti-Dumping Duties on Grain Oriented Flat Rolled Electrical Steel-from the United States WT/DS414/R
Continued Dumping and Subsidy Offset Act of 2000 WT/DS217/R
Italy v Commission [1999]1 CMLR1357. C-6/97
Tetra Pak International SA v Commission of the European Communities EUECJ T-51/89 (1990)
United States-Anti Dumping and Countervailing Measures on Steel Plate from India WT/DS206/R
United States-Definitive Anti-Dumping and Countervailing Duties On Certain Products From China WT/DS379/AB/R
United States-Definitive Anti-Dumping and Countervailing Duties On Certian Products From China WT/DS379/AB/R
United States-Subsidies on Upland Cotton WT/DS267/AB/R

Reports and Electronic Sources

Araujo J Jr, Macario C, Steinfatt K (2011) Antidumping in the Americas. Comercio Internacional, Division of Integration and International Trade, Chile. http://repositorio.cepal.org/bitstream/11362/4355/1/S2001718_en.pdf
Brown CP, McCulloh R (2012) The World Bank Development Research Group. Antidumping and Market Competition; Implications for Emerging Economies. Policy Research Working Paper, 6197. http://www.brandeis.edu/departments/economies/RePEc/brd/doc/Brandeis_WP50.pdf
Henrik I, Persson S (2012) The internal market in a global context. Externalizing the four freedoms. Komerskollegium, National Board of Trade. http://www.kommers.se/Documents/dokumentarkiv/Om oss/the-internal-market-in-a-global-context-externalising-the-four-free doms.pdf
Wootan I, Zanardi M (2012) Trade and competition policy: anti-dumping versus anti trust. www.gla.ac.uk/media/media_22263_en.pdf

Chapter 5
Unfolding the Intricacies of Trade Subsidies Through the WTO Rules of Origin

Abstract The discussion in this chapter continues from the previous chapters where the line of discussion follows that since the formation of the WTO, the international trade pattern has been progressing in the direction of free trade and has by and large been competitive and based on efficiency; nevertheless it is more beneficial to the multinationals. This has raised new forms of trade related issues that can be compared with benefits of several types, and one such is comparing the benefit obtained by multinationals, with the subsidies defined under the SCM Agreement.

As the present trend of trade between the Developed and Developing nations, in intermediate products is growing, so the legal requirement of the declaration of the nationality of the products and intermediate products is necessitated. Declaration of the nationality of the products will unfold the complexities involved whilst also strengthening the promotion of free trade. The declaration of the nationality of a product is the key feature of market transparency and at the procedural level, it also helps in applying the regulatory provisions. On the basis of these emerging concerns, it seems that the application of the "Rules of Origin" to determine the place of manufacture in the present day international trade is quite relevant. Furthermore, with regards to the trends in free trade, the manufacturing process of the products is no longer confined to one place or nation, but is becoming allocated to several countries. In today's complex trading system, more and more products are being given a final shape by obtaining intermediate parts from other nations, wherever they can be cheaply manufactured or are available. The choice of the place for the manufacturing of intermediary products can often be discriminatory, as the priorities are to attain cost efficient products. From the market observation, it can be said that this newly-developed pattern of trade, based on different production places, demands a new approach in the legal analysis to uncover the production intricacies. The WTO, as a trade regulating institution, has thus included a Rules-of-Origin Agreement, so as to determine the place from which the product has actually originated or is being produced.

In this chapter, an attempt has also been made to analyse the adverse effect of applying the Agreement on Rules of Origin by the Member States.

What can then be seen, are the challenges to free trade because of the preference given to the products based on the Rules-of-Origin. With the proliferation of regional-trade agreements such as NAFTA, ASEAN, CAFTA and several others, the WTO Member States, some of which are also the members of these regional

G. Singh, *Subsidies in the Context of the WTO's Free Trade System*,
DOI 10.1007/978-3-319-62422-8_5

trade agreements, prefer trading among themselves by giving tariff preferences. An examination from this standpoint also covers the broader issue of trade subsidies in terms of financial contribution and benefit, which from the WTO perspective, is a form of tension between legal values and the economic compulsions associated with international trade.

Testing such obtained trade gains, within the limits of subsidies classified as prohibited or actionable subsidies in the SCM Agreement, for restricting the subsidies of exports, finally raises questions concerning the new forms of subsidies. The study in this chapter is to inquire about the unconventional form of trade benefits obtained by applying the Rules of Origin, as the features of such profits can be compared with subsidies.

5.1 General Explanation About Free Trade and Rules of Origin

With the promotion of trade liberalisation policies, Member States are expected to apply the MFN clause to the imported products for non-discriminatory treatment, but there can be reasons why they would wish to distinguish between foreign products from the domestic products. For such differentiation, Member States are expected to follow certain norms, such as they need to define the reasons for the differentiation. Furthermore, in order to promote business transparency, Member States—needs to state the conditions under which it can be considered that a product originates in that particular country, so as to be granted either preferential treatment or is it another form of differentiation in practice.[1]

What is crucial here with regard to the objectives of the WTO in general, and for analysing the issues of subsidies in particular, that ascertaining the country of origin of product has become complicated. This is for several reasons, such as, technological changes, faster modes of transport, and the changing pattern of trade because of globalisation. Such complexities are commonly noticeable in the case of products such as clothing, computers, and telecommunication equipment. In these products much of the value addition lies in the intermediate inputs.[2] In addition to this, fragmentation of the production process and the apportionment of production centres at different locations have added to the complexities. For the multinational companies and for competitive business practices, such an approach may be a rational one, however, new legal questions often arise when determining the forms of subsidies oriented benefits. For example, while determining the extent of the subsidies in a trade deal, the question of finding out the specific country that can be considered as the place of origin. In case the intermediate products from several countries are used, or when part of the product is manufactured in one

[1]Vermulst et al. (1995), p. 8.

[2]Brenton et al. (2011), p. 165. www.worldbank.org.

country and some part in another, it is complex to locate place of origin for the legal purposes.[3]

It further adds to the deviation from the WTO objective, as major trading nations are following trade-practices also through special trade arrangements, in addition to the WTO trading system, which creates the possibility for a variation in tariffs measures, due to the preferential bias. Alternatively it can be said, there is no common basic norm for the tariff application for imports and exports among the WTO Member States. The necessity to identify the origin of the product therefore becomes an important issue also for these reasons.[4]

5.1.1 Rules of Origin and Free Trade Objectives, an Interface

The values and concepts inculcated by the WTO to promote free trade system among the Member State, generate an understanding that the place of origin of the product should not be the determining question, when buying a product. Therefore, the Agreement on the Rules of Origin, need not be applied for any trade restrictive purposes. The Agreement on Rules of Origin needs to be seen from the perspective of supporting-the trading system for meeting the WTO's basic objectives. Article 1 of the WTO Agreement on Rules of Origin, specifically demarcates the limits of the application of the Rules of Origin.[5] Prior to the formation of the WTO, trade lawyers tended to view market access negotiations solely in terms of tariff and non-tariff negotiations for the promotion of free trade, and the Rules of Origin were seen as assisting in the application or implementation of other basic trade instruments.[6]

---

[3]Brenton et al. (2011), p. 161. www.worldbank.org.

[4]For detail reference, see Rules of Origin, Gateway to Dubai's Prosperity, p. 2. www.dubaicustoms.gov.ae.

[5]Article 1 (Agreement on Rules of origin) For the purposes of parts I–IV of this Agreement, Rules of Origin shall be defined as those laws, regulations and administrative determinations of general applications applied by any Member, to determine the country of origin of goods provided such rules of origin are not related to contractual or autonomous trade regimes leading to the granting of tariff preferences going beyond the application of paragraph 1 of Article I of GATT 1994.

Article 1 para1 of the GATT 1994 states: With respect to customs duties and charges of any kind imposed or in connection with the importation or exportation or imposed on the international transfer of payments for imports or exports, and with respect to the method of levying such duties and charges, and with respect to all rules and formalities in connection with the importation and exportation, and with respect to all matters referred to in paragraphs 2 and 4 of Article III, of GATT any advantage, favor, privilege or immunity granted by any contracting party to any product originating in or destined for any other country shall be accorded immediately and unconditionally to the like product originating in or destined for the territories of all other contracting parties.

[6]Estevadeordal and Suominen (2008), p. 86.

Although, within the previous trade regulating organisation, GATT, Article XXIV recognised free trade areas and customs unions for the promotion of trade among the nations, however there was no such clear mention or references to the Rules of Origin.[7] Before the Uruguay Round, it was during the "Kyoto Customs Convention," negotiations in 1973,[8] that first attempt to evolve these rules was made. According to this Convention, the country of origin of a product was a country where the last substantial transformation took place.[9]

When attempting to determine the objectives of the Rules of Origin agreement, it can be said that the present agreement on the Rules of Origin promotes free trade,[10] but with exclusive preferences being given to the Developing countries and Less Developed countries, in order to provide more opportunities for their economic advancement.[11]

The conceptual basis in support of the Developing and Less-Developed countries through regulatory measures that also applies to the Rules of Origin Agreement lies in the preamble of the WTO. "*Relations in the field of trade and economic endeavour should be conducted with a view to raising standards of living, ensuring full employment and a large steadily growing volume of real income and effective demand, and expanding the production of trade in goods and services, while allowing for the optimal use of the world's resources….Being desirous of contributing to these objectives by entering into reciprocal and mutually advantageous*

[7]**Article XXIV** Clause 4, the contracting parties recognize the desirability of increasing freedom of trade by the development, through voluntary agreements, of closer integration between the economies of the countries parties to such agreements. They also recognize that the purpose of a customs union or of a free trade area should be to facilitate trade between the constituent territories and not to raise barriers to the trade of the other contracting parties with such territories. Under Clause 5, accordingly, the provision of this Agreement shall not prevent, as between the territories of contracting parties, the formation of a customs union or a free trade area or the adoption of an interim agreement necessary for the formation of a customs union or of a free trade area.

[8]International Convention on the Simplification and Harmonization of Custom Procedures, adopted in 1974 by the Custom Cooperation Council at its 41st and 42nd sessions held in Kyoto. In substance, Annex D1 did not provide for ready-to-use rules of origin.

[9]Harilal and Beena (2003), p. 10.

[10]**Article 2(c)** of the Rules of Origin Agreement, Rules of Origin shall not themselves create restrictive, distorting or disruptive effects on international trade. They shall not pose unduly strict requirements or require the fulfilment of a certain condition not related to manufacturing or processing, as a prerequisite for the determination of the country of origin. However, costs not directly related to manufacturing or processing may be included for the purposes of the application of an ad valorem percentage criterion consistent with subparagraph (a).

[11]**Relevant part of the preamble**. "Members, noting that ministers on 20 September 1986 agreed that the Uruguay Round of Multilateral trade negotiations shall aim to bring about further liberalization and expansion of world trade, strengthen the role of GATT and increase the responsiveness of the GATT system to the evolving international economic environment." Desiring to further the objectives of GATT 1994, Recognizing that clear and predictable Rules of Origin and their application facilitate the flow of international trade. Desiring to ensure that Rules of Origin themselves do not create unnecessary obstacles to trade, desiring to ensure that Rules of Origin do not nullify or impair the rights of members under GATT 1994.

arrangements....Resolved, therefore, to develop an integrated, more viable and durable multilateral trading system encompassing the General Agreement on Tariffs and trade.....[12]"

Based on the objectives mentioned in the preamble of the WTO, and in order to establish a certain level of balance between the free trade objectives and fair trade regulatory measures, the preamble of the Agreement on Rules of Origin, as a further sub-classification of the WTO objectives, draws the connecting lines from the WTO trading principles. It states *"Desiring to ensure that rules of origin themselves do not create unnecessary obstacles to trade; Desiring to ensure that rules of origin do not nullify or impair the rights of Members under GATT 1994; Recognizing that it is desirable to provide transparency of laws, regulations, and practices regarding rules of origin."*

5.1.2 Free Trade Between Developed and Developing Countries and the Rules of Origin

Focusing on the objectives of welfare and development, legal exemptions are created to the MFN clause for the accomplishment of these objectives. One such example is the "Generalised System of Preferences."[13]

The GSP clause was introduced as an exception to the general practices under the MFN clause of the WTO. Through the GSP,[14] the Developed countries unilaterally grant trade preferences to the Developing and the Less-Developed countries.[15] Although, such preferences seems contrary to the free trade system, however, the legal and economic rationality behind these preferences is that by developing export promotion opportunity, through the increase in trade of goods and services from the Developing and Less-Developed countries will lead to their economic growth and a reduction of poverty. The tariff concessions are given to the

[12]From the Preamble of the WTO.

[13]**Article 1 cl(2)** Rules of Origin referred to in paragraph 2 as mentioned above in the text, shall include all Rules of Origin used in non-preferential commercial policy instruments, such as in the application of: most-favoured-nation treatment under Article I, II, III, XI and XIII of the GATT 1994; anti-dumping and countervailing duties under Article VI of GATT 1994; safeguard measures under Article XIX of GATT 1994; origin making requirements under Article IX of GATT 1994; and any discriminatory quantitative restrictions of tariff quotas. They shall also include Rules of Origin used for government procurement and trade statistics.

[14]The principle of GSP was agreed at the United Nations Conference on Trade and Development, and is a facility granted to Developing countries by certain Developed Countries. GSP Rules of Origin are contained in Articles 66 to 97 and Annexes 13a to d, 16 to 18 and 21 Reg. 2454/93 (CCIP) [as amended by Regulation (EU) No. 1063/2010]. The list rules are contained in Annex 13a CCIP. (as amended by Regulation No. 1063/2010).

[15]These preferences are unilateral in the sense as that they do not involve any reciprocal preferences from them. The preferences are set and conditioned by the grantor countries alone, and can be modified or revoked by them at their discretion.

products from those countries which are party to the exclusive GSP treaties. The GSP authorises each Developed country to establish preference based, on a non-reciprocal trade relationship with the Developing and the Less-Developed countries.[16] These preferences often vary[17] with the exclusive set of features, depending upon the partner country so that a given set of the Rules of Origin applicable to one GSP may not be applicable to another. Pursuing trade through the GSP on the one hand and market system based on MFN clause on the other, requires, criteria to be established which can determine whether the product actually belongs to the Member State that is party to the preference treaty. These criteria become indispensable in the case of an intermediate products being imported from a preference country.[18]

Legal description concerning the WTO Rules of Origin can be that they are the legal rules used in international trade law to determine the original manufacturing place of a product.[19] These rules need to be consistent with the WTO objectives and for this they need to be transparent, and non-restrictive to free trade. *In the case of* ***United States-Rules of Origin for textiles and apparel products,***[20] India claimed that the United States' rules of origin for textiles and apparel products were inconsistent with paragraphs (b), (c), (d) and (e) of the Article 2 of the Rules of Origin Agreement.[21] India does in fact exports its greige fabrics to other countries, where they are further processed and then exported to the United States. Under the old rules, which were applied to determine the place of origin, these finished products were not deemed to originate in India. However, according to section 334(b) (1) (C),[22] the changed provisions, the same finished product would be counted as India's export to the United States and subject to restrictions.[23]

---

[16]Jones and Martin (2012), pp. 6–10. www.crs.gov. RL33663.

[17]*European Communities-Conditions for granting of Tariff Preferences to Developing Countries* WT/DS246/AB/R, Para 162. In sum, we read paragraph 3(c) as authorizing preference-granting countries to respond positively to needs that are not necessarily common or shared by all Developing countries. Responding to the needs of Developing countries may thus entail treating different Developing country beneficiaries differently. Para 163 However, paragraph 3(c) does not authorize any kind of response to any claimed need of Developing countries. First we observe that the types of needs to which a response is envisaged are limited to 'development, financial and trade needs.'

[18]Harris (2009), p. 7. www.iadb.org.

[19]Weiler et al. (2011), p. 3. http://www.jeanmonnetprogram.org/courses/wto/docs/unitiiirulesoforigin.pdf.

[20]WT/DS 243/R. On 21 July 2003, the DSB adopted the Panel report.

[21]See, WT/DS 243/R, para 1.3.

[22]WT/DS243/R, para 3.9. However, section 334(b) (1) (C) establishes a new rule, which fixes the origin of a fabric in the country where it is woven, knitted or otherwise formed in the greige state. No recognition of origin is given for any operations which follow the forming of the fabric, such as dyeing, printing or other finishing steps. This is a major departure from the previous rule, under which dyeing and printing as well as at least two additional finishing operations were deemed sufficient to transform greige fabric formed in one country into a new product of the country where finishing operations were performed.

[23]See WT/DS 243/R, para 3.31.

The dispute arose concerning application of the Rules of Origin by the United States on textile and apparel products and this further raises the question whether these Rules of Origin are used to pursue national trade objectives. The rules challenged by India in this case were based on the consideration that the United States Rules of Origin for textile and apparel products[24] were in-consistent with para (b),[25] (c),[26] (d) and (e) of the Article 2 of the Rules of Origin Agreement. The objectives of these provisions are that the Rules of Origin should not create restrictive and distortive effects on free trade.[27]

India in this case claimed that the US, by applying RoO on the imports of textiles and apparel products, under section 334 of the URA Act[28] of 1994, and by the subsequent modifications made in thereto by section 405 of the Trade and

[24]See Para 3.4 of the WT/DS243/R The United States Rules of Origin set out in section 334 of the Uruguay Round Agreements Act (section 334 or the 1996 rules of origin) and modified in section 405 of the Trade and Development Act of 2000 (section 405 or the 2000 rules of origin) and the customs regulations implementing these statutory provisions, and their application are inconsistent with the United States obligations under Article 2(b), (c), (d) and (e) of the Agreement on Rules of Origin.

[25]Article 2(b) notwithstanding the measure or instrument of commercial policy to which they are linked, the rules of origin are not used as instruments to pursue trade objectives directly or in directly.

[26]Article 2(c) Rules of Origin shall not themselves create restrictive, distorting, or disruptive effects on international trade. They shall not pose unduly strict requirements or require the fulfillment of certain conditions not related to manufacturing or processing, as a pre-requisite for the determination of the country of origin. However, costs not directly related to manufacturing or processing may be included for the purpose of the application of an ad-valorem percentage criterion consistent with sub paragraph (a).

The specific measures challenged by India in this case were the Rules of Origin set out in section 334 of the URAA (Uruguay Rounds of Agreement Act) and modified in section 405 of the trade development act of 2000.

[27]2(b) notwithstanding the measure or instrument of commercial policy to which they are linked, the rules of origin are not used as instruments to pursue trade objectives directly or in directly; 2(c) Rules of Origin shall not themselves create restrictive, distorting, or disruptive effects on international trade. They shall not pose unduly strict requirements or require the fulfillment of certain conditions not related to manufacturing or processing, as a pre-requisite for the determination of the country of origin. However, costs not directly related to manufacturing or processing may be included for the purpose of the application of an ad-valorem percentage criterion consistent with sub paragraph (a).

The specific measures challenged by India in this case were the Rules of Origin set out in section 334 of the URAA (Uruguay Rounds of Agreement Act) and modified in section 405 of the trade development act of 2000.

[28]Para 3.9. Section 334(b) (1) (c) establishes a new rule, which fixes the origin of a fabric in the country where it is woven, knitted or otherwise formed in the "greige" state. No recognition of origin is given for any operations which follow the forming of the fabric, such as dyeing, printing or other finishing steps. This is a major departure from the previous rule, under which dyeing and printing as well as at least two additional finishing operations were deemed sufficient to transform "greige" fabric formed in one country into a new product of the country where the finishing operations were performed.

Development Act of 2000, and additionally by applying the customs regulations, as set out in 19 CFR,[29] had used these measures, as an instrument to pursue trade objectives in its own interest. (CFR, Code of Federal Regulations, USA). According to India, this was a shift by the US from the basic trade practices being followed, and thereby the modified provisions became a matter of legal interpretation. India further stated that the US has modified its methods to determine Rules of Origin by creating exceptions. This according to India is based on inconsistent approach, and applying the RoO act, India therefore challenged the US measures.

As a matter of fact in this case, the cotton fabric was woven and exported to Portugal and the finishing touch was given by dyeing. After such changes had been made, the product was considered to be manufactured from Portugal. Subsequently, the same cotton fabric was used for the purpose of producing finished products, such as sheets, but then the origin of the product was resolved as Indian.[30] India further added to its claim that, the US has probably modified the rules to determine the place of Origin and this can be in order to harmonize it with other trading partners, mainly the European Union and Canada.[31]

India brought this case, as it considered that the United States had abused its rights, in determining the criteria of conferring the origin to the products. From the Indian perspective, this was for the purpose of protecting its own domestic industry by US and in order to favour the exports of their products and of their partner countries. These measures taken by the United States created a distorting effect because there was a shift in the basis, to determine the origin criteria from a country where the fabric was dyed and printed and other operations were carried out, to a country where the greige fabric was formed. India alleged that this was because the US favoured the export of products from the European Communities to the export interest of the Developing Countries.[32]

After assessing the facts and analysing the reasons, the case was not decided in India's favour. According to the Panel, India could not substantiate its argumentation with reasonable justification, that the United States was using the fabric formation rule to protect its domestic textile industry.[33] Further, the Panel stated that subject to Article 2(b) and (c) of the RoO Agreement, Members are free to make determinations for the harmonisation programme of the Rules of Origin,

[29]C.F.R, Code of Federal Regulations.

[30]See WT/DS243/R, para 3.47. These exceptions resulted in absurd cases. If cotton fabric is woven in India and exported to Portugal where it is dyed, printed and subject to two or more finishing operations, that fabric is now considered a product of Portugal. If, however, the same cotton fabric is now used in Portugal to produce a finished sheet, the origin reverts back to India. Therefore, even though operations were performed in Portugal on a Portuguese product, the origin of that product would be determined as Indian.

[31]See WT/DS243/R, para 3.36.

[32]*United States Rules of Origin for Textile Products*, WT/DS243/R, para 3.57.

[33]See para 6.76.

although India has challenged the US measures as contradicting para (b), (c), (d) and (e) of Article 2 of the Agreement on Rules Of Origin.

In this case, when the provisions of the RoO, interact with the modified US provisions, two different interpretations can be inferred. The Panel has derived the rationality for giving this decision on the basis of the final effect and in this concern has referred to Article 6.3 of the SCM Agreement to counter India's standpoint.[34] The Panel body by deriving such an analogy has tried to cover the substantive legal gap within the provisions, and for clarifying the two different interpretations, one by India and the other by US. As per the Panel body, Articles 2(b), (c), (d) of the RoO Agreement can be considered like guidelines rather than strict close ended provisions and therefore; India should have substantiated its claims. In this context, the Panel emphasised that India could not substantiate its claims beyond doubt to support that the US was applying the provisions for restrictive purposes and promoting its domestic market measures.

The arguments forwarded by India, may have a certain level of justification, however, India could not substantiate its claim, by showing the effect that it has to bear because of the protectionist policy adopted by the US.[35] Accordingly, the legal conditions have to be complied consistently and India's point could not stand.[36]

While applying the Rules of Origin in cross border trade, it is necessary to take into account that with the promotion of free trade, the growing trade between the Developed and Developing countries has not very often functioned smoothly as regards the expected trade pattern among the Member States, for achieving the WTO objectives.

---

[34]See para 3.224.

[35]Questions from the WTO Panel to India. **Question 26(c)** Would India agree that Article 6.3 of the SCM Agreement contemplate a showing of "actual" adverse effect? If so, is there any reason why the Panel, when interpreting the phrase "create" [.....] effects," should not seek inspiration from the provisions of Article 6.3 as well as the case law on Article III and IX of the GATT 1994?

[36]**Article 2** Until the work programme for the harmonization of Rules of Origin set out in part IV is completed, members shall ensure that: (a) when they issue administrative determinations of general application, the requirements to be fulfilled are clearly defined. In particular:

1. in cases where the criterion of change of tariff classification is applied, such a Rule of Origin and any exceptions to the rule must clearly specify the subheadings or headings within the tariff nomenclature that are addressed by the rule;
2. in cases where the ad-valorem percentage criterion is applied, the method for calculating this percentage shall also be indicated in the Rules of Origin;
3. in cases where the criterion of manufacturing or processing operation is prescribed, the operation that confers origin on the good concerned shall be precisely specified.

5.2 The Classification of Rules of Origin

Rules of Origin, for the purpose of determining the place of origin of a product are of a general nature. When these rules with the intention of applying specific policy measures, give preferences to imports, they are classified as Preferential and Non-preferential Rules of Origin.[37]

5.2.1 Preferential Rules of Origin

If we strictly follow the MFN clause, as stated in GATT Article I, clause 1,[38] specification of goods, through the rules of origin can be detrimental to free trade concepts. However, at the background of the application of trade preferences criteria for the specific objectives,[39] the preferential rules can be classified as the subset of rules, within the broader set of rules, and these preferential rules define the conditions under which an importing country could regard a product as originating from that specific exporting country and give tariff-preferences to the products from that country.[40] According to the practices followed, after the products are imported, the rules are applied to determine whether the imported products actually originated or were produced from that country.[41] Provisions specific with regard to the

[37]For detail references, see Agreement on Rules of Origin, Annex II Clause 1 Recognizing that some Members apply preferential Rules of Origin, distinct from non-preferential Rules of Origin, the Members hereby agree as follows. Clause 2 For the purpose of this Common Declaration, preferential Rules of Origin shall be defined as those laws, regulations and administrative determinations of general application applied by any member to determine whether goods qualify for preferential treatment under contractual or autonomous trade regimes leading to the granting of tariffs preferences going beyond the application of paragraph 1 of Article I of GATT 1994.

[38]GATT Article I clause 1, With respect to customs duties and charges of any kind imposed on or in connection with importation or exportation or imposed on the international transfer of payments for imports or exports, and with respect to the method of levying such duties and charges, and with respect to all rules and formalities in connection with importation and exportation, and with respect to all matters referred to in paragraphs 2 and 4 of Article III, any advantage, favour, privilege or immunity granted by any contracting party to any product originating in or destined for any other country shall be accorded immediately and unconditionally to the like product originating in or destined for the territories of all the contracting parties.

[39]As mentioned in Article 9 Clause 1, of the Rules of Origin, With the objectives of harmonizing rules of origin and, *interalia* providing more certainty in the conduct of world trade, the Ministerial Conference shall undertake the work programme set out below in conjunction with the CCC, on the basis of the following principles (a) rules of origin should be applied equally for all purposes as set out in Article1; (b) rules of origin should provide for the country to be determined as the origin of a particular good to be either the country where the good has been wholly obtained or, when more than one country is concerned in the production of the good, the country where the last substantial transformation has been carried out.

[40]Cadot et al. (2006), p. 73.

[41]De Wulf and Sokol (2005), p. 191.

Preferential Rules of Origin, inclusive of the conditions to be fulfilled by Member States, applying them are mentioned in the Annex II of the Agreement on Rules of Origin.[42]

A parallel between the market opportunities through free trade under the WTO, and the trade links established as a result of the Preferential Rules of Origin can be drawn to test, based on the following premises. Firstly, whether the market-preferential rules create a separate or quasi-trading system to the WTO's free trade system, and secondly, whether these trade links, through specific clauses, are consistent with the WTO provisions or not. These specific clauses are primarily the supportive provisions for the goods that genuinely originate in one of the treaty Member Countries, and therefore enjoy low tariffs or other benefits laid down under the specific clauses.[43] As a result of trade between the preference member country, firms may increase the export to partner countries at a lesser cost because of the favourable schemes. On the other hand, such preference based export generation will be supportive to employment generation in the exporting country. For these mutual benefits, two conditions are crucial. (1) The difference between the MFN tariff rates and the preferential tariff rates. (2) That the exporting firm chooses to trade with preference countries because of the large difference between the MFN rates and the preference rates.[44]

Such preferential access to the products can lead to trade creation and may even result to trade distortion as the resources are allocated based on preferences rather than following the norms of market competition.[45] Making further comparisons between the WTO objectives and the trade through preferential access, also leads to construction of the legal issues, such as the extent of balance between the free trade objectives and the opportunities created for the development by such preferential trade associations. One cannot ignore the fact that this balancing depends on conciliation, a flexible approach to the priorities, and a consideration of the overall interests. Preferential Rules of Origin often conclude as the trade arrangements in the form of regional trade agreements. Once trade relations through tariff preference are established, subsequent step is a preferential trade order within the WTO trading system leading to the formation of regional trade agreements. The extent of legality of a regional trade organisation can be determined, based on the legally determined limits of the trade between its members and in reality the trade practices followed beyond the limits, that affects the WTO objectives. Trade through these Preferential Rules of Origin, i.e., beyond the legally defined limits, rather creates

[42]Annex II, Clause 2. For the purposes of this Common Declaration, Preferential Rules of Origin shall be defined as those laws, regulations and administrative determinations of general application applied by any Member to determine whether the goods qualify for preferential treatment under contractual or autonomous trade regimes leading to the granting of tariff preferences going beyond the application of paragraph 1 of Article of GATT 1994.

[43]Barcelo (2006), pp. 3, 11–18, http://scholarship.law.cornell.edu/lsrp_papers/72.

[44]Hayakawa (2012), pp. 3–4. http://www.ide.go.jp/English/Publish/Download/Dp/pdf/366.pdf.

[45]Krishna and Krueger (1995), p. 2. http://www.iatp.org/files/Implementing_Free_Trade_Areas_Rules_of_Origin_.pdf.

regressive effects for attaining the objectives of the WTO through free trade. However, in practical terms, it is difficult to draw a common restrictive line for all the Member States by defining the limits of such rules. Preferential trade rules are country specific; therefore, the rules cannot be applied by general interpretation. Eventually, the extents of the varied possibilities of the interpretations, based on the objectives of the WTO and of the specific Regional Trade Organisation, or because of the provisional overlap between the different set of objectives of the organisations, then in such cases it is for the DSB to determine, in the instances where any party is affected by such policy measures.

Compared with the fundamental aspects and objectives of free trade, there may be minor legal justification for the regional trade agreements, other than that they serve the economic interests of the Developing and Less Developed countries through the supportive provisions. Some examples of the preferential rules of origin are (1) The African Trade Preference Act, (2) The North American Free Trade Agreement Implementation Act, (3) United States-Singapore Free Trade Agreement Act, and several others.

5.2.2 Non-preferential Rules of Origin

Non-preferential rules of origin are the rules applied to determine the country of origin of a product. In principle, these rules are not meant to apply for any preferences to a product based on nationality. Instead, they are primarily applied for distinguishing foreign products from domestic products. Article 1 of the Agreement on the Rules of Origin can be considered as the foundation provision for the Rules of Origin to be applied by the Member States and Article 1, Clause 2, of the Agreement on the Rules of Origin signifies the purpose of the Non-preferential Rules of Origin[46] in general.[47]

It is worth mentioning here that in the context of trade liberalisation policies, trading on the basis of Non-preferential Rules of Origin (just to know the place of Origin of the goods) is to allow, in the Member State's market, a newly evolving

[46]Article 1, Clause 2, Rules of Origin referred to in paragraph 1 shall include all Rules of Origin used in non-preferential commercial policy instruments, such as in the application of: Most-Favoured Nation treatment under Articles I,II,III,XI and XIII of GATT 1994; anti-dumping and countervailing duties under Article VI of GATT 1994; safeguard measures under Article XIX of GATT 1994;origin marking requirements under Article IX of GATT 1994; and any discriminatory quantitative restrictions or tariff quotas. They shall include Rules of Origin used for government procurement and trade statistics.

[47]**Article 1** of the Agreement on Rules of Origin. For the purposes of parts I to IV of this Agreement, rules of origin shall be defined as those laws, regulations and administrative determinations of general application applied by any member to determine the country of origin of goods provided such rules of origin are not related to contractual or autonomous trade regimes leading to the granting of tariff preferences going beyond the application of paragraph 1 of Article I of GATT 1994.

globalised economic approach and the existing domestic economic approach to co-exist and work together.

Under the Non-preferential rules, two main principles are applied to categorise goods. First, the goods must be wholly from any one particular country, i.e., a wholly obtained criteria, or second, the imported goods can be from more than one country. This criteria is based on substantial transformation.[48] In the second situation, origin of the product is determined as the last place in which it can be substantially transformed into a new and distinct article of commerce. For the purpose of legal qualification, it is noteworthy that the requirements of N.P.R.O are linked to the policy instruments of a more general nature that do not involve a preferential access for goods, rather remain specific to the identification of the place. An instance of this or reference for this can be, where a custom regime requires imports to bear special kinds of marks of origin.[49] Examples that can be quoted as Non-Preferential rules are; the MFN clause within the WTO, the Rules of origin applied for the safeguard measures, the conditions on the Origin of product applied for the government procurements, the application of rules for the general application of anti-dumping and countervailing duties, etc. According to the WTO provisions, Member States are supposed to grant MFN treatment to the products of all Member States except in exceptional cases. The US has not granted MFN status to Cuba and North Korea, so as to differentiate the products from these countries; Non-Preferential rules of Origin are applied.[50]

The MFN clause included in the WTO to establish free trade standards, also restricts discriminatory practices, such as allocating any sort of favourable treatment to a similar type of products originating from any particular country. Therefore, the objective application of the MFN clause raises further new issues of consistency. The MFN clause demands reasonable justification concerning the trade promotion based on Preferential and Non-preferential Trade Agreements.

5.3 Need for the Rules of Origin and the Promotion of Cross Border Trade

The application of the WTO Rules of Origin-provision determines the origin of a particular product, as either the country from where the product has been wholly obtained or, when more than one country is concerned in the production of the product, the country where the last substantial transformation has been carried out.[51]

[48]Jones and Martin (2012), p. 3. www.crs.gov.

[49]Jones and Martin (2012), p. 2. www.crs.gov.

[50]Jones and Martin (2012), p. 2. www.crs.gov. Footnote 6.

[51]**Article 3** clause (b) of the Agreement on Rules of Origin.

The trade between the Developed and Developing countries has grown faster, much more rapidly after the formation of the WTO. The pattern of trade has also diversified rather than remaining confined to raw materials and finished products. Nowadays, trade in intermediate goods covers a great proportion of export and import trade between the Developed countries and the Developing countries.

Along with this change, the sphere of production followed by the multinational companies has spread globally, rather than just remaining as a national matter. Consequently, the production process has become fragmented and divided between different countries around the world so as to attain maximum profit.[52] Multinational companies have also found a way of earning profit by outsourcing production. The production also forms the part of service sector as it depends upon human skills. Ironically, this newly emerged trading practice remains unregulated for several reasons, and one being that services sector are not covered under the SCM Agreement nor are they classified under the Rules of Origin Agreement. However, the affect of subsidies in the service sector[53] is recognised in the GATS.[54] Since the production process nowadays is distributed in several countries, and bearing in mind the scope of the WTO objectives, the emerging challenge is to maintain the standards of trade and level of transparency, which basically are part of treaty obligations among the Member States. These treaty obligations are based on basic level of trust among the Member States.

From the legal perspective, free trade should be based on some level of assumed values such as business transparency and fair trade policy measures, but how far it practically works, need to be tested.

While purchasing a product, when a customer observes a label stamped on any product denoting its origin, the general impression is that the product is from that particular country. But how far this is really true?

The dynamics of the markets are bringing changes as regards the places of production. Therefore to cover comprehensively the effective level of substantial production and the value addition, the Rules of Origin should be applied based on two main criteria.

1. A product wholly produced in one country.
2. Whether there are two or more countries involved in the production of the product. In such a case, the Rules of Origin will try to determine the origin of the product, based on the value addition.

The term value addition covers the value acquired as a result of working or processing or by incorporation of the parts, originating in the country of

[52]Varavithya and Esichaikul (2007), pp. 128–138.

[53]Article XV GATTS Cl (1) Members recognize that, in certain circumstances, subsidies may have distortive effects on trade in services. Members shall enter into negotiations with a view to developing the necessary multilateral disciplines to avoid such trade-distortive effects. Cl (2) Any Member which considers that it is adversely affected by a subsidy of another Member may request consultations with that Member on such matters.

[54]GATS: General Agreement on Trade in Services. Annex1B.

manufacture.[55] As there are several types of production functions carried out before the final product is ready, discerning the value addition in order to determine the origin of a product seems the simpler method. The added value of the imported intermediate parts can be calculated as, the price of the final product minus the value of non-originating material. Then, in a case of ascertaining the processing value added, the remaining amount should be subtracted by the value of raw materials from the place of origin (i.e., before addition from any other country is made).

In simple terms, it can be said that the extent of manufacturing or processing undergone in a country signifies the value added to the goods. There can be situations where a product is manufactured mainly from imported intermediate goods. Goods can retain the brand of origin of a specific country only if the added imported materials or components do not exceed a specified percentage of the value of the finished-product.[56]

Estimating the value addition of a product has far reaching significance in the WTO trading system, e.g. for the purpose of applying anti-dumping measures,[57] for determining the affect of subsidies when applying countervailing measures,[58] and as regards the safeguard measures mentioned earlier also.[59] In addition to the SCM Agreement, GATS Article XV[60] also covers such instances. The basic quantitative requirement for the application of any of the measure is above *de-minimis* threshold of the ratio of the product in question. From the international trade perspective, once a product is ready, the Rules of Origin can be applied on the basis of the value

---

[55] Inama (2009), p. 100.

[56] Inama (2009), p. 100.

[57] **Article 3.3** of the Anti-dumping agreement of the WTO "Where imports of a product from more than one country are simultaneously subject to anti-dumping investigations, the investigating authorities may cumulatively assess the effects of such imports only if they determine that (a) the margin of dumping established in relation to the imports from each country is more than *de minimis,* as defined in paragraph 8 of Article 5 and the volume of imports from each country is not negligible and (b) a cumulative assessment of the effects of the imports is appropriate in the light of the conditions of competition between imported products and the conditions of competition between the imported products and like domestic products."

[58] **Article 15.3** of the SCM agreement, "Where imports of a product from more than one country are simultaneously subject to countervailing duty investigations, the investigating authorities may cumulatively assess the effects of such imports only if they determine that (a) the amount of subsidization established in relation to the imports from each country is more than *de minimis* as defined in paragraph 9 of Article 11 and the volume of imports from each country is not negligible and (b) a cumulative assessment of the effects of the imports is appropriate in light of the conditions of competition between the imported products and the condition of competition between the imported products and the like domestic products."

[59] **Article 4 clause 2(b)** The determination referred to in subparagraph (a) shall not be made unless this investigation demonstrates, on the basis of objective evidence, the existence of the causal link between increased imports of the product concerned and serious injury or threat thereof. When factors other than increased imports are causing injury to the domestic industry at the same time, this shall not be attributed to increased imports.

[60] Article XV of the GATS deals with Subsidies.

added to the product, irrespective of the country in which it existed in the raw form.[61]

5.3.1 *The Trade Relationship Between Developed and Developing Countries and the New Forms of Cost Advantages*

The WTO by forming free trading system has also promoted a pattern of preferential trading between the Developed and Developing countries either through GSP or through other exclusive agreements such as GATS. Nowadays, the trade in services is also recognised as economic transactions among the Member States and the inclusion of GATS Agreement in the WTO is meant to cover such newly emerging trade practices. It is worth noting that in addition to the traditional business sectors, trade negotiations for the service sector create opportunities for development, as highlighted in the preamble of this Agreement.[62] This goes both way. However, it is important to put forward that the new type of trade agreements, within the free trade system of the WTO, may be mutually beneficial for the parties within the contractual obligations. On the other hand, it is relevant to keep in mind, that because of the lack of regulatory measures such opportunities may cause affects that are non-conducive to the dynamics of free trade and may create complexities for achieving the WTO objectives in a comprehensive manner.[63]

---

[61]**Article 9(b)** Rules of Origin should provide for the country to be determined as the origin of a particular product to be either the country where the product has been wholly obtained or, when more than one country is concerned in the production of the product, the country where the last substantial transformation has been carried out.

Article 3cl (b) Under their Rules of Origin, the country to be determined as the origin of a particular product is either the country where the product has been wholly obtained or, when more than one country is concerned in the production of the product, the country where the last substantial transformation has been carried out. This clause is applicable after the transition period that is a result of the harmonization work.

[62]Turning Hills into Mountains? Current Commitments, Under the GATS and Prospect for Change.

WTO, *Economic Research and Statistics Division* March, 2005, pp. 3–5. http://www.wto.org/english/res_e/reser_e/ersd201209_e.pdf.

From the Preamble. "*Recognizing* the growing importance of trade in services for the growth and development of the world economy…*Desiring* to facilitate the increasing participation of Developing countries in trade in services and the expansion of their service exports including, *inter alia*, through the strengthening of their domestic services capacity and its efficiency and competitiveness…Taking particular account of the serious difficulty of the Least-Developed countries, in view of their special economic situation and their development trade and financial needs."

[63]The trade in services as defined in GATS, Article 1 Clause 2. For the purposes of this Agreement, trade in services is defined as the supply of a service (a) from the territory of one Member into the territory of any other Member, (b) in the territory of one Member to the service consumer of any

Furthermore, with the growth of cross border trade, the trends in international trade shows an unconventional increase in the number of multinational companies, covering a wide variety of trade in goods and services. This has also led to the cross-border system of production networks making contributions at the various levels and these can be classified, as the ***trade practice of outsourcing, offshore assembly*** and ***production sharing agreements.***

Production sharing agreements[64] are formed between two or more independent enterprises and/or government agencies that specify the way in which and for what period of time, the signatories will share in the manufacturing of the output of a particular commodity. The production sharing agreement is a kind of alternative to the joint-venture enterprise, and is based on newly evolved way of business between two or more economic entities, with a common purpose of collaboration for the development and production of a commodity.[65]

The trade system of production-sharing process is beneficial where there is a difference both in currency value and the costs of the factors of production. Eventually, such economic conditions are suitable for establishing trade relationship between Developed and Developing countries, as it increases the trading opportunities.

In the context of the trading objectives mentioned, it can be observed that many of these new trade settings, due to the lack of strict regulatory measures, tends to be supportive for specific multinationals, which is contrary to the expected favourable opportunities for the Developing and Less-Developed countries. The effect on the WTO objectives, because of such mutually advantageous deals by the multinationals, can be formally compared with the basic factors for classifying subsidies, i.e., benefit, financial contribution, and specificity, and the trade distortive effects thus generated. In the mid-1960s, the multinational companies from the Developed countries, through product sharing agreements with the Developing countries had their products assembled at the lesser costs. For example, products such as semi-conductors, valves, turners and other components began to be assembled by international electronic firms in Hong Kong, Thailand, and Malaysia.[66] In the present day context, the trends are changing, the production sharing of the intermediate products has surged, rather than been confined to simple assembling. Imported intermediates are assembled at a cheaper rate from the places where the production

---

other Member (c) by a service supplier of one Member, through commercial presence in the territory of any other member (d) by a service supplier of one Member, through presence of natural person of a Member in the territory of any other Member.

[64]Athukorala (2010), p. 1.

[65]Global production sharing has evolved through three distinct phases. At the formative stage, the production sharing involved locating small fragments of the production process in a low-cost country and reimporting the assembled components to be incorporated in the final product. Subsequently, production networks began to encompass many countries engaged in the assembly process at different stages, resulting in multiple border crossings by product fragments before they were incorporated in the final product.

[66]Athukorala & Kohpaiboon (2011), p. 3. http://www.aae.wisc.edu/hoseae/d15.pdf.

assembly cost is less, hence benefitting the multinational companies.[67] The emphasis in the preamble of the RoO is to promote transparency regarding the origin of products; however, it seems difficult to determine the value addition, in order to quantify the benefit obtained by the multinationals through these production sharing agreements. The trade outcome of such production sharing agreement is that the final output so obtained can be sold further, as an export product, at a price, lesser than the competitors of the same product. So long as the benefits obtained by production sharing agreements are confined to welfare and development and creating trading opportunities for the Developing and Less–Developed countries, it can be considered as justifiable and within the parameters of the WTO objectives. However, the trade advantages obtained, without going through the required regulation, are distortive to the WTO objectives of free trade.

The term ***outsourcing*** can be explained as a business practice in which firms transfer management or day-to-day execution of business or business processes to an external service provider. Global outsourcing is enormously facilitated by technological innovations. With the improvements in electronic communication and the internet facilities, several services that were previously non-marketable can be traded across borders after the formation of the WTO. However, in these changing situations, and with the use of technology which creates complexities to demarcate the boundaries of rights and obligations, it is difficult to know the actual place of origin of the products. The trade practices of outsourcing have emerged rapidly between Developed and Developing countries, perhaps due to the availability of human services at a lesser price in the Developing countries.[68]

Within the WTO trading system, trade in services is defined under Article 1 Clause 2 of the GATS.[69] It is, however, noteworthy that in the light of the WTO objectives, the trade in services is promoted for the progress of the world economy and making special opportunities for the Welfare and Development of the Developing and Less-Developed countries. Such business practices promoted by the multinationals are not strictly based on the MFN trading principles, but rather on the scope of flexibilities based on the mutual interest of the trading countries. This may reasonably create the basis for several kinds of favoured concessions and grounds for subsidies.[70]

---

[67] Ventura and Lima (2001), p. 11.

[68] Minevich (2005), p. 3. www.globalequations.com/Global.

[69] For the purpose of this Agreement, trade in services is defined as the supply of a service:

(a) from the territory of one Member into the territory of any other Member;
(b) in the territory of one Member to the service consumer of any other Member;
(c) by a service supplier of one Member through commercial presence in the territory of any other Member;
(d) by a service supplier of one Member, through presence of natural persons of a Member in the territory of any other Member.

[70] GATS Article II for Most-Favoured-Nation Treatment 1. With respect to any measure covered by this Agreement, each Member shall accord immediately and unconditionally to services and service provider of any other Member treatment no less favourable than it accords to like service

Such policies are further encouraged by the Member States that promote outsourcing, in order to encourage foreign investment from the multinationals. Comparing the trade in services through outsourcing as one specific mode of business practices, with the general trading pattern promoted by the WTO, it can be noticed that the possibility of distortion both to the market efficiency and competition is higher in the case of trade in the service sector. The distortive effect because of the subsidies or through such favourable policies is acknowledged in the GATS Article XV.[71] As the free trade system is an institution based approach followed by the Member States through a treaty mechanism, it often has less normative support from the Member States. Therefore, the promotion of business interests at a mutual level, between the parties, superseding the objectives of the WTO cannot be discounted. How far such interests can be promoted, and drawing a restrictive line depends very much on case to case basis, as the matter falls into the grey area of substantive interpretation. The approach supporting the interest of the parties, despite the WTO regulations also has a substantial legal basis. The agreement to regulate subsidy practices also creates the scope of flexibilities for giving subsidies in the case of the development and welfare of the Developing and Less-Developed countries.

Offshore assembly programmes allow the firms to export component parts and then have them assembled overseas. This practice may be beneficial on bilateral basis, however considering the overall perspective of the WTO and the trading principles based on multilateralism, it creates new forms of challenge. The challenge for attaining the objectives through the free trade system is that most industrialised countries allow special favourable treatment such as 'tariff breaks' for domestically-produced components that are shipped abroad for further processing and re-imported into the home country.[72] In addition to the low currency value, availability of labour at a lesser rate is another major factor for the off-shore

suppliers of any other country. 2. A Member may maintain a measure inconsistent with paragraph 1, provided that such a measure is listed in, and meets the conditions of the Annex on Article II Exemptions. 3. The provisions of this Agreement shall not be so construed as to prevent any Member from conferring or according advantages to adjacent countries in order to facilitate exchanges limited to contiguous frontier zones of services that are both locally produced and consumed.

[71]Article XV GATTS Cl (1) Members recognize that in certain circumstances, subsidies may have distortive effects on trade in services. Members shall enter into negotiations with a view to developing the necessary multilateral disciplines to avoid such trade-distortive effects. Cl (2) Any Member which considers that it is adversely affected by a subsidy of another Member may request consultations with that Member on such matters.

[72]Finger (1976), pp. 598–611. [The US tariff contains an offshore assembly provision, (OAP). The tariff on certain imported goods is charged on the value of such goods less the value of incorporated domestically produced components, i.e., the tariff on an assembled product is applied only to the value-added in foreign assembly or processing if domestically produced components are used].

assembly of products.[73] This practice affects the market efficiency based on free competition as the countries form such business deals through bilateral treaties.

Once ready, the finished products are further re-exported to other countries by the multinationals. Undoubtedly, it is beneficial to the trading partners but on the other hand it limits the opportunities for the other Member States. Offshore assembly nevertheless raises concerns between free trade and other values that are mentioned in the preamble of the WTO. The offshore assembly considerations are based on means and end rationality and after cost-benefit analysis. Such trade practices depends on the economic rationality, i.e., if the benefit obtained by offshore assembly is greater than the job loss at the home country and it is profitable to transfer the intermediate level of production to the other countries, it is very likely that the Member State shall opt for it.[74] This point becomes further linked with the term benefit, as mentioned in the SCM Agreement on the one side, and the cost factor of retaining the local industrial set up and the employment level on the other side. The benefit attained by the multinationals is by using the factors of production in a Developing and Less-Developed country. Such externalisation of the production is based on co-operation among the other states. However, the practice of offshore assembly also affects the fair competition between the multinationals, relatively producing the same types of products, when such products produced and assembled domestically are somewhat more expensive because of the excess of the labour costs.[75] It cannot be ignored that such trade practices also create tension between rules and standards in theory and practice. Comparing the policy standards for the markets in the Developing and Less-Developed countries, there is a variance in WTO's legal position and the policy standards applied in many of the Member States. This further leads to the question of how effective the WTO system is in terms of cross border trade.

One cannot deny that there is a lack of mechanisms to determine transparency in part by part production processes. In matters of trade in services the market situation is not conventional. It is such that in the vast majority of international service transactions, the service providers have their presence in the market of the consumers, for example, an individual providing, professional advice or as some

[73]EC, community tariff schedules contain this provision. When a company import goods from outside the Community, they normally have to pay duty on the full customs value of the goods. When Community goods are exported outside the customs territory of the EC, they lose their Community status, and if they are later re-imported they are treated in the same way as non-Community goods, and are liable to duty on the full customs value. When using the **OPR procedure (outward processing relief procedure),** it will enable a company to claim relief from duty on the Community goods which have been exported for process, as long as it can be shown that the exported goods were used to produce, or are incorporated into, the products imported. Before claiming duty relief under OPR, however, a company must be authorised to use the arrangements. For detail reference, see [**Article 66** ***Special provision relating to non-originating goods, Article 235 of Proposal for the regulation of the European Parliament and of the Council laying down the Union custom code COM2012/64 final***].

[74]Trachtman (2008), pp. 226–227.

[75]Trachtman (2008), p. 227.

sort of entity (cooperation, agency, branch etc.) that is owned or controlled from abroad, although it might employ local resources such as personnels, buildings, in order to create the service.[76]

Hence, these preferential trade agreements, between Developed and Developing nations have also raised new forms of legal issues. While determining the place of origin of a product, from the perspective of trade between Developed and Developing country, several situations need to be considered. It may be that a product is produced wholly in a Developing country and receives WTO G.S.P preferences while being sold to a Developed country. In another situation, it may be that a product is partly processed in a Developing country and then exported directly to another Developed country.[77] The existing WTO G.S.P schemes create a preference for products deemed to have originated in a Developing and Less Developed country that has a special preference agreement with the respective Developed countries.

Hence, in the lack of coherence between the WTO objectives and the newly emerging trade practices through offshore service assistance, production sharing and outsourcing, trade issue arises, about the possibility of tension between the efficiency principles as promoted through free trade and trading based on preferential origin, if adopted as a policy measures. On the basis of this substantive background, the scope of legal provision gets tested, that to what level the trade benefits obtained by such practices can be justified, and if not justified how far restricted by the provisions of the agreements, such as SCM Agreement and GATS.

5.4 Rules of Origin and the Trade Subsidy Relationship

Member States often resort to seeking state support or similar practices in order to counter the growing market competition as a result of free trade. In the context of the WTO trading system, the use of subsidies is acceptable to the extent of developing comparative advantage by the Member States. However, subsidies are also used for the purpose of market gains, and circumventing the limitations of flexibility as provided under the provisions of the SCM Agreement. It is to be further noted that because of the economic differences and different technological and production capacity of the Member States and for the reasons of market compulsions, States follow even the unjustifiable trade practices of giving export subsidies. These export subsidies are often used for the trade practices of dumping which is inconsistent with the WTO objectives. However so, are the inconsistencies on the substantive level, it is to be noted that the WTO tries to regulate export trade through the SCM Agreement by categorising subsidies in the form of prohibited, actionable, and non-actionable.

[76]Vermulst et al. (1995), p. 19.

[77]Lloyd (2002), p. 180.

Despite the categorisation of subsidies in the form of prohibited and actionable in the SCM Agreement, it nevertheless cannot ensure restrictions on several indirect forms of state support whenever there is trade based on preferential trade agreement. A comparative analysis of the trade practices suggests, that these indirect methods of trade support cannot be determined by applying the provisions of SCM Agreement exclusively.

The Agreement on Rules of Origin is primarily intended to encourage greater industrialisation of the Developing countries.[78] For this, it specifically includes provision referring to the conditions, by virtue of which the origin rules define the level of substantial processing as an essential requirement for acquiring the place of origin status.[79] The application of value-of-parts rule, entailed crucial determinations about the origin of such parts.[80] In this free trade system, by applying the Rules of Origin, the determination of the origin of a product for the market purpose depends upon the place where the last substantial transformation or any such process that took place.[81] Free trade promotes efficiency in the market system. The WTO has covered various agreements to check the trade practices that distorts market efficiency. For the purpose of determining the distortion of trade, the Rules of Origin can be applied to determine the place of origin and the various steps followed in processing of a product. They are based on the trade situation, for example, when country A exports a part-produced product to country B and country B after further processing it into a final product, exports it to country C. The trade of product, very often in such a situation is considered as the export of country B to country C, without taking into account the contribution of country A in this trade. In such cases, the legal presumption that arises is the high possibility of giving preferences to products from country B by shadowing the role of country A in the world trade. This approach, adopted in international trade, has raised several questions in the mind of trade lawyers and researchers when analysing the discriminatory trade practices. In this instances it requires determining the dumping practices, or export of products affecting the sales of the competitor companies. The question from the subsidies perspective that arises, concerns the nature of financial contribution in the form of benefit to such exporting industries and in this discussion the specific impact to the export of inter-mediatory products. Such support can be compared with the criteria used to define export subsidies. In order to determine the connecting link between trade subsidies and the export of intermediate goods, the application of the Rules of Origin, besides demonstrating the place of the origin of the product may also uncover the objectives of such trade

[78]For detail reference, see the Preamble of the Agreement on Rules of Origin.

[79]Article 3(b) of the Agreement on Rules of Origin "Under their rules of origin, the country to be determined as the origin of a particular good is either the country where the good has been wholly obtained or, when more than one country is concerned in the production of the good, the country where the last substantial transformation has been carried out."

[80]Vermulst et al. (1995), p. 169.

[81]Brenton et al. (2011).

relationship and subsequently determine the subsidy aspect. The Rules of Origin are not only taken as a proposed measure to determine the origin of products.

Article 1.1(a) of the SCM Agreement covers the type of financial contribution that can be considered as a basic feature for testing a subsidy.[82] Article 1.1a (1) (ii) of the SCM Agreement states, 'government revenue that is otherwise due is foregone or not collected' (e.g.) [fiscal incentives such as tax credits].

Article 1.1a (1) (iii) of the SCM Agreement, 'a government provides goods or services other than general infrastructure, or purchases goods.' The term financial contribution used in the SCM Agreement also implies support of a type that is other than directly financial. Furthermore, to mention, about the term benefit. Article 1.1(b) of the SCM Agreement deals with the term "benefit" which can be presented in various forms, and is a constituting factor for substantially determining subsidies by specifying the objectives of such financial contributions. In the situation where there is trade between Developed and Developing countries and one is supplementing the other for some specific reasons, financial contribution can be provided in terms of tariff concessions on the use of imports of inter-mediatory products from a specific Member Country. In case of the use of inter-mediatory products, if conditioned upon being used for manufacturing by the preference given to the specific Developing countries, the possibilities of implicit form of subsidies cannot be discounted. Benefits can also arise because of the failure of the Developing countries to cover the externalities, such as checking the pollution level, maintaining the labour standards, and several other similar issues.[83] Assumptions of financial contribution also arises in the form of supportive investment policies encouraging foreign investment.[84] The growing trade in intermediate products between Developed and Developing countries necessitates that the provisions of the Subsidy Agreement and the Agreement on Rules of Origin can be used to cover the detailed aspects of trade transactions. The provisions of the two agreements can be applied together to study the cases related to the trade in intermediate products and the effects on the market concepts of efficiency based on the promotion of fair competition.

Moreover, the application of these rules helps to define the limits of preferential tariffs arrangements, which is a special relaxation to the WTO free trade agreements.

[82]Article 1, definition of subsidy (mentioned in the previous chapters).

[83]World Trade Report (2006), Exploring the links between subsidies, trade and the WTO, p. 49. http://www.wto.org/english/res_e/publications_e/wtr06_e.htm.

[84]Krishna and Krueger (1995), p. 4. http://www.iatp.org/files/Implementing_Free_Trade_Areas_Rules_of_Origin_pdf.

5.4.1 Trading Through Preferential Trade Agreements in the Multilateral Trading System

The concept of free trade among the member nations of the WTO is based mainly on comparative costs advantage and absolute advantage theories. The term "comparative costs advantage" refers to the lower opportunity costs[85] of the products compared with, those of competitors. Producers in one country do have a comparative advantage, if the opportunity cost in producing the product is lower for economic reasons than in the other country.

Comparing the present day trading situation with the position before the advent of the WTO, it is thus apparent, that the concept of free trade has changed the trading practices.[86] Nowadays, the diverse factors and the means of production are obtained from various countries rather than being produced domestically. It is often the case that the location of production is determined by the multinational companies keeping in mind the absolute advantage[87] and comparative advantage,[88] so as to attain high profits. This aim has further led to the adoption of fiscal policies with the primary objective of creating a conducive environment for exports. Governments supporting the export promotion, influence measures such as taxes, FDI (foreign direct investment), business regulation, support for the infrastructure, and other similar policies,[89] as these factors directly affect the economies of scale.[90] It is indeed an economic concern for any multinationals, from the investment perspective, if the intermediate product applied in manufactured output is from the preference given countries. Usually, multinationals, for buying intermediate inputs, try a broad range of the international market. The priority always is to acquire the inputs from a cost efficient source and that means prioritising the investment options based on mutual interests. Policy shifts, in support of export-

---

[85]Opportunity Cost is the cost of forgoing something because the company has opted for something else or it can be said as what the company has given up in order to obtain the item. *Illustration:*—A company employs three software engineers and commits to finish a project by using the services of all the three. The company also takes money in advance for this. Later, a larger opportunity is presented, as someone else is ready to pay more for the project, which can be used somewhere else. However, this is no longer possible because the three engineers are already occupied. Therefore, the cost of first project is not only the time and salary of the three engineers who are working as it is also the loss of revenue and market share that the company might have attained had the engineers worked either in partnership or separately on this new offer.

[86]The free trade measure signifies here the trade measures promoted by the WTO.

[87]Absolute advantage states that a particular individual or country can produce more of a specific commodity than another individual or country using the same amount of resources.

[88]Comparative advantage states that a particular country or individual can produce a specific commodity at a lower opportunity cost (in terms of forgone production in an alternative commodity) than another country or individual.

[89]Lloyd (2002), p. 172.

[90]When more units of a product or a service can be produced on a greater scale, with lower input costs, economies of scale are said to be achieved. Economies of scale are categorised in two forms. (1) Internal and External economies of scale. Södersten and Reed (1994), p. 335.

promoting measures for mutual gains can be observed both in the Developed and Developing countries.

The factors of production in some respect differ between Developing and Developed countries. In the majority of cases, Developing countries have an abundant of labour force, availability of raw materials at a cheaper rate and additionally, there can be several other factors of production which are less expensive in comparison to their prices in the Developed economies. In the free trade system, this provide gainful opportunities for the multinationals companies. The vertical intra-industry trade relation[91] reveals such practices by the multinational companies. The production process is based upon different stages, and each can be performed at different locations by taking advantage of the local economic conditions. China, for example, exports computer components, and electronic components and uses an abundantly available labour force to assemble these components in the labour intensive final production stage.[92]

The choice of the WTO system allowing preferential trade agreements in addition to free trade agreement is with the objective to promote welfare of the Developing and Less Developed countries through economic advancement. Taking into consideration, that free trade is the predominant policy of the WTO, the idea behind preferential trade organisation is to strengthen the prospects for sustainable domestic policy reforms along with trade liberalisation, mainly for economies in transition.[93]

Nevertheless, this new type of trade relationship has created business understanding that, mainly produces specific benefits between some Developed and Developing/Less-Developed countries rather than for the welfare and economic advantage of the population in general. The preferential trade organisations follows the Rules of Origin, while importing the products from the Member Nation of the regional trade organisation. Hence, local producers or producers within the preferential trade organisation are allowed to import inputs and raw material free of duty, as long as the final products contain a minimum percentage of local materials.[94] This newly formed trade practices gives wide room of discretion to the multinational, therefore such trade practices are often questionable from the perspective of the MFN clause.

Illustration

For explanation, an example is taken here of three countries **A, B &C**. It can be assumed that country A, can trade freely either with country B or C. That is, country A can import the product in question, either from B or C. Further, consider that country C is genuinely capable of supplying products at a lower price than B,

---

[91]Intra-industry trade arises if a country simultaneously imports and exports similar type of goods or services. Vertical intra-industry trade refers to the simultaneous exports and imports of goods classified in the same sector but at different stages of processing.

[92]Lindert (1986), p. 39.

[93]Holliday (1997), pp. 6–8. www.policyarchive.org/handle/10207/.../426.pdf.

[94]Holliday (1997), pp. 7–8. www.policyarchive.org/handle/10207/.../426.pdf.

because the production cost is less. Therefore, country A will have maximum imports from country C. Here, A follows the line of absolute and comparative cost advantage theories.

Now, suppose country A and B forms a free trade agreement (in the form of Regional Trade Agreements) between themselves, and A eliminates the import tariffs for the products from country B. Now country A can import the maximum of the products from country B. (But the free trade price from the perspective of the cost of production and the price because of production efficiency is less, in country C than in country B). Thus, trade is diverted from the more efficient supplier to a less efficient supplier.[95] The preferential trade organisation creates a preferential market system, by the reduction in tariffs for its own members, and that is based mainly on the economics of choices. This reduction of tariffs can be achieved or compensated by the subsidies for exports, but such practices are contrary to the WTO objectives.[96] In order to discover how this form of trade practice is a subsidy, a specific effect on the outcome, can be taken for comparison. The price of the product supported by the subsidy is lower than its normal price. In the case of products, preferably manufactured by using the intermediate parts from the regional trade agreement Member countries, the cost of the final product is less. Such trading practices are adopted with the goal of attaining benefit when there are several producers of the same product. Any such benefit obtained by exporting in a larger market outside the regional trade market, for the mutual gains with the Members of regional trade agreement countries can be compared with the term benefit, as defined under the subsidy Agreement.

The legal objective of this institution that is the general welfare of the people at large by promoting a free trade market approach towards international trade is also tampered with, due to product discrimination on the basis of nationality.

5.4.1.1 The Question of Trade Subsidies. An Example from NAFTA

The economic concept of the comparative cost advantage (discussed in the previous chapter) adopted by the WTO becomes overshadowed by the economic interests of regional trading organization. In other words, the Rules of Origin are applied as a protectionist measures that deprive consumers of the potential benefits by delivering the products not at the fair price, which is contrary to the WTO objectives.

Examples of such regional trade alliances are NAFTA, ASEAN, etc.

The case of NAFTA is described here, but prior to that, it is relevant to understand how trading works within the regional trade organisation, and its market influences in the system of free trade promoted by the WTO.

---

[95] Suranovic et al. (2011).

[96] **Article 3.1(a)** of Agreement on subsidies and countervailing measures the WTO prohibits, 'Subsidies contingent, in law or in fact, whether solely or as one of several other conditions, upon export performance, including those illustrated in Annex I.'

In a regional trade organisation also, member nations are placed in different economic categories. The trade relationship within this regional trade agreement is based upon upstream and downstream industry relationships.[97] Furthermore, from the conventions followed in international business practices, suggest that foreign direct investment is motivated by the desire to exploit the specific advantages of firms and manipulate the market system. Firms that are located in developed economies may have fewer opportunities to shift incomes, due to the competition they face in their own market. On the other hand, firms based in the developing economies may have several possibilities for arbitrage on primary resources utilised for the products, such as labour and capital markets. Hence, there is more foreign investment for upstream industries in the Developing countries. Upstream firms have the possibility to hire employees of various categories at lesser cost and consequently, downstream firms in the Developed economy can use the inputs, as low costs intermediate products of the upstream industries located in the Developing country. The trade situation of NAFTA is referred here as an example for understanding how the trading pattern based on buying inputs from the member group countries works in regional trading system.

The main criteria for NAFTA Rules of Origin are,[98]

1. Goods "wholly produced or obtained" in the NAFTA region, i.e., they contain no non-NAFTA material
2. Goods containing non-originating inputs, but meeting the product-specific Origin Rules;
3. Goods produced in the NAFTA region wholly from the originating materials, i.e., produced from materials that may contain non-NAFTA materials, but these materials -have met the NAFTA rules of origin.
4. Unassembled goods and goods classified in the same HS (Harmonized system) category as their parts, that do not meet product-specific origin rules, but contain sufficient North American regional value content.

The Rules of Origin, for the purpose of international trade, sets the guidelines to be adopted for acknowledging the place of origin of the final product, based on the value addition, once the product is ready as an export commodity. However, from the practices, it can be inferred that the trade pattern followed by the members of a preferential trade organisation, can be discriminatory, as the Member Nations of such an organisation distinguish products, that are from across the border of the regional trade group members and the product manufactured within the regional trade group. The discriminatory effect can be observed, as the products that fulfil the regional trade agreement criteria, are granted preferential tariff access. From these instances, it can be concluded that the Rules of Origin are applied for

[97] An upstream firm produces only the intermediate products, while a downstream firm produces the final product and buys the intermediate product in an open market. Strauss-Kahn (2005), p. 302.

[98] Inama (2009), p. 279.

discriminating products produced within the NAFTA region and one from outside the NAFTA.

In the case **of Canada-United States FTA and the Honda,**[99] the contended issue was that of the tariff criteria applied, based on the origin determination of the intermediate inputs and components. The trade agreement with specific clauses was signed between the parties, leading to Free Trade Agreement. After the formation of FTA, Free Trade Agreement between the US and Canada in 1989, Honda of Canada,[100] treated the engines used in the Civic Honda car model, manufactured in the United States, as eligible for importation into Canada under the FTA, and likewise market status was given to the Civics manufactured in Canada, without extra tariffs. Additionally, in line with the regional trade commitments, the two countries agreed on establishing a special bilateral procedure for settling disputes regarding the alleged government subsidies to their industry.

By the 1990s, Honda's compact model, the Accord, had shown a significant impact in the US market. The Accord was manufactured in Marysville.[101] As per the agreement between the US and Canada, there were two ways to earn duty-free status on trans-US-Canada trade.

1. When the product is wholly obtained or produced in one or both of the two countries.
2. When the product undergoes a substantial transformation either in the US or in Canada.

As the Honda Civic was not wholly obtained or produced either in the US or in Canada, the company needed to pass the second test to enter the US duty-free. As per the conditions mentioned in the provisions of the agreement, once the product entered in either of the country, the facts about the value additions were subsequently, reviewed by the respective custom authorities. In one such instance, as reported in this case, when imported cars entered the jurisdiction of the US customs,

[99]See United States International Trade Commission, 1992 ITC Lexis 195, Apr., 1992; Int'l Trade Rep. (BNA) (March 4, 1992) Chapter 20 of the NAFTA on the basic institutional arrangements and dispute settlement procedures established in Chapter 18 of the FTA. The Honda case involved a ruling by the US Customs service on March 2, 1992 that Canadian exports of Honda Civics during 1989/90 failed to qualify as North American products under FTA content rules, resulting in US duties being applied to the products. US Customs held that Canadian manufacturer had used engines made in the United States that contained too many foreign parts to qualify as North American. However, Revenue Canada had previously approved the engines on import into Canada as meeting rule-of-origin requirements. For further information, see "Customs Rules that Canadian Honda Civics Failed to meet Content Standards under FTA, International Trade Reporter", Vol. 9:10, March 4, 1992, 384, as cited in Winham (1992).

[100]The Japanese car making company in Canada.

[101]Marysville, Ohio. Honda's manufacturing operations in the United States began with a motorcycle plant in Marysville in 1979. Levin and Fleeter. (firm) *Honda in Ohio: The Economic Impact of the First 25 Years,* "A study prepared by June (2004)." Online Computer Library Centre (OCLC) number 60885765. http://dandftest.com/files/Download/Honda%20Economic%20Impact%20Study%20June%2004.PDF.

the United States customs investigation determined that the Honda Civic, manufactured in Canada and exported to the United States, did not meet the 50% requirement (transformation requirement) because it contained too many Japanese parts. The Honda Civics, was asked to pay an extra tariff.

In its claim before the US customs service, Honda of Canada contended that non-North American components, imported from Japan into Canada and applied in the Civics model, had already incurred a change in tariff classification in the process of the assembly of the cars.[102] The Honda cars exported to US were assembled in Canada. Furthermore, many non-Canadian components, notably the engines were manufactured in Ohio, and shipped to Canada. Hence, the value addition met the above 50% North American content requirement and thus could be counted as 100% North American by virtue of the roll-up rule.[103] On this basis, Honda argued that the completed cars met the 50% content requirement and hence could enter the United States duty-free.

Countering this argument pursued by the Honda of Canada, the US customs asserted that costs "reasonably" allocated to the production of goods can be used for the calculation of value addition only if they were directly incurred in the production of the goods. The US Customs refused to consider overhead cost or "general expenses of doing business" as direct costs and added that costs arising from the casting and machining of the head and block could not be reasonably allocated to the production of goods. Eventually, the US customs determined that the engine did not meet the 50% requirement for originating goods, as the car model contained too many Japanese parts by virtue of its value.[104]

---

[102]In calculating the domestic content requirement to 50% of the assembly costs, the CFTA (Canada Free Trade Area) utilises the direct costs methods, which requires 50% of the value of originating materials plus costs of processing be produced domestically. Direct costs are limited to direct labor, materials and processing costs. CFTA utilises the "roll up" method to calculate domestic content of automotive parts that consist of materials manufactured throughout the world.

[103]Kerr and Gaisford (2006), p. 135. **Roll up**:—If a member country of a regional trade agreement uses an input from a second country, perhaps to produce intermediate products, the product would be designated as that of the former country provided it satisfied the ad-valorem criterion. If that intermediate product is then used in the manufacture of a final product, a roll-up rule would allow that very intermediate product to be counted as a product that was 100% from the first country.

Roll-down system:—In the case of a roll-down system, a product would be treated as 0% from a country, in which one country used an input from a second country to produce an intermediate product and the second country did not fulfil the ad-valorem threshold. It is basically the subtraction of the entire price of the part that doesn't meet the ad-valorem standards to be considered as originating. (Roll-up and Roll-down methods are helpful in the case to determine product or intermediate product from the preferential trading region or outside).

[104]On the basis of the facts, the US Customs service reached the opposite conclusion. The US Customs determined that the Honda Civics did not qualify for the duty-free treatment given to cars under the FTA, because they contained too many Japanese parts, and thus did not meet the 50% local content requirement of the FTA.

After the US customs decision, the Canadian side reacted by saying that the decision would encourage assembly plants to be allocated in the US, which was more or less a subsidy in the form of tariff concessions.[105]

The US officials tried to play the controversy down by explaining that it was merely a dispute on technical grounds having no bearing on their overall attitude to the FTA.[106] Finally, the governments of Canada and the US agreed to settle the Honda dispute by drafting a new treaty.

The example stated above is not a WTO case rather a NAFTA case; nevertheless, from the perspective of free trade it can be inferred that the attitude adopted by the US is to encourage trade diversion for upstream intermediate goods.[107] The issue of subsidies, which is contrary to the objectives of the WTO, surfaces in this case, because of the policy measures encouraging exports and attracting investments in the regional trade organisations. Providing upstream goods at a cheaper rate to other countries, creates an incentive for obtaining either finished products or downstream products on a tariff-free basis among the members of the regional trade agreement, which is a trade promotion of the domestic industries contrary to the objectives of free trade which is to promote efficiency, creating equal trading opportunities for all the Member States. The growth of international trade in goods that are not manufactured in a single country, rather finished in several has made the rules for determining the "origin" of goods, one of the complex areas of preferential market access negotiations.[108] So long as the product origin rules are applied to the extent of distinguishing trade flows between preferential and other trading partners, and are not fundamentally violating the WTO objectives; such product differentiation can be said to have little distorting effect on the cross border flow of manufactured goods.[109]

As the market system works on the economic logic of profit and loss, nations therefore start to make choices, either trading based on WTO free trade principle or giving priority to trade with Member States from the regional trade organisation. From the perspective of the WTO free trade objective, such preferences create distortive affects and are also contrary to the efficiency principles.

Therefore, it can be suggested that preferential trading for producing final goods, for the purpose of exports, creates effects similar to "subsidies for exports," when selling those products to nations outside the regional trade organisations. What is missing in the SCM Agreement is the "legal requirement on this matter, demanding

---

[105]For Canada, the decision was important, Prime minister Mulroney said, "We are getting sides wiped, by American Japan-bashing." Others thought it was more like Canada-bashing, or at least confirmation of their negative views on the FTA in general. Canada feared that Honda and other third country automobile manufacturers would not benefit from the FTA, and they would simply relocate their assembly work in the United States. US customs in this case refused to allow North American costs as an amount spent for direct costs of processing in the US.

[106]Cantin and Lowenfeld (1993), p. 383.

[107]An upstream firm produces only the intermediate goods, while a downstream firm produces the final product and buys the intermediate product in an open market.

[108]Estevadeordal and Suominen (2008), p. 92.

[109]Vermulst et al. (1995), p. 8.

scrutiny through the various provisions of the subsidies agreement, the advantages sought in the form of benefits by trading within the members of a preferential trading agreement."[110]

5.5 Applying the Rules of Origin in Two Dimensions; Between Legality and Trade Benefits

Declaration of the nationality of a product is relevant so as to maintain transparency in the free trade system of the WTO, and this is referred to in the preamble of the Agreement on Rules of Origin.[111] The transparency criteria as a fair trade measures are indeed supportive to the free trade system. However, because of the restrictive scope of the provisions for determining the origin of products, inherent limitations are faced while interpreting the provisions in the broader perspectives of the WTO objectives. Therefore, supporting the nationality criteria for trade in products, for the reasons of developing the possibilities of comparative cost of the Developing countries economies, by shielding the effects of multinationals from the Developed countries may lead to misappropriations and restrictive market approach. In effect, in the free trade system, the market system is dynamic and competitive, hence on occasions, the classification, based on the place of origin, can be applied as a measure for restricting the imports of products of similar kinds to the domestic one, thus leading to the trends, which are the reverse of the free trade objectives. Such measures are protectionist.[112] As already discussed, that as a general trading principle, discriminating products for import and export on the ground of nationality, violates the MFN clause of the WTO, although on exceptional grounds, there is a possibility of restrictions to the free trade. As mentioned in the Agreement on Safeguard, Member State can restrict the import of a product, if the product that is being imported in an increased quantity causes or threatens to cause serious injury.[113] In several cases applying the Rules of Origin to enforce safeguard measures becomes a sensitive question. The application of the Rules of Origin, in

[110]Trade diversion means that a free trade area diverts trade away from a more efficient supplier outside the FTA, towards a less efficient supplier within the FTA.

[111]Members, noting that Ministers on 20 September, 1986 agreed that the Uruguay Round of Multilateral Trade Negotiations shall aim to "bring about further liberalization and expansion of world trade," "strengthen the role of GATT" and increase the responsiveness of the GATT system to the evolving international economic environment.

[112]**Article 2(d)** the Rules of Origin that they apply to imports and exports are not more stringent than the Rules of Origin they apply to determine whether or not a product is domestic and shall not discriminate between other Members, irrespective of the affiliation of the manufacturers of the goods concerned.

[113]**Article 2** of the 'Agreement on safeguards.' A member may apply a safeguard measure to a product only if that member has determined, pursuant to the provisions set below, that such product is being imported into its territory in such increased quantities, absolute or relative to domestic production, and under such conditions as to cause or threaten to cause serious injury to the domestic industry that produces like or directly competitive products.

the wake of competing interests of the Member States, for protectionist purpose[114] may have the objectives of providing benefits to an industry or some group of industries. The extent of the advantages given to a specific industry can be accounted and legally classified for distinction by further sub-categorisation, in the form of financial contribution and benefit to a specific industry or group of industries, through policy measures for comparing it with subsidies. **In the case of China-Measures Affecting Imports of Automobile Parts,**[115] the United States challenged the measures followed by China, as an import substitution 'subsidy,' in breach of Article 3.1(b) and 3.2 of the SCM Agreement. Additionally, the United States and the European Union contended that China's act of forgoing the revenue, by not imposing tariffs on the imports of auto parts, in some specified category and by applying less tariffs, if the manufacturer uses domestic over imported parts was in a way, discriminatory practice based on origin and in-consistent with Article 3.1(b) of the SCM Agreement[116] and was a form of subsidies covered under Article 1.1 of the ASCM.[117]

China, as a member of the WTO, like the other Member States, had undertaken to comply with the obligations as set out in the WTO agreement. It has undertaken to open up its markets, the non-compliance of which is a cause of dispute in this

[114]**Article 2(b)** Notwithstanding the measure or instrument of commercial policy to which they are linked, their rules of origin are not used as instruments to pursue trade objectives directly or indirectly;

Article2(c) Rules of Origin shall not themselves create restrictive, distorting or disruptive effects on international trade. They shall not pose unduly strict requirements or require the fulfillment of a certain condition not related to manufacturing or processing, as a prerequisite for the determination of the country of origin. However, costs not directly related to manufacturing or processing may be included for the purposes of the application of an ad valorem percentage criterion consistent with subparagraph (a).

[115]WT/DS342/R. On 12 January 2009, with respect to WT/DS340 and WT/DS342, the DSB adopted the Appellate Body reports and the Panel reports as modified by the Appellate Body reports.

[116]WT/DS342/R. para 3.4(g) Articles 3.1(b) and 3.2 of the SCM Agreement, by exempting domestic auto parts from charges imposed by the measures, as well exempting imported parts from charges imposed by the measures, as well as exempting imported parts from the charges if the motor vehicle manufacturer uses domestic over imported parts in order to meet the specified threshold.

[117]Para 4.36 The measure constitutes a financial contribution since 'government revenue' that is otherwise due is foregone or not collected, Article 1.17(a) (1) (ii) of the SCM agreement. "The appropriate bench mark for comparison is the revenue that China raises through duties on imports of auto parts that are automobile parts characterized as complete vehicles." China has established a duty rate which typically amounts to 25% of the value of the parts. If the local content requirements of the measures are not satisfied, this duty would be paid on imports of auto parts. If the imports, on the other hand, satisfy the local requirements, China has given up an entitlement to raise revenue that it could "otherwise" have raised. By charging this second category of parts imports with duties of typically only 10%, China has ignored the normative benchmark that it established for the first category of part's imports and thus, has forgone "government revenues that are otherwise due."

case. Despite these commitments, China introduced measures[118] imposing discriminatory internal charges on the imported auto parts.

Under the challenged measure, if vehicles manufactured in China exceeded certain thresholds of the imported auto parts, the manufacturers need to pay extra duty which indeed was a way to promote the use of domestic parts.

The Chinese tariff schedule provides for separate tariff lines for complete motor vehicles on the one hand, and for parts and accessories of such motor vehicles on the other.

1. The imported vehicle body and engine are deemed a whole vehicle and subject to 25% duty for the complete vehicle.[119]
2. The tariff of complete vehicle is imposed on SKD[120] and CKD[121] kits.

In another category, for the parts, China has established a duty rate of 25% of the value of parts where they do not fulfil local content requirements.

Such policies applied by China challenges the free trade objectives. From the perspective of the free trade objectives, it is significant to note, that the incidence of the policy measure are such that charges under the measures are levied, not at the border, but after the goods have entered into free circulation in the Chinese market and are incorporated into the manufactured vehicles. This policy was quite discriminatory as product origin rules were used for discriminatory purposes. It is also a protectionist measure supporting the Chinese automobile industry.

The WTO Panel decided that since China's measures were contingent upon the use of domestic over the imported components, so by adopting such measures it was conferring "benefits," trade advantage, within the meaning of Article 1.1(b) of the SCM Agreement. Furthermore, the Panel added that China's tariff provisions to the imported goods was, in a way, support to the domestic industry in the form of financial contribution within the meaning of Article 1.1(a) (1) (ii) of the SCM Agreement, as the auto manufacturers who fulfilled the local content requirements were being charged 10% and the ones who did not fulfil the criteria were being charged 25%.

The measures adopted by China were seen as protectionist and discriminatory measures. As a consequence of these measures, imported auto parts became more

[118]The EC, US and Canada identified policy measures as such. (1) Policy on the development of automotive industry that entered into force on 21 May, 2004. (See Para 2.1 of WT/DS 339/R, Order of the National Development and Reform Commission no. 8, Policy Order (that entered into force on 21 May 2004) (2) Administrative rules on the importation of automobile parts characterised as complete vehicle. (Decree of the People's Republic of China, No. 125 (Decree 125), which entered into force on 1 April 2005). (3) Rules on the verification of imported automobile parts characterised as complete vehicle. (Public announcement of the Customs General Administration of the People's Republic of China, no 4 of 2005 [announcement 4], which entered into force on 1 April 2005.

[119]See para 4.33.

[120]SKD Kit-Semi Knock Down Kit.

[121]CKD Kit-Complete Knock Down Kit.

expensive and less competitive than similar domestic auto parts. Furthermore, such measures also encouraged foreign investments in support of the local part-manufacturers. Such like policies were adopted to promote domestic industries. The import restrictive measures applied by China were an indirect form of subsidies to promote domestic industries.[122]

It is evident from this case, how far the policy measures are used to provide benefits to domestic industry. These trade subsidies are being used indirectly to promote domestic industry and the Rules of Origin or the nationality declaration of the product, supported by tariff concessions are measures applied to promote domestic goods[123] that are in competition with foreign goods. Preferences, classified or non-classified given to a domestic industry restricts free trade and is a trade subsidy, as challenged by the United States. In conclusion, it is suggested that the application of the Rules of Origin requires regulatory approach and to be in harmony with the free trade objectives of the WTO. Along with the free trade objectives, regulatory principles based on fair market approach need to be applied as supplementary measures so as to promote efficiency and equitable distribution of resources.

5.6 Ascertaining Subsidies for Dumping, Through the Rules of Origin

The trade practice of dumping is defined as the price discrimination or export of a product at a price below the domestic market price.

Economists have traditionally defined dumping as international price discrimination.[124]

Under the WTO classification of subsidies, export subsidies are regarded as the obvious measures adopted for dumping, as it supports a compensation of the cost burden generated as result of exports at a cheaper price. In cases where, a firm bears a loss because of exports at a cheaper price, the loss is compensated by the subsidies, or the same product is sold at a higher price in the domestic market.

[122]Article 1.1 (ii) of the SCM Agreement. 'Government revenue that is otherwise due is foregone or not collected, e.g. loan fiscal incentives such as tax credits.'

Article 3.1 (b) of the SCM Agreement 'Subsidies contingent, whether solely or as one of the several other conditions, upon the use of domestic over imported goods.'

[123]Appellate Body recommended that China bring its measures into conformity with the Agreement.

[124]Article 2 of the Agreement on Implementation of Article VI of the General Agreement on Tariffs and Trade 1994, 'For the purpose of this Agreement, a product is to be considered as being dumped, i.e. introduced into the commerce of another country at less than its normal value, if the export price of the product exported from one country to another is less than the comparable price, in the ordinary course of trade, for the like product when destined for consumption in the exporting country.'

Based on the same lines, comparison can be drawn from the instances where the use of intermediate products; that are, obtained at a lesser costs and the product is finally exported at a lesser price than the domestic market price. Nevertheless, the provisions with in the Subsidies and the Countervailing Measures Agreement have not directly covered the trade of the intermediate products, for testing the extent of justifiable support, if they are possibly obtained from cheaper places of production.

With the growing trade between the Developed and Developing countries, mainly in the production sectors, there is indeed increase in cooperation in the area of trade and commerce; however, in the lack of specific provisions in the SCM agreement, the complexities about finding various forms of trade gains have also increased. It becomes complicated to determine and check the trade practices such as dumping and trade-subsidies, when the intermediate parts in the final products might be from any place where the production cost is less.[125] However, by applying the Rules of Origin, it is possible to determine the place of the intermediate products and their final effects as in the case, see footnote (Hoesch Metals and Alloys GmbH v Hauptzollamt Aachen Case C-373/08.)

With the growing cross border trade of intermediate products, such provisions with in the SCM Agreement need to be added, in order to establish the trade links. After asserting the place of origin of the inputs used, the final cost of production can be calculated based on the appropriate data.

The agreement on the Rules of Origin, included in the WTO trading system, is composed of regulations and administrative guidelines, which a Member Nation uses to determine an imported product's country of origin. The WTO trading system, applies the Rules of Origin to verify the place of origin of the intermediate products, so as to finally determine the subsidies used for dumping.

The fair trade values that support the WTO objectives gets the substantive support as the Rules of Origin play an essential role for ascertaining the level of transparency in trade.[126]

5.7 Conclusions

The idea of the WTO, was a fundamental reform in the system of international trade. As already established, the main objectives of this institution is not the maximization of trade benefit, rather the welfare of the Developing and Less-Developed countries by creating more trading opportunities for them through the free trade market system. With this concern, trade opportunities for the Developing and Less-Developed countries are additionally promoted by granting special

---

[125]In the case of Case *C-373/08 Hoesch Metals and Alloys GmbH v Hauptzollamt Aachen* [2010] ECR I-951 p-228,247.

[126]From the Preamble of the RoO 'Desiring to ensure that rules of origin are prepared and applied in an impartial, transparent, predictable, consistent and neutral manner.'

preferences. The focus of the WTO is indeed to promote the idea of the free movements of goods, however it does not follow a formalistic approach for the practical application of the provisions. In order to allow a certain level of discretion to the Member States, for making economic choices, the WTO is flexible in the formation of regional trade organisations. This flexibility basically is with the intention to create further opportunities and maintain a clear level of certainty for the smaller economies.

The acceptance of flexibility however, is not only effective in the creation of opportunities, but the trade within the regional trade organization also creates a market structure that can affect comparative advantages, as manufacturers will prefer hedging as regards components subject to restrictions or preference. Such choices are somewhat discriminatory and such policies can even allow the production of goods of low competitive value, basically contrary to the WTO objectives. With the formation of regional trade agreements, there exists a rise in the trade of intermediate products between the members of regional trade organisation, which is not reasonably covered under the provision of the ASCM.

These recently evolved practices have raised the issue as to whether the trade within a Preferential Trade Organisation for the purpose of manufacturing and later exporting outside the regional organisation acts as a trade benefits. Such covert form of trade practices are contrary to the basic objectives of the free trade and it is also debatable how far it is justifiable.

However, with these effects, the issue of transparency emerges, as it seems that such trade preferences have not succeeded in evolving a pattern that can create a balance between the WTO system of free trade and economic development. As a consequence of the formation of regional trade organisation, it can be noticed that multinational companies find this as a business opportunity for buying or obtaining intermediate products from the emerging economies at a cheaper price. This business trend has led to diverting resources from development to profit-earning motives. Therefore at this backdrop, it is suggested that the Rules of Origin need to be applied for promoting transparency based on fair trade as a regulatory mechanism and for creating the regional trading system in harmony with the WTO objectives.

Linked with the production sector are the investment measures. The investment measures are influenced by mutual and other forms of trade benefits that lead to import substitution. Such preferences create deviations from the key objectives, instead of widening the development base for the, Developing and Less-Developed countries. These countries become keener to manufacture goods fetching short run profits, thus deprioritizing the social objectives of welfare and development. Moreover, it can be added here, that the effect of special trade relationship between Developed and Developing Member States, needs to be analysed by another factors also, rather than just from the development perspective.

Eventually, the trade and investment link established within the regional trade organization will affects the free trade market system. Therefore, from the economic point of view, value-added tests, based in relation to the total production cost of the product and not relative to the economic status of the producing countries involved, might deviate from the primary WTO objectives. From the analysis in this chapter, it seems fairly certain that members may digress from the core objectives of the WTO due to market compulsions.

For putting limitations on such practices, it is suggested that regulatory provisions be included in the WTO agreement, which can define the reasonable limits of trade within the Member States of the regional trade organisation.

However, there are some positive sides of the Regional Trade Organisations. A Regional Trade Organisation is beneficial for its members so that it creates the scope for market liberalisation along with some level of economic security for smaller economies. In the free trade market system, emerging and small market economies are at risks, as the larger economies may capture their market in a predatory manner. Therefore, trading at large with the regional trading partners, probably reduces that risk.

Within the WTO Agreement, the current origin rules are predominantly based on the criteria of value addition through substantial transformation. This criterion has some negative consequences, such as a bias being created for the localisation of the industries to promote the production process. Comparing the influence of regional trade organisations with the basic WTO objectives, one can safely say that trade with in the regional trade organisation, has in short, and regressed free trade as there is a lack of competition from more efficiently manufactured imported products.

As the trade among the regional Member States has progressed, Member States on some occasions have applied the provisions of the Agreement on Rules of Origin for the restrictive purposes by imposing higher tariffs. Restricting trade based on the origin of products are protectionist measures. Protectionist policies that are contrary to the MFN clause and tariff preferences are used specifically for the export promotion and have an effect analogues to that of a trade benefit under the SCM Agreement. There are substantive provisions for the legal regulation of such a form of trade behaviour as defined under actionable and prohibited subsidies. However, as regards the growing trade relationship with the Regional Trade Agreement and for the reason of applying protectionist measures by promoting products from the region based trade, such practices need to be broadly covered in the subsidies agreement, as subsidies agreement, in order to promote efficiency and to create equal trading opportunity among the Member States discourage special support to domestic producers of like product that can create market distortion.

Furthermore, it is proposed that within the subsidies agreement, provisions should be added to create more transparency in the market. With the addition of new provisions, trade regulations can be maintained. For example, if a country is giving a subsidy, or is practising dumping for inputs or intermediate products, the whole of that product can be restrained from entering the market, or tariffs to that extent can be imposed. In the light of these observations, it is further suggested that the WTO should follow an equity-based approach to maintain a balance between free trade and economic progress. The trade between the national economies, which are not at the same level, needs to be regulated from several perspectives, to avoid the use of resources available at cheaper price, which is just to support certain group of multinationals. For the greater welfare of the people, it is suggested that policy measures adopted by the Member States, remains basically focused on achieving the goal of development and welfare.

References

Kerr WA, Gaisford JD (2006) Handbook on International Trade Policy. Edward Elgar, Bodmin Cornwall
Cadot O, Estevadeordal A, Suwa-Eisenmann A, Verdier T (2006) The origin of goods-rules of origin in regional trade agreement. Oxford University Press, New York
Cantin FP, Lowenfeld AF (1993) Rules of origin: the Canada-U.S.FTA and The Honda Case. Am J Int Law 87(3):375–383. www.jstor.org/stable/2203644
Finger JM (1976) Trade and domestic effects of the offshore assembly provisions in the US tariff. Am Econ Rev 66(4):11–18
Inama S (2009) Rules of origin in international trade. Cambridge University Press, New York
Lindert PH (1986) International economics. Irwin Publications, Illinois
Lloyd PJ (2002) Country of origin in the global economy. World Trade Rev 1(2):171–118. https://doi.org/10.1017/S1474745602001143
Strauss-Kahn V (2005) Firms location decision across asymmetric countries and employment inequality. INSEAD Eur Econ Rev 49(2):299–320
Södersten B, Reed G (1994) International economics. The Macmillian Press Ltd, London
Trachtman JP (2008) The economic structure of international law. Harvard University Press, London
Ventura DV, Lima (2001) Production sharing in Latin American trade: a research note. United Nations Publications, International Trade and Integration Division, Santiago
Vermulst E, Waer P, Bourgeois J (1995) Rules of orgin in international trade: a comparative study. University of Michigan Press, Michigan
Winham GR (1992) Dispute settlement in NAFTA and FTA. International Trade Reporter, Dalhousie University 9(10):384. www.oldfraser.lexi.net/publications/...nafta/dispute.html
De Wulf L, Sokol JB (2005) Customs modernization handbook. World Bank, Washington, pp 192–197. ISBN-0-8213-5751-4. https://siteresources-worldbank.org

Cases

China-Measures Affecting Imports of Automobile Parts WT/DS342/R
European Communities-Conditions for Granting of Tariff Preferences to Developing Countries WT/DS246/AB/R
Hoesch Metals and Alloys GmbH v Hauptzollant Aachen [2010] ECR I-951. C-373/08
United States-Rules of Origin for Textile and Apparel Products WT/DS243/R

Reports and Electronic Sources

Athukorala P-C, Kohpaiboon A (2011) Global production sharing, trade patterns and industralization in Southeast Asia. http://www.aae.wisc.edu/hoseae/chapters/07d15.pdf

Athukorala P-C (2010) Production networks and trade patterns in East Asia: regionalization or globalization. Asian Development Bank: ADB Working Paper Series on Regional Economic Integration no, 56. www.adb.org/.../production-networks-and-trade-Patterns-east-asia-regionalisation

Barcelo B (2006) Harmonizing preferential rules of origin in the WTO system. Cornell Law Faculty Publications. http://scholarship.law.cornell.edu/Isrp_papers/72

Brenton P et al (2011) In: Chauffour J-P, Maur J-C (eds) Preferential trade agreement policies for development: a handbook. The World Bank, Washington. www.worldbank.org

World Trade Report (2006) Exploring the links between subsidies trade and the WTO. http://www.wto.org/english/res_e/publications_e/wtr06_e.htm

Turning hills into mountains? Current commitments, under the GATS and prospect for change. (March,2005). http://www.wto.org/english/res_e/reser_e/ersd201209_e.pdf

Estevadeordal A, Suominen K (2008) Gatekeepers of global commerce, rules of origin and international economic integration. WTO, Economic Research and Statistics Division, Washington DC. www.iadb.org

Harilal KN, Beena PL (2003) The WTO agreement on rules of origin, implications for South Asia. Working Paper 353. http://www.cds.edu/download_files/353.pdf

Harris JT (2009) Rules of origin for development: from the GSP to global free trade. Inter-American Development Bank Working Paper Series. www.iadb.org

Hayakawa K (2012) Impacts of FTA utilization on firm performance. Bangkok Research Centre, Japan External Trade Organization, Thailand: Institute of Developing Economies, IDE Discussion Paper No. 366. http://www.ide.go.jp/English/Publish/Download/Dp/pdf/366.pdf

Holliday G (1997) Regional trade agreements: implications for U.S. trade policy. CRS Report for Congress. www.policyarchive.org/handle/10207/.../426.pdf

Add....Rules of Origin, Gateway to Dubai's Prosperity. www.dubaicustoms.gov.ae

Jones VC, Martin MF (2012) International trade: rules of origin. CRS Report for Congress. www.crs.gov

Krishna K, Krueger A (1995) Implementing free trade areas: rules of origin and hidden protection. NBER working paper series working paper no 4983. http://www.iatp.org/files/Implementing_Free_Trade_Areas_Rules_of_Origin.pdf

Suranovic SM, Sophie Y, Lai N, Jeon H (2011) International trade theory and policy, free trade agreement: connect model. United Nations Association of South East Asian Nations. http://internationalecon.com/trade/tch110/T110-2A.php

Varavithya W, Esichaikul V (2007) Using the composite act frame technique to model rules of origin knowledge representations in e-government services. Electronic Commerce Research and Applications, Thailand, vol 6, issue 2. www.elsevier.com/locate/ecra

Minevich M, Richter F-J (2005) Going global ventures Inc. Global Outsourcing Report, Horasis. www.globalequations.com/Global

Weiler JHH, Cho S, Feichtner I (2011) International and regional trade law: the law of the World Trade Organisation Unit III: rules of origin. http://www.jeanmonnetprogram.org/courses/wto/docs/unitiirulesoforigin.pdf

Chapter 6
The Impact of Trade Subsidies on the Environment: A Problem for the WTO Trading System

Abstract The primary function of the WTO as a multilateral organisation is to regulate trade among the Member States, and this also implies discussion on issues with different set of values, such as the affect of free trade on the environment. The discussion concerning the 'impact of trade subsidies on the environment' revolves around two planes, (1) the principal objective of the WTO i.e., the promotion of free trade among its Member Nations together with the complex values, compounded, (2) such as sustainable development, the pursuit of which obviously goes alongside. It is ironical that within the WTO trading system, there are several agreements promoting free trade, but no explicit wide-ranging agreement, supporting environment-related issues on a parallel basis. While the WTO tries to promote free trade along with sustainable development, however, what adds to the biased position are the competing interests of the Member States in practice. The contradiction in practice is further deepened whenever the occasion arises for the multinationals to make a choice between trade and environment standards. From the analysis, it can be observed that the legislative bodies and the judicial bodies of many of the Member States follow an unbalanced approach, thus leading to a dilemma over the preference between trade and environment. This further draws attention to a question of whether the lack of a clear basis to make choices between the two objectives, also obstructs the evolution of a general normative set up of environmental values on a global basis. The issue of free trade and the environment sustainability, taken together also touches the institutional character of the WTO, which within the parameters of this discussion is tested through, several theories on environmental law.

A key concern when studying, the effect of subsidies on the environment is to analyse how far the WTO is capable of fulfilling a proper institutional role, by promoting sustainable development along with free trade. In the light of these propositions, this study seeks to make a comparative analysis, between the business attempt for benefit as a consequence of free trade, but at the cost of environment. The comparison is made by quoting several instances of the trade practices among the Member States. In this context, the benefits obtained are compared with trade subsidies for the purpose of broadly applying fair trade concepts as regulatory measures. Further, this study also attempts to examine the institutional and normative basis of the organisation, for a better understanding and in order to make informal recommendations about the WTO reform. The chapter begins by tracing the basic WTO objectives & Members State's relationships with issues related to

G. Singh, *Subsidies in the Context of the WTO's Free Trade System*,
DOI 10.1007/978-3-319-62422-8_6

trade protectionism and maintaining environment standards. Due to the lack of supportive agreements in the WTO and in order to protect environment, some authors have taken a critical perspective about the functioning of the WTO, however, it seems that the institutional balance between the objectives of free trade and sustainable development is the better option.

Free trade is distributing money but damaging the wealth of nature.

6.1 Free Trade and Sustainable Development, a Hard Choice

The study of subsidies from the free trade perspective that needs to be regulated by underlying fair trade values, identify the WTO as an institution promoting trade between nations, and also acting as an environmental regulatory organisation within the parameters of the general principles of international law. However, the instances that have arisen because of the lack of compatibility between the policies of trade liberalisation and the principles of sustainable development,[1] while de-escalating the protectionist trade policies of Member Nations, seems to have created new challenges for the WTO. Free trade, as the primary objective of the WTO has led to the dismantling of trade barriers, and has undoubtedly created many business opportunities for the Member States; ironically, it has also formed an inverse relationship between industrialisation and a healthy environment.

As a matter of fact, the problem of environmental pollution goes back to the early days of industrialisation, when industrial advancement was in its nascent stage. However, during those times, the impact of pollution on the environment remained within the limits of natural assimilation. With the advent of the WTO trading system, the possibility of the consequential effects on natural resources and the environment, because of the free trade market policies, cannot be discounted. Adopting market liberalisation policies has created not only trading opportunities but also competition in the internal market and export market. However, the unregulated promotion of free trade has affected the natural cyclical rejuvenation of the environment. It is often the case that Member States giving—priority to the trade objectives vis-a-vis, environmental standards, deprioritises the WTO objectives related to sustainable development.

In the free trade system, to continue in the long run, industries need to have both competitive advantage and some minimum amount of profit. Free trade, is indeed promoting economic freedoms, however this need not derogate opportunities for other forms of individual preferences.

[1]For protecting the environment.

The possibilities for tension between these two different objectives, free trade and sustainable development, arises in situations where free trade is being promoted, however, free trade is not consistent with the parameters regulated by law or with regard to the choice of implementation, such as:

1. The import restrictive measures claiming to protect the environment, if in one way or the other become linked with the unjustifiable benefits and financial contribution to the domestic industries/industry or the domestic industries exporting the same product.
2. State support to promote domestic industries for export that does not follow environmental standards (both in the case of Developing and Developed countries) or by allowing the use of such goods in domestic market,
3. In such cases where there are no such strictly established regulations for the specific industries to follow environment measures; this can also be considered as financial relaxation obtained at the cost of environment measures.

However, such interpretation is conditional, as the adoption of environmental standard may cost more to such industries. Further, making comparisons between such trade benefits with trade subsidies, and to draw a legal basis, reference is made to the provision of Article 1.1(a)(1) of the SCM agreement. The provision states that 'government revenue that is otherwise due is foregone or not collected (e.g. fiscal incentives such as tax credits).' Additionally, for the purpose of applying regulatory measures and for procedural purposes, similar support for trade to industries, as mentioned above, which are in conflict with basic parameters of sustainable development, can be considered with in the broader para meters of subsidies as the cost for environmental protection can be compared with trade benefits obtained.[2]

When trade restrictions on the grounds of environmental protection are based on health and safety standards and several other environmental standards, then such class of trade restrictions can be classified as restrictions based on fair trade regulatory measures,[3] otherwise, unregulated free trade may lead to trade with countries having lower environmental standards, which means conflict with ethical preferences.

For the purpose of this study, putting forward the general effect of unregulated free trade on the environment and from that approximate level, discussing the effect of unregulated subsidies, as one of the outcome of unregulated free trade, the term 'financial contribution' and 'benefit'[4] can be applied to analyse the short and long run objectives of the policies.

[2]Subsidies which is described as financial contribution providing benefit to a specific industry.

[3]De Sombre (1999), p. 1.

[4]For reference, see Article 1.1(a) (1) and Article 1.1 (b) of the SCM Agreement.

6.2 Tax, Subsidy and Environment: A Matter of Economic Choices

Subsidies can be considered as various forms of state support to a producer or manufacturer, as Luca Rubini states the "definition of subsidy is elusive as such and what is involved is the confrontation between different philosophical, political and societal conceptions of the role of state intervention in the economy."[5]

Trade subsidies in the context of the effect they make on the environment are the issues directly linked with sustainable development. In fact finding through converse relationship, i.e., if not following the expected level of environmental standard, while trading or during the business practices, whether can be considered as trade benefits in the form of subsidies? Such attempts to obtain trade benefits can be figured out by comparing such instances with the description of subsidies through various provisions of SCM Agreement.

While pursuing this discussion from the WTO perspective, it is relevant to point here that cross border trade mainly between the Developed countries on one side and Developing and Less Developed countries on the other side also need to be examined from the perspective of imperfect competition; the system of market structure that works everywhere.[6] Comparing between the types of market conditions that are favourable for attaining trade advantages, it is imperfect competition that firms and the undertakings find approachable to influence the price of their products. In the light of this fact it can be said that state support in the form of subsidies can play significant role in influencing the prices. State support may cause an increase in production for exports without safeguarding other effects, such as those on the environment, as free trade among the nations is mainly based on comparative cost.

The subsequent analysis of the effect on environment is based on the production variable. Once most of the Member States have followed the trade liberalisation policies, subsequently it is the market factors[7] that influence the production variables. It is natural in business practices that the key objective of the multinational companies is to gain profits by selling products. However, such ventures draw critical attention when attempted to be realised by undermining the fulfilment of the required environment measures.

The negative impact so caused to the environment, generated by the industries, can be measured in economic terms as externalities. Economists suggest subsidies or taxes as a matter of choice, from the initial stages itself, as two policy methods can be applied to restrict pollution generation by any firm or industry.[8] An option is to provide direct forms of subsidies, although tax concessions are also

---

[5]Biondi et al. (2004), p. 158.

[6]Imperfect competition, discussed in detail in the second chapter.

[7]Market factors mainly, "Demand and Supply."

[8]Pigou, Arthur Cecil, was an English economist. His famous work *Wealth and Welfare*, Macmillan and Co, London, 1912 brought welfare economics in to the scope of economic analysis.

acknowledged as forms of subsidies. Through tax measures, one probability is to impose higher taxes on the pollution generating industries or to provide tax concessions to the industries, stepping into the process of adopting environmental friendly methods of production. This effect is referred to as a "tax subsidy" which is connected to a normative or base line tax system.[9] As this causes extra stress on financial policies because of the loss of revenue, it means that other fiscal adjustments are needed to offset the effects. Finally, the choice between the two policy measures, tax or subsidies particularly depends upon the internal market system, as this plays a vital role in the trading policies of a country. The market system of every country is based on its specific economic concepts for establishing and promoting industry.

It is widely acceptable view that during the formative stages, industries often expect financial assistance from the state, either in the form of a subsidy[10] or tax relief which can also be termed state aid. In line with the objectives of sustainable development it can be further added that the use of subsidies in order to promote environmental protection or to alter the mode of production into an environmentally friendly mode is a justifiable use of state support. The fact remains that the practical implementations differ from one Member State to another.

For drawing the parameters, concerning the use of state support based on the WTO legal approach, the influence of trade subsidies for environmental objectives needs to be seen from two perspectives. First, the use of subsidies in order to promote and maintain environmental standards or for transforming the production process in an environmental friendly manner, needs to be further sub-categorised based on the limits of the justifiable use of subsidies. Secondly, the analysis of such state support through the extent of the financial contribution and benefit[11] to the export industry, bearing in mind that the use of subsidies is regulated by the SCM Agreement. Accordingly, judging the extent of state support, through 'financial contribution' and 'benefit' further draws the legal presumption to determine the externalities of trade practices. Subsidy based assertion is mainly linked with the premise, that not following environmental standards by an export industry can be considered as financial gains and benefit which was otherwise not possible.

[9]A normative tax system would take into account the optimum structure of taxes required to achieve the government's social objectives. "Subsidies in the Energy Sector: An overview," July, 2010, p. 24. http://siteresources.worldbank.org/EXTESC/Resources/Subsidy_background_paper.pdf.

[10]Although the November 1990, Subsidies Draft had contained such a provision (based on a 1989 EC proposal) it had been deleted from the December 1991 Dunkel Text. In particular, Mexico proposed that subsidies for the adaptation of existing facilities to new environmental requirements imposed by law and/or regulation be considered non-actionable if they, (1) were a one-time, non-recurring subsidy, (2) were limited to 20% of the cost of adaptation, (3) did not cover the cost of replacing and operating equipment, (4) were directly linked to pollution reduction, and (5) were available to all firms able to adopt the new equipment or production process. Mexico's Proposal was finally accepted and incorporated into the Final Agreement. The obsolete Article 8 of the SCM Agreement, also termed as Green Light subsidy. For detail reference, see Stewart (1999), p. 224.

[11]The two key testing elements for the trade practice of subsidies.

Locating such limits of trade benefits, in the absence of a normative basis to support the values for sustainable development, or any such provision mentioned in the agreement, then very much depends upon the interpretation of the DSB, and can vary from case to case.

At the initial stages of industrialisation, opting for subsidies instead of tax concessions, from the state/government, does have a comparative advantage, as regards, bearing the burden of expenses, so as to maintain environmental standards. Subsidies, creates possibilities for a diverse choice when using the financial support. This inherent feature of such financial support helps in achieving wide environmental standards, at various levels, such as its use in reducing emissions of greenhouse gases by altering to the use of clean energy. Additionally, the use of subsidies are preferable because the regulatory provisions for its use are flexible and this can cover wide variety of economic systems, in the matters of the trade policies of Developing and Less Developed countries.

Ironically, the objectives of sustainable development gets deprioritised while promoting industrialisation in the Developing and Less-Developed countries. The MFN clause is the main clause for promoting free movement of goods among the Member Nations. This clause also supports exceptions, such as SDT[12] (special and differential treatment) and GSP,[13] allowing the additional use of subsidies by the Developing and Less-Developed countries. Such provisions are meant to promote exports from the specific Developing countries.

These concessions do not comprehensively take into account all of the effects, as a downside it creates a wide room for interpretations allowing unregulated trade, without taking into account strictly the environmental measures. The MFN clause, and the exemption provisions, that are SDT and GSP provisions are more or less open-ended, not multi-layered by the supportive clauses or conditional clauses to determine the effects of free trade on the environment. Moreover, these clauses do not prohibit exclusive trade agreements with other preferential trade areas or the trade groups based on bilateral tax treaties. Such trade agreements although within the parameters of the overarching WTO free trade policy objectives, however, in the absence of any clause strongly supporting environmental standards, cannot check the consequential effects on fair standards for the environment. This can be illustrated by quoting here the examples of NAFTA.

---

[12]The WTO agreements contain special provisions which give Developing countries special rights and allow the Developed countries to treat Developing countries more favorably than over other WTO Members. Special and Differential treatment is related to the preferential provisions that apply to Developing and Less-Developed countries. The provisions are based to respond to the development needs of Developing countries. (Developing countries seek modifications to many provisions on the grounds that they need supportive policies for development needs).

[13]Between 1971 and 1976, most OECD countries, including the United States and the EU/EC, implemented the GSP by adopting national legislation, authorizing tariff preferences for Developing countries. The GSP is meant to provide reduced tariffs for industrial production and agricultural policy.

6.2.1 NAFTA

With the formation of NAFTA (on January 1, 1994) the production units of several industries in search of low price production venues, have shifted from one Member Country to another, mainly from the Developed to the Developing country, such as from the US and Canada to Mexico. One of the reasons for such a shift is that Mexico's currency, the Peso is of relatively lesser value in comparison to the Canadian and American dollar. The difference in exchange rate being competitively advantageous has promoted shifting of production base from the US to Mexico. The lesser production costs has led to great influx of industries into Mexico. But there is another side to this economic advantage. As a result of this shift in production bases, it has affected both the local surroundings and the natural diversity. One can easily presume, the reason for emergence of such an unbalanced situation is prioritising production of goods at the costs of environment.

In practical terms, the impact on the environment due to the unregulated industrialisation cannot be put into exact numerical figures, however, the aggregate change can be assessed by taking into account the impact on water, clean air and natural resources in those places.

In the context of these mentioned effects, it is worth quoting here, the example of Baja California[14] based 'maquiladoras' in Mexico.[15] It was found, that a company named *Metales y Derivados de Mexico, S.A (SECOFI, 2000)*[16] had abandoned at least 4729 tons of lead, cadmium and arsenic in the soil.

When NAFTA was created, expectations were that this trade agreement would favour the development of new technologies without disturbing much of the local environmental conditions. Evidently, Mexico gained in terms of technology followed by more investments and a shifting of the production centres.[17] However, it became a trend that the majority of the foreign production units started shifting their production centres to maquiladora dense places, such as Baja California, Chihuahua and Tamaulipas.[18] These localities consequently became swarmed with various industrial units.

---

[14]Baja California is both the northernmost and westernmost state of Mexico.

[15]The word "Maquiladora" comes from the past practices, where the millers charged a maquilla. A maquiladora is a Mexican Corporation which operates under a maquila program approved for it by the Mexican Secretariat of commerce and Industrial Development (SECOFI). A maquila program entitles the company, first to foreign investment participation in the capital and in management of up to 100% without need of any special authorization, second it entitles the company to special customs treatment, allowing duty free temporary import of machinery, equipment, parts and materials and administrative equipment such as computers and communications devices subject only to posting a bond guaranteeing that such goods will not remain in Mexico permanently.

[16]Metales y Derivados is a subsidiary of the New Frontier Trading Company, based in San Diego.

[17]Mayrand and Paquin (2003), p. 9. http://unisfera.org/IMG/pdf/Unisfera_-_NAFTA_effects.

[18]Term Maquiladora is used to describe companies that process (assemble and/or transform in some way) components imported into Mexico which are, in turn, exported- usually to the United States.

From the year, 1993 to 1998, the exports from maquiladora accounted for 41.5% of the average Mexican export value, but this has had negative consequences on the environment.[19] Studying into the reason for these consequences, it was found striking feature of the maquiladoras industry in Mexico is its degree of internationalisation (98% of the inputs are imported, 100% of the output is exported).[20] The situation certainly occurred due to the unregulated free trade. In the context of debate between free trade and sustainable development, the extent of industrialisation has further raised issue between short term objectives and its long term effects, leading to a conflict of interest.

The flow of wealth, as is evident, is because of surge in industrialisation, which indeed is a short term gain because of free trade objectives. However, to what extent it is in harmony with the sustainable development objectives, is a matter that remains within grey area and requires a reasonable balancing of interests in order to achieve the objectives from both the sides.

The example of NAFTA referred above, requires much broader discussions on the subject of trade and environment. With regard to the effect of trade on environment, from the WTO perspective, discussions will remain inconclusive, if these do not cover another key aspect of international trade relations, namely, border taxes. These tax treaties are in general concluded bilaterally between the nations, bearing the special trade relations that exist between the two treaty concluding states. Additionally, it is worth referring in the context of such like treaties, that the terms and conditions of these treaties are negotiated by the states on the basis of reciprocal business benefits. Concerning the principal aspect of these treaties, mainly they are business-based and are less concerned about the type of environmental measures adopted by the nations that are parties to the treaties. From the perspective of cross border trade issues, the effect of tax concessions on environment standards also require brief reference about tax havens.

Tax concessionary states are often nick named as tax havens. Such tax havens, enable multinationals to derive most of their income from abroad, irrespective of the fact whether they maintain environmental standards while trading or not and they are free of the host-countries taxation.[21] As Member States may lack norms in support of environmental measures, therefore even the domestic courts of those Member States, where multinationals are doing business, are less empowered to apply regulatory provisions in order to create a balance between trade and environment.

When studying the effect of subsidies in NAFTA regional trading system, it can be said that this sort of trade practices followed by the member countries is a stark instance of compromising environmental standards for the sake of trade benefits. Assessing the effects in economic terms and additionally for the purpose of quantifying trade benefits so obtained, the effects in relation to trade advantages

[19]Stromberg (2002), p. 5. www.eclac.org/publicaciones/.../lcmexl548eDocumento%20Completo.

[20]Stromberg (2002), p. 15. www.eclac.org/publicaciones/.../lcmexl548eDocumento%20Completo.

[21]Lang et al. (2005), p. 128.

so obtained can be studied under the scope of term "benefit" as described under the ASCM. Subsequently, the benefits so obtained can be linked with an "actionable subsidy," for analysing the policy level approach.

Within the regional trade agreements, it is mainly the policy promotion based on export criteria that support its functioning and regional cooperation, or often such policy designs can have features supporting export. When such policies for industrialisation are framed in some of the Developing countries, they often lack regulatory mechanism that can be applied to establish a balance between free trade and the environment. Additionally, there is lack of normative support, and the local people also remain unaware of the effect of the interaction between external treaty based policies and the position of internal support mechanisms. Hence, the far reaching consequences cannot be ascertained.

Bearing in mind that differences between justifiable subsidies and non-justifiable subsidies are often obscure; it may require the analysis of the production function. The production function can be separated into two stages. In the first stage, intermediate inputs and a primary composite of capital and labour would be used in fixed proportion to reach the output. In the second stage, capital and labour would be combined through CES (constant Elasticity of substitution) function to form the primary composite depending upon the demand and expected profit.[22] With the support of a subsidy, or by other supportive means, these production functions can be availed from the other countries at a lesser costs without giving due consideration to the environmental standards. Once the output level is attained, these factors subsequently help in export promotion. Usually, the criteria that is used to determine if a subsidy given is trade distorting, is based on the efficiency principle. The efficiency principle is more of an economic principle based on cost and demands. In order to maintain consistency with the WTO objectives, these efficiency principles on a product specific basis also needs to be related with the effect of production on environment. In the interest of individuals everywhere, a balanced approach between free trade and fair trade as a regulatory measure seems a suitable alternative.

6.3 Trade Subsidies Affecting the Environment

The consequence of trade subsidies are not only confined to market competition but have also created an impact on human and environment relationships. The link between trade subsidy and its effect on the environment is formed at a certain level of abstraction. In most of the instances, subsidies are provided for industrialisation or in the cases where society is transforming from an agrarian society to an industrial mode and state support, in terms of financial aid, is heavily required.

[22]For reference see Chap. 2.

Developing nations have their own explanation for the flexibilities adopted in terms of applying environmental measures while promoting industrialisation. For them, the promotion of exports is a priority to earn more of the foreign exchange, as their foremost challenge is to sustain their overwhelming population, and this forces them to follow industrialisation without strictly considering the regulatory measures.

On the other hand, the Developed nations are also in search of opportunities to save their business interests, as the sweeping industrialisation because of free trade has created robust competition in the market everywhere.

As an effect, this has formally led to the shifting of production bases from the Developed nations to the Developing and Less-Developed countries so that the products can be produced at a lesser expense. In addition, it is noteworthy, that the existing variance in the standard formations, while adopting environmental values by the Member States seems to create possibilities for trade bargains. Comparing this legal position of the Member States in the context of the WTO, it seems that such trade benefits have similar characteristics to that of the indirect form of subsidies as described under the ASCM. The term "benefit" explained in Article1.1 (b) of the ASCM refers to some form of financial gain or price support to the recipient.[23] A non-committal approach to the environmental standards for this cheaper production is comparable to the kind of trade benefit mentioned in the ASCM. Although the trade benefits so obtained at the cost of the environment are not formally covered in the ASCM, nevertheless, from the relevant illustrations as quoted in this text, the effects of a one sided approach, makes things clear, as one side is gaining and the other is loosing.

Following the shift in the location of specific industries, such as dismantling of ships industry and the paper industry from the Developed to the Developing countries and studying the after effects on the environment, it would be reasonable to say that there are also lack of provisions creating compatibility between free trade and sustainable development. From the scientific analysis, it is clear that these industries greatly contribute to the generation of greenhouse gases.[24] The reason for the shift of production bases of these industries, from the Developed to the Developing country, is because of economic advantages and not strictly maintaining environment standard.[25]

The example quoted here is that of the paper industry. Within the EU system, the provisions regulating environmental standards are stricter, and as a consequence several paper industries have shifted their production bases to the Developing

---

[23]Macrory et al. (2005), p. 692.

[24]The Iron and Steel industry produces greenhouse gases such as, Carbon dioxide, Carbon monoxide, Organic compounds, Sulphur oxides Nitrogen oxides and several other organic compounds.

[25]These economic advantages can be compared with financial contribution and benefit as described under the SCM Agreement.

countries. This is mainly to explore cheaper availability of resources and other benefits such as tax concessions so as to compete with their rivals.

6.3.1 *The Paper Industry*

The paper industry is undoubtedly, a major source of water pollution. The waste released from this industry and dumped into river water leads to the accumulation of toxic chemicals in the rivers, which is quite threatening to the environment. Chemicals that are used for making paper, such as chlorine compounds used to bleach and de-lignify pulp also have a toxic effect. Chlorine and the compounds of chlorine[26] are used in the bleaching of wood pulp, especially chemical pulps produced by the Kraft process[27] and the Sulphite-process.[28]

In addition to this, paper mills also releases conventional pollutants such as Carbon dioxide, Nitrous oxide and Sulphur oxide. With the promotion of free trade, and having realised the possibilities of production at a cheaper rate in the foreign places, the paper industries are shifting the production bases from the Developed to the Developing countries.

The case cited here, as an example is that of **"Stora-Enso,"** a Swedish-Finnish company.[29] This company also owns a large paper and pulp company, Veracel together with Aracruz.[30] Veracel is located in the south of Brazil, in the state of Bahia.[31] It is expected that this paper mill will produce the cheapest paper pulp in the world. This indeed is beneficial for the company, but the lesser cost of

[26]For detail references, see EPA Fact Sheet (Environment protection agency) The Pulp and Paper Industry, the Pulping Process, and Pollutant Releases to the environment. EPA-821-F-97-011, November 1997.

[27]The Kraft pulping process uses an alkaline cooking liquor of sodium hydroxide (NaOH) and sodium sulphide (Na_2S) to digest the wood. The cooking liquor in the sulphite pulping process is an acidic mixture of sulphurous acid (H_2SO_3). In preparing sulphite cooking liquors, cooled sulphur dioxide (SO_2) gas is absorbed in water containing one of four chemical bases, magnesium (Mg), ammonia (NH_3), sodium (Na), or calcium (Ca). The sulphite pulping process uses the acid solution in the cooking liquor to degrade the lignin bonds between wood fibres.

[28]The sulphite process uses different chemicals to attack and remove lignin. The sulphite process is characterised by its high flexibility compared to the Kraft process, which is a very uniform method, which can be carried out only with highly alkaline cooking liquor. The main sulphite processes are Acid (bi) Sulphite, Bisulphite (Magnetite), and Neutral sulphite (NSSC) and Alkaline sulphite.

[29]This is a public trading company registered in Helsinki and Stockholm. http://www.storaenso.com/About-Site/Pages/Stora-Enso-in-brief.aspx.

[30]**Aracruz cellulose** is one of the largest paper and Pulp Company in Brazil. This company produces nearly half of the total pulp exports from Brazil and is the world's largest producer of bleached eucalyptus pulp.

[31]Andersson, Måns and Örjan Bartholdson. "Swedish Pulp in Brazil: The case of Veracel, p. 5. http://www.swedwatch.org/sites/default/files/swedwatch_-_the_case_of_veracel.pdf.

production method will have negative consequences on the ecology in the long term basis. However, this one-sided and short term approach, while making choice between trade and environment has raised the concern for sustainable development, as the unregulated trade promotion has shadowed the environmental and other issues that are value based and also concern social aspects. These concerns can be highlighted through the following instances.

1. The expansion of the plantations for the production of paper pulp has started depriving local people, peasants, indigenous groups, and Afro-Brazilians, of their subsistence from the land. The displacement of the indigenous people is also an issue of constitutional rights.[32]
2. Plantations, specifically for the paper industry also had detrimental effects on the agriculture sector. Additional problems that have arisen are, such as the poor availability of clean water for basic necessities, gets reduced.
3. These plantations obstruct the regeneration of the Atlantic rainforest, as a plantation on a large scale for the paper industry has negative consequences for the sensitive flora and fauna in the region.[33]

It becomes further complicated to maintain a clean environment, because the pulp mill for this company is planned to be located 5 km from the river Jequitinhona.[34] Farm workers, associations, and environmental organisations have criticised Varcel for transforming diverse agricultural land with varied properties into monocultures.[35] Moreover, the company's acquisition of large areas has raised land prices and also reduced the economic possibility of establishing a more diverse form of agriculture. Gradually, all this has made the environment inhospitable for both, the people and the local fauna and flora, finally leading to the displacement of the native people.

This matter, does not seem to be related to trade subsidies primarily as the subject of subsidies is discussed within the framework of the SCM Agreement, however, it can be covered in the extended notion of subsidies. Analysing this position in the light of the WTO objectives, it would be fair to say, that had the industrial set up valued the required standard level, the concern for environment based objectives that are based on the principle of sustainable development on the one hand and the promotion of free trade on the other, then this would have been in harmony from the WTO perspective. Comparing such trade benefits, with the type of financial gains obtained but with negative consequences, would create a critical

[32]The Constitutional rights as quoted above should been seen here in the context of parameters quoted by Mattias Kumm such as, (1) Are rights trumps over competing considerations of policy? (2) Do they have priority over the good in some strong sense? (3) Are rights firewalls providing strong protections against demands made by the political community? Pavlakos (2007), p. 131.

[33]Andersson, Måns and Örjan Bartholdson. "Swedish Pulp in Brazil: The case of Veracel, p. 6. http://www.swedwatch.org/sites/default/files/swedwatch_-_the_case_of_veracel.pdf.

[34]Andersson, Måns and Örjan Bartholdson. "Swedish Pulp in Brazil: The case of Veracel, p. 24. http://www.swedwatch.org/sites/default/files/swedwatch_-_the_case_of_veracel.pdf.

[35]The use of land for growing one type of crop continuously.

perspective of such practices and would motivate for the regulatory measures to be adopted. It is very likely that such approach will create some proportional coherence between the objectives.

The main goal of the WTO, i.e., "trade liberalisation along with sustainable development," if not to be kept far from our reaches, requires that there should be a proper regulatory mechanism within the WTO framework that can help in obtaining balance between free trade and environment standards.

6.4 Concerning Trade-Benefits and the Environment; a Choice of Values and Standards

Michael Porter,[36] is known for describing competitive advantage of the nations based on the model for understanding the competitive position of a nation in global market. He has put forward the idea that environmental regulations are basically beneficial to the economy, as tough environmental regulations will encourage innovation and upgrading. On this basis, a proposition has been formulated to analyse the effect on environmental standards, because of the trade benefits acquired at the costs of not maintaining the required standards.[37]

Within the context of the debate between trade and environmental issues, it is worth adding here that environmentalist fear they are losing high standards of the environment, because of the current institutional arrangements at the WTO in particular. The WTO somehow allows trade with countries maintaining low environmental standards, which in a way is a challenge to attain environment objectives.[38]

Environmental sanctions, or restrictions in trade for sustainable objectives, create the scope of law, both substantive and procedural for the protection of environment. In fact, it is for the reason of tension between trade interests and the required proportionate priorities for environment interests, which finally leads to the discussion on sustainable development from various perspectives. In particular, the standards set up among the Member States, through these discussions contribute to the acceptability of positive trade discrimination, based on the effects on environment or for the reason of environmental effects, because of the specific production processes being followed. It can be said, that also for political reasons, it is essential to look at the threats of sanctions as those can be imposed in the pretext to safeguard environment. The sanctions for sustainable development essentially need to be based on fair trade regulatory measure.

The loss in environmental standards because of free trade can be further explained. In a market system based on free trade, promoted by the WTO, it is

[36]Michael Porter is professor at Harvard Business School.

[37]De Sombre (1999), p. 3. www.gmu.edu/programs/icar/ijps/vol4_1/desombre.htm.

[38]Srinivasan (2000), p. 67.

the price of a product which is the determining factor for a consumer, rather than the consumer making a sincere choice based on environmental values i.e., making distinction between the goods produced by maintaining environmental standards and goods that are not so produced. The underlying reason for making such choices is the economics of costs and benefits and the lack of normative support for environmental standards in many of the Member States.[39]

Acknowledging the influence of economic factors as primary reasons for the trade based effects on environment, it is further required to make a cost-and-benefit analysis of the production methods. The cost-and-benefit factors are basically based on the logic of market equilibrium,[40] essential for sustaining in the market. It gets necessitated that the WTO Member Nations adopt and reform domestic policies, conducive to the promotion of free trade and sustainable development. As a consequence of market liberalisation policies, the market systems of the nations are getting into competition with each other. This transitory situation remains open to the interpretation between what is justifiable and what is not. Therefore, the producers are influenced by market factors, as they are left with fewer options to survive market competition. The probable outcome is that an industry, in this kind of situation, will consider trade benefits as a priority rather than following the environmental standards, unless there is the possibility of punitive action for not complying with the environmental rules.

"Implementing free trade objectives and alongside maintaining the environmental standards," also requires trade analysis between the Developed and the Developing countries at the various levels. The development phase of the Member State is a transitory phase of the economy, leaving a wide area as an unregulated policy space. However, sustainable development is a principle adopted by the WTO, but the excess of competition due to the market dynamics promoted by market liberalisation undoubtedly makes trade related subjects, a matter of priority. For economic reasons, it is often hard for a Member State to choose between the competing interests, environmental standards on one side and free trade objectives on the other. We will here take the example of the dismantling of ships to illustrate how the trade advantages are obtained, due to the variance in adopting environmental standards.

The ship dismantling industry is an example explaining, the benefits obtained because of the difference in environmental standards among the Developed and Developing countries. The trade advantage, so obtained can be compared with the trade benefits, as defined under the SCM Agreement, ironically at the cost of human health and other basic environment necessities.

---

[39]Free trade is distributing money but damaging the wealth of nature.

[40]The Classical Economist such as Adam Smith, maintained that the free-market would tend towards economic equilibrium through the price mechanism. Any excess supply (market surplus or glut) would lead to price cuts, which decreases the quantity supplied (by reducing the incentive to produce and sell the product) and increase the quantity demanded (by offering consumers bargains), automatically abolishing the glut.

6.4.1 Dismantling of Ships: Environment Standards a Hard Choice for the Nations

Asbestos, one of the substances left behind after dismantling of a ship, is health hazardous. The waste released from a discarded ship at the time of dismantling is mainly.

1. Asbestos powder used for insulation,
2. Asbestos trapped in the coatings.[41]

In the Developed countries, taking into consideration the environment and health safeguard measures, the accessible part of the harmful pollutant is first isolated and then removed before dismantling a ship, and the rest is left as it is. On the contrary, the practices within the Developing countries are influenced by economic priorities. In terms of cost factors, the entire process of first separating the hazardous waste remains expensive and the law has less binding effect to enforce environment regulations.

The practice followed is such that within the Developing countries, the scrap mainly ferrous metal, which can be reused is all that is taken off while dismantling abandoned ships. Of course, one explanation for such a lenient attitude is the lack of technical knowledge and impropriety in the enforcement of environmental regulations, because the legal policies for protecting the environment have weaker impact in many countries. Substances like asbestos are not made ineffective, consequently, this leads to health complications such as, asbestosis and lung cancer.[42]

The Case of Clemenceau Ship[43] as an Example

In 2003, the French state handed over the "Clemenceau's" hull to the ship-decommissioning industry. The decommissioned ship was sent to India for dismantling. With regard to the quantity of asbestos, the French government claimed that altogether, the ship contained no more than 160 t of which 115 t had been removed. However, the fact was that the exact nature and quantity of the hazardous materials on board of the Clemenceau was difficult to ascertain as the French government failed to accomplish even the basic pre-requisite steps of estimating the extent of hazardous waste prior to the export.

This was in violation of the "Basel/Basle convention"[44] to which both France and India are parties. Therefore, in this case, India also shares responsibility for

[41]http://infochangeindia.org/kids/Peopletalk_clemenceau.php.

[42]BBC News Asbestos ship 'can sail to India' Friday, 30 December 2005. http://news.bbc.co.uk/2/hi/europe/4570246.stm.

[43]http://www.ban.org/pdfs/ban_clemenceau_summary_of_ violations.

[44]The Basel Convention on the control of Trans-boundary Movements of Hazardous Wastes and their disposal was adopted on 22 March 1989 by the Conference of Plenipotentiaries in Basel, Switzerland, in response to a public outcry following the discovery, in the 1980s, in Africa and other parts of the developing world of deposits of toxic wastes imported from abroad.

allowing the Clemenceau to be dismantled at Alang,[45] the shipbreaking yards without obtaining environmental clearance. The Basel/Basle Convention requires that no trans-boundary movement can occur without assurances that the destination facility is engaged in environmentally sound management, as defined in the convention. A requirements laid down in [Article 4, paragraph 2(e) and (g)][46] of the Basel/Basle Convention.

Finally, the matter was brought before the Pollution Control Board by the Gujarat government, (Gujarat a province of India) and subsequently also supported by the Basel Action Network.[47] Initially, permission for the dismantling of the decommissioned aircraft-carrier Clemenceau was granted by the government of India. Clause 2 of the agreement between the French government and the SDI i.e. (ship decommissioning industry) is as follows.

> On completion of this operation, the hull shall be exported to the ship yard for asbestos removal and ship-breaking purposes. Technopure, the French asbestos removal company, shall transfer its technology and know-how to the Luthra Group, the asbestos removal company from India. Additionally, as a part of deal, the Indian operators shall be trained during the major asbestos removal operation conducted in Toulon and be familiarised with the equipment's and techniques at the level of European standards. The final asbestos removal operation shall be carried out under the oversight and supervision of the French asbestos removal company.[48]

Unfortunately, what happened in practice was contrary to what has been reported. The French Government claimed that there was no more than 160 t of asbestos of which 115 t had been removed. With regard to PCB (poly-chlorinated biphenyls) another hazardous substance,[49] the French government failed to accomplish even the basic requisite step of declaring it before Egyptian authorities, the transit state and to India, the country to which the ship was finally destined.

---

[45]For detail reference, see [*Business Standard*, Tuesday, August 07, 2012], www.business-standard.com/india/news/alang-yard.

[46]Each party shall take appropriate measures to 2(e) Not to allow the export of hazardous wastes or other wastes to a state or group of states belonging to an economic and/or political integration organization that are parties, particularly Developing countries, which have prohibited by their legislation all imports, or if it has reason to believe that the wastes in question will be managed in an environmentally sound manner, according to the criteria to be decided on by the parties at their first meeting; (g) Prevent the import of hazardous wastes and other wastes if it has reason to believe that the wastes in question will not be managed in an environmentally sound manner.

[47]Basel Action Network (BAN) is a non-governmental organization (NGO) whose mission is to prevent the globalisation of the toxic chemical crisis. BAN is based in Seattle, Washington, USA.

[48]Orellana. "Insights Shipbreaking and Le Clemenceau Row," *American Society of International law*, Volume 10, Feb, (2006). http://www.asil.org.

[49]PCB is chemically stable/inert, heat resistant and non-flammable substance, which is used worldwide as a dielectric in electrical components (transformers and capacitors). Due to its low biodegradability in the environment and their tendency to bio-accumulation and bio-magnify, PCBs belong to the so called persistent organic pollutants (POPs).The Basel/Basle Convention strictly regulates the trans-boundary movements of hazardous wastes and their disposal.

As a result of this circumvention, the Basel Action Network challenged the French government, as they had failed to quantify the amount of hazardous material and were acting in contradiction of the Basel Convention. Eventually, the French government was found guilty of its attempts to tamper with the International obligations under the Basel Convention of 1989.

Based on the facts, it can be inferred that this case throws light on the extent, to which a Developed country has tried to seek trade benefits without caring, in reasonable terms, about the environmental and health effects on the people of Developing country. This practice of acquiring trade benefits can be compared with the subsidies defined under the WTO's SCM Agreement. Additionally, it can be argued that Developing countries violating environment commitments, in order to obtain the trade benefits are equally liable. These types of benefits provided by the Member States are no different from the non-permissible subsidies covered within the ambit of the ASCM of the WTO law. Further, referring this case in terms of the WTO objectives, the case illustrates how the Developed countries in collaboration with the Developing nations, are pursuing trade interests on a bilateral basis by forgoing the objectives of sustainable development.

6.5 The Choice Between Free Trade and Sustainable Development

Within the WTO trading system, there is no such general or specific agreement, dealing with the compliance of environment objectives, along with the trade liberalisation. There have been attempts to promote sustainable development measures along with free trade, but the possibilities of adapting and the compliance of such measures at the proportionate level or with the equitable concerns are not guaranteed by the provisions of any agreement. Nevertheless, in order to ascertain the long term consequences of unregulated free trade, its effects need to be tested through the legal provisions.

The need for legal discipline, to cover subjectively and to regulate the impact of trade on the environment can be explained from two perspectives. First, the right to a safe environment cannot be covered within the domain of property law and second, industrialisation is responsible for the pollution problem.

Explaining the first mode, the legal position with regard to the objectives of maintaining environmental standards for sustainable development and on that basis the acquired legal competency of an individual, if he suffers as a victim due to environmental pollution is still limited by the ambiguities of law and regulations. An individual has a remedy in tort law,[50] but the legal position is different with

[50]Yang and Moser (2011). The use of environmental tort claims to compensate pollution victims or to protect the environment and human health is still in an early stage of development in China. **Negligence** is a tort theory that permits someone who is injured by another's unreasonable conduct

regards to forging a balance between trade and the protection of the environment on a national basis or as a matter of policy measure.

Further, it can be added from the legal perspective, that the enforcement measures of the WTO treaty provision are not based on a uniform set of legal procedures nor does have any strong constitutional support from the Member States, rather in the majority of cases, a party can file for claims only after becoming affected and this situation provides enough room to bargain among the Member States. It is ironical, that Member States, instead of showing commitment to the WTO objectives, try to bargain with one another. These bargaining possibilities also become enhanced, as on the one hand, the WTO is promoting free trade, a favourable aspect for the Developed countries and on the other hand, it works for the objectives of welfare and development, a necessity based requirements for the Developing and Less-Developed countries.

Concerning the second instance, that industrialisation is responsible for pollution, a parallel can be drawn between the position of the Developed and the Developing countries in the matters of environmental protection. Besides economic reasons, the legal incapacity to maintain environmental safety standards, in the case of the Developing countries, is also due to the lack of environment protection norms. It would be worth referring here Mary E. Footer's view point, on the section 'Framework for analysis and structure of the WTO.'[51] She has put forward the idea of regime theory for understanding the practices of this organisation, vis-a-vis its Members. "On this basis, it seems that the WTO in its present status is inadequate of fulfilling proper institutional role and has failed in becoming a pillar for the global economic governance as long as its individual Members continue to shape the organisation to their own ends."[52] Well, how far the term global governance fits, when one of the key objectives of the WTO is welfare and development through free trade, is another issue and rather not a matter of debate in the present context. However, the point she has raised that individual Members States attempt to influence the WTO objectives through their personal aims and designs, is quite relevant in the context of acceptance of sustainable development as a general principle among the Member State. Further in this regard, the possibilities for the normative development in support of environment measures can be debated. Before a general principle for all the Member States on environment measure can be introduced, it can be debated, whether there are possibilities of norm creation, at the primary level by introducing soft law norm through treaty obligations.

---

to recover money damages. The primary element of a successful negligence case is proof of the defendant's wrongful conduct. **Nuisance** is a tort theory that protects someone's right to use and enjoyment of their real property. The Michigan Supreme Court described nuisance as follows: There are countless ways to interfere with the use and enjoyment of land, including interference with the physical condition of the land itself, disturbance in the comfort or conveniences of the occupant including his peace of mind, and threat of future injury that is a present menace and interference with enjoyment.

[51]Footer (2006), p. 6.

[52]Footer (2006), p. 6.

Thereafter, Member States would start following the general principle in the broader context. Such like measures probably can help to evolve common level of environmental standards among the Member states. In point of fact, the, environmental standards have not been given due consideration in proportion to the progress of free trade. Nevertheless, there are instances where free trade has been challenged with the help of the WTO legal provisions, so as to maintain some level of environmental standards.

6.5.1 Trade Restriction for Environmental Protection

The promotion of unregulated free trade has often faced counter arguments from environmental protection groups.[53] For the law to regulate trade, in support of environmental standards, the basic legal condition is authenticity *of reasonable grounds for trade restrictions* and for imposing limits on *import* restrictions. Such restrictions need to be applied by provisions that also create a distinction from the arbitrary protectionism.[54] The conflicting interests between trade restrictions for the purpose of environment protection and promotion of free trade or in other words between economic interests and environment values, arose in the case of the **United States-Import Prohibition of Certain Shrimp and Shrimp Products.**[55] According to the current legal scope, every nation, despite being a member of the WTO, is free to determine the extent of import restrictive measures, in relation to the developmental, environmental, and social policies that it deems appropriate. Such interpretive scope within the policy provisions can be characterised to create

[53]Some of the famous environmental groups are such as, (1) African Wildlife foundation, (2) Conservation International, (3) CREST (4) Green Peace (5) National Wildlife Federation...etc.

[54]AB while making findings, on the issue of Article XX of GATT, in the case of **United States-Standard for Reformulated and Conventional Gasoline WT/DS2/AB/R,** added in the conclusion that "the provisions of Article XX were not changed as a result of the Uruguay Round of Multilateral Trade Negotiations. Indeed, in the preamble to the WTO Agreement and in the decision on Trade and Environment, (Adopted by Ministers at the Meeting of the Trade Negotiations Committee in Marrakesh on 14 April 1994.) there is specific acknowledgement to be found about the importance of coordinating policies on trade and environment. WTO Members have a large measure of autonomy to determine their own policies on environment (including its relationship with trade), their environmental objectives and the environmental legislation they enact and implement. Concerning the WTO, that autonomy is circumscribed only by the need to respect the requirements of General Agreement and the other covered agreements."

[55]WT/DS58/AB/R. The guidelines adopted by State Department of the US for implementing Section 609 required the shrimp-harvesting nation to show that it had regulatory programme comparable to that of United States approved by the US National Marine Fisheries Service. **The dispute resolution Panel and the Appellate Body ruled that Section 609 and the Original Guidelines violated Article XI of the GATT because they barred the importation of goods. Article XI prohibits restrictions on the importation of goods. They also ruled that the Original Guidelines could not be justified by virtue of exceptions for environment under Article XX of the GATT.**

possibility for a balance between free trade and sustainable development, however without drawing a strict line between arbitrary protectionism and justifiable protectionism.[56]

Additional legal support measures, for the matters concerning environment, can be traced in Article XX of the GATT, also adopted by the WTO. These general exceptions in GATT Article XX are not protectionist measures; rather they are included for widening the scope of environment protection.[57]

In the context of the WTO objectives, in order to cover several key perspectives, both from the side of free trade and sustainable development, and then forming a balance, between the two, it seems that there is a need to evolve objective criteria based on the WTO preamble, and to determine trade restrictions on the grounds of environment protection.[58]

---

[56] Francioni (2001), p. 20.

[57] Article XX General Exceptions: Subject to the requirement, that such measures are not applied in a manner which would constitute a means of arbitrary or unjustifiable discrimination between countries where same conditions prevail, or a disguised restriction on international trade, nothing in this Agreement shall be construed to prevent the adoption or enforcement by any contracting party of measures:

(a) necessary to protect public morals;

(b) necessary to protect human, animal or plant life or health;

(c) relating to the importations or exportations of gold or silver;

(d) necessary to secure compliance with laws or regulations which are not inconsistent with the provisions of this Agreement, including those relating to customs enforcement, the enforcement of monopolies operated under paragraph 4 of Article II and Article XVII, the protection of patents, trademarks and copyrights, and the prevention of deceptive practices;

(e) relating to the products of prison labour;

(f) imposed for the protection of national treasures of artistic, historic or archaeological value;

(g) relating to the conservation of exhaustible natural resources if such measures are made effective in conjunction with restrictions on domestic production or consumption;

(h) undertaken in pursuance of obligations under any intergovernmental commodity agreement which conforms to criteria submitted to the CONTRACTING PARTIES and not disapproved by them or which is itself so submitted and not so disapproved;

(i) involving restrictions on exports of domestic materials necessary to ensure essential quantities of such materials to a domestic processing industry during periods when the domestic price of such materials is held below the world price as part of a governmental stabilization plan; provided that such restrictions shall not operate to increase the exports of or the protection afforded to such domestic industry, and shall not depart from the provisions of this Agreement relating to non-discrimination;

(j) essential to the acquisition or distribution of products in general or local short supply; provided that any such measures shall be consistent with the principle that all contracting parties are entitled to an equitable share of the international supply of such products, and that any such measures, which are inconsistent with the other provisions of the Agreement shall be discontinued as soon as the conditions giving rise to them have ceased to exist. The CONTRACTING PARTIES shall review the need for this sub-paragraph not later than 30 June 1960.

[58] The *Parties* to this Agreement, *Recognizing* that their relations in the field of trade and economic endeavour should be conducted with a view to raising standards of living, ensuring full employment and a large and steadily growing volume of real income and effective demand, and expanding the production of and trade in goods and services, while allowing for the optimal use of the world's resources in accordance with the objective of sustainable development, seeking both to protect and

Further, it would relevant to add here that the economic differences among the Member States are also a reason, for the lack of fair support for sustainable development. The disparity at the level of economic and technological development among the Member States gets compounded by the differences in the capacity of risk awareness and the assessment by the people in general. Thus, it aggravates the hindrance in meeting the objectives of sustainable development.

In the context of trade relationships between the Developed and Developing country the inequality is broadened when on the import side, there is a highly industrialised country and on the export side there are Less-Developed countries. It is important to note that Developing countries also try to influence the market of the Developed countries with a supply of goods produced at a cheaper rate, the example of garments factory fire in Pakistan is worth quoting here. Recently, fire broke out in a garment factory in the Karachi district of Pakistan, where at least 259 workers died. This garment factory produced jeans for the German textile and clothing retailer Kik at a lesser cost compared to the production cost in the Developed country. The human casualty would have been less, had the factory maintained the proper safety standards. The crucial feature with this case is that Developing countries are used as the production base, to produce the products at cheaper prices without proper safety standards applied.[59] Perhaps this is the reason why product production processes, within the WTO have not gained wider legal support among Developing countries, but are rather seen as a protectionist measure to counter the competition by the Developed countries.

In similar situations, due to the lack of clear cut regulatory provisions, or without any established set of standards at all, contextual construction can be formed by applying various provisions of the ASCM, so as to find out the economic impact on the environment due to the trade practices and subsequently applying the regulatory measures.

It is also of particular significance to note that the WTO dispute resolving bodies also play a significant role in the matters of policy interpretations and for resolving the ambiguities concerning preference between trade and environment. On most of the occasions, when the matter is brought before the DSB, it has tried to follow a midway approach between free trade-and maintaining environmental standards, as also premised in the Shrimp turtle case.[60] Briefly, it can be said that the Dispute

preserve the environment and to enhance the means for doing so in a manner consistent with their respective needs and concerns at different levels of economic development.

[59]Kazim, and Klawitter. *The value of Pakistani Worker*. Spiegel Online, 23 October, 2012. www.spiegel.de/international/world/criticism-over-damages.

[60]WT/DS58/AB/R, para 168 "...multilateral solutions based on international cooperation and consensus as the best and most effective way for the governments to tackle environmental problems of a trans-boundary or global nature. WTO Agreements and multilateral environmental agreements (MEAs) are representative of efforts of the international community to pursue shared goals, and in the development of a mutually supportive relationship between them, due respect must be afforded to both."

Settlement Body of the WTO, also applies balancing mechanism between free trade and maintaining the environment standards.

6.5.2 The North-South Divide on Environment Issues

The problems with regard to maintaining environmental standards are considered as mainly legal, social, and technical problems, but when the issue of standards becomes linked with the trade issues, they cover the economic aspects of the problem too. The economic gap and the limits due to the differences in standards and values that have emerged between the Developed and the Developing nations have made the term, "North-South divide" popular within the WTO circle.

It is relevant here to note, that there are differences in the policy measures between the Developed and the Developing countries concerning environmental issues. For the Developing and the Less-Developed countries, development by adopting the trade liberalisation policy is a primary objective and complying with the environmental rules is a secondary matter. In order to attain these objectives, there are also differences in the structures of trade-policy of the Developing countries. The general frame work of the industrial sector in the Developing countries is highlighted below, illustrating the reasons for the trade objectives being prioritised in comparison to environmental standards.[61] Bearing in mind the variance in the economic, social, and political context among the Developing countries group, there can be various sub-classifications based on several factors, for example, China, India, Brazil and several others are categorised as Developing countries but are in different economic positions.

Usually within the transforming economies:

1. There is a high tendency to achieve capital savings and more employment-generating methods, rather than capital intensive and quality promoting industry.
2. As the capital formation in the Developing and the Less-Developed country is not on a large scale, so transformation from cottage and small-scale industry is slow. Investment is mainly in the direction of goods and services suitable for mass consumption, rather than investment for research and quality up-gradation of the production method.
3. So as to reduce the production costs, there is use of local materials rather than the use of expensive materials obtained from foreign market.

The industrial policy structure shows in general, what the priorities of the Developing countries are. The trade situation of the NAFTA members, an example mentioned previously, can be referred to here in order to consider the industrial policy structure. After studying the range of measures, it can be said that the

[61] The Industrial structure of the developing countries is quoted here as an example, as that structure is affecting environment in higher proportion.

Developing economies expect immediate gains from their newly Developed industrial sectors, despite the fact that in their case, there is a sudden transfer from the agricultural economy to the industrial economy. To survive in the competitive market, nations work with the economic logic of costs and benefits. Therefore in order to realise the market necessities, upcoming economies try to obtain a place in the competitive market, and are compelled to surpass environmental standards to reduce production costs.

Ironically, with the free trade in progress, environmental protection is seen more from the perspectives of costs and benefits. Although, much is written in theory, it seems that there exists a considerable gap between environmental standards and their practical implementation.

The WTO as an institution, through its treaty provisions, can indeed actively assist in this kind of situation. As an institution, it can set out the conditions for regulating trade, promoting development, and, applying provisions for checking the compliance with environmental standards.

6.5.3 *Balancing Trade and Environment: A Complex Issue for the WTO*

Attempts to create balance between free trade and sustainable development have created a difference of opinions among the Member States. Developing nations are sceptical with regard to making a balance between trade and the environment. The reason being that following environmental standards at the same level as that of the Developed nations will off-set the meagre amount of trade profits which they earn. For the Developing countries, there is no alternative choice in this situation, as free trade and investment from the Developed economies are intertwined with and investors from the Developed nations in order to promote their industries, try to push forward their own terms and conditions.

Practically, it seems hard to attain a balance between trade and environmental objectives, as in many instances it is difficult to make a choices between the two. This type of complicated situation also arose during the Doha conference. Realising the existing indeterminate position of the environmental objectives, attempts were made to widen the scope of interpretation, by adding conditional clauses so that the balancing between the two sets of objectives is negotiable. The reference here is to "Para 31" of the Doha conference,[62] which broadens the scope of sustainable

[62]Para 31 of the DOHA conference (2001) With a view to enhancing the mutual supportiveness of trade and environment, we agree to negotiations, without prejudging their outcome, on: (1) the relationship between existing WTO rules and specific trade obligations set out in multilateral environmental agreements (MEA). The negotiations shall be limited in scope to the applicability of such existing WTO rules as among parties to the MEA in question; (2) procedures for regular information exchange between MEA Secretariats and the relevant WTO committees, and the criteria for the granting of observer status; (3) The reduction or, as appropriate, elimination of tariff

development and is based on "Specific Trade Obligations" (STO herein after). One can say that applying STO within the framework of the MEA[63] (multilateral environment agreement) is an attempt to create some sort of compatibility between the MEA and the WTO. This approach adopted various categories of trade obligations according to their specificity. However, such measures seem to favour more the interest of the Developed nations. Usually, the investment agreements between the Developed and Developing nations are based on mutual interests, covered through bilateral treaties. While making negotiations, the question often arises about the compatibility of the environmental standards with trade rules. By virtue of multilateral or bilateral agreements, parties among themselves can trade in specific products, whereas, alternately, the trade can be banned of the same products with the countries that have not signed the Agreement or are outside the commitments based on any agreement.[64] Developing nations are in need of foreign investments for development and for generating employment. In the lack of any regulatory mechanism for checking environment degradation, Developed nations use this as a bargaining power. Furthermore, because of the lack of enforcement mechanism the Environment objectives are considered as a soft law agenda.[65] The WTO indeed, through DSB, plays a positive role by trying to ensure that free trade does not make irreparable damage to the environment. Therefore, in this regard, besides the legal provisions of the agreements, creating obligations for the Member States to follow environment measures, various WTO conferences and the DSB (Dispute Settlement Body) also act to create harmony between trade and the environment.

The attainment of a balance between free trade and sustainable development has also been at odds due to the technicalities in the procedural aspects of treaty interpretations and the sovereign principles of the nations. In the case of **Canada-Certain Measures Affecting the Renewable Energy Generation Sector**,[66] besides other matters, the concerned issue, raised by the complainants, Japan[67]

---

and non-tariff barriers to environmental goods and services. We note that fisheries subsidies form part of the negotiations provided for in paragraph 28.

[63]Trade-related Measures and Multilateral Environmental Agreements, Economics and Trade Branch Division of Technology, Industry and Economics United Nations Environment Programme, 2007.

[64]For detail references, see 'Environment Negotiations' The Doha mandate on Multilateral Environmental Agreements. Doha Development Agenda. http://www.wto.org/english/tratop_e/envir_e/envir_neg_mea_e.htm.

[65]A distinction is often made between hard and soft international law. Hard international law generally refers to agreements or principles that are directly enforceable by a national or international body. Soft international law refers to agreements or principles that are meant to influence individual nations to respect certain norms or incorporate them into national law. Soft international law by itself is not enforceable. Also see Footer (2006), p. 244.

[66]WT/DS412/R, WTDS426/R and WT/DS412/AB/R, WT/DS426/AB/R.

[67]See WT/DS412/R, WTDS426/R, para 7.170, Japan submits that the challenged measures may be best characterized as "direct transfer of funds" because they involve payments on the part of the OPA that are analogous to a conditional grant.

and the European Union,[68] before the panel,[69] against Canada, was the policy measure support for the use of domestic over the imported product, hence according to them, violating Article 3.1(b) and 3.2 of the SCM Agreement.[70] Before approaching the panel, both EU and Japan raised the issue with Canada concerning the domestic content requirement in the feed-in tariff programme (FIT Programme[71]) established by the Canadian province of Ontario.[72] The Panel reasoned for not confirming the subsidy claims, was the approach forwarded by the complainants for benefit determination and secondly, Panel took into account the policy objectives of the government of Canada, to adopt environmental friendly policies on the one side and effective competitive circumstances in the market on the other.[73] The complainants requested before the A.B to reverse the findings of

---

[68]See WT/DS412/R, WTDS426/R, para 7.176 and 7.177, the European Union submits that the challenged measures may each be legally characterized as "financial contribution "in the form of a "direct transfer of funds" within the meaning of Article 1.1(a) (1) (i) of the SCM Agreement, or as a form of income or price support under the terms of Article1.1 (a) (2) of the SCM Agreement.

[69]WT/DS412/R, WTDS426/R, para 1.4 At its meetings on 20 July 2011 and 20 January 2012, the Dispute Settlement Body established two Panels respectively, Japan request in document WT/DS412/5, and European Union's request in WT/DS426/5, in accordance with Article 6 of the DSU.

[70]See para 1.6 of WT/DS412/AB/R●WT/DS426/AB/R.

[71]FIT Programme as described under Para 7.64 and 7.65 of the WT/DS412/R, WTDS426/R The FIT Programme can be generally described as a scheme implemented by the Government of Ontario and its agencies through which generators of electricity, produced from certain forms of renewable energy, are paid a guaranteed price per kWh of electricity delivered into the Ontario electricity system under 20-year or 40 year contracts with the OPA. In the case of wind power projects having a capacity to produce electricity that is greater than 10 kW, and solar projects with a capacity of up to 10 MW, a "Minimum Required Domestic Content Level" must be satisfied in the development and construction of the qualifying electricity generation facility. The FIT Programme was formally launched by the OPA on 1 October 2009, pursuant to the direction of the Ontario, Minister of Energy and Infrastructure acting under the authority of the Electricity Act of 1978, as amended by the Green Energy Act of 2009. The FIT Programme is the third in a series of initiatives adopted by the Government of Ontario since 2004 to increase the supply of electricity produced from renewable source of energy into the Ontario electricity system in order to diversify its supply-mix and help replace coal-fired facilities.

[72]Para 1.1 of the WT/DS412/R, WTDS426/R.

[73]WT/DS412/R, WT/DS426/R, para 7.320. We have carefully reviewed the parties, legal and factual arguments in the light of the legal standard for determining the existence of benefit that has to date been applied in WTO dispute settlement. In the particular circumstances of these disputes, we have concluded that determining whether the challenged measure confer a benefit on the basis of a benchmark derived from a competitive wholesale electricity, would mean that FIT and micro FIT contracts could be legally characterized as subsidies by means of a comparison with a market standard that has not been demonstrated to actually exist nor one that could be reasonably achieved in Ontario, a market standard that the complainants have not contested will only rarely, if at all attract sufficient investment in the generation capacity, to secure a reliable system of electricity supply even outside Ontario. In our view, such an outcome would fail to reflect the reality of modern electricity systems, which by their very nature need to draw electricity from a range of diverse generation technologies that play different roles and have different costs of production and environmental impacts. As we have emphasized on a number of occasions, it is only in exceptional

the Panel. Based on the observations and after analysing the arguments forwarded by the complainants, the A.B stated that Panel had erred in finding that both EU and Japan failed to demonstrate that the challenged measures conferred benefit within the meaning of Article 1.1(b) of the SCM Agreement.[74] During the course of hearings and at the time of proceedings from the Panel to the A.B, several new points have emerged concerning the choice between, subsidies for trade and subsidies for the environment in general, and, more specifically supporting the policies for the use of renewable energy. In the lack of any specific provisions supporting subsidies for environmental standards, Canada was defending its measures, on the basis of GATT III (8).[75] The A.B agreeing that governmental intervention for reduction in release of fossil fuel and for the promotion of energy from non-fossil may be essential. However, the A.B added that adopted measures should not be considered as preventing the identification of competitive benefit, for the analysis of benefit under Article 1.1 (b) of the SCM Agreement.[76] It is noteworthy for those supporting a green lobby, that the A.B because in the existing state that

circumstances that the generation capacity needed from all such technologies will be attracted into a wholesale market operating under effective competition. Thus, the competitive wholesale electricity market that is at the center of the complainant's main submission cannot be appropriate focus of the benefit analysis in these disputes.

[74]WT/DS412/AB/R●WT/DS426/AB/R, para 5.222. We have reversed the Panel's findings that the European Union and Japan failed to demonstrate that the challenged measures confer a benefit within the meaning of Article 1.1(b) of the SCM Agreement. Thus, the condition for us to consider the European Union's and Japan's alternative claims under Article 11 of the DSU is not met. Therefore, we do not address the alternative claims that the Panel failed to make an objective assessment of the matter according to Article 11 of the DSU.

[75]GATT Article III(8) (a) The provisions of this Article shall not apply to laws, regulations or requirements governing the procurement by governmental agencies of products purchased for governmental purposes and not with a view to commercial resale or with a view to use in the production of goods for commercial sale. (b) The provisions of this Article shall not prevent the payment of subsidies exclusively to domestic producers, including payments to domestic producers derived from the proceeds of internal taxes or charges applied consistently with the provisions of this Article and subsidies effected through governmental purchase of domestic products.

[76]WT/DS412/AB/R●WT/DS426/AB/R, para 5.185. Nevertheless, while introducing legitimate policy considerations into the determination of benefit cannot be reconciled with Article 1.1 (b) of the SCM Agreement, we do not think that a market-based approach to benefit benchmarks excludes taking into account situations where governments intervene to create markets that would otherwise not exist. For example, governments create electricity markets with constant and reliable supply. By regulating the quantity and the type of electricity that is supplied through the network (base-load, immediate load, or peak-load) and the timing of such supply, governments ensure that there is a continuous supply-demand balance between generators and consumers, thus avoiding imbalances that would destabilize the network and cause interruptions of power supply. Although this type of intervention has an effect on market prices, as opposed to a situation where prices are determined by unconstrained forces of supply and demand, it does not exclude per se treating the resulting prices as market prices for the purposes of a benefit analysis under Article 1.1 (b) of the SCM Agreement. In fact, in the absence of such government intervention, there could not be a market with a constant and reliable supply of electricity.

Article 8 of the SCM is obsolete, seems to have improvised the legal rationality (In Para 5.188) in favour of environmental based policies. In the para[77] 5.188 A.B states clearly that 'Nevertheless, *a distinction should be drawn between, on the one hand, government interventions that create markets that would otherwise not exist and, on the other hand, other types of government interventions in support of certain players in markets that already exist, or to correct market distortions therein.* Where a government creates a market, it cannot be said that the government intervention distorts the market, as there would not be a market if the government had not created it. Further, in support of government policies for renewable energy, the A.B states that comparison of cost for the generation of electricity, both with regard to renewable and non-renewable source is also essential along with the environment objectives and the support required to sustain such objectives. The A.B further added that government intervention in order to introduce new measures, also needs to be weighed in terms externalities.[78] With regard to a Member States' new set of legislation or new set of measure, the A.B clarified, supporting Japan's point, that characterisation of domestic law is itself not dispositive with regard to characterisation in terms of WTO Agreements. The A.B citing the reference of *US-section 211*,[79] states, a panel may examine whether a municipal law of a WTO Member State, complies with the obligations.[80] Such reference by the A.B also makes it possible to introduce a new set of government objectives for public good that may deviate from free trade objectives, but that are, however, consistent with the regulatory measures for public good rather than a circumvention from the key objectives.

Attempting to link environment measure with trade policies, by adding special condition based clauses to the MFN principles, such as ISO standards[81] and Global Eco labelling has generated counter arguments from the Developing nation's side. Once they find it is not feasible for them to follow such standards, then they probably consider "them as if it is the imposition of one country's national policies

[77]WT/DS412/AB/R● WT/DS426/AB/R, para 5.188.

[78]WT/DS412/AB/R● WT/DS426/AB/R, para 5.189. We further note that a comparison between renewable energy electricity generators and conventional energy electricity generators requires consideration of the full costs associated with the generation of electricity. In this respect, if, on the one hand, higher prices for renewable electricity have certain positive externalities, such as guaranteeing long-term supply and addressing environmental concerns, on the other hand, lower prices for non-renewable electricity generation have certain negative externalities, such as the adverse impact on human health and the environment of fossil fuel energy emissions and nuclear waste disposal. Considerations related to these externalities will often underlie a government definition of the energy supply-mix and thus be the reason why governments intervene to create markets for renewable electricity generation.

[79]WT/DS176/AB/R para 105.

[80]WT/DS412/AB/R, WT/DS426/AB/R, para 5.127.

[81]ISO standards: International Organization for Standardization.

on another country's sphere of domestic jurisdiction." This can also be construed from the Appellate Body of the WTO's legal reasoning in the Shrimp turtle case.[82]

Such a discrepant approach has raised a basic question concerning the extent of the possibility of the treaty's application after it has been subject to interaction with the fundamental principles of state sovereignty.[83]

What further hinders the balance between free trade and sustainable development are the doubts among the Member States, that perhaps these environmental standards can influence the established domestic rules and attempt to give them different interpretations that are suitable for the bigger economies.[84]

[82]WT/DS58/AB/R, para 177. "We have already observed that section 609, in its application, imposes a single, rigid and unbending requirement that countries applying for certification under Section 609 (b) (2) (A) and (B) adopt a comprehensive regulatory program that is essentially the same as the United States program, without inquiring into the appropriateness of that program for the conditions prevailing in the exporting countries. Furthermore, there is little or no flexibility in how officials make the determination for certification pursuant to these provisions. In our view, this rigidity and inflexibility also constitute 'arbitrary' discrimination."

[83]Francioni (2001), p. 13.

[84]*European Communities-Trade Description of Sardines*. WT/DS231/AB/R. [E]uropean Communities raised the issue of legal interpretation, concerning the product description of Sardines. In 1978, the Codex Alimentarius Commission (the "Codex commission"), of the United Nations Food and Agriculture Organization and World Health Organization, adopted a worldwide standard for preserved Sardines and Sardine-type products, which regulate matters such as presentation, essential composition and quality factors, food additives, hygiene and handling, labelling, sampling, examination and analyses, defects and lot acceptance. This standard, CODEX STAN 94-1981, Rev.1-1995("CODEX Stan 94"), covers preserved sardines or sardine-type products. This also included Section 6 of Codex Stan 94. Peru exports preserved products prepared from Sardinops sagax sagaax (Sardinops sagax), one of the species of fish covered by Codex Stan 94. This species is found mainly in the Eastern Pacific Ocean, along the costs of Peru and Chile. In appeal against the panel decision (para 35) The European Communities claims that the panel erred in concluding that Codex Stan 94 is a relevant international standard for purposes of Article 2.4 of the TBT agreement. The European Communities alleges further that the panel erred in law when interpreting the meaning of Codex Stan 94. According to the European Communities, the drafting history of Codex Stan 94 demonstrates that section 6.1.1(ii) of Codex stan 94 should be interpreted as allowing the common name for the species of fish to be a possible name for the preserved "sardine-type" product, and the word "sardine" does not have to be part of the name. Para 41, According to the European Communities, the EC regulation covers only Sardina pilchardus and does not regulate Sardinops sagax, nor fish of other species. The European Communities thus argues that the relevant part of Codex stan 94, for purpose of Article 2.4 of the TBT Agreement, is section 6.1.1(i), 'which states that the name "Sardines" is to be used exclusively for Sardina pilchardus. According to the European Communities section 6.1.1(i) of Codex Stan 94 is used "as a basis for" the EC regulation.' The European Communities contend that section 6.1.1(ii) is not a relevant part of the standard because it refers to products that are not regulated by the EC regulation. Therefore it need not be used "as a basis for" the EC regulation.

6.6 A Critique of Free Trade Policy, the Case of Subsidies for Fisheries

Discussions on Environmental issues are relevant with the objective of supporting the protection of nature and for broader level value based trade policies to be practically adopted. These value based policies can be sustained by applying fair trade regulatory measures. Several significant multilateral environmental agreements allow restrictions on free trade as essential for environmental regulations. Agreements such as the Convention on International Trade in Endangered Species (CITES)[85] regulates trade in animal and plant species or parts of these species, and fisheries. There are also environment conservation efforts, under the Law of Sea and from the institutional perspective other than the WTO, through United Nations Food and Agriculture Organization[86] regardless of a state's membership in the WTO.

Despite these specific agreements, the debate follows, that to promote free trade, the WTO has adopted several agreements such as, the Agreement on Subsidies and Countervailing Measures, the Anti-dumping law, Intellectual Property (TRIPS) and several others, but for the protection of the environment, on any required occasions, it depends upon the agreements outside the WTO trading system and the later formed "Committee on Trade and Environment[87] within the WTO system." In the background of these discussions, referring here about the effect of subsidies given for fisheries. The debate on subsidies for the commercial catch of fishes gets complex, when this issue is weighed between, responsibilities for the environment on the one hand and the liberty of free trade on the other. Apart from the discussions on sustainability and environment protection, as one common agenda for all the Member States, it nevertheless becomes divided and weakened for the sake of other priorities among the Member States. The Developing countries also try to obtain various forms of exemptions from following the environment commitments.

Subsidies for fisheries are considered by some of the Developing countries as a strategic tool for economic prosperity, therefore they claim state support as a necessary measure to modernise the infrastructure of fishing. It can be observed that States have an equivocal attitude towards the CITES aims. Some states, such as those strictly arguing for the protection of fisheries, claim that proper listing of the endangered species has not been done. On the other side, several of the Developing countries have followed a critical approach, pointing out and arguing that CITES's objectives are not sufficiently analysed and are rigidly related to one aspects only,

---

[85]American Society of International Law. http://www.cites.org/eng/disc/E-Text.pdf.

[86]Young (2010), p. 2. http://ssrn.com/abstract=1852904.

[87]The CTE was set up by the 1994 Marrakesh Ministerial Decision on Trade and Environment, which essentially mandates the committee to (1) identify the relationship between trade measures and environmental measures in order to promote sustainable development. (2) make appropriate recommendations on whether any modifications of provisions of the multilateral trading system are required, compatible with the open, equitable and non-discriminatory nature of the system.

rather than approaching the problem with the possibility of a sustainable catch. According to the Developing countries, conservation objectives can adversely affect commercial fishing as a means of employment, income generation, food security needs, and economic concerns about the rural population. This dichotomy has arisen probably as a consequence of a regime interaction between the WTO objectives and environmental law.[88] As a down side of the unregulated liberal trade policy measures adopted for economic prosperity, it nevertheless leads to over-fishing and over-exploitation of valuable fish stocks, which is contrary to the objectives of the environmental protection policies.[89] Thus, as far as the pursuance of economic objectives, along with regulatory measures for environmental protection is concerned, it can be said that different sets of laws create different obligations and these may even transpire to be contradictory obligations for the Member States.[90]

Discussions held during the formation of the WTO, certainly emphasised the impact of trade practices on the environment, if allowed without checks and balances. However, because of the conflicting interests and the trade priorities among the Member States, no balancing mechanism between free trade and the environment was accomplished. As an environment-safeguard measures, the over-arching principle suggested was sustainable development[91] along with free trade.

Drawing lessons from the unregulated use of subsidies on the environment, a specific example can be seen in the case of fisheries industry. The unregulated free trade has led to huge subsidies to promote the catching of fishes. As a result, the subsidies for expansion of the fishing industry have led to an uncontrolled expansion of the fisheries industry and consequently significant decline in the fish stocks. The stock of fish that are reduced includes heavily traded species, such as sharks, seahorses and one of the high in demand, the Bluefin tuna.[92] As of the 2010, data released by FAO, it demonstrates that 88% of tradable fisheries are over exploited in terms of quantity and consequently have depleted to the threshold of distinction.[93] Over-fishing nowadays is widely acknowledged as a growing threat to the sustainable management of the fishing resources. The example referred to in the

---

[88] Young (2010), p. 14. http://ssrn.com/abstract=1852904.

[89] Dugal and Walton (2011), p. 1.

[90] Young (2010), p. 2. http://ssrn.com/abstract=1852904.

[91] Preamble: Marrakesh agreement establishing the WTO "the parties to this agreement, recognizing that their relations in the field of trade and economic endeavor should be conducted with a view to raising standards of living, ensuring full employment and a large and steadily growing volume of real income and effective demand, and expanding the production of trade in goods and services, while allowing for the optimal use of the world's resources in accordance with the objective of sustainable development, seeking both to protect and preserve the environment and to enhance the means for doing so in a manner consistent with their respective needs and concerns at different levels of economic development."

[92] Young (2010), p. 3. http://ssrn.com/abstract=1852904.

[93] WTO fisheries subsidies negotiations and Pacific Island states. Dugal and Walton (2011), p. 1.

text concerning impact of fishing industry availing unregulated subsidies is covered in the broader discussions about the effect of subsidies on the environment.

This unregulated commercial activity is an outcome of the existing incoherence between national policies and treaty based obligations, compounded by the fact that many governments adopt subsidy policies for short term trade gain. "It has been found on the basis of case studies that there are programmes involving the provisions of loans and grants and risk-reduction programmes for vessel construction and modernisation."[94] Eventually, this has led to an increase in catch and therefore the depletion of several fishing species beyond the natural cycle of re-production level. We may take the cases of Canada, the EC, Japan, and the US.

From, 1954 to 1968, Canadian subsidies for fishing increased the capacity of the Northwest Atlantic offshore fishing fleet by more than 18 times, creating twice as much capacity as could be used for a sustainable level of catch. Despite the collapse of cod stocks, the Canadian fishery subsidy has increased the catch capacity five times the original annual quota by 1989.[95]

The EC and United States have also provided subsidies through low interest loans for their fishing fleet expansion and pursued a modernisation programme that has resulted in a further reduction of fish stocks. As an instance of support measures, the loan guarantees in the 1980s were for the construction of a large fleet of factory trawlers for the Alaska Pollock fishery of the Eastern Bearing Sea, the Aleutian Islands and the Gulf of Alaska. Another example is that of Japan, it has spent approximately US$ 2 billion annually on fishing ports and villages. Such infrastructure projects are used nowadays by the fishing industry.[96]

Until now, there have been no exclusive provisions within the WTO system to check the use of subsidies for commercial exploitation of marine life. Any such attempt to discipline the use of state support is possible through provisions on subsidies mainly under the SCM Agreement.[97] With regard to the growing concern about the depletion of fishing stock, during the Doha conference, the issue of fisheries subsidies was discussed emphatically. An attempt was made to find compatibility between trade and the environment with specific discussions on fishery subsidies.[98] Subsequent to the Doha Conference, during the Hong Kong

[94]Porter (2001), p. 11.

[95]Porter (2001), p. 11.

[96]Porter (2001), p. 11, 12–28.

[97]For detail reference see, Ongoing WTO Negotiations on Fisheries Subsidies (http://www.asil.org/insights/volume/8/issue/12/ongoing-wto-negotiations-fisheries subsidies), p. 1. Published on ASIL.

[98]WTO Doha Conference, (2001), para 28. Doha declarations "In the light of experience and of the increasing application of these instruments by members, we agree to negotiations aimed at clarifying and improving disciplines under the agreements on implementation of Article VI of the GATT 1994 and on Subsidies and Countervailing Measures, while preserving the basic concepts, principles and effectiveness of these agreements and their instruments and objectives, and taking into account the needs of Developing and Less-Developed participants. In the initial phase of the negotiations, participants will indicate the provisions, including disciplines on trade

conference,[99] some more substantive steps were taken, by outlining the measures that earlier were merely a subject of discussion during the Doha conference. The following is the chair's suggested draft proposal from the Hong Kong conference, which are,

1. Prohibiting a broad range of direct capacity promoting-or effort-enhancing fisheries subsidies, as well as any subsidies affecting fishing on unequivocally considered understocked fish,
2. Exempting several specific classes of subsidies from the prohibition (e.g., for vessel safety or reducing fishing capacity),
3. Subjecting most permitted fisheries subsidies to the conditions as set by, basic fisheries management system,
4. Allowing Developing countries to use most of the prohibited subsidies, but subject to fishing management and other conditions,
5. Creating a mechanism for involving the FAO in the review of measures, that fulfil fishing management criteria, and
6. Strengthening the WTO notification rules for fisheries subsidies.[100]

Free trade is undoubtedly an attempt to liberate markets for the proper distribution of resources and for adopting efficient production methods so that prosperity reaches the maximum number of people. This has also led to disagreements between the Member States of the WTO, which is noticeable when Member Nations of the WTO, try to prioritise between trade and the environment. *The issue that was not discussed during the formative period of the WTO, is what the actual limits to free trade should be.*

It seems essential here to regularise free trade and restrict the use of subsidies, bearing in mind the urgent need to save the environment.

---

distorting practices, which they seek to clarify and improve in the subsequent phase. In the context of these negotiations, participants shall also aim to clarify and improve WTO disciplines on fisheries subsidies, taking into account the importance of this sector to Developing countries."

[99] Sixth WTO Ministerial Conference, December (2005). "We ministers . . .recall our commitment at Doha to enhancing the mutual supportiveness of trade and environment. Note that there is broad agreement that the Group should strengthen disciplines on subsidies in the fisheries sector, including through the prohibition of certain forms of fisheries subsidies that contribute to overcapacity and overfishing, and call on participants promptly to undertake further detailed work to, inter alia, establish the nature and extent of those disciplines including transparency and enforceability. Appropriate and effective special and differential treatment for Developing and Least-Developed Members should be an integral part of the fisheries subsidies negotiation, taking into account the importance of this sector to development priorities, poverty reduction, and livelihood for food security concern."

[100] Fisheries Subsidies: A critical Issue for Trade and Sustainable Development at the WTO An introductory Guide, May 2008. http://www.unep.ch/etb/areas/fisherySub.php.

6.7 Conclusions

The focus of the Member States while trading and being involved in the related activities seems not in harmony with the two objectives, free trade, and sustainable development. Consequently, the unchecked industrialisation has lowered the quality of the environment. Based on the discussions formerly made in this text, concerning the balance between free trade and the environment, it is proposed that the trade relationship among the Member States needs to be based on some assumed environmental standards acceptable to all the Member States of the WTO.

However, attempts have been made to safeguard environment by creating standards for checks and balances while promoting free trade, nevertheless, the need for evolving general principles in support of long term objectives cannot be ignored.

In the present context, it seems that the existing provisions of the SCM agreement are not sufficiently comprehensive to cover free trade along with sustainable development at an equal level. Hence, the damage caused by industries in not following environmental obligations cannot be covered in appropriate terms by the existing legal provisions. The fact is that there is no mention of environment related trade benefits under the SCM Agreement; perhaps the progenitor of free trade could not foresee the trade impacts on the environment. However, with the deterioration of environmental conditions due to free trade, there seems to be a definite requirement for legal provisions within the ASCM, not only to regulate trade but also to compensate in economic terms, the affected parties. A shift of focus, by the policy makers towards sustainable development would allow for the adoption of necessity based environmental measures that could be seen as less disruptive of free trade and could be a way to distinguish, prejudiced trade protectionism from environmental protectionism.

Further, it should be noted that in order to ensure a safe and healthy environment for future generations, reforms in the WTO, which would include strict environmental measures are proposed. To accomplish such reforms, it is necessary that Member States also consider this as a part of their socio-political objectives. Adopting such objectives requires policy-reforms among the Member States within their domestic legal system, so as to cover environment-related issues from the global perspective.

Free trade, along with sustainable development, should be considered as common objectives of the WTO, and should function side by side. In order to attain this level of harmony between the two objectives, certain level of basic environment obligations need to be followed on a priority basis by the industrial sector of both the Developed and the Developing nations.

There is also an additional risk that putting too much emphasis on environment standards can create a protectionist approach, which is contrary to the objectives of free trade. Hence, an approach which can differentiate between the genuine grounds for trade restrictions versus protectionist propaganda needs to be adopted for environmental protection.

What can be suggested is a model that indicates the point when an optimum level of pollution control is reached and any further reduction can lead to greater costs in production and of less effective pollution control.

It is clear that the Developing nations avoid following environmental measures because they are likely to increase the cost of factors of production. An additional reason is that several of the Developing Member Nations are lacking the social norms to implement legal measures for the protection of environment. The WTO as a trade regulatory institution, with the objective of aiding sustainable development, needs to take initiatives to cover this normative gap through treaties that can bind the parties. It is also suggested that the existing differences between natural wealth and man-made capital, formed and distributed through free trade, requires a clear understanding and people need to be educated from this perspective.

There are indeed differences on several issues between the Developing and the Developed countries, but these difference of opinion should not go so far as to miss the main concerns such as the environmental issues. However, it could be useful to provide some alleviation based on the economic difference between the Member Nations.

The analysis of the subsidies to the fisheries industry, specifies the far-reaching consequences of the unregulated subsidies. These un-regulated subsidies can create critical damages to resources that people are dependent on for their livelihood. The subsidies have encouraged overproduction and thus exacerbated many of the ecological problems linked to overfishing and thus depleting stocks beyond sustainable limit.

Apart from the foregoing analysis, the positive side of using subsidies to promote trade cannot be ignored. As the means of production are the basis of free market-economies and Member Nations of the WTO are in the different economic situations, subsidies, compatible with the environment can play a positive role in the promotion of environmentally consistent and fair methods of production. Additionally, subsidies to reduce emissions of greenhouse gases or environmental-friendly methods of production have some justification.

The WTO as an institution has the responsibility of exploring or evolving a wider role in order to create a balance between trade subsidies and the environment, where subsidies are used, not mainly for the promotion of trade, rather making the production method environment friendly. The WTO has an inbuilt judicial mechanism, called the Dispute Settlement Body which can implement environmental friendly measures. Nevertheless, due to the lack of specific agreements in support of the environmental measures within the WTO, there are some limitations. As a result of this, the Dispute Settlement Body cannot take a strong line to secure obligations for maintaining environmental standards. Finally, it can be said that there is a need for the WTO to promote the principles of sustainable development along with trade liberalisation. This will be possible, once trade and the environment are taken as mutually supportive factors for meeting key objectives.

References

Biondi A, Eeckhout P, Flynn J (2004) The law of state aid in the European Union. Oxford University Press, New York
De Sombre ER (1999) Environmental harm as economic subsidy: new perspectives on the feasibility of trade sanctions for environmental protection. Int J Peace Stud 4(1). ISBN 1085-7494
Footer ME (2006) An institutional and normative analysis of the World Trade Organization. Martinus Nijhoff Publishers, Leiden
Francioni F (2001) Environment human rights and international trade. Hart Publishing, Portland
Lang M, Herlin J, Hofbauer I (2005) WTO and direct taxation. Kluwer Law Internationals, Alphen aan den Rijn
Macrory P, Appleton AE, Plummer MG (eds) (2005) The World Trade Organization: legal economic and political analysis, vol II. Springer, New York
Pavlakos G (2007) Law, rights and discourse; the legal philosophy of Robert Alexy. Hart, Oxford
Pigou AC (1912) Wealth and welfare. Macmillan and Co., London
Srinivasan TN (2000) Developing countries and the multilateral trading system: from the GATT to the Uruguay Round and the future. Westview Press, Colorado
Stewart TP (1999) The GATT Uruguay Round, a negotiating history, vol IV: the end game (part I). Kluwer Law International, The Hague
Yang T, Moser A (2011) Environment tort litigation in China: Santa Clara law digital common, vol 10. Faculty Publications, vol 10, pp 10895–10901. http://digitalcommons.law.scu.edu/facpubs/434
Young M (2010) Protecting endangered marine species: collaboration between the food and agriculture organization and the cites regime. Melb J Int Law 11(2):82–50. http://ssrn.com/abstract=1852904

Cases

Canada-Certain Measures Affecting the Renewable Energy Generation Sector WT/DS412/R
European Communities-Trade Description of Sardines WT/DS231/AB/R
United States-Import Prohibition of Certain Shrimp and Shrimp Products WT/DS58/AB/R
United States-Standard for Reformulated and Conventional Gasoline WT/DS2/AB/R

Reports and Electronic Sources

Andersson M, Bartholdson Ö (2006) Swedish pulp in Brazil: the case of Veracel. http://www.swedwatch.org/sites/default/files/swedwatch_the_case_of_veracel.pdf
Business Standard (2012) www.business-standard.com/india/news/alang-yard
Dugal M, Walton H (2011) WTO fisheries subsidies negotiations and Pacific Island states: trade negotiation insights. http://www.ictsd.org/.../trade-negotiations-insights/.../wto-fisheries-subsidies-negotiations
Environment Negotiations. The Doha mandate on multilateral environmental agreements. Doha Development Agenda. http://www.wto.org/english/tratop_e/envir_neg_mea_e.htm
Kazim H, Klawitter N (2012) The value of Pakistani worker. SPIE Online. www.spiegel.de
Benitah M (2004) Ongoing WTO negotiations on fisheries subsidies. Am Soc Int Law 8(12). http://www.asil.org/insights/volume/8/issue/12/

Orellana MA (2006) Insights shipbreaking and Le Clemenceau row. Am Soc Int Law. http://www.asil.org

Porter G (2001) United Nations environment programme. Fisheries subsidies and over fishing: towards a structured discussion. UNEP Publications, Geneva.ISBN 92-807-2126-7. Unep.ch/etb/etp/acts/capbld/rdtwo/FE_vol_1.pdf

Subsidies in the energy sector: an overview (2012) http://siteresresources.worldbank.org/EXTESC/Resources/Subsidy_background_paper.pdf

Chapter 7
Remedies: The Procedural Measures

Abstract The working of the WTO is based on specific set of objectives. The main objectives of the WTO are to promote trade liberalization and to create fair opportunities for development among its Member States. Following the liberal market policies based on the WTO system, the trading opportunities for the Member States has indeed grown, but they are obliged to follow specific set of rules as check and balances, restricting discriminatory, market distortionary and other inefficient trade practices.

This Chapter deals with the procedural measures to be applied for dispute resolution in case of disagreement between the parties. Member States are expected to follow the WTO rules and comply with the provisions of the SCM Agreement. Trade subsidies can be compared to the two sides of the same coin. For practical reasons, there can be relevant justifications for the state support in the form of subsidies, for example, during the initial phase of industrialization or when the society is transforming from agricultural to industrial mode.

After attaining membership, Member States are expected to formulate domestic policies consistent with the WTO Agreements. However, in cases where party is affected by the subsidy practices or due to the non-compliance, it has to recourse to the DSB. This chapter deals specifically with the procedure for the solutions if a party suffers from the subsidy practices by other Member States. Therefore, the discussion in this chapter is basically confined to the remedies because of the subsidies creating distortionary effect to the other parties.

7.1 Introduction

The WTO, as a trade regulating institution, expects all its Member States in pursuant of their trading practices to follow certain guidelines that are covered broadly through its foundation agreements. This implies that the trade policies and practices of the Member States need to be in-conformity with the WTO Agreements. Compliance of policies and principles are expected, also in order to meet the WTO objectives and for the smooth working and predictability of this trading system.

Keeping in mind the historical accounts of the trade relationship between the nations, Member States of the WTO, however, anticipated the possibilities of

G. Singh, *Subsidies in the Context of the WTO's Free Trade System*,
DOI 10.1007/978-3-319-62422-8_7

occurring business differences and conflict of interests due to the existence of diverse economic, political and social systems among themselves. With such a wide diversity among the Member States, and above all thanks to the interaction with common market liberalisation policies for all the Member States because of free trade concepts, it cannot be denied that the WTO trading system is vulnerable to several types of un-regulated, non-compatible, and unprincipled business practices. In order to create a balance between odds and evens, and in order to explore a solution within the framework of the various trading agreements of the WTO, Member States agreed to a Dispute Settlement mechanism acceptable to all. Eventually, this came in the form of an agreement, entitled "Understanding on Rules and Procedures Covering Settlement of Dispute" also termed the DSU.[1] On a formal basis, members are committed by the implications of Article 3[2] of the DSU to the basic principles under Article XXII[3] and XXIII[4] of GATT 1947 for the resolution of disputes.

7.1.1 *Aims and Purpose*

The WTO dispute settlement system, with its distinct features, can be further segmented in order understand the different roles played by the various classified bodies within its functional system. On the basis of responsibilities, one can distinguish between the political side of the institution, such as the Dispute Settlement Body and the independent, judicial type institutions, such as the dispute settlement panels and the standing Appellate Body.[5] The judicial body of this organisation and the DSB, works with the objective of safeguarding basic principles, such as, non-discrimination, equal market access opportunities, promoting the development measures for Developing and Less-Developed countries and maintaining the level of sustainability along with free trade. With due regard to the long term objectives of development of the Developing countries and

[1]Hodu (2006), p. 14.

[2]Article 3 Clause 1, Members affirms their adherence to the principles for the management of disputes here to fore applied under Articles XXII and XXIII of GATT 1947, and the rules and procedures as further elaborated and modified herein. Clause 2. The dispute settlement system of the WTO is a central element in providing security and predictability to the multilateral trading system. The Members recognize that it serves to preserve the rights and obligations of Members under the covered agreements, and to clarify the existing provisions of those agreements in accordance with customary rules of interpretation of public international law. Recommendations and rulings of the DSB cannot add to or diminish the rights and obligations provided in the covered agreements.

[3]Article XXII of the GATT 1947 encourages the parties to resolve the matter through consultation.

[4]Article XXIII of the GATT 1947 implies that if any benefit is hindered by the failure of the other party to fulfil its obligations, the party concerned can make a written proposal to consider the matter that has caused an adverse situation.

[5]Bossche (2008), p. 235.

Less-Developed countries; several clauses creating the scope of the flexible approach are included in various Articles. These are,

1. Article 4.10,[6] regarding special attention to the problems of the Developing countries during consultation among the Members,
2. Article 8.10,[7] deals with disputes between a Developing country member and a Developed country member,
3. Article 12.10,[8] with regard to measures taken by a Developing country member, the parties may agree to extend the time period and
4. Article 12.11[9] covers the situation where one or more of the parties is a Developing country member, the panel's report should mention in what respect an account has been taken of the special treatment, and this is included in the DSU.

As the Member States are categorised in terms of economic and technological basis, while deciding the cases and resolving the disputes, the adjudicating body works with an approach of following the systemic rationality of the institution and testing the issues in relation to the general WTO objectives.

Considering the level of economic and technological gap between the Developed and Less Developed countries, special consideration is given to the less-developed countries through exclusive Articles. These are Article 24[10] and Article 27,[11] which create an even wider scope for interpretation and maintaining a level of institutional balance between free trade objectives along with the promotion of fair

---

[6]Article 4.10 during consultations, Members should give attention to the particular problems and interests of the Developing country Members.

[7]When a dispute is between a Developing country Member and a Developed country Member, the panel shall, if the Developing country so requests, include at least one panelist from a Developing country Member.

[8]In the context of consultations involving a measure taken by a Developing country Member, the parties may agree to extend the periods established in paragraphs 7 and 8 of Article 4. If, after the relevant period has elapsed, the consulting parties cannot agree that the consultations have concluded, the chairman of the DSB shall decide, after consultation with the parties, whether to extend the relevant period and, if so, for how long. . .for detail reference, see the article.

[9]Where one or more of the parties is a Developing country Member, the panel's report shall explicitly indicate the form in which account has been taken of relevant provisions on differential and more favourable treatment for Developing country Members that form part of the covered agreements which have been raised by the Developing country Members in the course of the dispute settlement procedures.

[10]Article 24 Clause 1. At all stages of the determination of the cause of a dispute and of dispute settlement procedures involving a Least-Developed country Member, particular consideration shall be given to the special situation of Least-Developed country Members. Article 24 Clause 2 In dispute settlement cases involving a Least-Developed country Member, where a satisfactory solution has not been found in the course of consultations the Director-General or the Chairman of the DSB shall, upon request by a Least-Developed country Member offer their good offices, conciliation and mediation with a view to assisting the parties to settle the dispute, before a request for a panel is made. . .. For detail reference, see the Article.

[11]Article 27 Responsibilities of the Secretariat.

opportunities for economic and technological growth. Whenever matters are brought that require interpretation, the scope of the provisions, are defined keeping in mind the objectives of free trade principles, such as eliminating protectionist measures. If the specific situation so demands in any case, regulatory mechanisms are also applied, to promote other objectives on a rational and proportional basis, such as sustainable development, balanced economic growth and market stability. The regulatory methods also serve the purpose of adjusting free trade with other objectives. Alternatively, it can be said that several issues that are linked with trade matters, such as concerns about the environment, issue related to health and safety standards etc., are taken into account when the matter is brought before the DSB. At times, it can be observed that the issues of interest that Member States have brought for resolution or for the judicial body to act upon, are also based on the legal rights or remedies available to an individual as a claimant in the domain of the constitutional mechanism within their home countries.

In the cases where the matter under consideration requires interpretation different from what is conventionally followed, concepts and principles of International Law can be applied. Bearing in mind here that the WTO being a treaty-based organisation and taking into account the perspective of international law, it is more equitable for cases to be decided on the basis of *Lex posterior* principle. However, this principle should not be seen in the context that the later interpretation will prevail, but rather with the underlying idea that there cannot be any strict way of interpreting. There is always a possibility of applying legal provisions in a different way depending upon each case.[12]

7.2 The Parties, Amicus Curiae and Third Party

There is a general obligation among the Member States to settle the dispute with the concerned Members through a multilateral procedure, as prescribed in the agreement, the Understanding on Rules and Procedures Covering the Settlement of Disputes.[13] Once any issue under the covered agreements arises between the parties, the complaining Member is obliged to bring the dispute to the Dispute Settlement System. The Dispute settlement system is an adjudication body; allowing the governments of the Member States to bring claims. As the eligibility criteria to bring the matter before DSB permits only governments of the Member States to present the issues, individuals, companies and non-governmental organisations cannot participate as party before the dispute settlement system as they do

[12] *Japan Taxes on Alcoholic Beverages,* WT/DS8/AB/R WT/DS10/AB/R and/DS11/AB/R, A.B interpretation on the status of adopted panel reports, pp. 12–13.

[13] DSU Article 23 cl(1) When Members seek the redress of a violation of obligations or other nullification or impairment of benefits under the covered agreements or an impediment to the attainment of any objective of the covered agreements, they shall have recourse to, and abide by, the rules and procedures of this Understanding.

not have the right to participate in any direct form. The exclusive nature of the criteria that only a government can raise issue, leads to a question about the role of amicus curiae and third parties. Within the DSU, Article 13[14] was included to create the possibility for panel to accept and consider amicus curiae briefs.[15] However, such possibilities are marginal, with regard to A.B.[16] The possibilities for considering and accepting amicus curiae briefs by the A.B are guided by separate procedures determined as mentioned, under Art 17cl(9)[17]of the DSU. Despite separate procedure, conditions need to be satisfied, that these procedures should not be in conflict with the rules mentioned in the DSU. Rule 16(1)[18] of the Working Procedures for the Appellate review is rather specific in this regard, creating a discretionary, although a narrow possibility for the A.B to accept amicus curiae briefs, on a case to case basis only, rather than as a general rule.

It is quite often the case that other parties, in addition to the Member States directly involved in the issue for adjudication, intend to participate actively in the proceedings. Such additional parties are termed third parties. In the issues raised before for the adjudication, there can be occasions where the interest of the third parties may be indirectly connected to the dispute. Participation of third parties during the consultation process is possible in pursuant to the provisions of Article 4.11[19] of the DSU. It is clearly mentioned in Article 10 of the DSU, that during the panel stage, the interest of the third party should be give due consideration. Article 10, has a rather wider scope and covers the third party or any party having substantial interest that has been notified before the panel, and therefore, in essence,

[14]Right to seek information under Article 13cl (1) Each panel shall have the right to seek information and technical advice from any individual or body which it deems appropriate. However, before a panel seeks such information or advice from any individual or body within the jurisdiction of a Member it shall inform the authorities of that Member. . .. For detail reference, see the article.

[15]Bossche (2008), p. 192.

[16]Bossche (2008), p. 193.

[17]Article 17 cl (9) Working procedures shall be drawn up by the Appellate Body in consultation with the Chairman of the DSB and the Director-General, and communicated to the Members for their information.

[18]In the interests of fairness and orderly procedure in the conduct of an appeal, where a procedural question arises that is not covered by these rules, a division may adopt an appropriate procedure for the purposes of that appeal only, provided that it is not inconsistent with the DSU, the other covered agreements and these rules. Where such a procedure is adopted, the division shall immediately notify the parties to the dispute, participants, third parties and third participants as well as the other Members of the Appellate Body.

[19]Article 4.11 of the DSU Whenever a Member other than the consulting Member considers that it has a substantial trade interest in consultations being held pursuant to paragraph 1 of Article XXII of GATT 1994, paragraph 1 of Article XXII of GATS, or the corresponding provisions in other covered agreements, such Member may notify the consulting Members and the DSB, within 10 days after the date of the circulation of the request for consultation under said Article, of its desire to be joined in the consultations.

can be heard and can make a written submission.[20] With regard to the substantial effect of their opinion during the proceedings, third parties during the proceedings can indeed influence the decision of the panel body.[21]

Comparing the possibilities of third parties to put forward their views before the A.B, to those of the parties, directly involved, the third party's rights are confined up to the panel stage. By virtue of Article 17.4[22] of the DSU, a clear line has been drawn between the parties to the dispute and third parties, stating that only parties to the dispute and not the third parties may appeal to the A.B. However, in matters that are related to Para 2 of Article 10 DSU, where third parties have notified the DSB, the third party can be given an opportunity to be heard by the Appellate Body.[23] In precise terms, it can be said that the rights of a third party are fragile as nowhere in Article 10 of the DSU, has the term "right" been used for the third parties, which by implication places them in a secondary status position.

---

[20]Article 10.2 of the DSU Any Member having a substantial interest in a matter before a panel and having notified its interest to the DSB (referred to in this Understanding as a third party) shall have an opportunity to be heard by the panel and to make written submissions to the panel. These submissions shall also be given to the parties to the dispute and shall be reflected in the panel report.

[21]In the case of *Canada-Measures Affecting the Export of Civilian Aircraft*, WT/DS70/R. In this dispute between Canada and Brazil, the U.S acting as a third party gave significant submissions before the Panel Body. When the U.S requested before the Panel Body to withdraw its submissions, **See footnote 496** WT/DS70/R Brazil submitted a letter requesting the Panel to decline the request of the United States, in view of practical and substantive concerns over the request. In Brazil's view, complete deletion of the US submissions would pose logistical problems in these time-constrained proceedings, as both the section containing the US submissions, and all references in the parties' arguments to those submissions, would need to be removed. Substantively, Brazil states that such deletion would prejudice the rights of the parties, because parties (and all Members) have an interest in preserving an accurate and complete record of the proceedings; and because parties may have either developed or foregone particular lines of argument in response to arguments made by the United States. In Brazil's view, granting the request would prejudice these interests, and would be contrary to the twin goals of "security and predictability" identified by Article 3.2 of the DSU as central to the WTO dispute settlement system. Brazil believes that the Panel does not have the authority to fulfill the US request, in view of the provision of Article 10.2 of the DSU that third party submissions '*shall* be reflected in the panel report' (emphasis added by Brazil), and the provision of Rule XXV (2) of the Working Procedures for Appellate Review that third party written submissions, recorded oral statements and written answers to questions are part of the record of the panel proceedings. The **Panel**, in view of the practical difficulties of removing the US submissions and all references thereto from this report, in view of the strong opposition of one of the parties, and in view of the fact that the Panel had asked the parties to submit comments on specific aspects of the US submissions, declined the United States' request.

[22]Only parties to the dispute, not third parties, may appeal against a Panel Report. Third parties which have notified the DSB of a substantial interest in the matter pursuant to paragraph 2 of Article 10 may present written submissions, and be given an opportunity to be heard by the Appellate Body.

[23]DSU Article 17 cl 4. Only parties to the dispute, not third parties, may appeal a panel report. Third parties which have notified the DSB of a substantial interest in the matter pursuant to paragraph 2 of Article 10 may make a written submissions to, and be given an opportunity to be heard by the Appellate Body.

7.3 The DSU as Dispute Resolving System

Once an issue related to the treaty agreements has arisen within the Member States of the WTO, for finding a solution or to seek remedies or claims, with-in the normal course, it passes through several stages.

(1) Consultation process (2) Panel body (3) Appellate Body and the (4) Compliance.[24]

When any differences of opinion has arisen or has taken the form of a dispute, or the matter at issue concerns trade practices, and such practices violate the rights of the Member States of the WTO, the first step to resolve such like issue is by adopting the modes of consultation.[25] Once request for consultation has been made, the member to whom such a request is made is expected to reply within 10 days after the receipt of such a request. It is also expected that parties in good faith will enter into consultations within a period of 30 days of the receipt of such a request.[26] Furthermore, while following the procedure on remedies, special considerations are possible, so as to focus the approach during the consultation stage, depending upon the requirements and this is covered under Article 4.8[27] of the DSU.

With regard to the issues related to subsidies, the possibility to resolve a dispute by means of consultation is acknowledged. Provisions included within the SCM Agreement, specifically for consultation form a link with DSU, both in the case of prohibited and actionable subsidies. Whenever, an issue arises with regard to prohibited subsidies, or any Member State has reason to believe, that state support of such a category is being provided by another Member State, that affects its rights in terms of free trade or free trade objectives of the WTO or otherwise are contrary to the fair trade regulatory approach, it may request consultation by virtue of Article 4.1[28] of the SCM Agreement. There is an exclusive Article, Article 4[29] of the DSU dealing with the detailed procedures for consultations. It can also be mentioned here, that a similar approach is possible in the case of actionable subsidies. In trade matters where actionable subsidies are in case alleged, the legal possibility to initiate such consultations can be availed.[30] In given circumstances, supposing

---

[24]Covered under Article 4 for Consultations, Article 6 Establishment of Panels, Article 17 for the Appellate Body and Article 21 Surveillance of Implementation of Recommendations and Rulings.

[25]Article 3.7 of the DSU. Before bringing a case, a Member shall exercise its judgments as to whether action under these procedures would be fruitful. The aim of the dispute settlement mechanism is to secure a positive solution to a dispute.

[26]Article 4.3 of the DSU.

[27]Article 4.8 in cases of urgency, including those which concern perishable goods, Members shall enter into consultations within a period of no more than 10 days after the date of receipt of the request. If the consultations have failed to settle the dispute within a period of 20 days after the date of receipt of the request, the complaining party may request the establishment of a Panel.

[28]Whenever a Member has reason to believe that a prohibited subsidy is being granted or maintained by another Member, such a Member may request consultations with the other Member.

[29]Article 4, is further subdivided into 11 sub clauses.

[30]See Article 7.1 of the SCM Agreement.

that the affected Member State has sufficient reason to believe that state support by Member State in question has resulted in injury to the domestic industry or has led to any serious consequences, consultations can also be initiated through diplomatic channels. In the case of **Mexico-Provisional Countervailing Measures on Olive Oil from the European Communities,**[31] Mexico imposed provisional countervailing duty measures on imported olive oil from the European Communities. The EC considered that the imposition was not based on sufficient evidence to substantiate the claims that the domestic industry was suffering as a result of the subsidised import of Olive oil. The parties resorted to consultations in order to settle the matter. Until now, no dispute Panel has been established.

In the eventualities, when consultations are not successful in reaching consensus, disputes are then resolved through a codified procedure covered under the DSU. The WTO DSU is an integral part of the Uruguay Agreements, running to 27 Articles and four Appendices.[32] The rules and procedures covered under this agreement for the settlement of disputes are uniformly applicable to the members in general, however, with special consideration for Less-Developed countries as explicitly mentioned in Article 24 of the DSU.[33] The entire process is dealt with by special sub institutional arrangement i.e., DSB.

7.3.1 The Dispute Resolution by the DSB

The WTO dispute settlement system can be categorised into two different, but inter connected, sub-institutional frameworks. (1) The political establishment, which is the DSB[34] and (2) The judicial set up, that covers the panel body and the standing Appellate Body.[35] The General Council of the WTO which is composed of representatives of all the Member States, discharges the responsibilities of the DSB.[36] The DSB consists of representatives of all the Member States of the WTO. It has a

[31]DS 314. The consultations started on 18th August 2004 and no Panel Body was established.

[32]Read (2005), pp. 29–48.

[33]DSU Article 24 Cl (1) At all stages of the determination of the causes of a dispute and dispute settlement procedures involving a Less-Developed country Member, particular consideration shall be given to the special situation of the Less-Developed country Member. In this regard, Member shall exercise due restraint in raising matters under these procedures involving a Less-Developed country Member.

[34]Article 2 of the DSU. The Dispute Settlement Body is hereby established to administer these rules and procedures and, except as otherwise provided in a covered agreement, the consultation and dispute settlement provisions of the covered agreements. Accordingly, the DSB shall have the authority to establish Panels, adopt Panel and Appellate Body reports, maintain surveillance of implementation of rulings and recommendations and authorize suspension of concessions and other obligations under the covered agreements. (for detail reference see the Article 2 of the DSU).

[35]Bossche (2008), p. 235.

[36]www.wto.org (analytical index).

Chairman appointed by a consensus of the Member States. Whenever a, dispute between parties arise, the DSB is responsible for formulating the adjudicatory set-up and, the panel body to resolve the matter. In general terms, the functions of the DSB can be stated, as being to establish panels, adopt panels and the Appellate Body report, as defined in Article 2.1 of the DSU.[37] Additionally, as per the guidelines, the DSB formally directs compliance of the decisions by the parties if the compliance is still pending. Moreover, with regard to the adoption of reports, in formal terms, it can be said that once the DSB adopts the reports, the decision is automatically considered to be adopted and the parties need to fulfil their obligations.[38]

7.3.1.1 Panel Body After Consultations

The panel body is a judicial body, at the first stage of resolving trade disputes after consultation. If the consultation process has not succeeded, the complainant may request the establishment of the panel. There is no established panel body; rather it is formed in every case when the matter is brought before the DSB. The decision about the individuals serving on the panel in any particular case is taken by mutual agreement between the parties.[39] With regard to the matters of *prohibited subsidies*, in the cases where the parties cannot reach any solution within 30 days of the request for consultation, either of the parties can refer the matter to the DSB for the establishment of a panel.[40] The panel body is usually comprised of three members and in exceptional cases it has five members.[41] The details of the establishment and

[37]The Dispute Settlement Body is hereby established to administer these rules and procedures and, except as otherwise provided in a covered agreement, the consultation and dispute settlement provisions of the covered agreements. Accordingly, the DSB shall have the authority to establish panels, adopt panel and Appellate Body reports, maintain surveillance of implementation of rulings and recommendations, and authorize suspension of concessions and other obligations under the covered agreements.

[38]UNECLAC, Economic Commission for Latin American Countries. http://www.wto.org/english/tratop_e/dispu_e/dispu_te.htm#intro.

[39]Macrory et al. (2005), p. 1248.

[40]As per Article 4.3, if no mutually agreed solution has been reached within 30 days of the request for consultations, any Member, party to such consultations may refer the matter to the Dispute Settlement Body (DSB) for the immediate establishment of a panel, unless the DSB decides by consensus not to establish a panel.

[41]According to Article 8.5 of the DSU, panels shall be composed of three panelists unless the parties to the dispute agree, within 10 days from the establishment of the panel, to a panel composed of five panelists.

function of the panel body are covered under Article 6,[42] Article 7[43] and Article 8[44] of the DSU.

As a procedural requirement on a primary basis, it is laid down that the panel should make an objective assessment of the facts of the case presented to it. This assessment should be consistent with the relevant agreements of the WTO. In this regard, Article 11 of the DSU clarifies the legal role of the panel. The term objective assessment with regard to the panel's analysis was referred to in the case of the **United States-Safeguard Measures on Imports of Fresh Chilled or Frozen Lamb Meat from New Zealand and Australia.**[45]

Further, mentioning here in the context of objective analysis of the matter at issue, the panel is allowed additional possibilities to seek expert opinion as the disputes can be from diverse fields. The disputes brought before the panel body for adjudication may require the opinion of experts. In the matters before the panel body, where the resolution of the dispute requires the specific opinions of experts, Article 13[46] of the DSU creates the formal scope for the panel body to seek such information or report from experts. To encourage the practice of seeking advice from experts, and for making a better analysis of the case, Article 13 of the DSU endows the panel with the right to seek advice or information from any individual

[42]Article 6 deals with the establishment of the panels. Clause 1 of this Article states that based on the request of the complaining party, Panel shall be established.

[43]Article 7 deals with the terms of reference. Clause 1 states that the panel shall have the following terms of reference unless the parties to the dispute agree otherwise. "To examine in the light of the relevant provisions in (name of the covered agreement(s) cited by the parties to the dispute), the matter referred to the DSB by (name of party) in the document and make such findings as will assist the DSB in making the recommendations or in giving the rulings provided in that/those agreement(s)."

[44]Article 8 deals with the composition of the panel. Under Clause 1of this article, the Panel shall be composed of well qualified governmental and/or non-governmental individuals which includes persons who have served or presented a case before. An important condition to maintain integrity is covered in clause 3 of this Article. "Citizens of Members whose governments are parties to the dispute or third parties as defined in paragraph 2 of Article 10 shall not serve on a panel concerned with that dispute, unless the parties to the dispute agree otherwise."

[45]WT/DS178/AB/R The legal question mainly concerned the safeguard measures imposed by the U.S through the Agreement on Safeguard of the WTO. The Agreement on Safeguard sets forth the rules for application of safeguard measures pursuant to Article XIX of GATT 1994. Safeguard Measures are defined as "emergency" actions with respect to increased imports of particular products, where such imports have caused or threaten to cause serious injury to the importing Member's domestic industry. Para 103, 104, 105 of the A.B Report on this case, the A.B stated that the Panel was entitled to review whether the competent authorities had evaluated all the factors and whether the authorities had provided a reasoned and adequate explanation about the conclusions drawn. The A.B further added that this in brief involved taking into account, both the formal substantive aspect in order to make it an objective assessment and give a comprehensive picture of the issue.

[46]Article 13 clause 1, Each panel shall have the right to seek information and technical advice from any individual or body which it deems appropriate. However, before a panel seeks such information or advice from any individual or body within the jurisdiction of a Member it shall inform the authorities of that member.

expert or from the panel's group of experts. As subsidies and state support can be provided in various forms, the issue of subsidies in question can therefore be technical, from a policy perspective having several dimensions and the experts can help to analyse such issues. It is possible to establish a body of experts[47] by the Committee on Subsidies and Countervailing Measures (SCM Committee) under Article 24.3 of the Agreement on Subsidies and Countervailing Measure, in order to determine the question of subsidies and its effects.

The Committee on Subsidies and Countervailing Measure, establishes a **Permanent Group of Experts** composed of five independent persons well qualified in the matters of subsidy practices. Depending upon the facts and circumstances of the case, the panel body may request the assistance of the PGE (permanent group of experts).[48] This is to substantially clarify whether the measure at issue is a prohibited subsidy and what its effects can be.[49]

After the decision is given by the panel body, sufficient time is given to the concerned Member State, to consider and to act on it. When the issues before the panel body are related to the prohibited subsidies, within 30 days of the issuance of the report by the panel body, the report should be adopted by the DSB (1) unless it is decided by one of the parties, to appeal and (2) unless DSB decides by consensus not to adopt the report.[50]

If the matters are decided for the actionable subsidies,[51] then in such cases within 30 days of the issuance of report by the panel body, (1) it is expected that report should be adopted by the DSB, unless decided otherwise, or (2) unless one of the parties notifies for appeal.

7.3.1.2 Establishment of the Appellate Body

Where in the case decided, the party is not satisfied by the decision of the panel body and wants the decisions to be reviewed, the matter is referred to or appealed before the Appellate Body. The A.B is a permanent judicial body with its members serving for a 4 years term, and the term can be renewed for once.[52] This standing body is comprised of seven individuals, three of whom should have served on one of the case.

---

[47]Kazeri (2009), p. 1031.

[48]Appendix 4 of the DSU Clause 1. Expert review groups are under the Panel's authority. Their terms of reference and detailed working procedure shall be decided by the Panel, and they shall report to the Panel. Clause 2 Participation in expert review groups shall be restricted to persons of professional standing and experience in the field of question.

[49]Article 4.5 of the SCM Agreement.

[50]Article 4.8 of the SCM Agreement.

[51]Article 7.6 of the SCM Agreement.

[52]Article 17.1 and 2 of the DSU.

The working rules and procedures of the A.B are covered under Article 17[53] of the DSU. Article 17.1[54] of the DSU specifies that the A.B should be established to hear appeals from the panel cases, therefore the A.B's main role is to review an issue that is already decided on by the panel body. However, there is no such provision which expressly excludes *de-novo*[55] reviews by the A.B if the case so requires. By virtue of Article 17.6 of the DSU, the scope of the A.B is confined to the examination of the issue of law and analysing appropriateness of legal interpretation given by the panel. As in the hierarchical order, the A.B is a higher body, therefore it can uphold, modify or reverse the findings of the panel.

With regard to the jurisdictions, it is also worth mentioning here that both the panel body and the A.B have limitations when making legal interpretations. According to Article 19.2 of the DSU, the panel and the Appellate Body cannot make basic changes by making additions or by reducing any rights or obligations mentioned in the provisions of the covered agreements.[56] However, certain level of liberty is given to the A.B. In line with this approach, a special provision, referred as Article 17.9 is included. Article 17.9 of the DSU is a contextual provision that enables the working procedure to be drawn up by the A.B in consultation with the Chairman of the DSB and the Director General.

7.4 Constructive Remedies

While resolving the dispute, the possibilities of constructive remedies draw eminence in recognition to the concessionary possibilities for the Developing countries,

By using the term "constructive remedies," the idea is given of remedies beyond the strict context of the provisions. The price undertaking under Article 18 of the SCM Agreement, or improvising remedies during the consultation period under Article 4 or Article 7 of the SCM Agreement, create the possibilities for constructive remedies. Constructive remedies, how far can be strictly claimed or what the limits should be, was a matter before the panel body in the case of **European**

[53]Article 17 Clause 1 states that a standing Appellate Body established by the DSB shall hear appeals from the panel cases. Article 17 Clause 6 An appeal shall be limited to issues of law covered in the Panel Report and legal interpretations developed by the Panel. Article 17 clause 9 Working procedure shall be drawn up by the Appellate Body in consultation with the Chairman of the DSB and the Director-General, and communicated to the Members for their information. Article 17 clause 13 The Appellate Body may uphold, modify or reverse the legal findings and conclusions of the Panel.

[54]Article 17 cl 1. A standing Appellate Body shall be established by the DSB. The Appellate Body shall hear appeals from panel cases. It shall be composed of seven persons, three of whom shall serve on any one case. Persons serving on the Appellate Body shall serve in rotation. Such rotation shall be determined in the working procedures of the Appellate Body.

[55]From the beginning.

[56]Mitchell (2005), p. 197.

Communities Anti-dumping Duties on Imports of Cotton Type-Bed Linen from India.[57] India's claim for constructive remedies was based on Article 15[58] of the Agreement on Implementation of Article VI of the General Agreement on Tariffs and Trade 1994.

In addition to other issues, the parties i.e., India and the EC, in this case, have disagreed on the interpretative meaning of the term "constructive remedies."[59] India's view was that it is for the European Communities to find and propose such remedies for the Developing countries prior to the imposition of anti-dumping measures.[60] European Communities have considered the general price undertakings as the constructive remedies. Finally, the panel body attempted to clarify the use of the term constructive remedies for the purpose of the WTO trading system. In the first place the panel clarified that the decision not to impose an anti-dumping duty, as proposed by India, cannot be considered as "a constructive remedy" as it is stretching to an extreme the meaning of Article 9.1[61] of the Anti-Dumping Agreement.[62] Further, the panel stated that as the Agreement provides for the imposition of duties, and therefore the imposition of lesser duties or a price undertaking can be taken as constructive remedies.[63] It seems that India's claim for constructive remedies was with the presumption of Developing country's rights rather on the concessionary ground. Going literally by India's claim would affect the basic purpose of the legal provisions that is to restrict the practice of dumping. Therefore, the constructive remedies need to be seen as alternative possibilities within the scope of the agreement rather than in violation of it.

---

[57]WT/DS141/R **India is the complainant and the EC is respondent.** India requested for the establishment of the Panel Body, as the countervailing duties were imposed by the European communities on the cotton type bed linen from India. See para 1.1 and 2.1 of the WT/DS141/R.

[58]Article 15, It is recognized that special regard must be given by the Developed country Members to the special situation of Developing country Members when considering the application of anti-dumping measures under the Agreement.

[59]See para 6.227 of the WT/DS141/R Based on the foregoing understanding of Article 15 of the AD Agreement, we consider the issue before us in this case is, whether the EC authorities actively considered with an open mind the possibilities of price undertakings with Indian exporters prior to the imposition of final anti-dumping measures in the bed linen investigation.

[60]Para 6.228 India stresses that the Indian exporters and Texprocil made numerous arguments and submissions concerning the Developing country status of India, and the importance of the bed linen proceeding for Indian interests. India appears to be dissatisfied as a general matter with the European Communities failure to address these arguments in the various public notices, but makes no specific claims in this regard.... For detail reference see, the para in the details of the case.

[61]The decision on whether or not to impose an anti-dumping duty in cases where all requirements for the imposition have been fulfilled, and the decision whether the amount of the anti-dumping duty to be imposed shall be the full margin of dumping or less, are decisions to be made by the authorities of the importing Member.

[62]See WT/DS141/R, para 6.228.

[63]See WT/DS141/R, para 6.229. Wolfrum et al. (2008), p. 192.

7.5 Compliance

It is expected that the recommendations of the panel body or A.B will be duly complied within the time framework as mentioned in the provisions of the respective Agreements. After completion of the adjudication process by the panel body and subsequently decision being adopted by the DSB, parties have the option, either to accept the decision or to appeal against the decision. If parties not going for appeal after the decision of the panel, the respective parties according to the directions of the panel body are expected to comply, as per the guidelines drawn up through the provisions, mentioned as under Article 20[64] /Article 21[65] of the DSU, or in accordance with the relevant provisions of the Agreement. However, the respective parties also have an option to appeal the decisions given by the panel body. The possibility to appeal is available to all the Member States. In case parties to any dispute wish to appeal, this can be requested in writing, indicating the reason for such an appeal and the points they wish to be appealed before the A.B. Once the decision concerning an issue is finally given by the A.B, subsequently, it is adopted by the DSB.[66] Within 30 days after the adoption, a party must state its intentions to implement the recommendations of the rulings of the DSB.[67]

7.6 Procedure for Remedies in the Case of Trade Subsidies

Subsidies under the SCM Agreement are mainly classified as prohibited and actionable subsidies. When a matter in dispute concerns subsidies, the procedure followed in both the types of subsidies in question remains nearly the same. Remedies for the prohibited subsidies are provided under Article 4 of the SCM Agreement and remedies in the case of actionable subsidies are provided in Article 7 of the SCM Agreement.

[64]Article 20. Time frame for DSB Decisions. Unless otherwise agreed to the parties to the dispute, the period from the date of establishment of the panel by the DSB until the date DSB considers the panel or appellate report for adoption shall as a general rule not exceed 9 months where the panel report is not appealed or 12 months where the report is appealed. Where either the panel or the Appellate Body has acted, pursuant to paragraph 9 of Article 12 or paragraph 5 of 17, to extend the time for providing its report, the additional time shall be added to the above period.

[65]Article 21cl 1.Prompt compliance with recommendations or rulings of the DSB is essential in order to ensure an effective resolution of disputes to the benefit of all Members.

[66]Article 17 cl 14. An Appellate Body report shall be adopted by the DSB and unconditionally accepted by the parties to the dispute unless the DSB decides by consensus not to adopt the Appellate Body report within 30 days following its circulation to the Members. This adoption procedure is without prejudice to the right of Members to express their views on an Appellate Body.

[67]Article 21.3 DSU, at a DSB meeting held within 30 days after the date of adoption of the panel or Appellate Body report, the Member concerned shall inform the DSB of its intentions in respect of implementation of the recommendations and rulings of the DSB. If it is impracticable to comply immediately with the recommendations and rulings, the member concerned shall have a reasonable period of time in which to do so.

7.6.1 Procedural Steps in the Case of Obtaining Remedies for Prohibited Subsidies

In the case of prohibited subsidies, after the request for consultation as mentioned under Article 4.1 of the SCM Agreement is made, and this consultation has not resulted in resolving the matter within 30 days of the request, the Member State party to the dispute may refer the matter to the DSB for the formation of a panel, and in order to initiate its proceedings.[68] The panel is supposed to submit its report within 90 days of its composition on the terms of reference.[69]

Where the issue in question is found to be related to a prohibited subsidy, the panel should notify this in the decision and specify the time-period within which the measure should be withdrawn or made consistent with the SCM Agreement provisions. Pursuant to this, the report of the panel is to be adopted within 30 days in so far as no appeal has been made, as referred in the Article 4.8 of the SCM Agreement. Where the matter is appealed, the appeal goes to the Appellate Body. The Appellate Body will give its decisions to the parties within 30 days of the notice appeal, which can, depending upon the case extend up to 60 days.[70] The report of the A.B is almost final and should be adopted by the DSB. This correspondingly requires that the parties to the dispute abide by the report of the A.B unconditionally, unless the DSB decides by consensus not to adopt the report.

7.6.2 Procedural Steps in the Case of Obtaining Remedies for Actionable Subsidies

Article 6.6 of the SCM Agreement, covers the possibility of serious affects due to the subsidies covered under Article 5 of the SCM Agreement. These types of subsidies become actionable after an adverse effect is caused on the market of the importing Member State, or the Member State is indirectly affected because of such practices. Pursuant to Article 7 of the SCM Agreement, the first step for the remedies starts with the request for consultation. Article 7.2 in specific terms enables the Member States, if affected because of such practices to take the initiative for consultation where it has reason to believe that the subsidy practices referred to is causing injury to its domestic industry. The consultation must include a statement of evidence with regard to the nature of subsidy and the injury caused.[71]

In the event of unsuccessful consultations, the matter is referred to the panel body. Within 30 days of the making of panel report, it should be adopted by the

[68] Article 4.4 of the SCM Agreement.

[69] See Article 4.6 of the SCM Agreement.

[70] Article 4.9 of the SCM Agreement.

[71] For reference, see Article 7.2 of the SCM Agreement.

parties, unless one of the parties decides to appeal before the A.B or the DSB, by consensus, decides not to accept the report.[72] If the panel report is appealed, the A.B is to issue the report of investigation and other proceedings within 60 days, which can be extended to 30 more days.[73] Following this, the A.B report should be adopted by the DSB and thereafter to be adopted by the parties finally without any reservation, unless the DSB by consensus decides not to accept the report. Once the report is adopted, the party concerned is supposed to remove the measures causing the adverse effects or alternatively the complaining member can take countermeasures in the light of the nature and degree of the adverse-effects.[74]

With regard to actionable subsidies both the panel body and the A.B adopt the criteria of interpretation with the emphasis on the scope of the WTO objectives. In this context, while making interpretations, the usual practice is such that checks and limits are considered as part of the criteria to balance the measures between the aims of free trade and fair trade regulatory measures. Additionally, the panel and the A.B rationalise the choice for interpretation, to imbibe the values of fairness, also creating trade opportunities for all the Member States by following non-discrimination practices and promoting sustainability to protect environment, along with the promotion of free trade. When any matter goes to appeal before the A.B, for the reason of narrow interpretation of any provisions, or the concerned party considers that restrictive approach has been followed by the panel body, the A.B can add a substantive contribution by stretching the interpretations, for analysing various forms of state policies or business measures, such as in the case of Airbus-Boeing dispute. As the Member States are classified as Developed, Developing and Less-Developed countries, the emphasis while categorizing justifiable and non-justifiable use of state support, may also vary and the judicial bodies take into account the individual situations.

7.7 The Countervailing Measures

An alternative to the multilateral way of challenging the actionable and prohibited subsidies is by unilaterally taking such measures to counter[75] the affects of subsidies.[76] There are different set of rules for such a legal process covered under Article 10–23 of the SCM Agreement. Countervailing duties are imposed on subsidised imports based on the conditions such as;[77] (1) That there are imports receiving state

[72]See Article 7.6 of the SCM Agreement.

[73]See Article 7.7 of the SCM Agreement.

[74]Macrory et al. (2005), pp. 703–704. Also see Article7.9 of the SCM Agreement.

[75]Article 10 of the SCM Agreement, Application of Article VI of GATT 1994.

[76]Bossche (2008), p. 585.

[77]Article 11.2 of the SCM Agreement. An application under para1 shall include sufficient evidence of the existence of (a) a subsidy and, if possible, its amount (b) injury within the meaning of Article

support in the form of subsidies classified as actionable or prohibited (2) Such a legal measure adopted, needs to be substantiated based on the evidence that there is an injury due to the subsidised imports.

Article 10 of the SCM Agreement, primarily sets the procedural requirements and directs the Member States of the WTO to take steps in accordance with the provisions of Article VI of GATT 1994, before applying countervailing duties.

The countervailing measure mentioned under Part V,[78] of the SCM Agreement, also covers remedies against subsidies used for dumping in general, but not specifically dumping as such. Part V of the SCM Agreement draws general parameters of rules and procedures that Member States need to follow in the case of taking unilateral action against subsidy practices. Such action include investigation,[79] the presentation of evidence,[80] the consultation before the initiation of the investigation,[81] and once the investigation has started, the determination of the, calculation of the amount of subsidy as a benefit,[82] the determination of the injury,[83] discussions about the provisional measures,[84] suspension of the proceedings on the grounds of undertakings,[85] and imposition and collection of countervailing duties.[86] Once the investigation to determine the existence, degree and effect of any alleged subsidy is initiated, [87] the authorities concerned should check whether the amount of subsidy is *de minimis,* i.e., if the subsidy amount is less than 1 percent ad-valorem, or where for the purpose of comparison, the effect on the market is analysed by the volume of the subsidised import, but such volume is found not significant to create injury, should be considered *de minimis.*[88] There is always a possibility of consultation during the period when the investigations are on-going. After investigation,

---

VI of GATT 1994 as interpreted by this Agreement, and (c) a causal link between subsidised imports and the alleged injury.

[78]Part V of the SCM Agreement.

[79]Article 11 of the SCM Agreement.

[80]Article 12 ″.

[81]Article 13 ″.

[82]Article 14 ″.

[83]Article 15 ″.

[84]Article 17 ″.

[85]Article 18 ″.

[86]Article 19 of the SCM Agreement.

[87]Article 11.1 "Except as provided in paragraph 6, an investigation to determine the existence, degree and effect of any alleged subsidy shall be initiated upon a written application by or on behalf of the domestic industry."

[88]An application under paragraph1 shall be rejected and an investigation shall be terminated promptly as soon as the authorities concerned are satisfied that there is in sufficient evidence of either subsidization or of injury to justify proceeding with the case. There shall be immediate termination in cases where the amount of a subsidy is *de minimis*, or where the volume of subsidised imports, actual or potential, or the injury, is negligible. For the purpose of this paragraph, the amount of subsidy shall be considered to be *de minimis* if the subsidy is less than 1 percent *ad-valorem.*

the injury is determined based on the positive evidence.[89] Before the affirmative determination of injury, a provisional measure can also be applied if an investigation[90] has already started in pursuant to Article 17 of the SCM Agreement. As the test between state-aid and subsidy requires prospective and retrospective investigations based on some facts, the provisional measures can be imposed when a preliminary determination is made concerning the possibility of a subsidy and the measures are in order to restrict the injury for the remaining period of investigation. During the time of the investigation, the proceedings can be suspended or even terminated without the imposition of countervailing duties but upon the receipt of a voluntary undertaking, under which the party concerned accepts to restrain the alleged subsidies.[91] The undertakings by a party also create the possibility of constructive remedies.

7.7.1 *Imposition of Countervailing Duties*

Once the investigation authorities of the Member State find that market injury is caused because of the subsidies in question, countervailing duties are proposed. Subsequent to investigation, if, after reasonable attempts to find solutions through consultation have been exhausted, the authorities of the affected parties may impose countervailing duties in accordance with the provision.[92] Such imposed countervailing duties cannot be levied upon any imported product in excess of the amount of subsidy determined. There are limitations to the type of disputes that can be brought for the countervailing duty measures under Article 32.1 of the SCM Agreement[93] so that the Member State does not use this provision for protectionist purpose. The **Byrd amendment case**[94] is discussed in Chap. 4, i.e., on subsidies for dumping.

[89] Article 15.1 of the SCM Agreement "A determination of injury for purposes of Article VI of GATT 1994 shall be based on positive evidence and involve an objective examination of both (a) the volume of the subsidised imports and the effect of the subsidised imports on prices in the domestic market for like products and (b) the consequent impact of these imports on domestic producers of such products."

[90] Article 1.6 of the SCM Agreement allows the investigating authorities to initiate an investigation without receiving an application on behalf of the domestic industry, in circumstances in which they have sufficient evidence of the existence of a subsidy and the injury to the trade benefits because of it.

[91] Article 18 of the SCM Agreement.

[92] Article 19 of the SCM Agreement, Imposition and Collection of Countervailing Duties.

[93] No specific action against a subsidy of another Member can be taken except in accordance with the provisions of GATT 1994 as interpreted by this Agreement.

[94] WT/DS217/62.

7.8 The Puzzle of Double Remedies

The Member State claiming as affected party should seek remedies available through the provisions for remedies either by multilateral procedure of adjudication or by unilateral means, by applying for countervailing measures both in the case of prohibited or actionable subsidies. The question then arises as to whether, a party can opt for both the remedies, remedies through multilateral procedures and remedies by taking unilateral actions, simultaneously. The legal position is clear in this concern, as footnote 35 of the SCM Agreement, articulates that if the party affected is applying the provisions of Part II (that deal with Prohibited Subsidies) or Part III (Actionable Subsidies), parallel with the provisions of Part V (that covers countervailing measures), then only one form of relief can be sought. This can, either be a countervailing duty, if the requirements of Part V are met with or countermeasure under Article 4 or Article7 of the SCM Agreement.

The possibility of double remedies also arises in the case of trade relationship between subsidies and dumping practices. As discussed in the Chap. 4, that there are existing links between subsidies and dumping.[95] In the light of such links the issue, while making claims for compensation, the issue can arise, whether the claims for double remedies are justifiable, or remedies sought by applying the provisions of single instrument are sufficient and exhaustive. There is a possibility of availing the remedies for dumping separately under the agreement to restrict the dumping practices, on the other hand this also raises the concern for the remedial measures and the matters to determine compensation in lieu of the loss suffered because of subsidies as subsidies are also provided for dumping.

Remedies against the trade practices of dumping are available through Article 5, Article 7, Article 8, Article 9, and Article 17[96] of the Agreement on Implementation of Article VI of the General Agreement on Tariffs and Trade 1994" i.e., the Anti-Dumping Agreement.

A party that has suffered losses while making imports can benefit from one type of remedy either through the SCM Agreement or through the Anti-Dumping Agreement.

The opinion of the A.B and the panel body can be taken as a guiding line for an analysis, of the issue related to double remedies when the legal question involves the application of the provisions of the SCM Agreement and Anti-Dumping Measures.

In the case of **United States-Definitive Anti-Dumping and Countervailing Duties on Certain products from China,**[97] China claimed that the USDOC's, setting criteria[98] of certain procedural aspects for determining subsidies and

[95] *United States-Definitive Anti-Dumping and Countervailing Duties On Certain Products From China*, WT/DS379/AB/R.

[96] Article 5.

[97] WT/DS379/R and WT/DS379/AB/R.

[98] USDOC, United States Department of Commerce.

dumping and subsequent duty imposition on that basis, were inconsistent with the obligations under the covered WTO agreements.[99] As regards China's claim, the determination was based on four set of investigations and calculations under the US non-market economy (NME) methodology. This led to the imposition of the duty, but a failure to avoid the imposition of double remedies, as it also had offset the alleged subsidies that US has added while calculating antidumping duties.[100] China requested the establishment of a panel body to resolve this issue in the consequence of failed consultations.[101]

The legal grounds for raising the question of a double remedy were also based on the context, as mentioned in Article 19.3 and 19.4 of the SCM Agreement for the justifiable level of countervailing duties.[102]

The panel reasoned that the countervailing duties were the duties collected for the purpose of "offsetting subsidies." Therefore, countervailing duties need to be a precise amount, as the amount collected should not need exceed the amount of subsidy found to exist. The panel body in reply to China's claim concerning the overlap of duties stated, that the antidumping duties calculated under this methodology may have the effect of offsetting a subsidy in totality or in parts, however it does not extinguish the subsidies. Therefore, China's claim about the use of NME methodology leading to twice the calculation for the remedies is not relevant.[103]

Regarding the claims by China under Article 19.4 of the SCM Agreement, the panel stated that Article 19.4 imposes only discipline with respect to the levying of countervailing duties for investigations conducted in accordance with the SCM Agreement. Further, concerning the matter at issue, the panel agreed to some extent with China's point but with its reservations. The panel stated, the fact that anti-dumping duties calculated under the NME methodology may offset the subsidies granted, however, it does not change the characteristics of duties as, basically as anti-dumping,[104] therefore does not provide the legal basis for making claims about the double remedies being imposed. With respect to this point, the Panel body cited

[99]WT/DS379/R, para 2.1.

[100]See WT/DS379/R, para 2.1.

[101]See WT/DS379/R, para 1, The consultations concerned definitive anti-dumping and countervailing duties imposed by the United States on imports of four products from China (circular welded carbon quality steel pipe, pneumatic of-the-road tires, light walled rectangular pipe and tube, laminated woven sacks. China and the United States held consultations on 14th November 2008. These consultations failed to resolve the dispute. The definitive anti-dumping and countervailing duties were imposed by the United States on four products (1) Circular Welded Carbon quality Steel pipe (CWP) (2) Certain New Pneumatic off-the Road Tires (OTR) (3) Light-Walled Rectangular Pipe and Tube (LWR) (4) Laminated Woven Sacks (LWS).

[102]Article 19.3 "When a countervailing duty is imposed in respect of any product, such a countervailing duty shall be levied, on the appropriate amounts in each case, on a non-discriminatory basis on imports of such product from all sources found to be subsidized and causing injury, except as to imports from those sources which have renounced any subsidies in question or from which undertakings under the terms of this Agreement has been accepted."

[103]See para 14.113 WT/DS379/R.

[104]See para 14.114.

the reference of Article VI:5 in comparison to Article VI:3 of the GATT 1994 and referred to the fact that Article VI:5 is limited to export subsidies and does not cover the situations where domestic subsidies are granted on goods for export.[105] Additionally, the panel body considered that the purpose of Article 19.4 is not concerned with the issue of double remedies but is rather confined to the levying of countervailing duties not in excess of the subsidies.[106]

The decision of the panel on double remedies, and interpretation of relevant provisions was appealed by China before the A.B.[107] After the hearing, the A.B disagreeing with the panel's interpretation stated, that double remedies may arise when both countervailing duties and anti-dumping duties are imposed on the same imported product. In order to make a comparative analysis before reaching a conclusion, the A.B also related the term double remedies to double counting, referring to the simultaneous application of antidumping and countervailing duties on the same imported product.[108] Based on the relationship between these two instruments, and the provisions established on that basis, the A.B further discussed in detail the relationship between dumping margin and domestic subsidies in the case of NM economies and the subsequent imposition of countervailing duties. For a product from an NM economy, the investigating agency calculates the dumping margin in an anti-dumping investigation by comparing the export price to the normal price based on surrogate costs from a third country. The reason for taking a third country price is that prices in the case of an NME calculation reflects not only price discrimination but also economic distortions that affects the producers cost of production. Considering the overall economic affects, as a consequence of such state support, the A.B clarified that these economic distortions are linked with the specific forms of subsidies.[109] Therefore, the antidumping duties may also offset the domestic subsidies to the extent, that it lowered the price for exports.[110] If the countervailing duties are additionally imposed on the same imports, the same domestic support is counted for a second time. In this regard the A.B followed the approach that concurrent imposition of anti-dumping and countervailing duties based on NME methodology may result in offsetting the subsidies twice, therefore leading to double remedies.[111]

The main point of interpretation before the A.B was the extent of "the appropriate amount and moreover, whether it would be appropriate to levy countervailing duties concurrent to the imposition of the anti-dumping duties," or whether they are

---

[105] See para 14.117.

[106] See para 14.119.

[107] See para1 and para7 of WT/DS379/AB/R.

[108] See para 541 WT/DS379/AB/R.

[109] See 542, 543 WT/DS379/AB/R.

[110] See para 543 WT/DS 379/AB/R.

[111] See para 543 WT/DS 379/AB/R.

likely to result in the imposition of double remedies.[112] The A.B referring to Article VI.5[113] of the GATT stated that Article VI.5 prohibits the concurrent application of anti-dumping and countervailing duties to compensate for the same situation of dumping or export subsidisation. The A.B further added to its interpretation that in the situation where subsidisation and dumping are coincidental, the application of the concurrent duties would amount to the application of double remedies to compensate for or offset the situation covering dumping due to subsidies.[114] Therefore, the A.B reversed the panel's interpretation of Article 19.3 and its findings that the imposition of anti-dumping duties calculated under N.M.E methodology had no gross impact on the amount of the countervailing duty collected concurrently. To make it clear, whether such imposition is justified or not, the A.B explicitly stated that "it finds instead the imposition of double remedies that is the offsetting of the same subsidization twice."[115]

The issue it seems was decided by the A.B keeping in view the basic aims and objectives of the SCM Agreements and the Agreement to check dumping practices. The restriction on subsidies and dumping practices is basically a trade regulatory measure. While making an interpretation of the dumping margin in this case, the A. B also considered subsidies that were in the form of domestic subsidies in the case of NME and the link established with the dumping margin. Rather than going for a theoretical interpretation, the practical and economic affect of the remedies was used, as the basis for the approach which was adopted by the A.B to determine the outcome of the subsidies and the extent of the regulation required in that respect.

[112]WT/DS379/AB/R, para 540 of the A.B report. China appeals this findings and requests us to (1) find that the Panel erred in its interpretation and application of Article 10, 19.3 ,19.4 and 32.1 of the SCM Agreement and Article VI:3 of the GATT 1994 (2) reverses the Panel's finding that China did not establish that the United States had acted inconsistently with its obligations under these provisions by imposing anti-dumping duties calculated under its NME methodology concurrently with the imposition of countervailing duties on the same products, without taking steps to avoid offsetting the same subsidies twice; and (3) complete the analysis and conclude that USDOC acted inconsistently with the obligations of the United States under Article 10, 19.3, 19.4 and 32.1 of the SCM Agreement and Article VI:3 of the GATT 1994, in all of the investigations at issue, by failing to take steps to avoid offsetting the same subsidies twice.

[113]Article VI.5 of the GATT "No product of the territory of any contracting party imported into the territory of any contracting party shall be subject to both anti-dumping and countervailing duties to compensate for the same situation of dumping or export subsidization."

[114]See AB report, para 568.

[115]See WT/DS379/AB/R, para 583.

7.9 Arbitration

Arbitration is an acknowledged method to resolve disputes in the WTO system.[116] It is an alternative approach followed for dispute settlement rather than going through panel and the Appellate Body. Resorting to this method is possible on the basis of the mutual consent of the parties. The general outline for arbitration, as a mode to resolve dispute is referred under Article 25 of the DSU.

In case if the issues are related to compliance within the time frame and the party has not acted upon or fulfilled its obligations within the timeframe prescribed by the DSB, arbitration is possible under Article 21.3(c).[117] Furthermore, arbitration as a means to resolve any issue is also used, if it a matter of providing compensation or suspension of compensation or if recommendations are not implemented within reasonable time.[118]

7.10 Conclusions

The rationality behind the functioning of DSB is to decide disputes related to trade matters between the Member States. Meaning that the losing parties will bring the challenged measures in conformity with the WTO provisions. In the cases brought before, where the losing party is a Less-Developed country and is supposed to alter its measures and pay the penalty, the situation can be difficult and may in fact be contrary to the WTO objectives. Provisions in support of the Less-Developed countries are fragile in such circumstances.

The DSB is meant to resolve the disputes, however in some of the cases has been used as a Chess Board by the parties. It seems the intention between the two sides was to snub each other rather than pursuing them on the grounds of legal merits. Such was the case with the Airbus dispute, India's balance of payments case, the EC-Bed linen case, and there can be some other such examples. It is unfair that DSB

---

[116]Article 25 of the DSU covers the procedure concerning the Arbitration. Article 25 cl (1) Expeditious arbitration within the WTO as an alternative means of dispute settlement can facilitate the solution of certain disputes that concern issues that are clearly defined by both parties.

[117]*European Communities-Regime for the Importation,* WT/DS27/15, the European Communities requested for the consultations with the complaining parties in this case Ecuador, Guatemala, Honduras, Mexico and the United States. As both sides could not reach agreement, the complaining parties requested on 17th November 1997, for arbitration in order to resolve the matter that is implementation of the DSB decision within the reasonable time set. (See Introduction WT/DS27/15). The Arbitrator was appointed to find the solution. The complaining party stated before the arbitrator that to discover whether the EC intended to implement the recommendations of the DSB within the reasonable time period. Finally, the arbitrator in the context of Article 21.3(c) suggested a reasonable period time for the EC to implement the recommendations and rulings of the DSB. The time period assigned was from 25th September 1997 to 1st January 1999.

[118]Article 22.6, Article 22.7 of the DSU.

is used for applying measures to circumvent the procedures, rather than for promoting free trade.

Another legal question the DSB has to deals with is the rights of the third party. As far as the presence of third parties is concerned, there is no clear-cut established position of the rights of the third party, although they are often indirectly affected. By including their rights through provisions, more transparency and integrity will be brought within the system. Despite some short comings, the positive aspect of the DSB is that Member States, by and large, trust the WTO system, and in case of any dispute try to find solutions through the codified Dispute Settlement Procedures. It is an achievement that Member States, despite largescale political, social and economic differences, do manage to overcome them and accept a single procedural system to resolve the matters.

References

Bossche P (2008) The law and policy of the World Trade Organization. Cambridge University Press, Cambridge

Hodu YN (2006) The WTO dispute settlement system and the issue of compliance. Faculty of Law, University of Helsinki, Helsinki

Kazeri J (2009) Permanent group of experts under the SCM agreement. J World Trade 43 (5):1031–1045

Macrory P, Appleton AE, Plummer MG (eds) (2005) The World Trade Organization, legal, economic and political analysis, vol I. Springer, New York

Mitchell AD (2005) Challenges and prospects for the WTO. Cameron May Ltd, UK

Wolfrum R, Koebele M, Tobias P (2008) WTO trade remedies. Martinus Nijhoff Publishers, Leiden

Cases

Canada-Measures Affecting the Export of Civilian Aircraft WT/DS70/R

European Communities Anti-Dumping Duties on Imports of Cotton Type-Bed Linen from India WT/DS141/R

European Communities Anti-Dumping Duties on Imports of Cotton Type-Bed Linen from India WT/DS141/R (chk)

European Communities-Regime for the Importation WT/DS27/15

Japan-Taxes on Alcoholic Beverages WT/DS8/AB/R

Japan-Taxes on Alcoholic Beverages WT/DS11/R

Mexico-Provisional Countervailing Measures on Olive Oil from the European Communities DS314

United States-Continued Dumping and Offset Act of 2000 WT/DS217/AB/R

United States-Definitive Anti-Dumping and Countervailing Duties On Certain Products from China WT/DS379/AB/R

United States-Safeguard Measures on Imports of Fresh Chilled or Frozen Lamb Meat from New Zealand and Australia WT/DS178/AB/R

United States-Safeguard Measures on Imports of Fresh Chilled or Frozen Lamb Meat from New Zealand and Australia WT/DS178/AB/R

Reports and Electronic Sources

Read R (2005) Trade dispute settlement mechanisms: the WTO dispute settlement understanding in the wake of the GATT. Lancaster University Management School. http://www.lums.lancs.ac.uk/publications

UNECLAC Economic Commission for Latin American Countries. http://wto.org/english/tratop_e/dispu_te.htm#intro

Chapter 8
Conclusions and Suggestions

The conclusions on the use of subsidies are based on discussions that start from an abstract level. Further, within the discussion, giving general explanations in terms of values to be followed while adopting the free trade market approach, both with regard to the industrial and agricultural sector, and in order to meet the objectives broadly considered as opportunities for development and welfare are advocated.

As the principal objective of the WTO is to promote free trade market system among its Member States, covering both the industrial and agricultural sectors of the economy, undoubtedly, along with the other agreements, the SCM Agreement is an endeavour to establish a delicate balance between a free trade system and fair-trade values. Taking into account the wide range of economic diversity among the Member States, as also considered in this study, and various other determining factors, discussed within the chapters, it can be reasoned that subsidies either for industrial or agricultural purposes are not justifiable except in the case of some classifications and exceptions.

However, within the WTO, 'what really is a subsidy' does not start from the abstract level; nevertheless, in order to determine whether state support is a subsidy, the elements such as financial contribution and benefit are included as basic features and this indeed is an improvement to the GATT system. In addition to the acceptable use of subsidies for welfare and development, the justifiable and non-justifiable use varies, as it is a matter of free market compulsion, varying somewhat among the Member States. While analysing the use of subsidies based on country classifications, through the parameters determining prohibited or actionable subsidies, the necessity based criteria and the clear outlining of its use for welfare and development approach seems missing in the SCM Agreement.

After making a comparative analysis in this study, it is suggested that the EU's expression concerning state-support can be an option here. Within the EU system, state support at the initial level is seen as state-aid but if contested from the common market perspective, the effects can be compared with competition policy, which practically, seems a more comparative method of assessment.

G. Singh, *Subsidies in the Context of the WTO's Free Trade System*,
DOI 10.1007/978-3-319-62422-8_8

That business practices among the Member States need to be regulated by a certain accepted set of values, was a debate entered into before the formation of the WTO, when theories on laissez faire were propounded. Probably, in the light of that debate, some of the agreements within the WTO system acted as instruments to sustain the level of fairness, once the promotion of trade-liberalisation policies had began. Remarkably, the promoters of the free trade market concept were leaders and intellectuals from industrially and technologically-advanced countries. It is probable that, they thought the theory of free trade could work as a means of deliverance for the freedom of choice, which according to them was fundamental for the disposition of liberty.

The legal perspective in this work takes the line that concepts of free trade in the Developed countries are linked with the ideas of liberty and their judicial system is safeguarding that Liberty. Testing the WTO system of free trade, from this constitutional context, it seems that the individual perspective of rights and the normative safeguards for those rights under the WTO, lacks a strong legal basis, even at the remedial stages. The present framework of the WTO seems to be based on some selected principles and objectives, and only after practical experience is it possible to know the value of these principles and objectives. Based on this position, the conclusion of this study, in the light of the WTO objectives, also raises the issue that which stratum of the population of the Developing countries and the Less-Developed countries, are reaping the benefits of free trade, and which stratum of the population in these countries are losing their basic rights otherwise prescribed in their constitutions needs to be taken seriously. This matter was also discussed in the chapter on the impact of trade subsidies on the environment and the chapter on agricultural subsidies.

Furthermore, as regards the basic elements adopted by the SCM Agreement to determine subsidies, the key elements considered to determine the effects of subsidies are, financial contribution and benefits, as stated previously; How far they succeed to cover state support of various characteristics within the ambit of subsidies is a debatable issue. Based on the intended purpose of the SCM Agreement, the affects highlighted for the purpose of drawing conclusions are:

1. The subsidies to promote technology (as in the Airbus/Boeing case) and the subsequent use of that technology for industrial purposes affecting fair competition in the market. In fact, there is no general agreement on competition policy among the Member States; therefore, there is rarely any possibility to apply such provisions to raise questions about how to regulate such types of subsidies. The suggestion in this regard is to include competition-policy objectives, in the WTO system, that can allow state support, but, if it affects fair competition in the market, it should be considered as unjustifiable.
2. The emphasis of the SCM Agreement is to reduce trade protectionism and market distortion. The question then arises of, how far the level of environmental standards can be retained by giving restrictive amount of state support in order to safeguard the environment. This is a matter of a dilemma between free trade and fair trade objectives and conversely, it should also be realised that subsidies for

the promotion of free trade do have a negative impact on the environment. Covering new issues showing the effect on environment because of unregulated trade practices, there are examples explaining the effect of subsidies both on fisheries and, the use of subsidies for the plantation of biofuels, are also discussed in the chapters. Therefore, after making the study it is concluded, that in the lack of provisions classifying non-actionable subsidies, or any state support for environment purposes, the DSB has attempted to cover the grey area, such as in the case of Canada-Certain Measure Affecting the Renewable Energy, by striking a balance between free trade objectives in the market and fair-trade goals. Due to the lack of specific agreements on the environment, the DSB is playing a responsive role in resolving trade related ambiguities and, moreover, maintaining opportunities for trade while restricting such opportunities if they degrade the environment beyond the level of sustainability.

3. The question of agricultural subsidies is linked to the general definition of trade-subsidy, common to both agricultural and industrial purposes. It is worth noticing that the objectives of providing agriculture subsidies by the Developed countries and the Developing/Less-Developed countries are different and classifying these in general terms as export subsidies or domestic support measures may create confusion and prevent reaching any long term solution. Despite the classification of Member States and the justification of subsidies on the grounds different from the Developed countries, the subject of subsidies for export tends to become overlapped, so export subsidies in the matters of agriculture need to be relatively tested based on the objectives of the Member State.

Related to this is the unresolved issue of agricultural subsidies between the Developed and the Developing/Less-Developed countries. Despite several efforts to resolve the question of subsidies given for agricultural purposes either directly or indirectly, this still remains one of the crucial topics for discussions. Moreover, within the WTO, the key issue that revolves constantly during agricultural trade discussions is the export subsidies and high tariffs of the industrialized nations, such as the EU/EC, which undermine the Developing countries and Less-Developed countries' efforts to build up their economies through free trade.

Agricultural products are modeled as part of the free trading system, mainly by reducing restrictions on trade in (1) agricultural products (2) reducing the domestic support, mainly in the form of agricultural subsidies. In order to enable the consistent working of free trade, it is suggested here that there is a further requirement for changes at the policy level by the Developed, Developing and Less-Developed countries in order to promote free trade in agricultural products. However this, may unfortunately not be possible at the present stage because of rigidity and market compulsion.

While testing the effects of subsidies in various market sectors and at different level of production, also requires seeing things from various practical perspectives and distinguishing the area of study. Concerning such development, subsidies for biofuels has been referred to as an example in this study. Biofuels are nowadays a growing necessity and a prospective commodity for large scale trade, however, their cropping has once again raised debate both from environmental and agricultural perspectives. This has created division among the Member States. Nowadays, with the rise in market demand for biofuels, the planting of biofuel crops has caused a reduction in cereal crops production. A comparative analysis in the study reveals that promotion of biofuel plantation in the Developing and Less-Developed countries is creating new types of challenges, such as a rise in food prices, in the Less-Developed countries, which is discussed in detail in the chapter on agricultural subsidies. With the lack of domestic support policies to stabilize prices, there has also been a rise in prices of the crops. Consequently, this has led to incidences of food riots in Senegal, which requires a critical evaluation of the free trade policies. After such an evaluation, the conclusion reached is that these problems do not receive due acknowledgement when applying the provisions of the SCM Agreement in the present frame work.

Comparing the subsidies for biofuels among the Member States and their effects both from the economic and legal perspective, it may not be incorrect to assume that unregulated biofuel production can have implications beyond the balancing capacity of the WTO, under the present working position.

Furthermore, after examining several economic factors, it can be suggested that claims made by the Member States do not seem to be based on a consideration of all the relevant factors. For the sake of meeting the objectives of the WTO, it is suggested from both the economic and legal perspective, that standards for the categorisation of Developing countries and the permissible use of subsidies require periodic evaluation. It is noticeable that, some of the Developing countries are taking advantage of the situation of the Less-Developed countries. These Developing countries provide subsidies to promote their own industry and later export their products to the Less-Developed countries, and these products have an effect on the indigenous cottage industries of the Less-Developed countries. The China-Africa trade relationship is an example for this. Exports from African countries to China are mainly raw materials, petroleum, and timber, while China exports finished products ranging from machinery, textiles and consumer electronics.

While studying the effect of subsidies on the natural equilibrium of demand and supply in the market, the effect of subsidies is also analysed from the macro-economic perspective mainly by scrutinising the impact of artificial currency rates, the example was taken of the Chinese currency, as quoted in the market at lower rate to increase exports. The present SCM Agreement lacks the provisions to check such superficial policy-measures by governments. Hence, bearing in mind the effects from a broader perspective, it is suggested that the addition of provisions within the SCM Agreement to check such types of government measures in a qualified manner will enable fairness in trade practices.

Although for the promotion of free trade by the WTO, Member States have started reducing the level of restrictions both in the agricultural and in industrial sectors, this has undoubtedly increased the choice of products and also the availability of products at a reasonable price. Nevertheless, the international companies apply strategic business tactics of predatory pricing in order to capture the market of other countries. The reasons for such practices are, the absence of a general competition policy criteria for Member States within the WTO trading system. There are no provisions to check many forms of indirect subsidies, as referred to in the case of China. The inclusion of competition-policy measures can also help the efficient allocation of resources.

Free trade is linked with scientific progress and the use of technology. The scientific and technical research, which in the future has a high prospect of being traded on a broader level, cannot have an independent existence, devoid of legal parameters. The insights of the WTO's determination of subsidies in the form of the use of technology were revealed in the Airbus case. Subsidies for research in the case of the Airbus-Boeing dispute have been discussed in detail. The suggestion concluded from this dispute is that there is a need for wider parameters to judge the impact of such subsidies.

From the previously mentioned facts, it can be further stated that evolving a standard of fairness is a gradual process, as consumers are often unable to obtain correct information. The trading under the free trade system is based on the relative advantages and disadvantages of the Member States. Moreover, studies from the economic perspective reveals that the diversity within the Developing countries and Less-Developed countries is wide, often traditional and difficult to define on the basis of specific concepts.

However, one cannot deny that permissible limits of subsidies play a significant role in the economic development of the Developing and Less-Developed countries. In order to meet the objectives of the WTO it is also necessary to keep in mind the social and political realities of the respective group of countries. The basic factors for the fair-trade policies need to be effective and prudent, and although this is easy to state, in practice the reality is very far different.

The harmonization of market and trading principles are still far from a practical achievement, because this may require changes in the entire business-law system. Therefore, general policies on subsidies may not be suitable in every case. Basically, it is in the consumer's interest to have a fair-trading system. The formation of the WTO after GATT has raised many expectations and the WTO has proved itself by performing better than GATT, which is apparent as the membership of this organisation is growing. The transformation from GATT to the WTO was made for various reasons, not just for the purpose of trade, but also in order to achieve several development objectives by decreasing the barriers on trade; however, achieving all the goals may not be feasible in the short term. Briefly, it is suggested here that to understand trade subsidies and their effects as regards the Developed, Developing and Less-Developed countries, a broader legal plane covering the effects of subsidies in the areas such as Industrial, Agricultural, Environmental and Social can be highly supportive for a comparative understanding of the WTO's aims and objectives.

Finally, it can be said that the subsidy issue falls within justifiable and non-justifiable limits. On the basis of the trading pattern established among the Member States, and the role the SCM Agreement plays as a subsidies regulatory instrument, it can be said that market practices driven by fair-trade values have started progressing towards the WTO objectives even with the reasonable number of shortcomings.

List of Cited Cases

WTO Appellate Body Decisions

Argentina: Measures Affecting Imports of Footwear, Textiles, Apparel and other Items.

WT/DS56/AB/R, Complainant:United States, Respondent:Argentina, the DSB adopted the report on 22 April 1998. Implementation of the report, 30 May 1999.

Brazil-Export Financing Programme for Aircraft.

WT/DS46/AB/R, Complainant:Canada, Respondent:Brazil, the DSB adopted the report on 4 August 2000. On 12 December 2000, Brazil informed the DSB of the compliance. However, Canada remaining unsatisfied initiated compliance proceedings on 22 January 2001.

Brazil-Measures Affecting Desiccated Coconut.

WT/DS22/AB/R, Complainant:Philippines, Respondent:Brazil, the DSB adopted the report on 20 March 1997.

Canada-Certain Measures Affecting the Automotive Industry.

WT/DS139/AB/R, Complainant:Japan, Respondent: Canada, the DSB adopted the report on 19 June 2000. Implementation of the report, 19 July 2000.

Canada-Certain Measures Affecting the Automative Industry.

WT/DS142/AB/R, Complainant:European Communities, Respondent:Canada, the DSB adopted the report on 19 June 2000. Implementtion of the report, 19 July 2000.

Canada-Measures Affecting the Export of Civilian Aircraft.

WT/DS70/AB/R, Complainant:Brazil, Respondent:Canada, the DSB adopted the report on 4 August 2000. Implementation thereafter as stated.

China-Measures Affecting Imports of Automobile Parts.

WT/DS340/AB/R, Complainant:United States, Respondent:China, the DSB adopted the report on 12 January 2009. Implementation of the report, 1 September 2009.

G. Singh, *Subsidies in the Context of the WTO's Free Trade System*,
DOI 10.1007/978-3-319-62422-8

China-Measures Affecting Imports of Automobile Parts.

WT/DS339/AB/R, Complainant:European Communities, Respondent:China, the DSB adopted the report on 12 January 2009. Implementation of the report, 1 September 2009.

China-Measures Affecting Imports of Automobile Parts.

WT/DS342/AB/R, Complainant:Canada, Respondent:China, the DSB adopted the report on 12 January 2009. Implementation of the report, 1 September 2009.

Canada-Measure Affecting the Importation of Milk and the Exportation of Dairy Products.

WT/DS103/AB/RWT2, WT/DS113/AB/RW2, Complainant: United States, Respondent:Canada, the DSB adopted the report on 17 January 2003. Mutually agreed solution 9 May 2003.

Canada-Measure Affecting Imports of Fresh Chilled and Frozen Beef.

WT/DS103/AB/R, Complainant:United States, Respondent:Canada, the DSB adopted the report on 27 October 1999. On 9 May 2003, Canada and the United States informed the DSB that they had reached a mutually agreed solution.

Canada-Measures Relating to the Export of Wheat and treatment of Imported grains.

WT/DS276/AB/R, Complainant:United States, Respondent:Canada, the DSB adopted the report on 27 Sep 2004. Implementation of the report, 1 August 2005.

Canada-Measures Relating to the Feed- in Tariff Program.

WT/DS412/AB/R, WT/DS426/AB/R, Complainant: European Union, Respondent:Canada, the DSB adopted the report on 24 May 2013. Implementation of the report on 5 June 2014.

Chile — Price Band System and Safeguard Measures Relating to Certain Agricultural Products.

WT/DS207/AB/R, Complainant: European Union, Respondent:Canada, the DSB adopted the Appellate Body report and the panel report, as upheld by the Appellate Body on 22 May 2007.

European Communities-Conditions for Granting of Tariff Preferences to Developing Countries. WT/DS246/AB/R, Complainant: India, Respondent: European Communities, the DSB adopted the report on 20 April 2004. Implementation of report by 1 July 2005.

European Communities-Export Subsidies for Sugar.

WT/DS265/AB/R, Complainant:Australia, Respondent:European Communities, the DSB adopted the report on 19 May 2005. Implementation of the report, 8 June 2006.

European Communities-Measures Affecting Trade in Large Civil Aircraft.

WT/DS316/AB/R, Complainant:United States, Respondent:European Communities; France; Germany; Spain; United Kingdom, the DSB adopted the report on 1 June 2011. On 17 June 2011, the European Union expressed its intention to implement the report. However, on 30 March 2012, the United States requested the establishment of the compliance panel.

European Communities-Trade Description of Sardines.

WT/DS231/AB/R, Complainant:Peru, Respondent:European Communities, the DSB adopted the report on 23 October 2002. Implementation of the report, 25 July 2003.

India's Quantitative Restrictions on the Imports of Agricultural, Textile and Industrial Products.

WT/DS90/AB/R, Complainant:United States, Respondent:India, the DSB adopted the report on 22 September. Implementation of the report, 1 April 2001.

Japan Taxes on Alcoholic Beverages.

WT/DS8/AB/R, WT/DS10/AB/R and WT/DS11/AB/R, Complainant:United States, Respondent: Japan, the DSB adopted the report on 1 November 1996. Matter went for binding arbitration before implementation. Implementation expected by 1 February 1998.

Korea-Measures Affecting Imports of Fresh Chilled and Frozen Beef.

WT/DS161/AB/R, Complainant:United States, Respondent: Republic of Korea, the DSB adopted the report on 10 January 2001. Implementation of the report, 2 February 2001.

United States-Countervailing Duty Investigation on Dynamic Random Access Memory Semiconductors (DRAMS) from Korea.

WT/DS296/AB/R, Complainant: Korea, Republic of, Respondent: United States, the DSB adopted the report on, 20 July 2005. Implementation of the report, 7 November 2005.

The United States-Rules of Origin for Textiles and Apparel Products.

WT/DS/339/AB/R, Complainant:European Communities, Respondent:China, the DSB adopted the report on 12 January, 2009. Implementation of the report, 27 February 2009.

United States- Measures Affecting Trade in Large Civil Aircraft–Second Complaint.

WT/DS353/AB/R, Complainant: European Communities, Respondent: United States, the DSB adopted the report on 23 March 2012. On 23 September, US notified the withdrawal of subsidies. However, on 11 October, 2012, the European Union requested the establishment of the compliance panel.

United States Import Prohibition of Certain Shrimp and Shrimp Products.

WT/DS58/AB/R, Complainant:India, Malaysia, Pakistan, Thailand.Respondent: United States, the DSB adopted the report on 6 November 1998. Implementation expected by, 6 December 1999 (reported about implementation, 21 Nov 2001).

United States-Continued Dumping and Offset Act of 2000.

WT/DS234/AB/R, Complainant:Canada; Mexico, Respondent:United States, the DSB adopted the report on 27 January 2003. For implementation, on 26 January, 2004, the DSB decided to refer the matter for arbitration.

United States-Continued Dumping and Subsidies and Offset Act of 2000.

WT/DS217/AB/R, Complainant:Australia, Brazil, Chile; European Communities; India; Indonesia; Japan; Korea, Republic of; Thailand, Respondent:United States, the DSB adopted the report on 27 January 2003. Implementation of the report, 1 February 2006.

United States-Countervailing Measures Concerning Certain Products from the European Communities.

WT/DS212/AB/R, Complainant:European Communities, Respondent:United States, the DSB adopted the report on 8 January 2003. Implementation of the report agreed between the parties, 8 Jan 2003 to 8 Nov 2003.

United States-Definitive Anti-Dumping and Countervailing Duties on Certain Products from China.

WT/DS379/AB/R, Complainant:China, Respondent:United States, the DSB adopted the report on 25 March 2011. Implementation of the report, 11 May 2012.

United States-Final Countervailing Duty Determination with Respect to Certain Softwood Lumber from Canada.

WT/DS257/AB/R, Complainant:Canada, Respondent:United States, the DSB adopted the report on 20 December 2005. Implementation of the report, 12 October 2006.

United States-Imposition of Countervailing Duties on Certain Hot-Rolled Lead and Bismuth Carbon Steel Products Originating in the United Kingdom.

WT/DS138/AB/R, Complainant: European Communities, Respondent:United States, the DSB adopted the report on 7 June 2000. Implementation of the report, 5 July 2000.

United States-Safeguard Measures on Imports of Fresh Chilled or Frozen Lamb Meat from New Zealand and Australia.

WT/DS178/AB/R, Complainant:Australia, Respondent:United States, the DSB adopted the report on 16 May 2001. Implementation of the report, 15 Nov 2001.

United States-Standards for Reformulated and Conventional Gasoline.

WT/DS2/AB/R, Complainant:Venezuela, Republic of Bolivarian, Respondent: United States, the DSB adopted the report on 20 May 1996. Implementation of the report, 19 August 1997.

United States-Subsidies on Upland Cotton.

WT/DS267/AB/R, Complainant:Brazil, Respondent:United States, the DSB adopted the report on 20 June 2008. Implementation of the report, 30 September 2012.

United States-Tax Treatment for Foreign Sales Corporation.

WT/DS108/AB/RW, Complainant:European Communities, Respondent:United States, the DSB adopted the report on 14 March 2006. Implementation of the report, 11 May 2006.

WTO Panel Decisions

Brazil-Measures Affecting Desiccated Coconut.

WT/DS22/R, Complainant:Philippines, Respondent:Brazil. The Panel report was circulated on 17 October 1996.

Brazil-Export Financing Programme for Aircraft.

WT/DS46/R, Complainant:Canada, Respondent:Brazil. The Panel report was circulated on 14 April 1999.

China-Countervailing and Anti-Dumping Duties on Grain Oriented Flat-rolled Electrical Steel from the United States.

WT/DS414/R, Complainant:United States, Respondent:China. The Panel report was circulated on 15 June 2012.

Canada-Certain Measures Affecting the Automotive Industry.

WT/DS139/R, Complainant:Japan, Respondent:Canada. The Panel report was circulated on 1 February 1999.

Canada-Measures Affecting the Export of Civilian Aircraft.

WT/DS70/R, Complainant:Brazil, Respondent:Canada. The Panel report was circulated on 14 April 1999.

Canada — Certain Measures Affecting the Renewable Energy Generation Sector.

WT/DS412/R, Complainant: Japan, Respondent: Canada. The Panel report was circulated on 19 December 2012.

China-Measures Affecting Imports of Automobile Parts.

WT/DS339/R, Complainant:European Communities, Respondent:China. The Panel report was circulated on 18 July 2008.

China-Measures Affecting Imports of Automobile Parts.

WT/DS340/R, Complainant:United States, Respondent:China. The Panel circulated the report on 18 July 2008.

China-Measures Affecting Imports of Automobile Parts.

WT/DS342/R, Complainant:Canada, Respondent:China. The Panel circulated the report on 18 July 2008.

Canada-Measures Affecting the Importation of Milk and the Exportation of Dairy Products

WT/DS103/R, Complainant:United States, Respondent:Canada. The Panel report was circulated on 17 May 1999.

European Communities Anti-dumping Duties on Imports of Cotton Type-Bed Linen from India. WT/DS141/R, Complainant:India, Respondent:European Communities. The panel report was circulated on 30 October 2000.

European Communities-Export Subsidies on Sugar.

WT/DS265/R, Complainant:Australia, Respondent:European Communities. The Panel circulated its report on 15 October 2004.

European Communities-Measures Affecting Trade in Large Civil Aircraft.

WT/DS316/R, Complainant:United States, Respondent:European Communities; France; Germany; Spain; United Kingdom. The Panel report was circulated on 30 June 2010.

European Communities-Regime for the Importation, Sale and Distribution of Bananas,

WT/DS27/15, Complainant:Ecuador;Guatemala;Honduras; Mexico;UnitedStates, Respondent:European Communities. Case for Arbitration.

European Communities—Trade Description of Sardines.

WT/DS231/R, Complainant:Peru, Respondent:European Communities. The Panel report was circulated on 29 May 2002.

India-Quantitative Restrictions on Imports of Agricultural, Textile and Industrial Products.

WT/DS90/R, Complainant: United States, Respondent: India.

The Panel report was circulated on 6 April 1999.

Japan-Taxes on Alcoholic Beverages.

WT/DS8/R, Complainant:European Communities, Respondent:Japan. The Panel report was circulated on 11 July 1996.

Japan-Taxes on Alcoholic Beverages.

WT/DS11/R, Complainant: United States, Respondent:Japan. The Panel report was circulated on 11 July 1996.

Korea-Measures Affecting Imports of Fresh, Chilled and Frozen Beef.

WT/DS161/R, Complainant:United States, Respondent: Republic of Korea. The Panel report was circulated on 31 July 2000.

Korea-Measures Affecting Trade in Commercial Vessels.

WT/DS273/R, Complainant:European Communities, Respondent: Republic of Korea. The Panel report was circulated on 7 March 2005. The DSB adopted the Panel report on 11 April 2005.

Mexico-Definitive Countervailing Measures on Olive Oil from the European Communities.

WT/DS341/R, Complainant:European Communities, Respondent:Mexico. The Panel report was circulated on 4 September 2008.

Mexico-Provisional Countervailing Measures on Olive Oil from the European Communities.

WT/DS314/1, Complainant:European Communities, Respondent:Mexico. Case for Arbitration.

United States-Anti-Dumping and Countervailing Measures on Steel Plate from India.

WT/DS206/R, Complainant:India, Respondent:United States. The Panel report was circulated on 28 June 2002.

United States-Continued Dumping and Subsidy Offset Act of 2000.

WT/DS217/R, Complainant:Australia; Brazil; Chile; European Communities; India; Indonesia; Japan; Korea, Republic of Thailand, Respondent:United States. The Panel report was circulated on 16 September 2002.

United States-Continued Dumping and Subsidy Offset Act of 2000.

WT/DS234/R, Complainant:Canada; Mexico, Respondent:United States. The Panel report was circulated on 16 September 2002.

United States-Definitive Anti-Dumping and Countervailing Duties on Certain Products from China. WT/DS379/R, Complainant:China, Respondent: United States. The panel report was circulated on 22 October 2010.

United States-Final Countervailing Duty Determination with respect to certain Softwood Lumber from Canada.

WT/DS257/R, Complainant:Canada, Respondent:United States. The Panel report was circulated on 29 August 2003.

United States-Import Prohibition of Certain Shrimp and Shrimp Products.
WT/DS58/R, Complainant:India; Malaysia; Pakistan; Thailand, Respondent: United States. The Panel report was circulated on 15 May 1998.
United States-Measures Affecting Trade in Large Civil Aircraft — Second Complaint.
WT/DS353/R, Complainant:European Communities, Respondent:United States. The Panel report was circulated on 31 March 2011.
United States-Measures Treating Export Restraints as Subsidies.
WT/DS/194/R, Complainant:Canada, Respondent:United States. The Panel report was circulated on 29 June 2001.
United States-Rules of Origin for Textiles and Apparel Products.
WT/DS243/R, Complainant:India, Respondent:United States. The Panel report was circulated on 20 June 2003.
United States-Standards for Reformulated and Conventional Gasoline.
WT/DS2/R, Complainant:Venezuela, Republic of Bolivarian, Respondent: United States. The Panel report was circulated on 29 January 1996.
United States-Subsidies on Upland Cotton.
WT/DS267/R, Complainant: Brazil, Respondent: United States. The report of the Panel was circulated on 8 September 2004.
United States Tax Treatment for Foreign Sales Corporation.
WT/DS108/R, Complainant:European Communities, Respondent:United States. The Panel report was circulated on 8 October 1999.

GATT Panel Decisions

United States-Imposition Of Countervailing Duties On Certain Hot-Rolled Lead And Bismuth Carbon Steel Products Originating In France Germany And The United Kingdom.
SCM/185, Complainant:European Communities, Respondent:United States. Circulation of the GATT Panel report 15 November 1994.

EU/EC Cases Cited

AKZO Chemie BV v Commission of the European Communities, CaseC-62/86
Banks v British Coal and Secretary of State, (European Coal and Steel Community (ECSC) Treaty case), Case C-390/98
Belgium v Commission, Case C-234/84
European Commission v EDF (Électricité de France), Case C-124/10
Fediol v Commission, Case C-188/85

Fédération National du Commerce Extérier des Produits Alimentaires and Syndicat National des Négociants et Trsnsformateurs de Saumon vFrench Republic, Case C-354/90

Hoesch Metals and Alloys GmbH v Hauptzollamt Aachen, Case C-378/08

Italy v Commission, Case C-6/97

Preussen Elektra v Schleswig, Case C-379/98

Tetra Pak International SA v Commission of the European Communities, Case C-333/94

Cases Cited from US Courts

Downs. V. United States, the Customs Court Certiorari: 434 U.S. 1060, 98 S.Ct. 1231, 55 L.Ed.2d 760 (1978).

Zenith Radio Corp. V. United States U.S. Supreme Court case 437U.S.443 (1978)

Other Sources

Business vs. Safety (Le Clemenceau case). Case code BECG062 1997-2006

Canada-United States FTA and the Honda case, March 2, 1992 (Arbitration) International Trade Reporter, Vol.9:10, March 4, 1992, 384

List of Agreements and Treaties Referred

Agreement on Agriculture (WTO)

Agreement on implementation of Article VI of the General Agreement on Tariffs and Trade 1994

Agreement on Rules of Origin

Agreement on Subsidies and Countervailing Measure

Agreement on Trade-Related Aspects of Intellectual Property Rights

Basel Convention 1989

Bali Conference 2013

Canada-United-States Free Trade Agreement

Cotonou Agreement

Cancún Ministerial Conference

Committee on Agriculture, Special Session

Doha Declaration

Environmental Goods for Development; Committee on Trade and Environment Special Session

Economic Partnership Agreement

General Agreement on Trade in Services

GATT- General Agreement on Tariffs and Trade

Hong Kong Conference

Kyoto custom convention

Lomè convention

Lisbon treaty

November, 2005. Negotiating Group on Rules.

North American Free Trade Agreement

Technical Barriers to Trade Agreement

Treaty on the Functioning of the European Union

Treaty of Rome establishing EC/EU and EEC Treaty

Treaty Establishing European Community

Tokyo Round Subsidies Code

Trade Related Aspects of Intellectual Property Rights

G. Singh, *Subsidies in the Context of the WTO's Free Trade System*,
DOI 10.1007/978-3-319-62422-8

Uruguay Rounds of Agreement
United Nations Framework Convention on Climate Change
Vienna Convention on the Law of Treaties 1969
Yaoundè convention

Important Statutes Referred

Biofuels Market Expansion Act of 2011
Clean Air for Europe Programme
Competition Act, 2002 (India)
Continued Dumping and Subsidy Offset Act, U.S.
Code of Federal Regulations, U.S.
Council Regulation No 17(EEC):First Regulation Implementing Articles 85 and 86 of the treaty (at present Articles 81 and 82) Articles 101 and 102 TEFU
ETI Act (Extra-territorial Income Exclusion Act, U.S.)
Energy Policy Act, U.S.
Energy Tax Act of 1978, U.S.
Indian Companies Act 2002
Internal Revenue Code, U.S.
Monopolies and Restrictive Trade practices Act 1969 (India)
Price Anderson Act, U.S.
Pollution Prevention Act of 1990, U.S.
Tariff Act of 1930, U.S.
The US Endangered Species Act of 1973
Volumetric Ethanol Excise Tax Credit Repeal Act.

Annex I: Appendix to be Read with Agreement on Agriculture

The WTO negotiations produced general rules that apply to all Members, and specific commitments made by individual Member governments. The specific Commitments are listed in documents called "Schedules of concessions," which reflect specific tariff concessions and other commitments that they have given in the context of trade negotiations, such as the Uruguay-Round. In the case of agricultural products, these concessions and commitments also relate to tariff-rate quotas, limits on export subsidies, and some kinds of domestic support. All the WTO Members have a schedule of concessions which is either annexed to the Marrakesh Protocol to the GATT 1994 or to a Protocol of Accession. The content of the schedules change over time to take account of different modifications, such as GATT Article XXVIII negotiations or rectification procedures. This is the reason why determining a Member's concession for a specific tariff line could involve, in some cases, examining several different legal instruments.

Each schedule consist of four parts:

Part 1 Most-favoured nation or MFN concessions, tariffs to goods from other WTO members.

Part 1 is divided into

Section 1A—tariffs on agriculture products

Section 1B—tariff quotas on agriculture products

Section II—other products

Tariffs are taxes or the amount of money a country needs to pay for trading products. Quotas are the limitations on what is traded, how much is traded, how much is paid for each product traded, and where it is traded.

G. Singh, *Subsidies in the Context of the WTO's Free Trade System*,
DOI 10.1007/978-3-319-62422-8

Annex II: Structural Overview of EC/EU Farming[1]

Mixed cropping accounted for 12% of all agricultural holdings (commercial and small holdings), while specialist cropping and general field cropping each accounted for around 10%. Farms specialist in rearing sheep and goats and other grazing livestock accounted for 8% of the EU-27s farms in 2007, as did farms with a combination of various crops and livestock. Outside of these most frequently occurring types of farming, 6.0% of agricultural holdings in the EU-27 were specialized in Olive growing (mainly found in the Mediterranean) Permanent crops (such as citrus and olive plantations and vineyards) accounted for a relatively high proportion of the utilized agricultural area in most Mediterranean countries and Portugal, but particularly in Greece and Cyprus, where they comprised approximately one quarter of the land used for agricultural production. The majority (60.5%) of the utilized agricultural area in the EU-27 was devoted to arable land in 2007. This proportion rose to over 90% in Denmark and Finland, while the largest arable area in the EU was recorded in France.

[1]Food: from farm to fork statistics, 2011 edition. Luxembourg: Publications office of the European Union. Printed in Belgium. Eurostat European Commission pp. 24–25.ISBN 978-92-79-20239-1.

G. Singh, *Subsidies in the Context of the WTO's Free Trade System*,
DOI 10.1007/978-3-319-62422-8

Annex III: The EU'S Classification of AB and C Sugar

The price system for the sugar regime uses four institutional support prices. These are the target price, the intervention price, the basic beet price, and the minimum beet price. They are fixed annually and are applied to a sugar marketing year. A marketing year generally means October/September, except for Greece and Italy. The EU member states allocate an A quota and B quota to each sugar producing operation, iso-glucose -producing operation, and each inulin syrup-producing operation established in their territory.

Isoglucose is syrup obtained by isomerisation of glucose in fructose under the action of particular enzymes. The raw material is wheat or maize from which starch is extracted. The basic industrial product is glucose.

Inulin syrup Inulin syrup has a very high fructose content of 80% obtained by hydrolysis of inulin extracted from chicory roots. Inulin production began in the 1980, when appropriate industrial hydrolysis and extraction processes were developed. The food industry uses inulin powder and its oligo fructose derivatives for their nutritional and dietary qualities rather than as a sweetener.

There are two types of quota, the A quota (initially determined in accordance with domestic consumption) and the B quota (additional amount to fulfil export potential). Production quotas were set to distribute production of sugar amongst the Member States and to keep overall production within certain limits. They represent the maximum quantity of sugar eligible for price support.

C-sugar "C-isoglucose and C-inulin syrup refer to any quantity of sugar, isoglucose or inulin sugar which is produced outside the sum of total A and B quotas. According to EU legislation, C sugar must be sold on the world market without export subsidies or carried over to the following marketing year. To ensure that the "C" production is exported, a time limit is applied.

As with other CAP commodities there is a common intervention price at which the national intervention agencies will buy all the Union-produced sugar offered within the quota. This intervention price applies for the processed product (white sugar) and is set at 95% of the target price. The common intervention price is increased in those countries which are regarded as being in deficit.

G. Singh, *Subsidies in the Context of the WTO's Free Trade System*,
DOI 10.1007/978-3-319-62422-8

Annex IV

DGFT - Public Notices - 2012
To be published in the Gazette of India Extraordinary Part-I, Section-I
Government of India
Ministry of Commerce and Industry
Department of Commerce
Directorate General of Foreign Trade
Public Notice No. 89 (RE-2010)/2009-2014
New Delhi, Dated the 6th January, 2012 Sub: Allocation of 10,000 MTs of white sugar for the year 2011-12 (October, 2011- September, 2012) for Export to EU under CXL Quota.

(1) In exercise of the powers conferred under Paragraph 2.4 of the Foreign Trade Policy,2009-14, as amended from time to time, the Director-General of Foreign Trade hereby allocates a total quantity of 10,000 MTs (Ten thousand metric tons) of white Sugar for export of CXL Concessions Sugar to European Union (EU) for the period October,2011 to September,2012.
(2) As per HS code 170100 00 in the Schedule-2 of ITC (HS) Classification of Export and Import items, as amended, M/s Indian Sugar Exim Corporation Limited, New Delhi is the designated agency for the export of Sugar to the EU under Preferential Quota.
(3) As per Article 10 of the European Union Regulation (EC) no.891/2009 of 25.9.2009 "release for free circulation for the quotas of CXL concession sugar with order no. 09.4321 shall be subject to the presentation of a certificate of origin issued by the competent of the third country concerned in accordance with articles 55 to 65 of Regulation (EEC) No. 2454/93." Accordingly, the entries to be made in the export authorization document EUR and GSP are as follows:-
    i) CXL Concessions Sugar
    [Application of Regulation (EC) No. 891/2009 under Schedule CXL (European Communities). CXL Concessions sugar Serial No 09.4321

G. Singh, *Subsidies in the Context of the WTO's Free Trade System*,
DOI 10.1007/978-3-319-62422-8

(4) GSP Certificate as per details given in para (3) above shall be issued by Export Inspection Agency/Directorate General of Foreign Trade and EUR Form is to be endorsed by Customs at the Port of Shipment.

Appendix

Instances of business subsidies in Finland. For further reference see ETLA No:-1225 (dated 3.11.2010)

The ship building industry as a result of free trade policies, is also subject to international competition. Studies on this subject have revealed that to seek ship-building contracts companies apply their own business strategies. Conversely, nations also try to attract companies by giving various types of state supports and facilities because of their economic interest as the shipbuilding industry generates huge foreign investment, and furthermore this industry provides employment. In other words, contracts are allotted on the basis of mutual gains. The example referred to here is of the shipbuilding industry in Finland, there are mainly 6 ship-yards in Finland, Helsinki, Turku, Turku Repair Yard, Naantali, Rauma and the UKI Workboat in Uusikaupunki. STX Finland OY, (the company building ships) is the major shareholder in three shipyards in Finland: Turku Shipyard, Rauma Shipyard, and Arctech Helsinki Shipyard Oy. STX Finland Oy belongs to the STX Europe[2] group, an international shipbuilding group with a wide variety of ship-building and related industries. Furthermore, the company STX Europe's principal shareholder is the Korean-based international industrial group STX Business group,[3] which has approximately 70,000 employees.

[2]For Detail reference see, www.shipcruise.org/cruise-articles/495-ship-building-companies **STX Offshore &Shipbuilding founded in 1962 headquarters in Jinhae, South Korea. STX Europe founded 2004, headquarters in Oslo, Norway.** An STX subsidiary, combining the activities of Aker and Kvaerner shipbuilding companies and with a majority share of the shipyards in St Nazaire (the former "Chantiers del' Atlantique") and in Lorient. Main business divisions and products-cruise and ferry ships by STX France Cruise SA and STX Finland Cruise Oy (shipyards at Helsinki, Turku and Rauma); offshore and specialized ships (sub-sea support-arctic, fishing, research and coast guard vessels) at the yards in Norway, Vietnam and Brazil, while hulls are often constructed in Romania.

[3]For detail reference see, STX Corporation http://wwwstx.co.kr.

G. Singh, *Subsidies in the Context of the WTO's Free Trade System*,
DOI 10.1007/978-3-319-62422-8

The Employment Reports suggest that the years 2003 and 2004 were difficult years in Europe with regard to employment. However, the situation is now getting better as new jobs are created. Most of the shipyards have better employment possibilities.

So far as the question of subsidies is concerned, the general practice is such that domestic companies apply for business subsidies and there is a demand for loans, for the building of the new ships by the South Korean company STX in the Turku Yard. In this category, the state supports may be in the form of loans, guarantees and R&D subsidies. As Finnvera[4] supports the governments regional policy goals, firms outside southern Finland are likely to receive favorable decisions (as from the reports).[5] Shipbuilding firms may also receive support from Tekes.[6] The Helsinki Sanomat published an article (dated 15.12.2012) stating that support by subsidies was spreading between various technical sectors. However, giving subsidies to the Korean ship company was finally denied by the state of Finland. Consequently, this company made the deal with France. As a matter of the latest political development, the new Finnish minister Mr, Jan Vapaavuori managed to obtain the possible construction of two smaller ships for Germany, thus attempting to save jobs as the contract did not succeed with the Korean company. The construction of these two ships is for the German cruise line called TUIAG.[7] The State of Finland has given a subsidy of 16 million Euros to the STX shipyard in Turku and it is expected that 15 million will also be provided on the completion of the ships. This seems paradoxical, as previously the Korean ship building company was denied subsidies for the construction of ships at the Turku shipyard.[8]

This incidence can be compared with the subsidy given for the manufacturing of aircrafts as discussed in the Airbus-Boeing case. Although this issue is not before the WTO however, the same analogy can be applied in order to compare the fairness in this matter of international trade. The pattern of state support that is formed in this case is somewhat unusual, because it is not a question of a subsidy for infrastructure development but for various companies that are competing for shipbuilding contracts. Once they obtain a contract, the companies demand state support, which becomes further linked with employment issues and therefore the government is left with less-choices.

The inference drawn is that the WTO needs to formulate its policies on subsidies covering several other forms of state support, which probably were not apparent when the SCM Agreement was formulated in the present context and this possible

---

[4]Finnvera is a specialised financing company owned by the state of Finland and it is the official Export Credit Agency of Finland.

[5]ETLA No:- 1225 (dated 3.11.2010) Authors are Heli Koski and Jukka Tuuli Pg no 23.

[6]**Tekes,** is the Finnish funding Agency for technology and Innovation. **Tekes** provides funding for innovative projects aimed at generating new Know-how and new kinds of products, processes and service or business contracts.

[7]For reference see, Helsingin Sanomat dated 28.2.2013.

[8]For reference see, Helsingin Sanomat dated 27.2.2013.

subsidy for shipbuilding to foreign companies is an instance. Overall, this practice also puts a question mark on the objectives of free trade objectives.

An Instance of a Business Loan Provided by the Government

In recent years, as a consequence of outsourcing due to globalisation, investment in heavy machinery and equipment has been comparatively lower in the Developed countries. The industrial future is seen as being in the ICT sector (Information and Communication Technology Sector). Therefore, private investment and fund raising has increased for this sector also in Finland. Moreover, ICT is nowadays also seen as a job promoting sector. It was reported in the Helsingin Sanomat dated 26.2.2013 that a sum of 700,000 euros from Tekes, (see footnote 1109) is possibly being awarded to Pekka Himanen, a friend of the Finnish Prime Minister, for the future economic plans for Finland. This kind of supports often raises the issues of competition policy.

However, at the WTO free market level, this further leads to the question of whether loans provided by government to industries, in the case of a shift in demand and supply can be termed subsidies and if so, how can this form of subsidy be categorized?[9]

[9]Investoinnit Suomessa. Kehitys ja kansainvälinen vertailu (Investment in Finland. Development and International Comparison) ETLA discussion papers, no 1267,Dated 30.1.2012 by Ville Kaitila and Pekka Ylä-Anttila.

Kolibri 360 GmbH
Ferdinand-Jühlke-Straße 7
99095 Erfurt, Deutschland
produktsicherheit@kolibri360.de